Illustrated Series™

Microsoft® Office 365®
Excel® 2021
Comprehensive

Australia • Brazil • Canada • Mexico • Singapore • United Kingdom • United States

**Illustrated Series® Collection Microsoft® Office 365®
& Excel® 2021 Comprehensive**
Lynn Wermers

SVP, Product: Erin Joyner

VP, Product: Thais Alencar

Product Director: Mark Santee

Senior Product Manager: Amy Savino

Product Assistant: Ciara Horne

Learning Designer: Zenya Molnar

Content Manager: Grant Davis

Digital Delivery Quality Partner: Jim Vaughey

Developmental Editor: Mary-Terese Cozzola

VP, Product Marketing: Jason Sakos

Director, Product Marketing: Danaë April

Executive Product Marketing Manager: Jill Staut

IP Analyst: Ann Hoffman

IP Project Manager: Ilakkiya Jayagopi

Production Service: Lumina Datamatics, Inc.

Designer: Erin Griffin

Cover Image Source: 4khz/Getty Images 472630254

For product information and technology assistance, contact us at
Cengage Customer & Sales Support, 1-800-354-9706 or support.cengage.com.

For permission to use material from this text or product, submit all requests online at **www.copyright.com.**

Library of Congress Control Number: 2022904922

Student Edition ISBN: 978-0-357-67510-6
Looseleaf ISBN: 978-0-357-67511-3*
*Looseleaf available as part of a digital bundle

Cengage
200 Pier 4 Boulevard
Boston, MA 02210
USA

Cengage is a leading provider of customized learning solutions with employees residing in nearly 40 different countries and sales in more than 125 countries around the world. Find your local representative at **www.cengage.com.**

To learn more about Cengage platforms and services, register or access your online learning solution, or purchase materials for your course, visit **www.cengage.com.**

Printed in the United States of America
Print Number: 01   Print Year: 2022

Brief Contents

Contents

Illustrated Series™

Microsoft® Office 365®
Excel® 2021

Comprehensive

Getting to Know Microsoft Office Versions

Cengage is proud to bring you the next edition of Microsoft Office. This edition was designed to provide a robust learning experience that is not dependent upon a specific version of Office.

Microsoft supports several versions of Office:

- **Office 365:** A cloud-based subscription service that delivers Microsoft's most up-to-date, feature-rich, modern productivity tools direct to your device. There are variations of Office 365 for business, educational, and personal use. Office 365 offers extra online storage and cloud-connected features, as well as updates with the latest features, fixes, and security updates.

- **Office 2021:** Microsoft's "on-premises" version of the Office apps, available for both PCs and Macs, offered as a static, one-time purchase and outside of the subscription model.

- **Office Online:** A free, simplified version of Office web applications (Word, Excel, PowerPoint, and OneNote) that facilitates creating and editing files collaboratively.

Office 365 (the subscription model) and Office 2021 (the one-time purchase model) had only slight differences between them at the time this content was developed. Over time, Office 365's cloud interface will continuously update, offering new application features and functions, while Office 2021 will remain static. Therefore, your onscreen experience may differ from what you see in this product. For example, the more advanced features and functionalities covered in this product may not be available in Office Online or may have updated from what you see in Office 2021.

For more information on the differences between Office 365, Office 2021, and Office Online, please visit the Microsoft Support site.

Cengage is committed to providing high-quality learning solutions for you to gain the knowledge and skills that will empower you throughout your educational and professional careers.

Thank you for using our product, and we look forward to exploring the future of Microsoft Office with you!

Using SAM Projects and Textbook Projects

SAM Projects allow you to actively apply the skills you learned live in Microsoft Word, Excel, PowerPoint, or Access. Become a more productive student and use these skills throughout your career.

To complete SAM Textbook Projects, please follow these steps:

SAM Textbook Projects allow you to complete a project as you follow along with the steps in the textbook. As you read the module, look for icons that indicate when you should download **sam** your SAM Start file(s) and when to upload **sam** the final project file to SAM for grading.

Everything you need to complete this project is provided within SAM. You can launch the eBook directly from SAM, which will allow you to take notes, highlight, and create a custom study guide, or you can use a print textbook or your mobile app. Download IOS or Download Android.

To get started, launch your SAM Project assignment from SAM, MindTap, or a link within your LMS.

Step 1: Download Files

- Click the "Download All" button or the individual links to download your **Start File** and **Support File(s)** (when available). You <u>must</u> use the SAM Start file.

- Click the Instructions link to launch the eBook (or use the print textbook or mobile app).

- Disregard any steps in the textbook that ask you to create a new file or to use a file from a location outside of SAM.

- Look for the SAM Download icon **sam** to begin working with your start file.

- Follow the module's step-by-step instructions until you reach the SAM Upload icon **sam**.

- Save and close the file.

Step 2: Save Work to SAM

- Ensure you rename your project file to match the Expected File Name.

- Upload your in-progress or completed file to SAM. You can download the file to continue working or submit it for grading in the next step.

Step 3: Submit for Grading

- Upload the completed file to SAM for immediate feedback and to view the available Reports.

  - The **Graded Summary Report** provides a detailed list of project steps, your score, and feedback to aid you in revising and re-submitting the project.

  - The **Study Guide Report** provides your score for each project step and links to the associated training and textbook pages.

- If additional attempts are allowed, use your reports to assist with revising and resubmitting your project.

- To re-submit the project, download the file saved in step 2.

- Edit, save, and close the file, then re-upload and submit it again.

For all other SAM Projects, please follow these steps:

To get started, launch your SAM Project assignment from SAM, MindTap, or a link within your LMS.

Step 1: Download Files

- Click the "Download All" button or the individual links to download your **Instruction File**, **Start File**, and **Support File(s)** (when available). You <u>must</u> use the SAM Start file.

- Open the Instruction file and follow the step-by-step instructions. Ensure you rename your project file to match the Expected File Name (change _1 to _2 at the end of the file name).

Step 2: Save Work to SAM

- Upload your in-progress or completed file to SAM. You can download the file to continue working or submit it for grading in the next step.

Step 3: Submit for Grading

- Upload the completed file to SAM for immediate feedback and to view available Reports.

  - The **Graded Summary Report** provides a detailed list of project steps, your score, and feedback to aid you in revising and resubmitting the project.

  - The **Study Guide Report** provides your score for each project step and links to the associated training and textbook pages.

- If additional attempts are allowed, use your reports to assist with revising and resubmitting your project.

- To re-submit the project, download the file saved in step 2.

- Edit, save, and close the file, then re-upload and submit it again.

For additional tips to successfully complete your SAM Projects, please view our Common Student Errors Infographic.

Getting Started with Excel

CASE ▶ You have been hired as an assistant at JCL Talent, a company that provides recruitment services for employers and job seekers. You report to Dawn LaPointe, the director of technical careers. As Dawn's assistant, you create worksheets to analyze data from various company offices to help her make sound decisions on company expansion, investments, and new recruiting opportunities.

Module Objectives

After completing this module, you will be able to:

- Explore Excel
- Enter data
- Edit data
- Copy and move cell data
- Enter formulas and use AutoSum
- Copy formulas with relative cell references
- Copy formulas with absolute cell references
- Enter a formula with multiple operators
- Insert a function
- Switch worksheet views
- Choose print options

Files You Will Need

IL_EX_1-1.xlsx   IL_EX_1-4.xlsx
IL_EX_1-2.xlsx   IL_EX_1-5.xlsx
IL_EX_1-3.xlsx

Explore Excel

Learning Outcomes
• Define key spreadsheet terms
• Open and save an Excel file
• Identify Excel window elements

Microsoft Excel is an **electronic spreadsheet program**, a computer program used to perform calculations and analyze and present numeric data. An Excel file, a **workbook**, is a collection of related worksheets contained within a single file with the file extension xlsx. A workbook is made up of one or more worksheets. A **worksheet** contains a grid of columns and rows where you can enter and manipulate data, perform calculations with data, and analyze data. **CASE** *You decide to review the distribution of technical postings in JCL's North American offices, to learn more about where and when these types of jobs have been posted.*

STEPS

TROUBLE

If you don't see the extension .xlsx on the filenames in the Save As dialog box, don't worry; Windows can be set up to display or not to display the file extensions.

1. **sam ↓ Click the Start button ⊞ on the Windows taskbar, type Excel, click Excel, click Open, navigate to the location where you store your Data Files, click IL_EX_1-1.xlsx, then click Open**

2. **Click the File tab, click Save As on the navigation bar, click Browse, navigate to the location where you store your Data Files if necessary, type IL_EX_1_Postings in the File name box, then click Save**

   Using **FIGURE 1-1** as a guide, identify the following items:

QUICK TIP

You can open a blank workbook by clicking Blank workbook rather than Open.

   • The **Name box** is the box to the left of the formula bar that shows the cell reference or name of the active cell. "A1" appears in the Name box.
   • The **formula bar** is the area above the worksheet grid where you enter or edit data in the active cell.
   • The **worksheet window** is an area of the program window that displays part of the current worksheet, which can contain a total of 1,048,576 rows and 16,384 columns. The columns and rows intersect to form cells, where you can enter and manipulate text, numbers, formulas, or a combination of all three. Every cell has its own unique location or **cell address**, a cell's location, expressed by its column letter and row number such as A1.
   • The **cell pointer** is a dark rectangle that outlines the active cell in a worksheet. In the figure, the cell pointer outlines cell A1, so A1 is the active cell.
   • By default, a workbook file contains one worksheet named Sheet1—but you can have as many sheets as your computer's memory allows in a workbook. The New sheet button to the right of Sheet1 allows you to add worksheets to a workbook. **Sheet tab scrolling buttons** are triangles that let you navigate to additional sheet tabs when available; they're located to the left of the sheet tabs.
   • You can use the scroll bars to move around in a worksheet that is too large to fit on the screen at once.
   • The status bar provides a brief description of the active command or task in progress. The **mode indicator** on the left end of the status bar indicates the program's status, such as the Edit mode in Excel. You are in Edit mode any time you are entering or changing the contents of a cell. You can use the Zoom In and Zoom Out buttons in the status bar to increase or decrease the scale of the displayed worksheet.
   • You can use the **Search box** on the title bar to find a command or access the Excel Help system.
   • The AutoSave button on the Quick Access Toolbar is on if you are working on a file saved on OneDrive. When AutoSave is on, your file will be automatically saved as you make changes.

3. **Click cell B4**

   Cell B4 becomes the active cell. To activate a different cell, you can click the cell or press the arrow keys on your keyboard to move to it.

QUICK TIP

The button that opens in the lower-right corner of a range is the Quick Analysis tool.

4. **Click cell B4, drag ✛ to cell B11, then release the mouse button**

   You selected a group of cells and they are highlighted, as shown in **FIGURE 1-2**. A series of two or more adjacent cells in a column, row, or rectangular group of cells, notated using the cell address of its upper-left and lower-right corners, such as B4:B11, is called a **range**; you select a range when you want to perform an action on a group of cells at once, such as moving them or formatting them.

FIGURE 1-1: Open workbook

FIGURE 1-2: Selected range

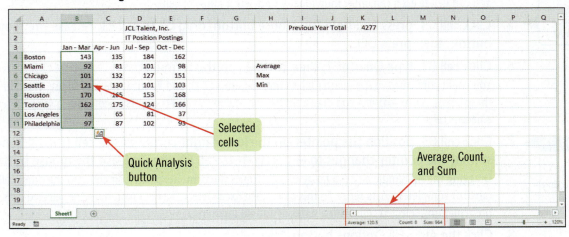

Excel

Navigating a worksheet

With over a million cells available in a worksheet, it is important to know how to move around in, or navigate, a worksheet. You can use the arrow keys on the keyboard ↑, ↓, →, or ← to move one cell at a time, or press PAGE UP or PAGE DOWN to move one screen at a time. To move one screen to the left, press ALT+PAGE UP; to move one screen to the right, press ALT+PAGE DOWN.

You can also use the pointer to click the desired cell. If the desired cell is not visible in the worksheet window, use the scroll bars or use the Go To command by clicking the Find & Select button in the Editing group on the Home tab on the ribbon. To quickly jump to the first cell in a worksheet, press CTRL+HOME; to jump to the last cell, press CTRL+END.

Enter Data

Learning Outcomes
• Enter labels
• Enter values
• Copy data using the fill handle
• Enter a series of data with Auto Fill

To enter content in a cell, you can type in the formula bar or directly in the cell itself. **Labels** are descriptive text or other information that identifies data in rows, columns, or charts, not included in calculations, such as "2021 Sales" or "Expenses". **Values** are numbers, formulas, and functions used in calculations.

CASE ▸ *You want to enter and edit information in the Postings workbook.*

STEPS

QUICK TIP
If you change your mind and want to cancel an entry in the formula bar, click the Cancel button ☒ on the formula bar.

1. **Click cell F3, type Total, then click the Enter button** ☑ **on the formula bar**
   Clicking the Enter button accepts the entry without moving the cell pointer to a new location. The new text is left-aligned in the cell because labels are left-aligned by default. Excel recognizes an entry as a value if it is a number or it begins with one of these symbols: +, –, =, @, #, or $. When a cell contains both text and numbers, Excel recognizes it as a label.

2. **Click cell A12, type Vancouver, then press TAB**
   Pressing TAB accepts the entry and moves the active cell to the right, to cell B12.

3. **With B12 as the active cell, type 120, press TAB, type 130, press TAB, type 117, press TAB, type 130, then press TAB**
   The quarterly data is displayed for the Vancouver office, as shown in **FIGURE 1-3**. The numbers are right-aligned because values are right-aligned by default. You want to replace the monthly labels in row 3 with quarter labels.

QUICK TIP
If you want to clear a cell's content, including its formatting, click the Clear button ◇ in the Editing group, then click Clear All.

4. **Click cell B3, then press DEL**
   You can delete each cell entry individually or delete a range of cells.

5. **Click cell C3, press and hold the mouse button, drag ✛ to cell E3, release the mouse button, then press DEL**

6. **Click cell B3, type Quarter 1, then click** ☑ **on the formula bar**
   You could continue to type quarter labels into columns C, D, and E, but it is easier to use Auto Fill to enter these labels. **Auto Fill** lets you drag a fill handle to copy a cell's contents or continue a selected series into adjacent cells.

QUICK TIP
You can insert a worksheet into a workbook by clicking the New sheet button ⊕.

7. **Click cell B3, position the pointer on the lower-right corner of the cell (the fill handle) so that the pointer changes to ✛, drag ✛ to cell E3, then release the mouse button**
   Dragging the fill handle across a range of cells copies the contents of the first cell into the other cells in the range or completes a data series. In this case, since Excel detected a data pattern in the selected cells, it filled the remaining selected cells with a series of annual quarters.

8. **Click the Auto Fill Options button** 🔳
   Options for filling the selected range include Fill Series, which is selected, as shown in **FIGURE 1-4**. The other available options allow you to change to copying cells, fill the cells with formatting only, or fill the cells without formatting.

9. **Save your work**

FIGURE 1-3: Vancouver data entered

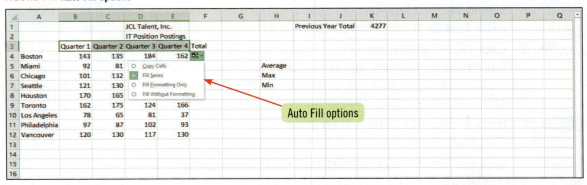

Vancouver data

FIGURE 1-4: Auto Fill options

Auto Fill options

Inserting and deleting selected cells

As you add formulas to your workbook, you may need to insert or delete cells. To insert cells, click the Insert arrow in the Cells group on the Home tab, then click Insert Cells. The Insert dialog box opens, asking if you want to insert a cell and move the current active cell down or to the right of the new one. To delete one or more selected cells, click the Delete arrow in the Cells group, click Delete Cells, and in the Delete dialog box, indicate which way you want to move the adjacent cells. When using this option, be careful not to disturb row or column alignment that may be necessary to maintain the accuracy of cell references on the worksheet. You can also click the Insert button or Delete button in the Cells group to insert or delete a single cell. Excel automatically adjusts cell references within the formulas of any moved cells to reflect their new locations.

Using Auto Fill and Flash Fill

Auto Fill is an Excel feature that lets you drag a fill handle to copy a cell's contents or continue a series into adjacent cells. This can be used to enter the months of the year, days of the week, and custom lists of a series. Flash Fill, although similar to Auto Fill, isn't used to fill in a series of data. It is an Excel feature that looks for patterns in the data you enter and automatically fills or formats data in remaining cells based on those patterns. The filled data must be adjacent to the example data. Flash Fill often detects the pattern as you enter data and shows the new data in a light font. Pressing ENTER accepts the suggestion and enters the data. If Excel doesn't detect a pattern automatically, you can click the Flash Fill button in the Data Tools group on the Data tab to fill in the data.

Edit Data

You can change, or edit, the contents of an active cell at any time. To do so, double-click the cell, and then click in the formula bar or just start typing. Excel switches to Edit mode when you are making cell entries. Different pointers, shown in **TABLE 1-1**, guide you through the editing process. **CASE** *You noticed some errors on the worksheet and want to make corrections.*

STEPS

1. **Click cell B4, then click to the left of 4 in the formula bar**

   As soon as you click in the formula bar, a blinking vertical line called the **insertion point** appears on the formula bar at the location where new text will be inserted. See **FIGURE 1-5**.

2. **Press DEL, type 3, then click the Enter button ✓ on the formula bar**

   Clicking the Enter button accepts the edit, and the Boston first quarter posting is 133. You can also press ENTER to accept an edit. Pressing ENTER to accept an edit moves the cell pointer down one cell.

3. **Click cell B6, then press F2**

   Excel switches to Edit mode, and the insertion point blinks in the cell. Pressing F2 activates the cell for editing directly in the cell instead of the formula bar. Whether you edit in the cell or the formula bar is simply a matter of preference; the results on the worksheet are the same.

4. **Press BACKSPACE, type 9, then press ENTER**

   The value in the cell changes from 101 to 109, and cell B7 becomes the active cell.

5. **Click cell H6, then double-click the word Max in the formula bar**

   Double-clicking a word in a cell selects it. When you selected the word, the Mini toolbar automatically opened.

6. **Type Maximum, then press ENTER**

   When text is selected, typing deletes it and replaces it with the new text.

7. **Double-click cell H7, click to the right of n, type imum, then click ✓**

   Double-clicking a cell activates it for editing directly in the cell. Compare your screen to **FIGURE 1-6**.

8. **Save your work**

Recovering unsaved changes to a workbook file

You can use Excel's AutoRecover feature to automatically save (Autosave) your work as often as you want. This means that if you suddenly lose power or if Excel closes unexpectedly while you're working, you can recover all or some of the changes you made since you saved it last. (Of course, this is no substitute for regularly saving your work; it's just added insurance.) To customize the AutoRecover settings, click the File tab, click Options, then click Save. AutoRecover lets you decide how often and in which location it should AutoSave files. When you restart Excel after losing power, you will see a new section, Recovered files, above the listing of recent files. You can click Show Recovered Files to access the saved and AutoSaved versions of files that were open when Excel closed.

FIGURE 1-5: Worksheet in Edit mode

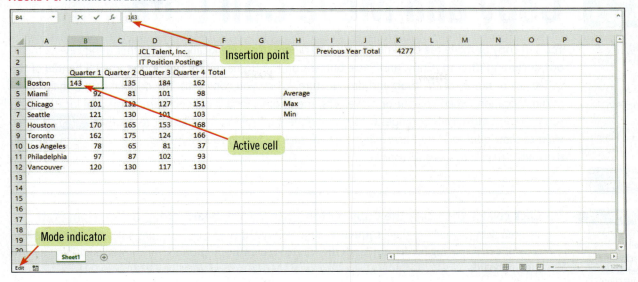

FIGURE 1-6: Edited worksheet

TABLE 1-1: Common pointers in Excel

name	pointer	use to	visible over the
Normal	✛	Select a cell or range; indicates Ready mode	Active worksheet
Fill handle	+	Copy cell contents or series to adjacent cells	Lower-right corner of the active cell or range
I-beam	I	Edit cell contents in active cell or formula bar	Active cell in Edit mode or over the formula bar
Move	✛	Change the location of the selected cell(s)	Perimeter of the active cell(s)
Copy	▷⁺	Create a duplicate of the selected cell(s)	Perimeter of the active cell(s) when CTRL is pressed
Column resize	↔	Change the width of a column	Border between column heading indicators

Excel

Copy and Move Cell Data

Learning Outcomes
- Copy cell data to the Clipboard
- Paste a Clipboard entry
- Move a range

You can copy or move the contents in cells and ranges from one location to another using several methods, including the Cut, Copy, and Paste buttons on the Home tab on the ribbon, the fill handle of the active cell or range, or the drag-and-drop feature. When you copy cells, the original data remains in its original location; when you cut or move cells, the original data is deleted from its original location. You can copy and move cells or ranges within a worksheet or from one worksheet to another. **CASE** *You want to show totals and statistical information for each quarter in your worksheet, so you decide to copy and move selected cells to speed up your task.*

STEPS

1. **Click cell F3, then click the Copy button 🗐 in the Clipboard group on the Home tab**

   The cell data is copied to the **Clipboard**, a temporary Office storage area that holds the selections you copy or cut. A moving border surrounds the selected cell until you press ESC or copy an additional item to the Clipboard.

2. **Click the dialog box launcher 🗔 in the Clipboard group**

   The Office Clipboard opens in the Clipboard task pane, as shown in **FIGURE 1-7**. When you copy or cut an item, it is cut or copied both to the Clipboard provided by Windows and to the Office Clipboard. The Office Clipboard can hold up to 24 of the most recently cut or copied items from any Office program. Your Clipboard task pane may contain more items than are shown in the figure.

3. **Click cell A13, then click the Paste button 🗐 in the Clipboard group**

   A copy of the contents of cell F3 is pasted into cell A13. Notice that the information you copied remains in the original cell, F3; if you had cut instead of copied, the information would have been deleted from its original location once it was pasted. You can also paste an item by clicking it in the Office Clipboard.

4. **Click the Paste Options button 🗐 (Ctrl) ▾**

   The Paste Options open, as shown in **FIGURE 1-8**. These options allow you to determine what you want pasted and how you want the pasted data to appear on the worksheet. Review the three categories, Paste, Paste Values, and Other Paste Options. The current pasted data doesn't need any change in formatting.

5. **Press ESC twice, then click the Close button ❌ on the Clipboard task pane**

6. **Select the range H5:H7, point to any edge of the selected range until the pointer changes to 🖝, drag the range to cell A15, then release the mouse button**

   The move pointer displays an outline of the range you are dragging. When you release the mouse button, you "drop" the selection to the range A15:A17. When pasting an item from the Clipboard, you only need to specify the upper-left cell of the range where you want to paste the selection. If you press and hold CTRL while dragging and dropping, the information is copied instead of moved.

FIGURE 1-7: Copied data in Office Clipboard

Paste button

Copy button

Clipboard dialog box launcher

Item in Office Clipboard

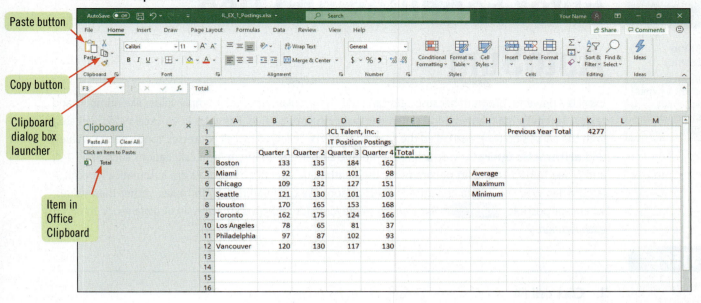

FIGURE 1-8: Paste options

Cell contents being copied

Paste options

Copied label

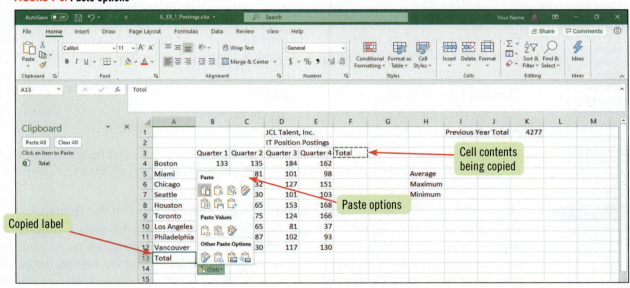

Using Paste Options and Paste Preview

You can selectively paste copied or cut formulas, values, or other data by using the Paste Options button that opens on the worksheet after you paste data or use the Paste arrow in the Clipboard. The Paste Preview feature shows how the current selection will look when pasted. When you click the Paste Options button (or simply press [Ctrl] or the Paste arrow), a gallery of paste option icons opens, organized by category. The Paste category includes pasting formulas, pasting formulas and number formatting, pasting using the source formatting, pasting with no borders (to remove any borders around pasted cells), pasting with the source column widths, and pasting transposed data so that column data appears in rows and row data appears in columns. The Paste Values category includes pasting values only (without formatting), pasting values and number formatting, and pasting values with source formatting. The Other Paste Options category includes pasting formatting, links, pictures, and linked pictures. Clicking Paste Link in this category creates a link to the source data so that in the future, changes to the copied data update the pasted data. Clicking Picture in this category pastes the data as a picture where the picture tools can be used to format it, resize it, or move it.

Excel

Enter Formulas and Use AutoSum

Learning Outcomes
- Use cell references to create a formula
- Build formulas with the AutoSum button

Excel is a powerful program because cells can contain formulas rather than simply values like numbers and text. A **formula** is a mathematical statement that calculates a value. Formulas in an Excel worksheet start with the equal sign (=), also called the **formula prefix**, followed by cell addresses, range names, values, and **arithmetic operators**, which are symbols that perform mathematical calculations such as +, –, *, and /. See **TABLE 1-2** for a list of commonly used arithmetic operators. Formulas are automatically recalculated when worksheet data changes. For this reason, use cell references in formulas, rather than values, whenever possible. **CASE** *You want to create formulas in the worksheet that calculate yearly totals for each location.*

STEPS

1. Click cell F4

This is the first cell where you want to insert a formula. To calculate the yearly total for the Boston location, you need to add the quarterly totals.

2. Type =, click cell B4, type +, click cell C4, type +, click cell D4, type +, then click cell E4

Compare your formula bar to **FIGURE 1-9**. The blue, red, purple, and green cell references in cell F4 correspond to the color of the cells. When entering a formula, clicking cells rather typing the cell addresses helps avoid typing errors.

3. Click the Enter button ✓ on the formula bar

The result of the formula =B4+C4+D4+E4, 614, appears in cell F4.

4. Click cell B13

You want this cell to total first quarter positions for all the locations. You might think you need to create a formula that looks like this: =B4+B5+B6+B7+B8+B9+B10+B11+B12. However, there's an easier way to achieve this result.

5. On the ribbon, click the AutoSum button Σ in the Editing group on the Home tab

The SUM function is inserted in the cell, and a suggested range appears in parentheses. A **function** is a predefined procedure that returns a value; it includes the **arguments** (the information necessary to calculate an answer) as well as cell references and other unique information. Clicking the AutoSum button sums the adjacent range (that is, the cells next to the active cell) above or to the left, although you can adjust the range if necessary by selecting a different range before accepting the cell entry. Using the SUM function is quicker than entering a formula, and using the range B4:B12 is more efficient than entering individual cell references.

6. Click ✓ on the formula bar

Excel calculates the total contained in cells B4:B12 and displays the result, 1082, in cell B13. The cell actually contains the formula =SUM(B4:B12), but it displays the result. Compare your screen to **FIGURE 1-10**.

7. Save your work

FIGURE 1-9: Entering a formula

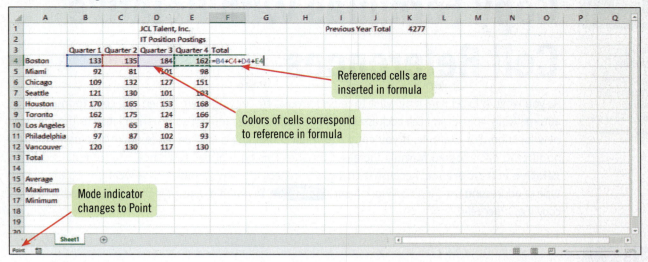

Referenced cells are inserted in formula

Colors of cells correspond to reference in formula

Mode indicator changes to Point

FIGURE 1-10: SUM function in a worksheet

Enter button

AutoSum button

SUM function in cell

Result of the function

TABLE 1-2: Excel arithmetic operators

operator	purpose	example
+	Addition	=A5+A7
–	Subtraction or negation	=A5–10
*	Multiplication	=A5*A7
/	Division	=A5/A7
%	Percent	=35%
^ (caret)	Exponent	=6^2 (same as 6^2)

Copy Formulas with Relative Cell References

Learning Outcomes
- Copy formulas with relative cell references
- Use the fill handle to copy formulas

As you work in Excel, you may want to reuse formulas by copying them. When you copy formulas, Excel automatically adjusts any cell addresses in the formula so they remain consistent relative to the formula's new location. For example, if you copy a formula containing a cell reference down a column, the row number in each copied formula increases by one. This type of cell reference in a formula is called a **relative cell reference**, because it changes to reflect the new formula's new location; it's the default type of addressing used in Excel worksheets. **CASE** *You want to reuse a formula you created, so you will copy it to other cells.*

STEPS

1. **Click cell F4, then drag the fill handle down to cell F12**

   The formula for calculating the total for all four quarters is copied into the range F5:F12.

2. **Click cell F5**

   A copy of the formula from cell F4 appears in cell F5, with the new result of 372, as shown in **FIGURE 1-11**. Notice in the formula bar that the cell references have changed so that cells in row 5 are referenced instead of row 4. This formula contains relative cell references, which tells Excel to substitute new cell references within the copied formulas as necessary. In this case, Excel adjusted the cell references in the formula in cell F5 by increasing the row number references by one from 4 to 5.

3. **Click cell F6**

   Because the location of this cell is two rows below the original formula, Excel adjusted the cell references in the copied formula by increasing the row number references by two from 4 to 6.

4. **Click cell B13, then drag the fill handle to the right to cell F13**

   A formula similar to the one in cell B13 now appears in the range C13:F13.

5. **Click cell C13**

   In copying the formula one cell to the right, the cell references in the formula bar are adjusted by increasing the column letter references by one from B to C. Compare your worksheet to **FIGURE 1-12**.

6. **Save your work**

FIGURE 1-11: Formula copied using the fill handle

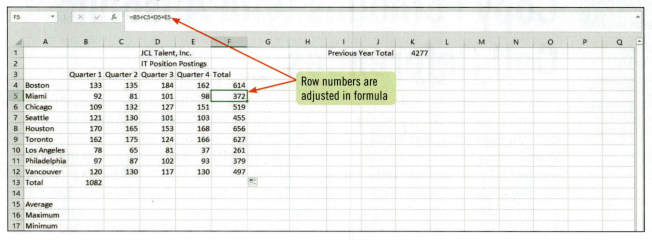

FIGURE 1-12: Formula column references changed

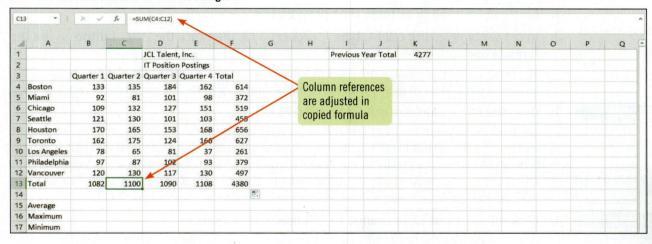

Inserting functions into formulas

You can insert a function on its own or as part of another formula. For example, you have used the SUM function on its own to add a range of cells—for example, =SUM(B5:B9). You could also use the SUM function within a formula that adds a range of cells and then multiplies the total by a decimal—for example, =SUM(B5:B9)*.5.

Copy Formulas with Absolute Cell References

Learning Outcomes
- Create an absolute cell reference
- Use the fill handle to copy absolute cell references

When copying formulas, you might want one or more of the cell references in the formula to remain unchanged. For example, you might have a price in a specific cell that you want to use in all the copied formulas, regardless of their location. If you use relative cell referencing, the formula results would be incorrect, because the formula would reference a different cell every time you copy it. In this situation, you need to use an **absolute cell reference**, which refers to a specific cell and does not change when you copy the formula. Absolute cell references display a dollar sign ($) before the column letter and row number of the address (for example, $A$1). You can either type the dollar sign when typing the cell address in a formula, or you can select a cell address on the formula bar and then press F4, and the dollar signs are added automatically. When copying a formula, absolute cell references remain fixed in the copied formulas. **CASE** *You decide to calculate each location's percentage of the total postings.*

STEPS

1. **Click cell G3, type % of Total, then press ENTER**

2. **In cell G4 type =, click cell F4, type /, click cell F13, then click the Enter button ☑ on the formula bar**

   The result, 14.02%, appears in cell G4. This value represents the total positions for Boston (in cell F4) divided by the total for all locations (in cell F13). You want to calculate this percentage for each location.

3. **Drag the fill handle from cell G4 to cell G12**

   The resulting values in the range G5:G12 are the error messages #DIV/0!. Because you used relative cell addressing in the formula in cell G4, the copied formula adjusted so that the formula in cell G5 is =F5/F14; because there is no value in cell F14, the result is a division by 0 error. You need to use an absolute reference for cell F13 in the formula to keep the denominator from adjusting in a relative way as the formula is copied. That way, the denominator will always reference the total for all locations in cell F13.

4. **Click cell G4, press F2 to change to Edit mode, then press F4**

   When you press F2, the range finder outlines the arguments of the equation in blue and red. The insertion point appears next to the F13 cell reference in cell G4. When you press F4, dollar signs are inserted in the F13 cell reference, making it an absolute reference. See **FIGURE 1-13**.

5. **Click ☑, then drag the fill handle from cell G4 to cell G12**

   Because the formula correctly contains an absolute cell reference, the correct percentage values appear for each location in cells G5:G12. Compare your worksheet to **FIGURE 1-14**.

6. **Save your work**

FIGURE 1-13: Absolute reference created in formula

Absolute cell reference in formula

Incorrect values from relative referencing in previously copied formula

FIGURE 1-14: Correct percentages calculated

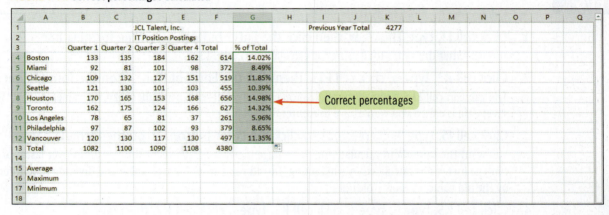

Correct percentages

Using a mixed reference

Sometimes when you copy a formula, you want to change the row reference, but keep the column reference the same. This type of cell referencing, where one factor remains constant and the other one varies, is a **mixed reference**. For example, when copied, a formula containing the mixed reference C$14 would change the column letter relative to its new location, but not the row number.

In the mixed reference $C14, the column letter would not change, but the row number would be updated relative to its location. Like an absolute reference, a mixed reference can be created by pressing F4 with the cell reference selected. With each press of the F4 key, you cycle through all the possible combinations of relative, absolute, and mixed references (C14, $C$14, C$14, and $C14).

Excel

Enter a Formula with Multiple Operators

Learning Outcomes
- Understand the order of operations
- Create a formula with multiple operators

Formulas often contain more than one arithmetic operator. In these formulas, Excel follows the **order of operations**, the sequence in which operators are applied in a mathematical calculation. Instead of calculating simply from left to right, this order calls for calculations in parentheses to be performed first, exponent calculations second, then multiplication and division, and finally addition and subtraction. If there are multiple occurrences of an operation, such as two multiplication operations, they are calculated from left to right. If your formula requires addition or subtraction to be calculated before multiplication or division, you can change the calculation order by using parentheses around the addition or subtraction. For example, the formula to average the numbers 100, 200, and 300 is (100+200+300)/3 to make sure the numbers are totaled before the division operation. **TABLE 1-3** shows more examples of how calculations are performed in Excel. **CASE** ▶ *You need to analyze the percentage increase of this year's total for the North American locations from last year's total.*

STEPS

1. **Click cell J3, type This Year, then click the Enter button ✓ on the formula bar**
   You will enter this year's total using the calculation in cell F13.

2. **Click cell K3, type =, click cell F13, then click the Enter button ✓ on the formula bar**
   The value in cell F13 is copied to cell K3. You entered a cell reference rather than the value, so if any worksheet data is edited you won't have to reenter this total.

3. **Click cell J5, type % Increase, then click the Enter button ✓ on the formula bar**
   You want the formula to calculate the percentage increase of this year's total postings over last year. Percentage increase is calculated by subtracting the old value from the new value and dividing that difference by the old value, or (new – old)/old.

4. **Click cell K5, type =, type (, click cell K3, type -, click cell K1, then type)**
   In this first part of the formula, you are finding the difference in totals between this year and last year. You enclosed this calculation with parentheses so it will be performed before any other calculations, because calculations in parentheses are always calculated first. Compare your screen to **FIGURE 1-15**.

5. **Type /, click cell K1, then click the Enter button ✓ on the formula bar**
   The second part of this formula divides the difference in yearly totals by the total for the previous year to find the percentage of the growth. Because you enclosed the subtraction calculation in parentheses, it was calculated before the division calculation. The value in cell K5 is in decimal format. You want to display this value as a percentage with two decimal places.

6. **Click the Percent Style button % in the Number group on the Home tab, then click the Increase Decimal button ⬆ in the Number group twice**
   The percentage increase in cell K5 is 2.41%, as shown in **FIGURE 1-16**.

7. **Save your work**

FIGURE 1-15: Formula with parentheses

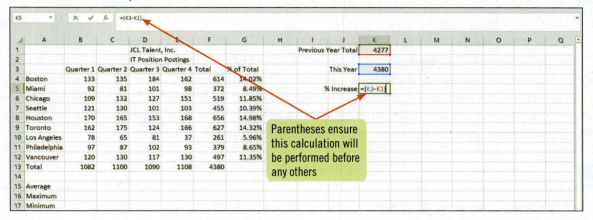

FIGURE 1-16: Formula with percentage increase

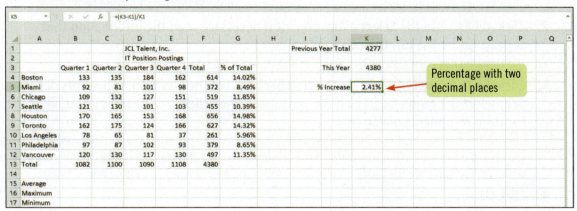

TABLE 1-3: Calculation results in Excel formulas

formula	result
10+20+40/2	50
(10+20+40)/2	35
10+5*2	20
(10+5)*2	30
20–10/2	15
(20–10)/2	5

Insert a Function

You can insert functions in several ways. So far, you have used the AutoSum button on the ribbon to add the SUM function. To choose from all available functions you can use the Insert Function dialog box. This is especially valuable if you're not sure of the name of the function you need, because functions are organized into categories, such as Financial, Date & Time, and Statistical, and you are guided through the process. Other ways to insert a function include manually typing it in a cell and using the AutoSum arrow to insert commonly used functions. **CASE** *You need to calculate the average, maximum, and minimum location postings for the first quarter of the year and decide to use functions to do so.*

STEPS

1. **Click cell B15, then click the Insert Function button 𝑓ₓ on the formula bar**

   An equal sign (=) is inserted in the active cell, and the Insert Function dialog box opens, as shown in **FIGURE 1-17**. In this dialog box, you specify the function you want to use by clicking it in the Select a function list of recently used functions, clicking the Or select a category arrow to choose a desired function category, or typing the function name, or its description, in the Search for a function field.

   > **TROUBLE**
   > If AVERAGE is not in the function list, type AVERAGE in the Search for a function box, then click Go.

2. **Click AVERAGE in the Select a function list if necessary, read the information that appears under the list, then click OK**

   The Function Arguments dialog box opens, as shown in **FIGURE 1-18**.

3. **Click the Collapse button ⬆ in the Number1 field of the Function Arguments dialog box, select the range B4:B12 on the worksheet, then click the Expand button ⬇ in the Function Arguments dialog box**

   Clicking the Collapse button minimizes the dialog box so that you can select cells on the worksheet. When you click the Expand button, the dialog box is restored. You can also begin dragging on the worksheet to automatically minimize the dialog box; after you select the desired range, the dialog box is restored.

4. **Click OK**

   The Function Arguments dialog box closes, and the calculated value is displayed in cell B15. The average postings per location for Quarter 1 is 120.222.

5. **Click cell B16, type =, then type m**

   Because you are manually typing this function, you must manually type the opening equal sign (=). Once you type an equal sign in a cell, each letter you type acts as a trigger to activate the Excel **Formula Auto-Complete**, a feature that automatically suggests text, numbers, or dates to insert based on previous entries. Because you entered the letter *m*, this feature suggests a list of function names beginning with "M."

   > **QUICK TIP**
   > In the AutoComplete list, if you click a function instead of double-clicking, a ScreenTip displays more detailed information about the function.

6. **Double-click MAX in the list, select the range B4:B12, then click the Enter button ✓ on the formula bar**

   The result, 170, appears in cell B16. When you completed the entry, the closing parenthesis was automatically added to the formula.

7. **Click cell B17, type =, type m, double-click MIN in the list of function names, select the range B4:B12, then press ENTER**

   The result, 78, appears in cell B17.

8. **Select the range B15:B17, drag the fill handle to the range C15:E17, then save your work**

   The average, maximum, and minimum values for all the quarters appear in the selected range, as shown in **FIGURE 1-19**.

FIGURE 1-17: Insert Function dialog box

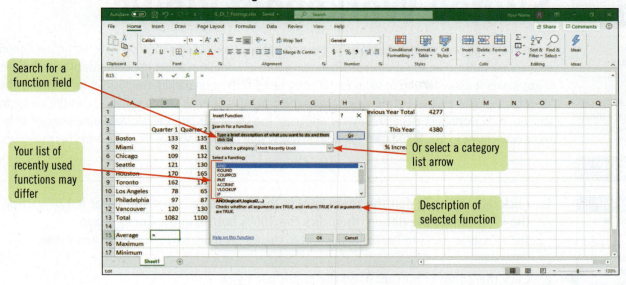

Search for a function field

Your list of recently used functions may differ

Or select a category list arrow

Description of selected function

FIGURE 1-18: Function Arguments dialog box

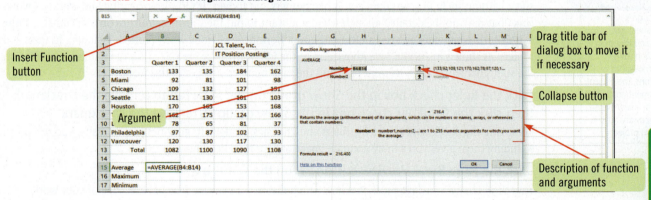

Insert Function button

Argument

Drag title bar of dialog box to move it if necessary

Collapse button

Description of function and arguments

FIGURE 1-19: Completed AVERAGE, MAX, and MIN functions

	A	B	C	D	E	F	G	H	I	J	K
1			JCL Talent, Inc.						Previous Year Total		4277
2			IT Position Postings								
3		Quarter 1	Quarter 2	Quarter 3	Quarter 4	Total	% of Total		This Year		4380
4	Boston	133	135	184	162	614	14.02%				
5	Miami	92	81	101	98	372	8.49%		% Increase		2.41%
6	Chicago	109	132	127	151	519	11.85%				
7	Seattle	121	130	101	103	455	10.39%				
8	Houston	170	165	153	168	656	14.98%				
9	Toronto	162	175	124	166	627	14.32%				
10	Los Angeles	78	65	81	37	261	5.96%				
11	Philadelphia	97	87	102	93	379	8.65%				
12	Vancouver	120	130	117	130	497	11.35%				
13	Total	1082	1100	1090	1108	4380					
14											
15	Average	120.222	122.222	121.111	123.111						
16	Maximum	170	175	184	168						
17	Minimum	78	65	81	37						
18											

Switch Worksheet Views

Learning Outcomes
- Change worksheet views
- Zoom a worksheet
- Adjust page breaks in a worksheet

You can change your view of the worksheet window at any time, using either the View tab on the ribbon or the View buttons on the status bar. Changing your view does not affect the contents of a worksheet; it just makes it easier for you to focus on different tasks, such as preparing a worksheet for printing. The View tab includes a variety of viewing options, such as View buttons, zoom controls, and the ability to show or hide worksheet elements such as gridlines. The status bar offers fewer View options but can be more convenient to use. **CASE** *You want to review your worksheet before sharing it with your colleagues.*

STEPS

QUICK TIP

You can use the Zoom button to select the worksheet magnification level or the Zoom to Selection button to zoom into the cell or range that is selected on the worksheet.

1. **Click cell A1, verify that the zoom level in the Zoom area of the status bar is 120%, click the View tab on the ribbon, then click the 100% button in the Zoom group**

   The worksheet zooms to 100%. Another way to change the zoom level is to use the Zoom slider on the status bar.

2. **Click the Zoom in button ⊞ on the status bar twice**

   The worksheet zooms in 10% at a time, to 120%.

3. **Click the Page Layout button in the Workbook Views group on the View tab**

   The view switches from the default view, Normal, to Page Layout view. **Normal view** shows the worksheet without including certain features like headers and footers; it's ideal for creating and editing a worksheet but may not be detailed enough when you want to put the finishing touches on a document. **Page Layout view** provides an accurate view of how a worksheet will look when printed, including headers and footers, as shown in **FIGURE 1-20**. Above and to the left of the page are rulers. A page number indicator on the status bar tells you the current page and the total number of pages in this worksheet.

QUICK TIP

Although a worksheet can contain more than a million rows and thousands of columns, the current document contains only as many pages as necessary for the current project.

4. **Click the Ruler check box in the Show group on the View tab to remove the checkmark, then click the Gridlines check box in the Show group to remove the checkmark**

   Removing the checkmarks hides the rulers and gridlines. By default, gridlines in a worksheet do not print, so hiding them gives you a more accurate image of your final document.

5. **Click the Page Break Preview button ▥ on the status bar**

   Your view changes to Page Break Preview, which displays a reduced view of each page of your worksheet, along with page break indicators that you can drag to include more or less information on a page.

6. **Drag the pointer ↕ from the bottom page break indicator to the bottom of row 20, as shown in FIGURE 1-21**

   When you're working on a large worksheet with multiple pages, sometimes you need to adjust where pages break; in this worksheet, however, the information all fits comfortably on one page.

QUICK TIP

Once you view a worksheet in Page Break Preview, the page break indicators appear as lines after you switch back to Normal view or Page Layout view.

7. **Click the Page Layout button in the Workbook Views group, click the Ruler box in the Show group, then click the Gridlines box in the Show group**

   Adding checkmarks to the check boxes displays the rulers and gridlines. You can show or hide View tab items in any view.

8. **Click the Normal button in the Workbook Views group, then save your work**

FIGURE 1-20: Page Layout view

Turns ruler on/off

If header is added, it appears here

Workbook Views group

Turns gridlines on/off

Horizontal ruler

Vertical ruler

Add header

		JCL Talent, Inc.						Previous Year Total	4
		IT Position Postings							
	Quarter 1	Quarter 2	Quarter 3	Quarter 4	Total	% of Total		This Year	4
Boston	133	135	184	162	614	14.02%			
Miami	92	81	101	98	372	8.49%		% Increase	2.4
Chicago	109	132	127	151	519	11.85%			
Seattle	121	130	101	103	455	10.39%			
Houston	170	165	153	168	656	14.98%			

Current page and total number of pages

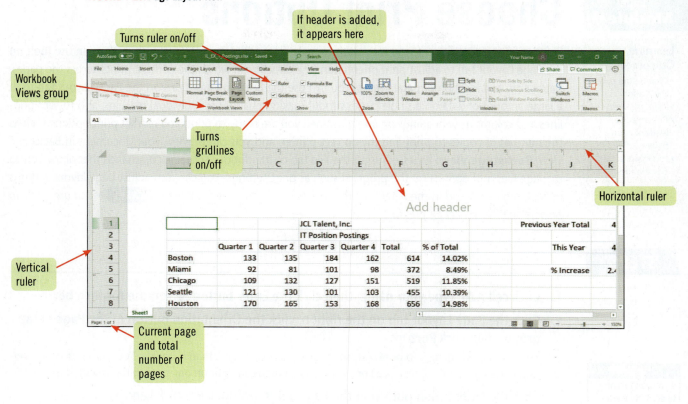

FIGURE 1-21: Page Break Preview

Drag to row 20

Bottom page break indicator

Choose Print Options

Before printing a document, you may want to make final adjustments to the output. You can use tools on the Page Layout tab to adjust print orientation (the direction in which the content prints across the page), paper size, and location of page breaks. You can use the Scale to Fit options on the Page Layout tab to fit a large amount of data on a single page without making changes to individual margins, and to turn gridlines and column/row headings on and off. When you are ready to print, you can set print options such as the number of copies to print and the correct printer, and you can preview your document in Backstage view. **Backstage view**, accessed using the File tab of the ribbon, contains commands that allow you to manage files and options for the program such as print settings. You can also adjust page layout settings in Backstage view and immediately see the results in the document preview. **CASE** *You are ready to prepare your worksheet for printing.*

STEPS

1. **Click cell A20, type your name, then click the Enter button** ☑ **on the formula bar**

2. **Click the Page Layout tab on the ribbon, click the Orientation button in the Page Setup group, then click Portrait**

   The orientation changes to **portrait**, so the printed page is taller than it is wide. You can see from the vertical dotted line, indicating a page break, that all columns don't fit on one page in this orientation.

   QUICK TIP

   If you don't want to print gridlines or headings, make sure to clear the Print check boxes for both options in the Sheet Options group; clearing the View check boxes does not affect what prints.

3. **Click the Orientation button in the Page Setup group, then click Landscape**

   The paper orientation returns to **landscape**, so the printed page is wider than it is tall. Now all the content fits on one page.

4. **Click the Gridlines Print box in the Sheet Options group on the Page Layout tab, then save your work**

   Printing gridlines makes the data easier to read, but the gridlines will not print unless the Gridlines Print box is selected. You can also print row numbers and column letters by clicking the Headings Print box. If you don't want to print gridlines or headings, make sure these boxes are not selected.

   QUICK TIP

   You can choose to print an entire workbook or a selected area of the worksheet by clicking the Print Active Sheets button in the Settings list, then clicking Print Entire Workbook or Print Selection.

5. **Click the File tab, click Print on the navigation bar, then select an active printer if necessary**

   The Print tab in Backstage view displays a preview of your worksheet exactly as it will look when it is printed. To the left of the preview, you can also change a number of document settings and print options. Compare your screen to **FIGURE 1-22**. You can print from this view by clicking Print, or you can return to the worksheet without printing by clicking the Back button ⊙.

6. **Click the Page Setup link in the Settings list, click the Margins tab in the Page Setup dialog box, click the Horizontally check box in the Center on page section, click the Vertically check box in the Center on page section, then compare your screen to FIGURE 1-23**

   The printed worksheet will be centered on the page.

   QUICK TIP

   You can change the number of printed pages of your worksheet by clicking the Page Layout tab, then clicking the Width and Height arrows in the Scale to Fit group.

7. **Click OK, then click Print**

   One copy of the worksheet prints.

8. **sam↑ Save your workbook, submit your work to your instructor as directed, click File, click Close, then click the Close button** ☒ **on the title bar**

FIGURE 1-22: Worksheet in Backstage view

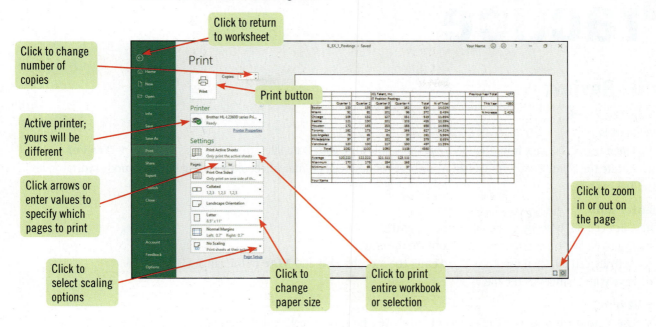

Click to return to worksheet

Click to change number of copies

Print button

Active printer; yours will be different

Click arrows or enter values to specify which pages to print

Click to zoom in or out on the page

Click to select scaling options

Click to change paper size

Click to print entire workbook or selection

FIGURE 1-23: Page Setup dialog box

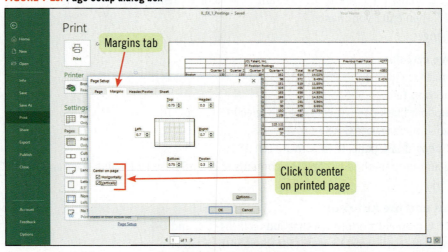

Margins tab

Click to center on printed page

Setting a print area

If you want to print a selected worksheet area repeatedly, it's best to define a **print area**, so that the Quick Print feature prints only that portion of the worksheet area. To define a print area, select the range you want to print on the worksheet, click the Page Layout tab on the ribbon, click the Print Area button in the Page Setup group, then click Set Print Area. A print area can consist of one contiguous range of cells, or multiple ranges in different parts of a worksheet. To clear a print area, click the Page Layout tab on the ribbon, click the Print Area button in the Page Setup group, then click Clear Print Area.

Scaling to fit

If you have a large amount of data that you want to fit to a single sheet of paper, you can control how much of your work to print on a single sheet by clicking the No Scaling arrow in the Settings list in the Print screen in Backstage view, then clicking Fit Sheet on One Page, Fit All Columns on One Page, or Fit All Rows on One Page. Another method for fitting worksheet content onto one page is to click the Page Layout tab on the ribbon, then change the Width and Height settings in the Scale to Fit group to 1 page each. You can also click the Page Setup link in the Print screen in Backstage view, click the Page tab if necessary in the Page Setup dialog box, click the Fit to option button, then enter 1 in the page(s) wide by and tall fields.

Practice

Skills Review

1. **Explore Excel.**
   a. Start Excel.
   b. Open IL_EX_1-2.xlsx from the location where you store your Data Files, then save it as **IL_EX_1_Travel**.
   c. Locate the Name box, formula bar, worksheet window, cell pointer, sheet tab scrolling buttons, mode indicator, and Tell me box.

2. **Enter data.**
   a. Click cell B3, type **Jan**, then confirm the entry.
   b. Click cell D7, type **202497**, then confirm the entry.
   c. Activate cell B3, then use Auto Fill to enter the months **Feb** and **Mar** in the range C3:D3.
   d. Save your changes to the file.

3. **Edit data.**
   a. Use F2 to correct the spelling of Maimi in cell A6 (the correct spelling is Miami).
   b. Click cell C7, then use the formula bar to change the value to **188270**.
   c. Click cell A17, then enter your name.
   d. Save your changes.

4. **Copy and move cell data.**
   a. Select the range G4:G6.
   b. Copy the selection to the Clipboard.
   c. Open the Clipboard task pane, then paste the selection to cell A10.
   d. Delete the labels in the range G4:G6.
   e. Close the Clipboard task pane, then activate cell A8.
   f. Use the drag-and-drop method to copy the contents of cell A8 to cell E3. (*Hint:* Press and hold CTRL while dragging.)
   g. Save your work.

5. **Enter formulas and use AutoSum.**
   a. Activate cell E4, then enter a formula that adds cells B4, C4, and D4.
   b. Use AutoSum to enter the total expenses for the month of January in cell B8.
   c. Save your changes.

6. **Copy formulas with relative cell references.**
   a. Activate cell E4, then use the fill handle to copy the formula in cell E4 to the range E5:E7.
   b. Activate cell B8, then use the fill handle to copy the formula in cell B8 to the range C8:E8.
   c. Save your work.

7. **Copy formulas with absolute cell references.**
   a. Enter **% of Total** in cell F3.
   b. In cell F4, create a formula that divides the value in cell E4 by the value in cell E8 using an absolute reference to cell E8.
   c. Use the fill handle to copy the formula in cell F4 to the range F5:F7.
   d. Save your work.

Skills Review (continued)

8. Enter a formula with multiple operators.

  a. Enter a formula in cell B10 that calculates the average travel expenses for the month of January. Use a formula that contains cell references and not a function. (*Hint:* The formula is =(B4+B5+B6+B7)/4.)

  b. Review the use of the parentheses in the formula.

  c. Save your work.

9. Insert a function.

  a. Use the Insert Function button to create a formula in cell B11 that calculates the maximum travel expense for January.

  b. In cell B12, enter a function to calculate the minimum travel expenses for January.

  c. Select the range B10:B12, then use the fill handle to copy the functions into the range C10:D12.

  d. Save your work.

10. Switch worksheet views.

  a. Click the View tab on the ribbon, then switch to Page Layout view.

  b. Verify that the Ruler and Gridlines check boxes contain checkmarks.

  c. Switch to Page Break view and adjust the page break so it comes at the bottom of row 20.

  d. Switch to Normal View, use a button in the Zoom group of the View tab to zoom the worksheet to 100%, then use the Zoom buttons in the Status bar to zoom the worksheet back to 120%.

  e. Save your changes.

11. Choose print options.

  a. Use the Page Layout tab to change the orientation to Portrait.

  b. Turn on gridlines for printing using a check box in the Sheet Options group of the Page Layout tab.

  c. Preview the worksheet in Backstage view, then use the Page Setup dialog box to center the worksheet vertically and horizontally on the page. (*Hint:* The commands are located on the Margins tab.) Compare your screen to **FIGURE 1-24**.

  d. Save your changes, submit your work to your instructor as directed, close the workbook, then exit Excel.

FIGURE 1-24

	Reed & Allen Legal Services				
	Travel Expenses				
	Jan	Feb	Mar	Total	% of Total
New York	220,125	187,012	240,185	647,322	24.26%
Los Angeles	289,134	302,184	219,750	811,068	30.39%
Miami	157,368	207,305	257,217	621,890	23.30%
Chicago	197,516	188,270	202,497	588,283	22.04%
Total	864,143	884,771	919,649	2,668,563	
Average	216,036	221,193	229,912		
Maximum	289,134	302,184	257,217		
Minimum	157,368	187,012	202,497		
Your Name					

Independent Challenge 1

The CFO at Riverwalk Medical Clinic has hired you to help him analyze departmental insurance reimbursements. He also would like to see what quarterly revenues would look like with a 20% increase in quarterly reimbursements. You've been given a worksheet for this project that contains some but not all of the data.

  a. Open IL_EX_1-3.xlsx from the location where you store your Data Files, then save it as **IL_EX_1_Reimbursements**.

  b. Enter the data shown in **TABLE 1-4** in the range E4:E11.

  c. Type your name in cell A17.

  d. Move the label in cell F2 to cell A15.

Independent Challenge 1 (continued)

e. Use the Clipboard to copy and paste the label in cell F3 to cell A12.

f. Use the formula bar to correct the spelling error in the label in cell A6. (*Hint:* The correct spelling is Immunology.)

g. Edit cell A8 to correct the spelling error in the label. (*Hint:* The correct spelling is Ophthalmology.)

h. Type **Quarter 1** in cell B3, then use Auto Fill to enter Quarter 2, Quarter 3, and Quarter 4 in the range C3:E3.

i. Create a formula in cell F4 that uses cell references and totals the quarterly reimbursements for the Cardiology department.

j. Use the fill handle to copy the formula in cell F4 to the range F5:F11.

k. Using AutoSum, create a formula in cell B12 that totals the first quarter reimbursements for all the departments.

l. Copy the formula in cell B12 to the range C12:E12.

m. Enter a formula in cell B14 to calculate a 20% increase in the first quarter reimbursement total in cell B12. (*Hint:* You need to add B12 to B12 multiplied by .20. Use parentheses if necessary to follow the order of operations.)

n. Enter a function, using the help of AutoComplete, in cell B15 that calculates the average first quarter reimbursement amount for the departments.

o. Copy the formulas in the range B14:B15 to the range C14:E15.

p. Switch to Page Break view and adjust the page break to the bottom of row 18.

q. Switch to Normal View, then zoom the worksheet to 120%.

r. Turn on gridlines for printing.

s. Change the page orientation to landscape.

t. Preview the worksheet in Backstage view, then use the Page Setup dialog box to center the worksheet horizontally and vertically on the page. Compare your screen to FIGURE 1-25.

u. Submit your work to your instructor as directed.

v. Close the workbook, then exit Excel.

TABLE 1-4

cell address	value
E4	67247.90
E5	45581.20
E6	43000.60
E7	48539.20
E8	38125.00
E9	28909.50
E10	39216.90
E11	71189.10

FIGURE 1-25

	Quarter 1	Quarter 2	Quarter 3	Quarter 4	Total
Riverwalk Medical Clinic					
Insurance Reimbursements					
	Quarter 1	Quarter 2	Quarter 3	Quarter 4	Total
Cardiology	61,762.00	61,738.20	72,076.60	67,247.90	262,824.70
Dermatology	36,109.90	40,214.60	44,374.00	45,581.20	166,279.70
Immunology	43,877.60	44,719.80	46,702.10	43,000.60	178,300.10
Neurology	41,321.00	45,897.40	46,790.60	48,539.20	182,548.20
Ophthalmology	51,827.70	30,045.20	36,611.20	38,125.00	156,609.10
Orthopedics	15,682.50	26,103.00	27,650.20	28,909.50	98,345.20
Pediatrics	33,715.00	36,561.40	83,403.50	39,216.90	192,896.80
Psychology	72,950.60	66,427.60	73,403.60	71,189.10	283,970.90
Total	357,246.30	351,707.20	431,011.80	381,809.40	
20% increase	428,695.56	422,048.64	517,214.16	458,171.28	
Average	44,655.79	43,963.40	53,876.48	47,726.18	
Your Name					

1   of 1

Independent Challenge 2

As the assistant to the Dean of STEM (science, technology, engineering, and mathematics) at West Shore Community College, it is your responsibility to review the budgets for the departments in the division and help with a budget forecast for the upcoming academic year. You've decided to use Excel formulas and functions to help with this analysis.

a. Open IL_EX_1-4.xlsx from the location where you store your Data Files, then save it as **IL_EX_1_Budgets**.

b. Move the labels in the range A6:A11 to the range A5:A10.

c. Enter **Total** in cell A11, then use AutoSum to calculate the total 2020 expenses for all departments in cell B11.

d. Enter **Average** in cell A12, then use the AutoSum arrow to enter a function in cell B12 that calculates the average 2020 expenses for all departments. (*Hint:* make sure you include only the department data.)

e. Use the fill handle to copy the formulas in the range B11:B12 to the range C11:C12.

f. Using cell references, enter a formula in cell D5 that calculates the 2022 Budget for the engineering department, using the increase shown in cell F2 over the 2021 expenses in cell C5. Use absolute cell references where necessary. (*Hint:* Multiply the percentage in cell F2 by the 2021 expenses in cell C5, then add that amount to the 2021 expenses in cell C5.)

g. Use the fill handle to copy the formula in cell D5 to the range D6:D10.

h. Use the fill handle to copy the formulas in the range C11:C12 to the range D11:D12.

i. Enter a formula in cell F5 that calculates the percentage increase in total expenses from 2020 to 2021. (*Hint:* The 2020 total is in cell B11 and the 2021 total is in cell C11.)

j. Change the page orientation to landscape, then turn on gridlines for printing.

k. Enter your name in cell A14.

l. Preview the worksheet in Backstage view. Compare your screen to **FIGURE 1-26**.

m. Save your work, then submit the worksheet to your instructor as directed.

n. Close the workbook and exit Excel.

FIGURE 1-26

West Shore Community College					2022 Budget Increase		
STEM Division					2.15%		
Departmental Budgets							
Department	2020 Expenses	2021 Expenses	2022 Budget		% Increase in Expenses 2020 to 2021		
Engineering	$50,124.17	$52,457.65	$53,585.49		6.01%		
Computer Science	$45,287.23	$55,214.98	$56,402.10				
Biology	$36,784.98	$36,799.88	$37,591.08				
Chemistry	$58,214.78	$59,847.47	$61,134.19				
Physics	$61,002.27	$62,178.78	$63,515.62				
Math	$37,512.32	$39,781.33	$40,636.63				
Total	$288,925.75	$306,280.09	$312,865.11				
Average	$48,154.29	$51,046.68	$52,144.19				
Your Name							

Visual Workshop

Open IL_EX_1-5.xlsx from the location where you store your Data Files, then save it as **IL_EX_1_Royalties**. Complete the worksheet shown in **FIGURE 1-27** using the skills you learned in this module. Use functions to calculate the values in B8:B11 and C8. The values in column C are calculated by multiplying the gross revenues in column B by the percentage in cell E2. Adjust your zoom level as necessary to match the figure. Enter your name in cell A14. Submit your work to your instructor as directed.

FIGURE 1-27

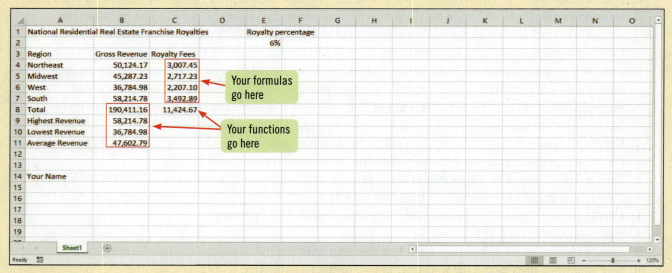

Getting Started with Excel

Formatting a Worksheet

CASE Cheri McNeil, the manager of the Boston office at JCL Talent, has gathered data from all JCL recruiters on technology position postings for the first quarter of the year. Cheri has created a worksheet listing this information, and she asks you to format the worksheet to make it easier to read and understand.

Module Objectives

After completing this module, you will be able to:

- Format values
- Change font and font size
- Change font styles and alignment
- Adjust column width
- Insert and delete rows and columns
- Apply colors, borders, and documentation
- Apply conditional formatting
- Rename and move a worksheet
- Check spelling

Files You Will Need

IL_EX_2-1.xlsx   IL_EX_2-4.xlsx
IL_EX_2-2.xlsx   IL_EX_2-5.xlsx
IL_EX_2-3.xlsx

Format Values

When you **format** a cell, you enhance the appearance of information by changing its font, size, color, or alignment. Formatting changes only the appearance of a value or label; it does not alter the actual data in any way. To format a cell or range, first you select it, then you apply the formatting using the ribbon, Mini toolbar, or a keyboard shortcut. You can apply formatting before or after you enter data in a cell or range.

CASE ▶ *Cheri has provided you with a worksheet that details technology postings, and you're ready to improve its appearance. You start by formatting some cells to better reflect the type of information they contain, such as currency, percentages, and dates.*

STEPS

1. **sam** ⬇ **Start Excel, open IL_EX_2-1.xlsx from the location where you store your Data Files, then save it as IL_EX_2_Tech**

   This worksheet is difficult to interpret because all the information is crowded and looks the same. In some columns, such as D, the contents appear cut off because there is too much data to fit given the current column width. You decide not to widen the columns yet, because the other changes you plan to make might affect column width and row height.

2. **Select the range G3:G15, then click the Accounting Number Format button $ in the Number group on the Home tab**

   A **number format** is applied to values to express numeric concepts, such as currency, date, and percentage. The default Accounting number format adds dollar signs and two decimal places to the expense data, as shown in **FIGURE 2-1**.

3. **Select the range H3:H15, then click the Comma Style button ⁹ in the Number group**

   The values in column H display the Comma Style format, which does not include a dollar sign but can be useful for some types of accounting data.

4. **Click cell M1, click the Number Format arrow, click Percentage, then click the Increase Decimal button 🔼 in the Number group**

   The revenue rate is now formatted with a percent sign (%) and three decimal places. The Number Format arrow lets you choose from popular number formats and shows an example of what the selected cell or cells would look like (when multiple cells are selected, the example is based on the first cell in the range). Each time you click the Increase Decimal button, you add one decimal place; clicking the button twice would add two decimal places.

5. **Click the Decrease Decimal button 🔽 in the Number group three times**

   All three decimal places are removed from the revenue rate value.

6. **Select the range C3:C15, then click the launcher ⌐ in the Number group**

   The Format Cells dialog box opens with the Date category already selected on the Number tab.

7. **Click the 14-Mar format in the Type list box, as shown in FIGURE 2-2, then click OK**

   The dates in column C appear in the 14-Mar format.

8. **Select the range I3:J15, right-click the range, click Format Cells on the shortcut menu, in the Category list click Currency, in the Decimal places box type 2 if necessary, then click OK**

   This number format looks similar to the Accounting format but aligns currency symbols and decimal points slightly differently. Compare your worksheet to **FIGURE 2-3**.

9. **Select the range G3:I15, click the Decrease Decimal button 🔽 in the Number group twice, press CTRL+HOME, then save your work**

   The cell values in this range now use a custom format that doesn't display decimal places. This format is applied to all cells in the range, including the cells in column H that display the $ symbol.

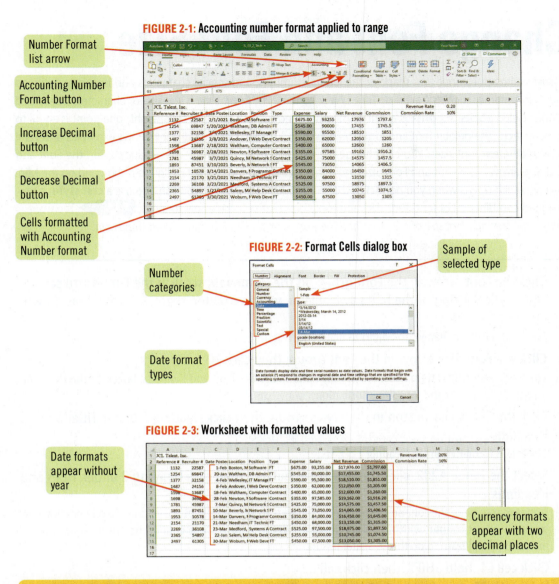

FIGURE 2-1: Accounting number format applied to range

Number Format list arrow

Accounting Number Format button

Increase Decimal button

Decrease Decimal button

Cells formatted with Accounting Number format

FIGURE 2-2: Format Cells dialog box

Number categories

Sample of selected type

Date format types

FIGURE 2-3: Worksheet with formatted values

Date formats appear without year

Currency formats appear with two decimal places

Working with online pictures, other images, and symbols

You can illustrate your worksheets using online pictures and other images. To add a picture to a worksheet, click the Illustrations button on the Insert tab, click Pictures, then click Online Pictures. The Online Pictures dialog box opens. Here you can search for online pictures from the Bing search engine or OneDrive, as shown in **FIGURE 2-4**. To search, type one or more keywords in the search box, then press ENTER. When you double-click an image in the Search Results window, the image is inserted at the location of the active cell. Clicking an image selects it and adds resizing handles. To resize an image proportionally, drag any corner sizing handle. If you drag an edge sizing handle, the image will be resized nonproportionally. You can add alternative text to an image by right-clicking it, clicking Edit Alt Text on the shortcut menu, then entering the text in the Alt Text pane. To move an image, point inside the image until the pointer changes to ⊹, then drag it to a new location. To delete a picture, select it, then press DEL. To work with an image it must be selected. You

FIGURE 2-4: Results of Online Picture search

Type keyword(s) here, then press ENTER to begin search

Your available images may differ

can select an image, or any object, by clicking it. To work with multiple images at once, hold CTRL while clicking each image. You can insert a symbol in a worksheet by clicking the Insert tab, clicking the Symbols button in the Symbols group, clicking Symbol, clicking a symbol from the Symbols tab in the Symbol dialog box, clicking Insert, then clicking Close to close the Symbol dialog box.

Change Font and Font Size

Learning Outcomes
- Change a font
- Change a font size

A **font** is the appearance and shape of the letters, numbers, and special characters and is usually designed with a font name, such as Calibri or Times New Roman. The **font size** is the size of characters, measured in units called points. A **point** is a unit of measure used for font size and row height; one point is equal to ½₂ of an inch. The default font and font size in Excel is 11-point Calibri. **TABLE 2-1** shows examples of several fonts in different font sizes. You can change the font and font size of any cell or range using the Font and Font Size arrows. The Font and Font Size arrows are located on the Home tab on the ribbon and on the Mini toolbar, which opens when you right-click a cell or range. To save time, you can also use a **cell style**, a pre-designed combination of font, font size, and font color that you can apply to a cell. **CASE** *You want to change the font and font size of the labels and the worksheet title, so this information stands out.*

STEPS

1. **Click the Font arrow in the Font group on the Home tab, scroll in the Font list to see an alphabetical listing of the fonts available on your computer, then click Calibri, as shown in FIGURE 2-5**

   The font in cell A1 changes to Calibri to match the rest of the worksheet.

QUICK TIP

You can also use the Increase Font Size button A^ to increase the font size by one point or the Decrease Font Size button to decrease it by one point. You specify an exact size by entering the size in the Font Size box.

2. **Click the Font Size arrow in the Font group, then click 20**

   The worksheet title is formatted in 20-point Calibri, and the Font and Font Size boxes on the Home tab display the new font and font size information.

3. **Click the Cell Styles button in the Styles group, then click Heading 1 under Titles and Headings**

   The title is formatted in the Heading 1 cell style.

4. **Select the range A2:J2, click the Cell Styles button, then click Heading 2 under Titles and Headings**

   Notice that some of the column labels are now too wide to appear fully in the column. Excel does not automatically adjust column widths to accommodate cell formatting; these column widths must be adjusted manually. You'll learn to do this in a later lesson.

QUICK TIP

Holding CTRL while selecting cells allows you to select multiple nonadjacent cells.

5. **Click cell L1, hold SHIFT, then click cell L2**

   Holding SHIFT while clicking a cell selects that cell and any cells between it and the cell first selected. In this case there are only two cells selected.

6. **Click the Cell Styles button, then click Heading 4 under Titles and Headings**

   The revenue and commission rate labels are now formatted consistently. Compare your worksheet to **FIGURE 2-6**.

7. **Save your work**

TABLE 2-1: Examples of fonts and font sizes

font name	12 point	24 point
Calibri	Excel	Excel
Playbill	Excel	Excel
Comic Sans MS	Excel	Excel
Times New Roman	Excel	Excel

FIGURE 2-5: Font list

Font list arrow

Active cell displays preview of selected formatting change

Font size list arrow

Click a font to apply it to the selected cell

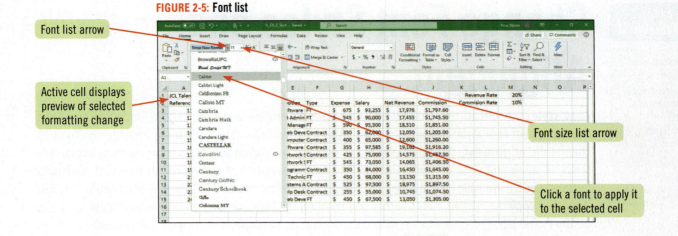

FIGURE 2-6: Worksheet with formatted headings and column labels

Cell Styles

Title formatted in Heading 1 cell style

Rate labels are formatted in Heading 4 cell style

Column labels are formatted in Heading 2 cell style

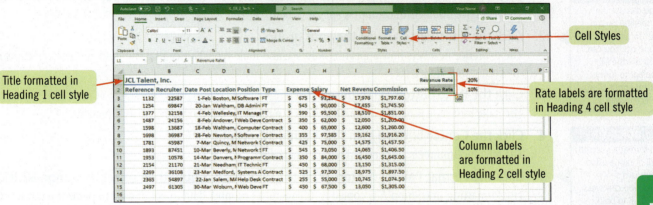

Working with cell styles

You can modify any style in the Cell Styles gallery. In the Cell Styles gallery, right-click the cell style that you want to modify, on the shortcut menu shown in **FIGURE 2-7**, click Modify, select the style options from the Style Includes list in the Style dialog box, click the Format button to choose new customized formatting, then click OK twice. To create a new cell style, click New Cell Style at the bottom of the Cell Styles gallery, enter a name in the Style name box, select style options from the Style Includes list, click the Format button to choose customized formatting for your style, then click OK twice. You can merge styles from a different workbook by opening the workbook that contains the cell styles that you want to copy, clicking Merge Styles at the bottom of the Cell Styles gallery, clicking the workbook

FIGURE 2-7: Shortcut menu in Cell Styles gallery

in the Merge styles from list, then clicking OK. If styles in the workbooks have the same name, you will be asked if you want to merge those styles.

Change Font Styles and Alignment

**Learning
Outcomes**
• Apply formatting
• Use the Format
  Painter
• Change cell
  alignment

Font styles are formats that indicate how characters are emphasized, such as bold, underline, and italic. You have seen font styles applied with cell styles, and you can also apply them individually. You can change the **alignment**, the placement of cell contents in relation to a cell's edges, such as left or centered, of labels and values in cells. See **TABLE 2-2** for a description of common font style and alignment buttons that are available on the Home tab. Once you have formatted a cell the way you want it, you can "paint" or copy the cell's formats to other cells by using the Format Painter button in the Clipboard group on the Home tab. This is similar to using copy and paste, but instead of copying cell contents, it copies only the cell's formatting. **CASE** *You want to further enhance the worksheet's appearance by adding bold and underline formatting and centering some of the labels.*

STEPS

1. **Select the range A3:A15, then click the Bold button** B **in the Font group on the Home tab**
   The reference numbers in column A appear in bold.

2. **Click the Italic button** I **in the Font group**
   The reference numbers now appear in boldface and italic type. Notice that the Bold and Italic buttons in the Font group are selected.

3. **Click the Italic button** I **to deselect it**
   The italic font style is removed from the reference numbers but the bold font style remains.

4. **Click the Center button** ≡ **in the Alignment group**
   The reference numbers are centered within their cells.

5. **Click the Format Painter button** 🖌 **in the Clipboard group, then select the range B3:B15**
   The formatting in column A is copied to the recruiter number data in column B. To paint the formats to more than one selection, double-click the Format Painter button to keep it activated until you turn it off. You can turn off the Format Painter by pressing ESC or by clicking 🖌.

6. **Click cell A1, select the range A1:J1, then click the Merge & Center button** 🔲 **in the Alignment group**
   The Merge & Center button creates one cell out of the ten cells across the row, then centers the text in that newly created, merged cell. The title "JCL Talent, Inc." is centered across the ten columns you selected. To split a merged cell into its original components, select the merged cell, then click the Merge & Center button 🔲 to deselect it. Occasionally, you may find that you want cell contents to wrap within a cell. You can do this by selecting the cells containing the text you want to wrap, then clicking the Wrap Text button 🔲 in the Alignment group on the Home tab on the ribbon.

7. **Compare your screen to FIGURE 2-8, then save your work**

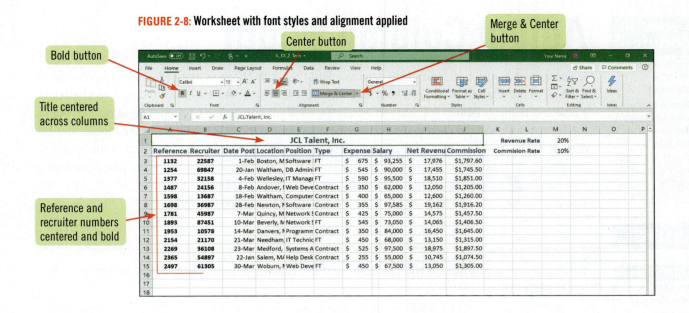

FIGURE 2-8: Worksheet with font styles and alignment applied

Bold button

Center button

Merge & Center button

Title centered across columns

Reference and recruiter numbers centered and bold

TABLE 2-2: Common font style and alignment buttons

button	description
B	Bolds cell content
I	Italicizes cell content
U	Underlines cell content
	Centers content across columns; also merges two or more selected, adjacent cells into one cell; also unmerges previously merged cells
	Aligns content at the left edge of the cell
	Centers content horizontally within the cell
	Aligns content at the right edge of the cell
ab⇄c	Wraps long text into multiple lines to fit within a column
	Aligns content at the top of a cell
	Aligns content at the bottom of a cell
	Aligns content in the middle of a cell

Rotating and indenting cell entries

In addition to applying fonts and font styles, you can rotate or indent data within a cell. To rotate text within a cell, click the Home tab, select the cells you want to modify, then click the dialog box launcher in the Alignment group to open the Alignment tab of the Format Cells dialog box. Click a position in the Orientation box or type a number in the Degrees box to rotate text from its default horizontal orientation, then click OK. You can indent cell contents by clicking the Increase Indent button in the Alignment group, which moves cell contents to the right one space, or the Decrease Indent button, which moves cell contents to the left one space.

Excel

Adjust Column Width

As you format a worksheet, you might need to adjust the width of one or more columns to accommodate changes in the amount of text, the font size, or font style. The default column width is 8.43 characters, a little less than 1". With Excel, you can adjust the width of one or more columns by using the mouse, the Format button in the Cells group on the Home tab, or the shortcut menu. Using the mouse, you can drag or double-click the right edge of a column heading. The Format button and shortcut menu include commands for making more precise width adjustments. **TABLE 2-3** describes common column formatting commands. **CASE** *You have noticed that some of the labels in columns A through L don't fit in the cells. You want to adjust the widths of the columns so that the labels appear in their entirety.*

STEPS

1. **Position the pointer on the line between the column C and column D headings until it changes to ╫**

   See **FIGURE 2-9**. A **column heading** is a box that appears above each worksheet column and identifies it by a letter. You positioned the mouse pointer here because in order to adjust column width using the mouse, you need to position the pointer on the right edge of the column heading for the column you want to adjust.

2. **Click and drag ╫ to the right until the column fully displays the column label Date Posted (approximately 12.71 characters or 94 pixels)**

   As you change the column width, a ScreenTip opens listing the column width.

3. **Position the pointer on the line between columns D and E until it changes to ╫, then double-click**

   Column D automatically widens to fit the widest entry. Double-clicking the right edge of a column heading activates **AutoFit**. This feature adjusts column width or row height to accommodate its widest or tallest entry.

4. **Use AutoFit to resize columns E, F, G, H, and L**

5. **Position the pointer in the column heading area for column I until it changes to ↓, then drag to select columns I and J**

6. **Click the Format button in the Cells group, then click Column Width**

   The Column Width dialog box opens. Column width measurement is based on the number of characters that will fit in the column when formatted in the Normal font and font size (in this case, 11-point Calibri).

7. **Type 14 in the Column width box, then click OK**

   The widths of columns I and J change to reflect the new setting. See **FIGURE 2-10**.

8. **Click cell A1, then save your work**

FIGURE 2-9: Preparing to change the column width

Resize pointer

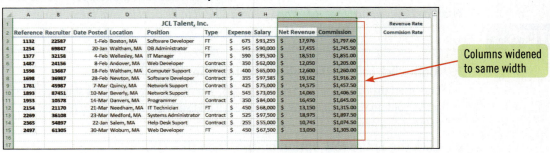

FIGURE 2-10: Worksheet with column widths adjusted

Columns widened to same width

TABLE 2-3: Common column formatting commands

command	description	available using
Column Width	Sets the width to a specific number of characters	Format button; shortcut menu
AutoFit Column Width	Fits to the widest entry in a column	Format button; mouse
Hide & Unhide	Hides or displays selected column(s)	Format button; shortcut menu
Default Width	Resets column to worksheet's default column width	Format button

Changing row height

Changing row height is as easy as changing column width. Row height is calculated in points, the same unit of measure used for fonts. The row height must exceed the size of the font you are using. Normally, you don't need to adjust row height manually, because row heights adjust automatically to accommodate font size changes. If you format something in a row to be a larger point size, Excel adjusts the row to fit the largest point size in the row. However, you have just as many options for changing row height as you do column width. Using the mouse, you can place the ✛ pointer on the line dividing a row heading from the heading below it, and then drag to the desired height; double-clicking the line AutoFits the row height where necessary. You can also select one or more rows, then use the Row Height command on the shortcut menu, or click the Format button on the Home tab, then click the Row Height or AutoFit Row Height command.

**Learning
Outcomes**
• Use the Insert
  dialog box
• Use column and
  row heading
  buttons to insert
  and delete

Insert and Delete Rows and Columns

As you modify a worksheet, you might find it necessary to insert or delete rows and columns to keep your worksheet current. For example, you might need to insert rows to accommodate new inventory products or remove a column of yearly totals that are no longer necessary. When you insert a new row, the row is inserted above the cell pointer and the contents of the worksheet shift down from the newly inserted row. When you insert a new column, the column is inserted to the left of the cell pointer and the contents of the worksheet shift to the right of the new column. To insert multiple rows, select the same number of row headings as you want to insert before using the Insert command. **CASE** ▶ *You want to improve the overall appearance of the worksheet by inserting a row between the company name and the column labels. Also, you have learned that row 9 and column K need to be deleted from the worksheet.*

STEPS

1. **Right-click cell F2, then click Insert on the shortcut menu**

   The Insert dialog box opens. See **FIGURE 2-11**. You can choose to insert a single cell and shift the cells in the active column to the right, insert a single cell and shift the cells in the active row down, or insert an entire column or a row.

2. **Click the Entire row option button, then click OK**

   A blank row appears between the company name and the column labels, visually separating the worksheet data, and the Insert Options button 🖌 opens next to cell F3.

3. **Click the Insert Options button 🖌, then review your choices**

   This menu lets you format the inserted row in Format Same As Above (the default setting, already selected), Format Same As Below, or Clear Formatting.

4. **Click 🖌 to close the menu without making changes, then click the row 9 heading**

   All of row 9 is selected, as shown in **FIGURE 2-12**.

5. **Click the Delete button in the Cells group; do not click the Delete arrow**

   Excel deletes row 9, and all rows below it shift up one row. You must use the Delete button or the Delete command on the shortcut menu to delete a row or column; pressing DEL on the keyboard removes only the *contents* of a selected row or column.

6. **Click the column K heading**

   The column is empty and isn't necessary in this worksheet.

7. **Click the Delete button in the Cells group**

   Excel deletes column K. The remaining columns to the right shift left one column.

8. **Save your work**

FIGURE 2-11: Insert dialog box

Entire row option button

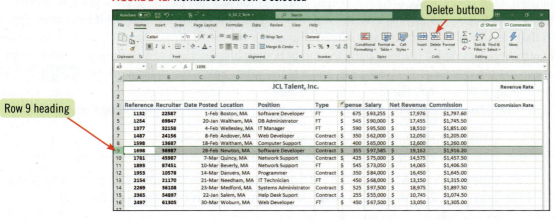

FIGURE 2-12: Worksheet with row 9 selected

Delete button

Row 9 heading

Hiding and unhiding columns and rows

When you don't want data in a column or row to be visible, but you don't want to delete it, you can hide the column or row. To hide a selected column, click the Format button in the Cells group on the Home tab, point to Hide & Unhide, then click Hide Columns. A hidden column is indicated by a dark green vertical line in its original position. This green line is removed when you click elsewhere on the worksheet, but a thin double line remains between the column headings to remind you that one or more columns are hidden. You can display a hidden column by selecting the column headings on either side of the hidden column, clicking the Format button in the Cells group, pointing to Hide & Unhide, then clicking Unhide Columns. (To hide or unhide one or more rows, substitute Hide Rows and Unhide Rows for the Hide Columns and Unhide Columns instructions.)

Create and apply a template

A **template** is a predesigned, preformatted Office file that contains default text formats, themes, placeholder text, headers and footers, and graphics that you can replace with your own information for hundreds of purposes, including budgets, flyers, and resumes. Template files have a file extension of .xltx. You can create your own template to provide a model for creating a new workbook by saving a workbook with this extension. To use a template, you apply it, which means you create a workbook based on the template. A workbook based on a template has the same content, formulas, and formatting defined in the template but is saved in the standard workbook format, .xlsx. The template file itself remains unchanged. To save a file as a template, click the File tab, click Save As, click This PC if necessary, click More options, click the Save as type arrow, click Excel Template in the list of file types, as shown

FIGURE 2-13: Save menu file types

Excel Template (*.xltx)

in **FIGURE 2-13**, type a name for the new template in the File name box (the default save location is the Custom Office Templates folder), then click Save.

Excel

Apply Colors, Borders, and Documentation

You have seen how you can use cell styles to add predesigned formatting, including colors and borders to a worksheet. If a cell style doesn't capture the formatting you need for a worksheet, you can add this formatting individually. Color options are based on the worksheet theme. A **theme** is a predefined, coordinated set of colors, fonts, graphical effects, and other formats that can be applied to a spreadsheet to give it a consistent, professional look. In Excel, applying a theme to one sheet applies it to all other sheets in that workbook. You can also add a **header** and/or a **footer** to provide useful text, date and other information, including a graphic, along the top or bottom of every page of a worksheet. A header prints above the top margin of the worksheet, and a footer prints below the bottom margin. **CASE** *You want to add a border and color to the reference numbers on the worksheet to make them stand out from the other information. You also want to add information about the worksheet in a header and footer.*

STEPS

1. **Select the range A4:A15, click the Fill Color arrow** 🎨 **in the Font group, then click the Blue-Gray, Text 2, Lighter 80% color (second row, fourth column from the left)**

   The color is applied to the background (or fill) of this range. When you change fill or font color, the color on the Fill Color or Font Color button changes to the last color you selected.

2. **Click the Borders arrow** ⊞ **in the Font group, review the Borders menu, as shown in FIGURE 2-14, then click Right Border**

   You can use the options at the bottom of the Borders menu to draw a border or to change a border line color or style.

3. **Click the Font Color arrow** 🅰 **in the Font group, then click the Blue-Gray, Text 2 color (first row, fourth column from the left)**

   The new color is applied to the labels in the selected range. This color will make the first column reference numbers stand out.

4. **Click the Insert tab, click the Text button, then click the Header & Footer button**

   The header is divided into three sections, as shown in FIGURE 2-15, where you can enter or edit text. The Header & Footer tab includes elements and options for customizing the header or footer.

5. **Click the Sheet Name button in the Header & Footer Elements group on the Header & Footer tab**

   The & [Tab] code is added, which will display the current sheet name in this location. Using codes instead of manually typing the information ensures this information is always up to date.

6. **Click the Go to Footer button in the Navigation group, enter your name in the center footer section, click any cell on the worksheet, click the Normal button** ⊞ **in the status bar, then press CTRL+HOME**

   The header and footer are only visible in Page Layout view and Print Preview.

7. **Click File, then click Print**

   Your header and footer will provide useful information to others viewing the worksheet.

8. **Click the Back button** ⬅ **to return to your worksheet, then save your work**

FIGURE 2-14: Borders menu

Borders menu

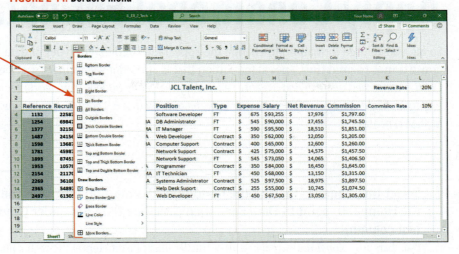

FIGURE 2-15: Header & Footer tab

Go To Footer button

Options for header

Three sections of header

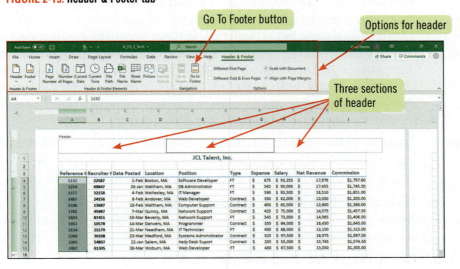

Checking worksheet accessibility

Part of successfully formatting your worksheets includes checking to see if any format presents accessibility problems. **Accessibility** is the quality of removing barriers that may prevent individuals with disabilities from interacting with data or an app. You can check for accessibility issues by clicking the Check Accessibility button in the Accessibility group on the Review tab. The Accessibility pane opens and displays an Inspection Results listing, as shown in **FIGURE 2-16**. You can click the errors and/or warnings to see additional information below the results, as well as steps to take to fix the issue.

FIGURE 2-16: Accessibility Checker pane

Warnings

Apply Conditional Formatting

Learning Outcomes
- Create a Data Bars rule
- Create a Highlight Cells rule

So far, you've used formatting to change the appearance of different types of data, but you can also use **conditional formatting**, special formatting that is applied if values meet specified criteria. **CASE** ▶ *Cheri is concerned about hiring expenses exceeding the yearly budget. You decide to use conditional formatting to highlight certain trends and patterns in the data so that it's easy to compare net revenue and spot the highest expenses.*

STEPS

QUICK TIP

You can create a custom data bar rule by clicking the Conditional Formatting button, pointing to Data Bars, clicking More Rules, adjusting the options in the New Formatting Rule dialog box, then clicking OK.

1. **Select the range I4:I15, click the Conditional Formatting button in the Styles group on the Home tab, point to Data Bars, then click Blue Data Bar under Gradient Fill (first row, first column)**

   Data bars are colored horizontal bars that visually illustrate differences between values in a range of cells.

2. **Select the range G4:G15, click the Quick Analysis button 🖼 that opens next to the selection, then click the Greater Than button on the Formatting tab**

   The Greater Than dialog box opens, displaying an input box you can use to define the condition and a default format (Light Red Fill with Dark Red Text) selected for cells that meet that condition. You can define the condition using the input box and assigning the formatting you want to use for cells that meet that condition. The Quick Analysis tool offers a powerful but limited number of options. To set more conditions, you can click the Highlight Cells Rules option on the Conditional Formatting menu instead. For example, you can create a rule for values that are between two amounts. Values used in input boxes for a condition can be constants, formulas, cell references, or dates.

QUICK TIP

You can highlight duplicate values in a selected range by clicking the Conditional Formatting button in the Styles group, pointing to Highlight Cells Rules, clicking Duplicate Values, then selecting a formatting option.

3. **Type 500 in the Format cells that are GREATER THAN box, click the with list arrow, click Light Red Fill, compare your settings to FIGURE 2-17, then click OK**

   All cells with values greater than $500 in column G appear with a light red fill.

4. **Click cell G4, type 499, then press ENTER**

   Because of the rule you created, the appearance of cell G4 changes because the new value no longer meets the condition you set. Compare your results to **FIGURE 2-18**.

5. **Press CTRL+HOME, then save your work**

Formatting data with icon sets

Icon sets are a conditional format in which different icons are displayed in a cell based on the cell's value. In one group of cells, for example, upward-pointing green arrows might represent the highest values, while downward-pointing red arrows represent the lower values. To add an icon set to a data range, select a data range, click the Conditional Formatting button in the Styles group, point to Icon Sets, then click an icon set. You can customize the values that are used as thresholds for color scales and icon sets by clicking the Conditional Formatting button in the Styles group, clicking Manage Rules, clicking the rule in the Conditional Formatting Rules Manager dialog box, clicking Edit Rule, entering new values, clicking OK, clicking Apply, then clicking OK to close the dialog box.

FIGURE 2-17: Greater Than dialog box

Input box

With arrow

Format for cells meeting the condition

FIGURE 2-18: Worksheet with conditional formatting

	A	B	C	D	E	F	G	H	I	J	K	L
1					JCL Talent, Inc.						Revenue Rate	20%
2												
3	Reference	Recruiter	Date Posted	Location	Position	Type	Expense	Salary	Net Revenue	Commission	Commision Rate	10%
4	1132	22587	1-Feb	Boston, MA	Software Developer	FT	$ 499	$93,255	$ 18,152	$1,815.20		
5	1254	69847	20-Jan	Waltham, MA	DB Administrator	FT	$ 545	$90,000	$ 17,455	$1,745.50		
6	1377	32158	4-Feb	Wellesley, MA	IT Manager	FT	$ 590	$95,500	$ 18,510	$1,851.00		
7	1487	24156	8-Feb	Andover, MA	Web Developer	Contract	$ 350	$62,000	$ 12,050	$1,205.00		
8	1598	13687	18-Feb	Waltham, MA	Computer Support	Contract	$ 400	$65,000	$ 12,600	$1,260.00		
9	1781	45987	7-Mar	Quincy, MA	Network Support	Contract	$ 425	$75,000	$ 14,575	$1,457.50		
10	1893	87451	10-Mar	Beverly, MA	Network Support	FT	$ 545	$73,050	$ 14,065	$1,406.50		
11	1953	10578	14-Mar	Danvers, MA	Programmer	Contract	$ 350	$84,000	$ 16,450	$1,645.00		
12	2154	21170	21-Mar	Needham, MA	IT Technician	FT	$ 450	$68,000	$ 13,150	$1,315.00		
13	2269	36108	23-Mar	Medford, MA	Systems Administrator	Contract	$ 525	$97,500	$ 18,975	$1,897.50		
14	2365	54897	22-Jan	Salem, MA	Help Desk Suport	Contract	$ 255	$55,000	$ 10,745	$1,074.50		
15	2497	61305	30-Mar	Woburn, MA	Web Developer	FT	$ 450	$67,500	$ 13,050	$1,305.00		
16												

Managing conditional formatting rules

If you create a conditional formatting rule and then want to change a condition, you don't need to create a new rule; instead, you can edit the rule using the Rules Manager. Click the Conditional Formatting button in the Styles group, then click Manage Rules. The Conditional Formatting Rules Manager dialog box opens, as shown in **FIGURE 2-19**, listing any rules you have set. Use the Show Formatting rules for arrow to see rules for other parts of a worksheet or for other sheets in the workbook. Select the rule you want to edit, click Edit Rule, then modify the settings in the Edit the Rule Description area in the Edit Formatting Rule dialog box. To change the formatting for a rule, click the Format button in the Edit the Rule Description area, select the formatting styles you want the cells to have, then click OK three times to close the Format Cells dialog box, the Edit Formatting Rule dialog box, and the Conditional Formatting Rules Manager dialog box. To delete a rule, select the

FIGURE 2-19: Conditional Formatting Rules Manager dialog box

Edit Rule button

Delete Rule button

rule in the Conditional Formatting Rules Manager dialog box, then click the Delete Rule button. You can quickly clear conditional formatting rules by clicking the Conditional Formatting button in the Styles group, pointing to Clear Rules, then clicking Clear Rules from Selected Cells or Clear Rules from Entire Worksheet.

Rename and Move a Worksheet

Learning Outcomes
• Rename a sheet
• Apply color to a sheet tab
• Reorder sheets in a workbook

By default, an Excel workbook initially contains one worksheet named Sheet1, although you can add sheets anytime. Each sheet name appears on a sheet tab at the bottom of the worksheet. To move from sheet to sheet, you can click any sheet tab at the bottom of the worksheet window. The **sheet tab scrolling buttons** let you navigate to additional sheet tabs when available; they are located to the left of the sheet tabs and are useful when a workbook contains too many sheet tabs to display at once. To make a workbook more accessible, you can rename worksheets with descriptive names. Worksheets are easier to identify if you add color to the tabs. You can also organize worksheets in a logical order. **CASE** ▶ *In the current worksheet, Sheet1 contains detailed information about technical job postings in the Boston office. Sheet2 contains commission information, and Sheet3 contains no data. You want to rename these sheets to reflect their contents. You also want to add color to a sheet tab to easily distinguish one from the other and change their order.*

STEPS

1. **Click the Sheet2 sheet tab**
   Sheet2 becomes active, appearing in front of the Sheet1 tab; this worksheet contains the commission information. See **FIGURE 2-20**.

2. **Click the Sheet1 tab**
   Sheet1, which contains the detailed job posting data, becomes active again.

3. **Double-click the Sheet2 tab, type Commission, then press ENTER**
   The new name for Sheet2 automatically replaces the default name on the tab. Worksheet names can have up to 31 characters, including spaces and punctuation.

4. **Right-click the Commission tab, point to Tab Color on the shortcut menu, then click the Blue, Accent 5, Darker 25% color (fifth row, second column from the right), as shown in FIGURE 2-21**

5. **Right-click the Sheet1 tab, click Rename on the shortcut menu, type Boston Tech, then press ENTER**
   Notice that the color of the Commission tab changes depending on whether it is the active tab; when the Boston Tech tab is active, the color of the Commission tab changes to the blue tab color you selected. You decide to rearrange the order of the sheets so that the Commission tab is to the right of the Sheet3 tab.

6. **Click the Commission tab, hold down the mouse button, drag it to the right of the Sheet3 tab, as shown in FIGURE 2-22, then release the mouse button**
   As you drag, the pointer changes to 🖑, the sheet relocation pointer, and a small black triangle just above the tabs shows the position where the moved sheet will be when you release the mouse button. The last sheet in the workbook is now the Commission sheet. See **FIGURE 2-23**. You can move multiple sheets by pressing and holding SHIFT while clicking the sheets you want to move, then dragging the sheets to their new location.

7. **Right-click the Sheet3 tab, click Delete on the shortcut menu, press CTRL+HOME, then save your work**
   The sheet is deleted.

FIGURE 2-20: Sheet tabs in workbook

Sheet2 tab

Sheet1 tab

Sheet3 tab

FIGURE 2-21: Tab Color palette

Blue, Accent 5, Darker 25%

Sheet2 renamed

FIGURE 2-22: Moving the Commission sheet

Sheet relocation pointer

FIGURE 2-23: Reordered sheets

Commission sheet is the last sheet

Copying, adding, and deleting worksheets

There are times when you may want to copy a worksheet. For example, a workbook might contain a sheet with Quarter 1 expenses, and you want to use that sheet as the basis for a sheet containing Quarter 2 expenses. To copy a sheet within the same workbook, press and hold CTRL, drag the sheet tab to the desired tab location, release the mouse button, then release CTRL. A duplicate sheet appears with the same name as the copied sheet followed by "(2)" indicating that it is a copy. You can then rename the sheet to a more meaningful name. To copy a sheet to a different workbook, both the source and destination workbooks must be open. Select the sheet to copy or move, right-click the sheet tab, click Move or Copy in the shortcut menu, then complete the information in the Move or Copy dialog box. Be sure to click the Create a copy check box if you want to copy rather than move the worksheet. Carefully check your calculation results whenever you move or copy a worksheet. You can add multiple worksheets quickly by pressing and holding SHIFT, clicking the number of existing worksheet tabs that correspond with the number of sheets you want to add, clicking the Insert arrow in the Cells group on the Home tab, then clicking Insert Sheet. You can delete multiple worksheets from a workbook by clicking the Home tab on the ribbon, pressing and holding SHIFT, clicking the sheet tabs of the worksheets you want to delete, clicking the Delete arrow in the Cells group, then clicking Delete Sheet.

Excel

Check Spelling

Excel includes a spell checker to help you ensure that the words in your worksheet are spelled correctly. The spell checker scans your worksheet, displays words it doesn't find in its built-in dictionary, and suggests replacements when they are available. To check all the sheets in a multiple-sheet workbook, you need to display each sheet individually and run the spell checker for each one. Because the built-in dictionary cannot possibly include all the words that anyone needs, you can add words to the dictionary, such as your company name, an acronym, or an unusual technical term. Once you add a word or term, the spell checker no longer considers that word misspelled. Any words you've added to the dictionary using Word, Access, or PowerPoint are also available in Excel. **CASE** ▶ *Before you share this workbook with Cheri, you want to check the spelling.*

Learning Outcomes
• Change the spelling using a suggestion
• Replace text using Find & Select

STEPS

QUICK TIP
You can click the Thesaurus button in the Proofing group to open a Thesaurus pane with a list of synonyms for a selected word in a cell.

1. **Click the Boston Tech sheet tab, click the Review tab on the ribbon, then click the Spelling button in the Proofing group**

   The Spelling: English (United States) dialog box opens, as shown in **FIGURE 2-24**, with "Commision" selected as the first misspelled word on the worksheet, and with "Commission" selected in the Suggestions list as a possible replacement. For any word, you have the option to Ignore this case of the flagged word, Ignore All cases of the flagged word, Change the word to the selected suggestion, Change All instances of the flagged word to the selected suggestion, or Add to Dictionary to add the flagged word to the dictionary.

2. **Click Change**

   Next, the spell checker finds the word "Suport" and suggests "Support" as an alternative.

3. **Verify that the word "Support" is selected in the Suggestions list, then click Change**

   When no more incorrect words are found, Excel displays a message indicating that the spell check is complete.

4. **Click OK**

QUICK TIP
If you want to find text, click Find & Select in the Editing group, then click Find.

5. **Click the Home tab, click Find & Select in the Editing group, then click Replace**

   The Find and Replace dialog box opens. You can use this dialog box to replace a word or phrase. It might be a misspelling of a proper name that the spell checker didn't recognize as misspelled, or it could simply be a term that you want to change throughout the worksheet.

6. **Type Contract in the Find what text box, press TAB, then type Temp in the Replace with text box**

   Compare your dialog box to **FIGURE 2-25**.

QUICK TIP
You can find and replace cell formatting by clicking the Options button in the Find and Replace dialog box, then clicking the Format arrows to select the desired formatting.

7. **Click Replace All, click OK to close the Microsoft Excel dialog box, then click Close to close the Find and Replace dialog box**

   Excel made six replacements, changing each instance of "Contract" on the worksheet to "Temp."

8. **Click the File tab, click Print on the navigation bar, click the Custom Scaling setting in the Settings section on the Print tab, then click Fit Sheet on One Page**

9. **sam▲ Click the Back button ⬅ to return to your worksheet, save your work, submit it to your instructor as directed, close the workbook, then close Excel**

   The completed worksheet is shown in **FIGURE 2-26**.

Translating text

You can translate text in a worksheet by clicking the Review tab, clicking the Translate button in the Language group, then, if necessary, clicking Turn on when asked if you want to use intelligent services. The Translator pane opens and allows you to select the From language and the To language from menus of world languages. The translated text appears in the To language box.

FIGURE 2-24: Spelling: English (United States) dialog box

Misspelled word

Suggested replacements for misspelled word

Click to ignore all occurrences of misspelled word

Click to add word to dictionary

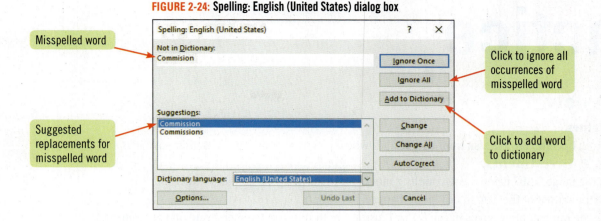

FIGURE 2-25: Find and Replace dialog box

FIGURE 2-26: Completed worksheet

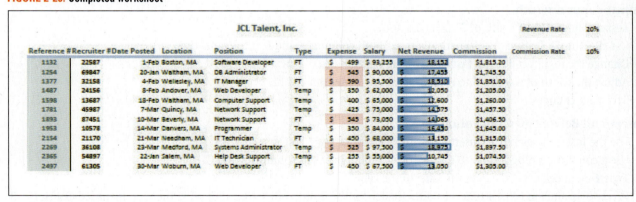

Using Find & Select features

You can navigate to a specific place in a workbook by clicking the Find & Select button in the Editing group on the Home tab, clicking Go To, typing a cell address, then clicking OK. Clicking the Find & Select button also allows you to quickly go to notes, formulas, constants, data validation, and conditional formatting in a worksheet. You can use the Go to Special dialog box to navigate to cells with special elements such as different types of formulas or objects. Some Go to Special commands also appear on the Find & Select menu. Using this menu, you can also change the mouse pointer shape to the Select Objects pointer so you can quickly select drawing objects when necessary. To return to the standard Excel pointer, press ESC.

Practice

Skills Review

1. **Format values.**
   a. Start Excel, open IL_EX_2-2.xlsx from the location where you store your Data Files, then save it as **IL_EX_2_Investments**.
   b. Format the range B3:B7 using the Accounting number format.
   c. Change the format of the date in cell B9 so it appears as 18-Jun.
   d. Increase the number of decimals in cell D1 to 1, using a button in the Number group on the Home tab.
   e. Save your work.

2. **Change font and font size.**
   a. Select the range A3:A7.
   b. Change the font of the selection to Calibri.
   c. Increase the font size of the selection to 11 point.
   d. Increase the font size of the label in cell A1 to 11 point.
   e. Save your changes.

3. **Change font styles and alignment.**
   a. Apply the Heading 2 cell style to cell A1.
   b. Use the Merge & Center button to center the label in cell A1 over columns A and B.
   c. Apply the italic and bold font formats to the label in cell C1.
   d. Use the Format Painter to copy the format in cell C1 to the label in cell A9.
   e. Change the alignment of cell B2 to Align Right using a button in the Alignment group on the Home tab.
   f. Save your changes.

4. **Adjust column width.**
   a. Resize column C to a width of 21.00 characters.
   b. Use the AutoFit feature to automatically resize both columns A and B at the same time.
   c. Change the text in cell B2 to **Total Managed Assets**.
   d. Adjust the width of column B to display all of the content in cell B2.
   e. Save your changes.

5. **Insert and delete rows and columns.**
   a. Use the Insert dialog box to insert a new row between rows 1 and 2.
   b. Use a column heading button to insert a new column between columns B and C.
   c. Type **Fee** in cell C3 and center the label in the cell.
   d. Create a formula in cell C4 that calculates the fee for the Boston office by multiplying the total managed assets in cell B4 by the annual fee percentage in cell E1. (*Hint:* Make sure you use the correct type of cell references in the formula.)
   e. Copy the formula in cell C4 to the range C5:C8.
   f. Use a row heading button to delete the Philadelphia row from the worksheet.
   g. Save your changes.

6. **Apply colors, borders, and documentation.**
   a. Add an outside border around the range A3:C7.
   b. Apply the Green, Accent 6, Lighter 80% fill color (second row, last column) to the range D1:E1.
   c. Change the color of the font in the range A9:B9 to Green, Accent 6, Darker 50% (last row, last column under Theme Colors).
   d. Add a header in the center section of the worksheet that contains the sheet name.

Formatting a Worksheet

Skills Review (continued)

e. Enter your name in the center section of the worksheet footer.

f. Save your changes.

7. Apply conditional formatting.

a. Select the range C4:C7, then create a Highlight Cells rule that changes cell contents to green fill with dark green text if the value is greater than 50000.

b. Select the range B4:B7, then apply Gradient Fill green data bars. (*Hint:* Click Green Data Bar in the Gradient Fill section.)

c. Open the Conditional Formatting Rules Manager dialog box and view the conditional formatting rules for the worksheet. (*Hint:* Click Manage Rules on the Conditional Formatting menu, then click the Show formatting rules for arrow.)

d. Review the rules for the worksheet, making sure your rules are correct, then close the dialog box.

e. Save your changes.

8. Rename and move a worksheet.

a. Rename the Sheet1 tab to **Active Management** and rename the Sheet2 tab to **Passive Management**.

b. Add a sheet to the workbook, then name the new sheet **Total Fees**.

c. Change the Active Management tab color to Green, Accent 6, Darker 50%.

d. Change the Passive Management tab color to Blue, Accent 5, Darker 50%.

e. Reorder the sheets so that the Total Fees sheet comes before (to the left of) the Active Management sheet.

f. Delete the Total Fees sheet.

g. Activate the Active Management sheet, then save your work.

9. Check spelling.

a. Move the cell pointer to cell A1.

b. Use the Find & Select feature to replace the word "Boston" with **New York**.

c. Use the Spelling tool to check the spelling on the worksheet and correct any spelling errors, using suggestions as appropriate.

d. Save your changes, then compare your Active Management sheet to **FIGURE 2-27**.

e. Preview the Active Management sheet in Backstage view, submit your work to your instructor as directed, then close the workbook and close Excel.

FIGURE 2-27

	A	B	C	D	E	F
1		CGS Investments			*Annual Fee Percentage*	1.1%	
2						
3	Office	Total Managed Assets	Fee			
4	New York	$ 5,426,324.35	$ 59,689.57			
5	Los Angeles	$ 4,895,714.77	$ 53,852.86			
6	Cincinnati	$ 3,415,981.19	$ 37,575.79			
7	Indianapolis	$ 4,213,257.23	$ 46,345.83			
8						
9	*Report date:*	18-Jun				
10						

Independent Challenge 1

As an accountant for Riverwalk medical clinic, you have been asked to review the expenses for the emergency room. You've organized the data in an Excel workbook, and now you want to format the data to improve its readability and highlight trends in expenses.

a. Start Excel, open IL_EX_2-3.xlsx from the location where you store your Data Files, then save it as **IL_EX_2_Riverwalk**.

b. Format the values in the Total column in the Accounting number format with two decimal places.

c. Format the values in the % of Total column as Percent format with two decimal places.

d. Format the values in the Inv. Date column with the Date format 14-Mar.

e. Apply bold formatting to the column labels and increase the font size of the labels to 12.

f. Italicize the inventory Type items in column A.

g. Change the font of the Sales Tax label in cell K1 to Calibri.

h. Apply the Title cell style to cell A1.

i. Delete column I, then delete row 13.

j. Merge and center the title in cell A1 over columns A1:I1.

k. Resize column widths as necessary, using AutoFit or by dragging, so that all columns are wide enough to display the data and labels.

l. Use the Format Painter to copy the date format in the Inv. Date column to the values in the Inv. Due column.

m. Change the fill color of the sales tax information in the range J1:K1 to the Light Gray, Background 2 color (first row, third column from the left).

n. Change the font color of the sales tax information in the range J1:K1 to the Blue-Gray, Text 2 color (first row, fourth column from the left).

o. Add a bottom border to the column labels.

p. Use conditional formatting to apply blue gradient data bars to the Total column data. Do not include the total in cell H38 at the bottom of the column.

q. Add the 3 Arrows (Colored) (first set in the Directional group) icon set to the Quantity column to illustrate the relative differences between quantities. Do not include the total in cell E38 at the bottom of the column in this format.

FIGURE 2-28

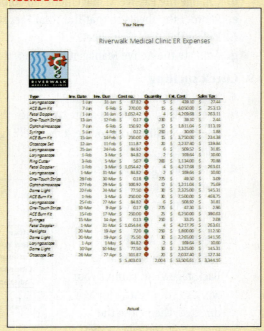

r. Rename Sheet3 to **Budget** and rename Sheet1 to **Actual**. Change the color of the Budget sheet to Red in the Standard colors. Change the color of the Actual sheet to Purple in the Standard colors.

s. Move Sheet2 to the right of the Budget sheet.

t. Activate the Actual Sheet and spell check the worksheet. Correct any spelling errors.

u. Using Find and Select, replace all instances of Maxi on the worksheet with ACE.

v. Delete Sheet2, enter your name in the center section of the Actual worksheet header, enter the sheet name in the center section of the worksheet footer, then save the file.

w. Preview the Actual worksheet. Compare your worksheet to **FIGURE 2-28**.

x. Submit your work to your instructor as directed, close the workbook, then close Excel.

Independent Challenge 2

You are assisting the head of business operations at First Financial Services. You have been asked to format a worksheet showing the first-quarter business services for the company's five branches. As part of this effort, you want to illustrate service trends among the branches.

a. Start Excel, open IL_EX_2-4.xlsx from the location where you store your Data Files, then save it as **IL_EX_2_FinancialServices**.

b. Enter a formula in cell B8 for the Main total, then copy the formula to the range C8:F8.

c. Enter a formula in cell G3 for the Credit card processing total, then copy the formula to the range G4:G8.

d. Apply the Title cell style to cell A1, apply the Heading 4 cell style to the column headings in row 2, and apply the Total cell style to the range A8:G8.

e. Merge and center the title in cell A1 across the range A1:G1.

f. Format the range B3:G8 using the Accounting number format. AutoFit the widths of all columns and format the range with no decimal places.

g. Format the date in cell B9 using the first 14-Mar-12 date format.

h. Rotate the label in cell A2 up by 45 degrees. Copy this rotated format to the other column headings.

i. Format the range A9:B9 with a Blue-Gray, Text 2, Lighter 80% (second row, fourth column from the left) fill.

j. Format the range A9:B9 with a Blue, Accent 1, Darker 50% (last row, fifth column from the left, under Theme Colors) font color.

k. Create a conditional format in the range G3:G8 so that entries less than 25,000,000 appear in light red fill with dark red text.

l. Create a conditional format in the range B8:F8 to add the 3 Stars Ratings icon set. Widen the columns as necessary to fully display the data and formatting.

m. Use the Spelling tool to check spelling in the sheet.

n. Rename Sheet1 to **First Quarter**. Copy the First Quarter sheet and rename the copied sheet **Second Quarter**. Move the Second Quarter sheet if necessary so it is to the right of the First Quarter sheet.

o. On the Second Quarter sheet, delete the data in the range B3:F7 and delete the date in cell B9.

p. Activate the First Quarter sheet. Compare your worksheet to FIGURE 2-29.

q. Enter your name in the center header section, change the worksheet orientation to landscape, then save your work.

r. Preview the worksheet, make any final changes you think are necessary, then submit your work to your instructor as directed.

s. Close the workbook, then close Excel.

FIGURE 2-29

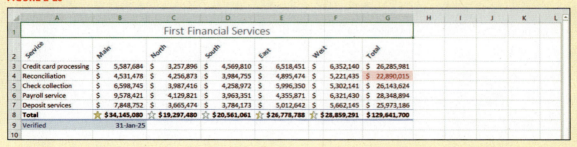

Visual Workshop

Open IL_EX_2-5.xlsx from the location where you store your Data Files, then save it as **IL_EX_2_EngineeringServices**. Use the skills you learned in this module to format the worksheet so it looks like the one shown in FIGURE 2-30. (Note that cell A1 is selected in the figure.) Use the blue gradient fill for the data bars in the Total column. Use the Title cell style for the company name in cell A1, the Heading 1 cell style for the column labels in row 2, and the Total cell style for the total values in the last row. The font color for the service packages listed in column A is Dark Blue in the standard colors. (*Hint:* A row has been deleted from the worksheet.) Enter your name in the upper-left section of the header, check the spelling on the worksheet, save your changes, then submit your work to your instructor as directed.

FIGURE 2-30

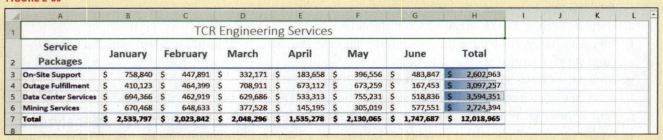

Service Packages	January	February	March	April	May	June	Total
On-Site Support	$ 758,840	$ 447,891	$ 332,171	$ 183,658	$ 396,556	$ 483,847	$ 2,602,963
Outage Fulfillment	$ 410,123	$ 464,399	$ 708,911	$ 673,112	$ 673,259	$ 167,453	$ 3,097,257
Data Center Services	$ 694,366	$ 462,919	$ 629,686	$ 533,313	$ 755,231	$ 518,836	$ 3,594,351
Mining Services	$ 670,468	$ 648,633	$ 377,528	$ 145,195	$ 305,019	$ 577,551	$ 2,724,394
Total	$ 2,533,797	$ 2,023,842	$ 2,048,296	$ 1,535,278	$ 2,130,065	$ 1,747,687	$ 12,018,965

TCR Engineering Services

Analyzing Data Using Formulas

CASE ▶ Ellie Schwartz, the vice president of Finance at JCL, wants to know how North American revenues have performed compared to last year and relative to projected targets. She asks you to prepare a worksheet that summarizes and analyzes this revenue data.

Module Objectives

After completing this module, you will be able to:

- Enter a formula using the Quick Analysis tool
- Build a logical formula with the IF function
- Build a logical formula with the AND function
- Round a value with a function
- Build a statistical formula with the COUNTA function
- Enter a date function
- Work with equation tools
- Control worksheet calculations

Files You Will Need

IL_EX_3-1.xlsx	IL_EX_3-4.xlsx
IL_EX_3-2.xlsx	IL_EX_3-5.xlsx
IL_EX_3-3.xlsx	

Enter a Formula Using the Quick Analysis Tool

Learning Outcomes
- Create a formula using the Quick Analysis tool
- Create a formula to find a percentage increase

So far, you have used the AutoSum button on the ribbon to quickly add simple formulas that sum and average selected data. You can also add formulas using the Quick Analysis tool, which opens when you select a range of cells. This tool allows you to quickly format, chart, or analyze data by calculating sums, averages, and other selected totals. **CASE** *To help Ellie evaluate revenues at JCL, you want to calculate yearly revenue totals for each North American office and compare the yearly performance of each office to the previous year.*

STEPS

1. **sam↓ Start Excel, open IL_EX_3-1.xlsx from the location where you store your Data Files, then save it as IL_EX_3_Revenue**

2. **Select the range B3:E12, click the Quick Analysis button 📶 that appears below the selection, then click the Totals tab**

   The Totals tab in the Quick Analysis tool displays commonly used functions, as shown in **FIGURE 3-1**. This tab includes two Sum buttons, one that inserts the SUM function in a row beneath the selected range, and one that inserts the SUM function in the column to the right of the range.

3. **Click the Sum button displaying the gold column**

   The newly calculated totals display in the column to the right of the selected range, in cells F3:F12.

4. **Click cell H3, type =(, click cell F3, type -, click cell G3, then type)**

   This first part of the formula finds the difference in total revenue from the previous year to this year. You enclosed this operation in parentheses to make sure this difference is calculated first.

5. **Type /, then click cell G3**

   The second part of this formula divides the difference in revenue by the total revenue for the previous year, to calculate the increase or decrease.

6. **Click the Enter button ✓ on the formula bar**

   The result, .75405003, appears in cell H3. The column isn't wide enough to fully display this value but the number of decimal places will be adjusted in the next formatting step.

7. **Click the Percent Style button % in the Number group, then click the Increase Decimal button ⊞ in the Number group twice**

   The formatted percentage, 75.41%, appears in cell H3.

8. **Drag the fill handle from cell H3 to cell H12, then save your work**

   The percentage changes in annual revenue for each office appear in column H, as shown in **FIGURE 3-2**.

FIGURE 3-1: Quick Analysis tool

FIGURE 3-2: Percentage changes

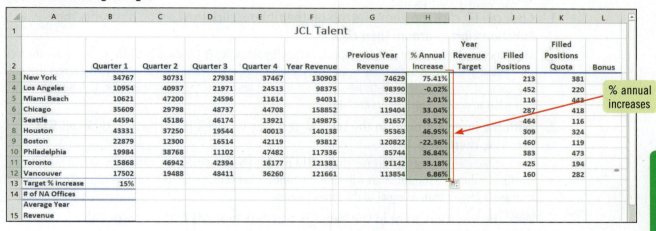

Excel

Build a Logical Formula with the IF Function

Learning Outcomes
- Build a logical formula using the IF function
- Apply comparison operators in a logical test

You can build a formula in a worksheet using a **logical function** that returns a different value depending on whether the given condition is true or false. An **IF function** is a logical function that assigns a value to a cell based on a logical test. A **logical formula** makes calculations based on criteria that you create, called **stated conditions**. For example, you can build a formula to calculate bonuses based on a person's performance rating, where the stated condition is 5. If a person is rated a 5 on a scale of 1 to 5, he or she receives an additional 10% of his or her salary as a bonus; otherwise, there is no bonus. The IF function has three parts, including the **logical test**, which is the first part of the function. This test is a condition that can be answered with a true or false response. If the logical test is true, then the second part of the function is applied; if it is false, then the third part of the function is applied. When entering the logical test portion of an IF statement, you often use some combination of the comparison operators listed in **TABLE 3-1**.

CASE ▸ *Ellie asks you to calculate whether each office met or missed its revenue target for the year.*

STEPS

1. **Click cell I3, click the Formulas tab on the ribbon, click the Logical button in the Function Library group, then click IF**

   The Function Arguments dialog box opens, displaying three boxes for the three parts of a logical function: the Logical_test, which in this case tests if the annual increase is greater than or equal to the target increase; the Value_if_true box, which tells what to do if the test results are true; and the Value_if_false box, which tells what to do if the test results are false.

2. **With the insertion point in the Logical_test box click cell H3, type > =, click cell B13, press F4, then press TAB**

   The symbol (>) represents "greater than." B13 needs to be formatted as an absolute reference because it is a fixed value in a formula that will be copied into other cells. So far, the formula reads, "If the annual increase is greater than or equal to the target increase..."

3. **With the insertion point in the Value_if_true box type MET, then press TAB**

   This part of the function tells Excel to display the text MET if the annual increase equals or exceeds the target increase of 15%. Quotation marks are automatically added around the text you entered.

4. **Type MISSED in the Value_if_false box, then click OK**

   This part tells Excel to display the text MISSED if the results of the logical test are false—that is, if the increase does not equal or exceed the target. The function is complete, and the result, MET, appears in cell I3, as shown in **FIGURE 3-3**.

5. **Drag the fill handle to copy the formula in cell I3 into the range I4:I12**

   Compare your results with **FIGURE 3-4**. Most offices met their target increase but four offices did not.

6. **Save the workbook**

FIGURE 3-3: Worksheet with IF function

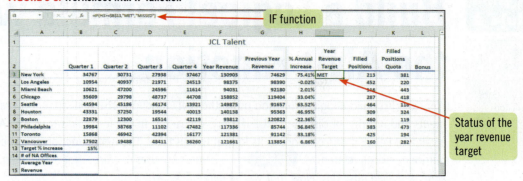

FIGURE 3-4: Worksheet showing yearly revenue status

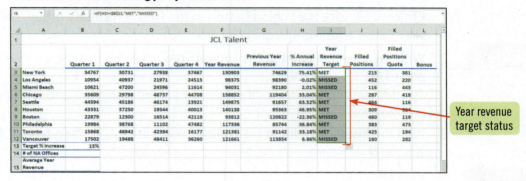

TABLE 3-1: Comparison operators

operator	meaning	operator	meaning
<	Less than	<=	Less than or equal to
>	Greater than	>=	Greater than or equal to
=	Equal to	<>	Not equal to

Nesting IF functions

You can nest IF functions to test several conditions in a formula. A nested IF function contains IF functions inside other IF functions to test these multiple conditions. To create a nested IF function, enter the second IF statement in the value_if_false argument of the first IF statement. For example, the nested statement =IF(H3<0%,"Warning",IF(H3<50%,"No Bonus","Bonus")) tests whether a warning should be issued based on the percentage increases for an office. Assuming the percentage increase of an office is in cell H3, the nested IF statement first checks to see if the increase was less than 0. If that first test is true, the text "Warning" will appear. If the first test is false, a second test will be performed to check to see if the increase is less than 50%. If that second test is true (values are less than 50%), the text "No Bonus" will appear. If that second test is false, the text "Bonus" will be displayed.

**Learning
Outcomes**
• Build a logical
formula using the
AND function
• Apply logical tests

Build a Logical Formula with the AND Function

You can also build a logical function using the AND function. The AND function evaluates all of its arguments and returns, or displays, TRUE if every logical test in the formula is true. The AND function returns a value of FALSE if one or more of its logical tests is false. The AND function arguments can include text, numbers, or cell references. **CASE** *JCL awards bonuses to offices that meet targets for both annual revenue and filled positions. Now that you've determined which offices met their revenue goal, you need to see which offices are eligible for a bonus by meeting both this target and the filled positions target.*

STEPS

1. **Click cell L3, click the Logical button in the Function Library group, then click AND**
    The Function Arguments dialog box opens.

2. **With the insertion point in the Logical1 box, click cell J3, type >=, click cell K3, then press TAB**
    This part of the formula reads, "If the number of filled positions is greater than or equal to the filled positions quota…"

3. **With the insertion point in the Logical2 box, click cell I3, then type = "MET"**
    This part of the formula reads, "If the revenue goal was met…"

4. **Click OK**
    The function is complete, and the result, FALSE, appears in cell L3, as shown in **FIGURE 3-5**, because both stated conditions were not met. Although the revenue target was met, the number of filled positions was not greater than or equal to the quota.

5. **Drag the fill handle to copy the formula in cell L3 into the range L4:L12**
    Compare your results with **FIGURE 3-6**.

6. **Enter your name in the center section of the footer, preview the worksheet, then save your work**

Using the OR and NOT logical functions

The OR logical function follows the same syntax as the AND function, but rather than returning TRUE if every argument is true, the OR function will return TRUE if any of its arguments are true. It will only return FALSE if all of its arguments are false. The NOT logical function reverses the value of its argument. For example, NOT(TRUE) reverses its argument of TRUE and returns FALSE. You might want to use this function in a worksheet to ensure that a cell is not equal to a particular value. See **TABLE 3-2** for examples of the AND, OR, and NOT functions.

FIGURE 3-5: Worksheet with AND function

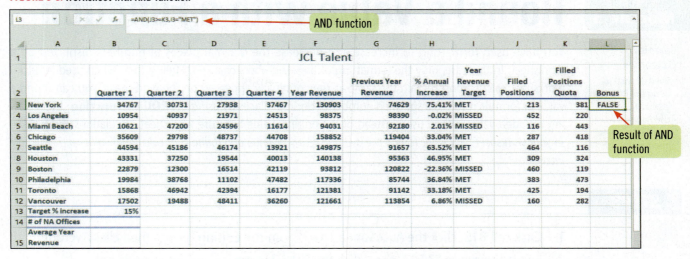

FIGURE 3-6: Worksheet with bonus status evaluated for all offices

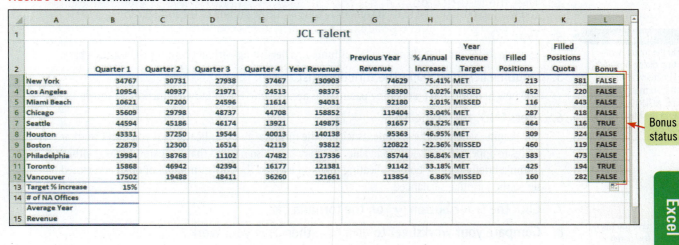

TABLE 3-2: Examples of AND, OR, and NOT functions (cell A1=10, cell B1=20)

function	formula	result
AND	=AND(A1>5,B1>25)	FALSE
OR	=OR(A1>5,B1>25)	TRUE
NOT	=NOT(A1=0)	TRUE

Round a Value with a Function

You have used formatting to increase and decrease the decimal places of numbers displayed on a worksheet. In this case, only the formatting of these numbers changes. Their values, when used in future worksheet calculations, remain the same as they originally appeared on the worksheet. You can round a value or formula result to a specified number of decimal places by using the **ROUND function**; the resulting rounded value is then used instead of the original value in future worksheet calculations. **CASE** ▶ *In your worksheet, you want to find the average yearly revenue and round that calculated value to the nearest integer.*

STEPS

1. **Click cell B15, click the AutoSum arrow ∑ ▾ in the Editing group, then click Average**

2. **Select the range F3:F12, then click the Enter button ✓ on the formula bar**
   The result, 122636.4, appears in cell B15.

3. **Click to the right of = in the formula bar**
   You want to position the ROUND function here, at the beginning of the formula.

4. **Type RO**
   Formula AutoComplete displays a list of functions beginning with RO beneath the formula bar.

5. **Double-click ROUND in the functions list**
   The new function and an opening parenthesis are added to the AVERAGE function, as shown in **FIGURE 3-7**.

6. **Press END, then type ,0)**
   The comma separates the arguments within the formula, and 0 indicates that you don't want any decimal places to appear in the calculated value. You may have also noticed that the parentheses at either end of the formula briefly became bold, indicating that you entered the correct number of open and closed parentheses so the formula is balanced.

7. **Click the Enter button ✓ on the formula bar**

8. **Compare your worksheet to FIGURE 3-8, then save your work**

FIGURE 3-7: ROUND function added to an existing function

ROUND function and opening parenthesis inserted in formula

ScreenTip indicates needed arguments

FIGURE 3-8: Rounded year average

Round function surrounds average formula

Calculated value with no decimals

Using Excel rounding functions

You can use other rounding functions besides ROUND to fine-tune the rounding results you want to see. The **MROUND function** rounds a number to the nearest multiple of another number. The syntax is: MROUND(number, multiple). For example, MROUND(14,3) returns the value 15 because 15 is the nearest multiple of 3 to 14. The **ROUNDDOWN function** works like the ROUND function except that rather than rounding a number to the next closest value, it always rounds down. The syntax is ROUNDDOWN(number, num_digits). For example, =ROUNDDOWN(15.778, 2) returns a value of 15.77 because this is the nearest two-digit number below 15.778. The **ROUNDUP function** works similarly but rounds a number up. The syntax is ROUNDUP(number, num_digits). For example, =ROUNDUP(15.778, 2) returns a value of 15.78.

Build a Statistical Formula with the COUNTA Function

When you select a range, a count of cells in the range that are not blank appears in the status bar. For example, if you select the range A1:A5 and only cells A1, A4, and A5 contain data, the status bar displays "Count: 3." To count nonblank cells more precisely, or to incorporate these calculations in a worksheet, you can use the COUNT and COUNTA functions. The **COUNT function** tallies the number of cells in a range that contain numeric data, including numbers, dates, and formulas. The **COUNTA function** tallies how many cells in a specified range contain any entries (numbers, dates, or text). For example, the formula =COUNT(A1:A5) returns the number of cells in the range that contain numeric data, and the formula =COUNTA(A1:A5) returns the number of cells in the range that are not empty. **CASE** ▶ *In your worksheet, you want to calculate the number of offices in the North America region. You also want to format some worksheet values using a custom format, so that the data looks exactly the way you want.*

STEPS

1. **Click cell B14, click the Formulas tab on the ribbon, click the More Functions button, then point to Statistical**
   A gallery of statistical functions opens, as shown in **FIGURE 3-9**.

2. **Scroll down the list of functions if necessary, then click COUNTA**
   The Function Arguments dialog box opens.

3. **With the insertion point in the Value1 box select the range A3:A12, then click OK**
   The number of offices, 10, appears in cell B14.

4. **Select the range H3:H12, click the Home tab on the ribbon, click the Format button in the Cells group, then click Format Cells**
   Currently, the negative values in this range are difficult to distinguish from the positive values.

5. **Click the Number tab if necessary, click Custom in the Category menu, click after % in the Type box, type ;[Red](0.00%) as shown in FIGURE 3-10, then click OK**
   The negative percentages in cells H4 and H9 now appear in red with parentheses.

6. **Select the range B3:G12, press and hold CTRL, then click cell B15**
   Holding CTRL allows you to select multiple ranges and cells.

7. **Click the Accounting Number Format button $ in the Number group, then click the Decrease Decimal button .00→.0 twice**
   Formatting these revenue figures makes them easier to read. Compare your worksheet to **FIGURE 3-11**.

FIGURE 3-9: Statistical functions

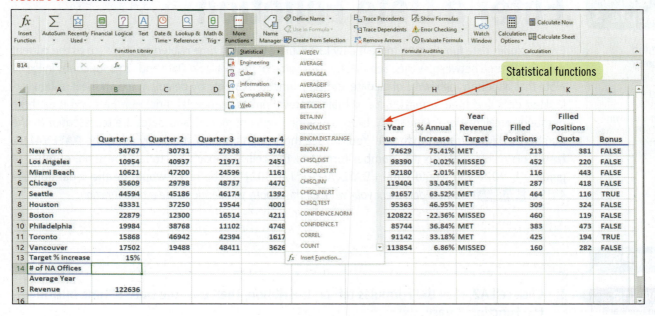

FIGURE 3-10: Custom number format

FIGURE 3-11: Formatted worksheet

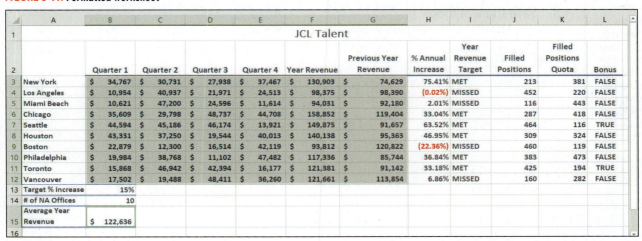

Enter a Date Function

Excel includes date functions to make it easy to calculate date and time related results, such as the current date or the time between events. See **TABLE 3-3** for some of the available Date and Time functions in Excel. Note that although the results of all date and time functions appear by default in a worksheet in familiar-looking date and time formats, Excel actually stores them as sequential serial numbers and uses these numbers in calculations. January 1, 1900 is assigned serial number 1 and dates are represented as the number of days following that date. You can see the serial number of a date by using the **DATEVALUE function** or by applying the Number format to the cell. For example, to see the serial number of January 1, 2021 you would enter =DATEVALUE("1/1/2021"). The result would be the serial number 44197. **CASE** ▶ *To help document your work on this report, you decide to use a date function.*

STEPS

1. Click cell **A2**, click the **Formulas tab** on the ribbon, then click the **Date & Time button** in the Function library

   A list of date and time functions opens, as shown in **FIGURE 3-12**.

2. Scroll if necessary, click **TODAY**, then click **OK** in the dialog box

   The **TODAY function** displays the current date and updates each time a worksheet is opened. However, you want the workbook to show the date it was completed, rather than the date the workbook is opened.

3. Press **DEL**, click the **Date & Time button** in the Function Library, then click **DATE**

   The **DATE function** uses three arguments, year, month, and day, to enter a date.

4. With the insertion point in the Year box type **2025**, then press **TAB**

5. With the insertion point in the Month box type **2**, then press **TAB**

6. Type **24** in the Day box, then click **OK**

   The function is complete, and the result, 2/24/2025, appears in cell A2.

7. Click the **Home tab** on the ribbon, click the **Cell Styles button** in the Styles group, then click **20% Accent1** in the Themed Cell Styles group

   Compare your worksheet to **FIGURE 3-13**.

8. Save the workbook

FIGURE 3-12: Date & Time functions

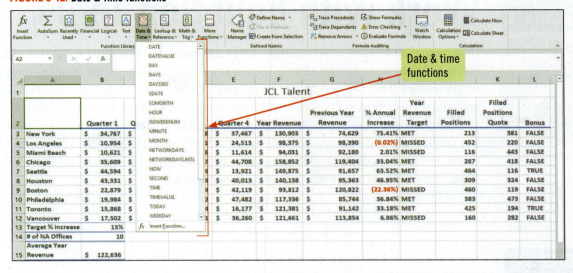

Date & time functions

FIGURE 3-13: Formatted date

Formatted date

	2/24/2025	Quarter 1	Quarter 2	Quarter 3	Quarter 4	Year Revenue	Previous Year Revenue	% Annual Increase	Year Revenue Target	Filled Positions	Filled Positions Quota	Bonus
												JCL Talent
3	New York	$ 34,767	$ 30,731	$ 27,938	$ 37,467	$ 130,903	$ 74,629	75.41%	MET	213	381	FALSE
4	Los Angeles	$ 10,954	$ 40,937	$ 21,971	$ 24,513	$ 98,375	$ 98,390	(0.02%)	MISSED	452	220	FALSE
5	Miami Beach	$ 10,621	$ 47,200	$ 24,596	$ 11,614	$ 94,031	$ 92,180	2.01%	MISSED	116	443	FALSE
6	Chicago	$ 35,609	$ 29,798	$ 48,737	$ 44,708	$ 158,852	$ 119,404	33.04%	MET	287	418	FALSE
7	Seattle	$ 44,594	$ 45,186	$ 46,174	$ 13,921	$ 149,875	$ 91,657	63.52%	MET	464	116	TRUE
8	Houston	$ 43,331	$ 37,250	$ 19,544	$ 40,013	$ 140,138	$ 95,363	46.95%	MET	309	324	FALSE
9	Boston	$ 22,879	$ 12,300	$ 16,514	$ 42,119	$ 93,812	$ 120,822	(22.36%)	MISSED	460	119	FALSE
10	Philadelphia	$ 19,984	$ 38,768	$ 11,102	$ 47,482	$ 117,336	$ 85,744	36.84%	MET	383	473	FALSE
11	Toronto	$ 15,868	$ 46,942	$ 42,394	$ 16,177	$ 121,381	$ 91,142	33.18%	MET	425	194	TRUE
12	Vancouver	$ 17,502	$ 19,488	$ 48,411	$ 36,260	$ 121,661	$ 113,854	6.86%	MISSED	160	282	FALSE
13	Target % increase	15%										
14	# of NA Offices	10										
15	Average Year Revenue	$ 122,636										

TABLE 3-3: Date and Time functions

function	calculates	example formula	example result
DAY	The day of the month using a date serial number	=DAY(44197)	1
NOW	The current date and time	=NOW()	1/1/2021 10:00
MONTH	The month number using a date serial number	=MONTH(44197)	1
TIME	A serial number in time format from hours, minutes, and seconds	=TIME(5,12,20)	0.216898
TIMEVALUE	A serial time in text format	=TIMEVALUE("5:15:24")	.219028
YEAR	The year portion of a date	=YEAR(44197)	2021
HOUR	The hour portion of a time	=HOUR("6:45:21 PM")	18
MINUTE	The minute portion of a time	=MINUTE("6:45:21 PM")	45
SECOND	The second portion of a time	=SECOND("6:45:21 PM")	21
WEEKDAY	The day of the week from a serial date (1 =Sunday, 2 = Monday…)	=WEEKDAY("6/21/2021")	2
WORKDAY	A serial number in date format after a certain number of working days	=WORKDAY(44198,5)	44204 (When formatted as a date: 1/8/2021)

Work with Equation Tools

Learning Outcomes
• Select an equation structure
• Enter an equation using the equation tools

Excel's equation tools allow you to insert many common equations, such as the area of a circle and the Pythagorean theorem, in a worksheet. The worksheet does not display the results of these expressions, it simply displays them with the correct syntax and structure. This can be helpful to illustrate the thinking behind a formula or to share mathematical information with others, such as algebraic formulas. You can also compose your own equations and formulas using structures such as fractions, exponents, radicals, and matrices along with many available mathematical symbols. **CASE** *Before sending the workbook to Ellie, you want to document the process you used to determine the revenue percentage increase. You have started this process on a separate worksheet in the workbook.*

STEPS

QUICK TIP
If your device is touch-enabled, you can click the Ink Equation button in the Tools group of the Equation tab to write a math equation using your mouse, a stylus, or your fingertip.

1. Click the Formula Documentation sheet tab, click the Insert tab on the ribbon, click the Symbols button if necessary to expand the Symbols group, then click the Equation button in the Symbols group

   The Equation tab opens and the Shape Format tab becomes available. An equation placeholder that reads, "Type equation here," is added to the worksheet.

2. With the Equation tab active, click the Fraction button in the Structures group, then click the Stacked Fraction button (first row, first column)

   The structure of a fraction is placed on the worksheet with a blank numerator and denominator, as shown in FIGURE 3-14.

3. Click the upper box (the numerator), then type (Year Revenue – Previous Year Revenue)

4. Click the lower box (the denominator), then type Previous Year Revenue

5. Select the equation if necessary, place the Move pointer ⊕ on the edge of the equation, drag the equation so the upper-left corner is in cell A9, then click cell A1

6. Compare your worksheet to FIGURE 3-15, then save your work

Analyzing Data Using Formulas

FIGURE 3-14: Fraction structure added to worksheet

FIGURE 3-15: Completed equation

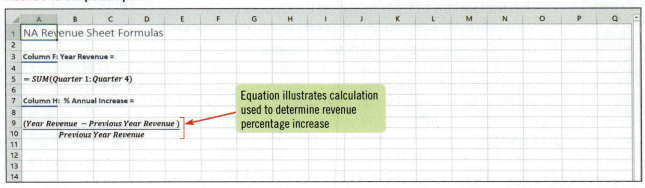

Using Draw tools

On a touch-enabled device you can use your mouse, a stylus, or even your finger to draw or write. If your device is touch-enabled, the Touch/Mouse Mode button appears on the Quick Access toolbar and the Draw tab automatically becomes available on the ribbon. You can add or remove the Touch/Mouse Mode button by clicking the Customize Quick Access Toolbar button ⬇, then clicking Touch/Mouse Mode. Touch mode adds space between the buttons on the ribbon, making them easier to access with your fingertip. You can manually turn on the Draw tab by clicking the File tab, clicking Options, clicking Customize Ribbon in the Excel Options dialog box, selecting the Draw box in the Main Tabs list, then clicking OK.

Clicking the Draw button in the Input Mode group of the Draw tab allows you to select a pen, pencil, or highlighter. If you click the selected instrument you can change its thickness and color. As you work, you can correct drawing mistakes using the Eraser tool, also in the Drawing Tools group. Clicking the Ink to Shape button in the Convert group before beginning to draw converts your completed drawing to a geometric shape. The Ink to Shape feature works with pens and pencils but not highlighters. The Convert group includes an Ink to Math button that converts a handwritten mathematical expression to text. If you wish to see the steps followed in creating drawings on the worksheet, use the Ink Replay button in the Replay group to replay each step.

To modify an ink shape, you must select it, either by using the lasso button in the Drawing Tools group to enclose it or by using the lasso tool or arrow tool to click the shape. Once a shape is selected, you can format it using the Shape Format tab.

Control Worksheet Calculations

Learning
Outcomes
• Control formula
  calculations
• Calculate work-
  sheet formulas

Whenever you change a value in a cell, Excel automatically recalculates all the formulas on the worksheet based on that cell. This automatic calculation is efficient unless you create a worksheet so large that the recalculation process slows down data entry and screen updating. Worksheets with many formulas, data tables, or functions may also recalculate slowly. In these cases, you might want to apply the **manual calculation** option to turn off automatic calculation of worksheet formulas, allowing you to selectively determine if and when you want Excel to perform calculations. When you turn on the manual calculation option, Excel stops automatically recalculating all open worksheets. **CASE** *Because you have added several formulas to the worksheet, you decide to review the formula settings in the workbook and see whether changing from automatic to manual calculation improves performance.*

STEPS

QUICK TIP

You can also change the formula calcu-lation to manual by clicking the Formulas tab, clicking the Calculation Options button in the Calcu-lation group, then clicking Manual.

1. **Click the NA Revenue sheet tab, click the File tab on the ribbon to open Backstage view, click Options, then click Formulas on the Options screen**

   The options related to formula calculation and error checking appear, as shown in **FIGURE 3-16**.

2. **Under Calculation options, click the Manual option button**

   When you select the Manual option, the Recalculate workbook before saving check box automatically becomes active and contains a checkmark. Because the workbook will not recalculate until you save or close and reopen the workbook, you must make sure to recalculate your worksheet before you print it and after you finish making changes.

3. **Click OK**

   Ellie informs you that the first quarter revenue for the New York office is incorrect and needs updating.

4. **Click cell B3**

   Before proceeding, notice that in cell F3 the year revenue for the New York office is $130,903.

QUICK TIP

The Calculate Now command calculates the entire workbook, not just the work-sheet. You can also manually recalculate a workbook by pressing F9. Pressing SHIFT+F9 recalcu-lates only the current worksheet.

5. **Type 34305, then click the Enter button ☑ on the formula bar**

   Notice that the year revenue in cell F3 does not adjust to reflect the change in cell B3. The word "Calculate" appears in the status bar to indicate that a specific value on the worksheet did indeed change and remind-ing you that the worksheet must be recalculated.

6. **Click the Formulas tab, click the Calculate Sheet button in the Calculation group, click cell A1, then save the workbook**

   The year revenue in cell F3 is now $130,441. The other formulas on the worksheet affected by the value in cell B3 changed as well, as shown in **FIGURE 3-17**. Because this is a relatively small worksheet that recalcu-lates quickly, you decide that the manual calculation option is not necessary.

QUICK TIP

If your worksheet contains a table, such as a complex payment schedule, you may want to use manual recalculation just for the table. To do so, click the Automatic Except for Data Tables option.

7. **Click the Calculation Options button in the Calculation group, then click Automatic**

   Now Excel will automatically recalculate the worksheet formulas any time you make changes.

8. **sam'↑ Save your changes, activate cell A1, submit the workbook to your instructor as directed, close the workbook, then close Excel**

FIGURE 3-16: Excel formula options

Click to select manual calculation of worksheet formulas

FIGURE 3-17: Worksheet with updated values

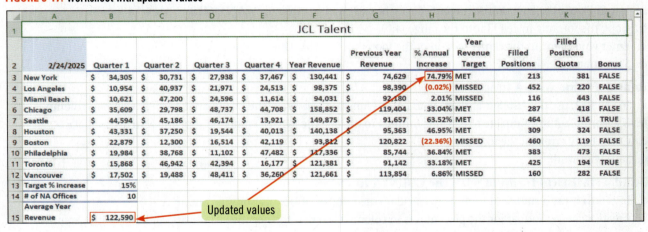

Updated values

Showing and printing worksheet formulas

Sometimes you need to show or keep a record of all the formulas in a worksheet. You might want to do this to show exactly how you came up with a complex calculation, so you can explain it to others. To display formulas rather than results in a worksheet, first open the workbook. Click the Formulas tab on the ribbon, then click the Show Formulas button in the Formula Auditing group to select it. When the Show Formulas button is selected, formulas rather than resulting values are displayed on the worksheet, and any entered values appear without number formatting. You can print the worksheet to save a record of all the formulas. The Show Formulas button is a toggle: click it again to show the values, rather than the formulas, on the worksheet.

Excel

Practice

Skills Review

1. **Enter a formula using the Quick Analysis tool.**
   a. Start Excel, open IL_EX_3-2.xlsx from the location where you store your Data Files, then save it as **IL_EX_3_Labs**.
   b. On the First Quarter worksheet, select the range B3:D9, then use the Quick Analysis tool to enter the first quarter revenue totals in column E.
   c. In cell G3, use the revenue totals in cells E3 and F3 to calculate the percent increase in revenue from the previous quarter to the first quarter.
   d. Format the value in cell G3 using the percent style with two decimal places.
   e. Copy the formula in cell G3 into the range G4:G9.

2. **Build a logical formula with the IF function.**
   a. In cell H3, use the Function Arguments dialog box to enter the formula **=IF(G3>=$B$10,"Met","Missed")**.
   b. Copy the formula in cell H3 into the range H4:H9.
   c. Save your work.

3. **Build a logical formula with the AND function.**
   a. In cell J3, use the Function Arguments dialog box to enter the formula **=AND(H3="Met",I3>=4)**.
   b. Copy the formula in cell J3 into the range J4:J9.
   c. Enter your name in the center section of the footer for the First Quarter sheet.
   d. Save your work.

4. **Round a value with a function.**
   a. In cell B12, use the AutoSum list arrow to enter a function to average the first quarter revenue values in column E.
   b. Use Formula AutoComplete to edit this formula to include the ROUND function showing zero decimal places.
   c. Correct any errors in the formula.
   d. Save your work.

5. **Build a statistical formula with the COUNTA function.**
   a. In cell B11, use a statistical formula to calculate the number of lab locations in column A.
   b. Create a custom format for the percentages in column G so that the negative values appear in red with parentheses.
   c. Format the revenue values in the range B3:F9 and in cell B12 using the Accounting Number Format with no decimal places.
   d. Save your work.

6. **Enter a date function.**
   a. In cell D12, enter **Report Date**.
   b. In cell E12, use the TODAY function to enter today's date.
   c. Delete the TODAY function in cell E12, then use the DATE function to enter the date 4/3/2025.
   d. Use the Cell Style Rose, 20% - Accent 1 (the first row and first column in the Themed Cell Styles group) to format the range D12:E12.
   e. Activate cell A1, then save your work.

7. **Work with equation tools.**
   a. Activate the Formula Documentation sheet.
   b. Add a stacked fraction to the worksheet.
   c. Enter **(First Quarter Revenue – Previous Quarter Revenue)** as the numerator.
   d. Enter **Previous Quarter Revenue** as the denominator.

Skills Review (continued)

e. Move the equation to place its upper-left corner in cell A9.

f. Activate cell A1, then save your work.

8. **Control worksheet calculations.**

a. Activate the First Quarter sheet.

b. Open the Formulas category of the Excel Options dialog box.

c. Change the worksheet calculations to manual.

d. Change the value in cell B3 to **72000**.

e. Recalculate the worksheet manually.

f. Change the worksheet calculation back to automatic using the Calculation Options button on the Formulas tab of the ribbon, then save the workbook.

g. Preview the worksheet. Compare your screen to **FIGURE 3-18**.

h. Save your changes, submit your work to your instructor as directed, close the workbook, then close Excel.

FIGURE 3-18

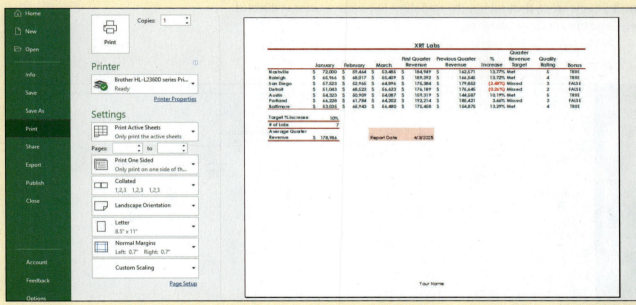

Independent Challenge 1

The manager at Riverwalk Medical Clinic has hired you to analyze patient accounts and insurance reimbursements for their Boston imaging facility. He would like you to flag overdue accounts and calculate the average procedure amount.

a. Open IL_EX_3-3.xlsx from the location where you store your Data Files, then save it as **IL_EX_3_Accounts**.

b. Use the DATE function to return the date 5/18/2021 in cell B3.

c. Enter a formula in cell C5 that calculates the statement age by subtracting the statement date in cell B5 from the report date in cell B3. (*Hint:* The formula needs to use an absolute reference for the report date in cell B3 so this cell address doesn't change when copied.)

d. Copy the formula in cell C5 to the range C6:C11.

Independent Challenge 1 (continued)

e. In cell F5, enter an IF function that calculates the patient responsibility. (*Hint:* The Logical_test should check to see if the procedure amount is greater than the insurance payment, the Value_if_true should calculate the procedure amount minus the insurance payment, and the Value_if_false should be 0.)

f. Copy the IF function in cell F5 to the range F6:F11.

g. In cell G5, enter an AND function to find accounts that are past due. Accounts are past due if a patient is responsible for a balance due and the statement age is over 30 days. (*Hint:* The Logical1 condition should check to see if the statement age is more than 30, and the Logical2 condition should check if the patient responsibility is greater than 0.)

h. Use the fill handle to copy the AND function in cell G5 into the range G6:G11.

i. In cell B13, enter a COUNTA function to calculate the number of accounts in column A.

j. Enter a function in cell B14 that averages the procedure amounts in column D.

k. Use Formula AutoComplete to enter a function to round the average in cell B14 to zero decimal places.

l. Enter your name in the center section of the footer.

m. Preview the worksheet. Compare your screen to **FIGURE 3-19**.

n. Save your work, then submit the worksheet to your instructor as directed.

o. Close the workbook and Excel.

FIGURE 3-19

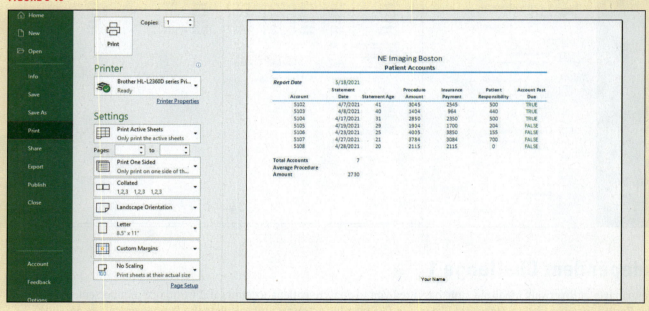

Independent Challenge 2

As the senior loan officer at North Shore Bank, one of your responsibilities is reviewing the quarterly loan portfolios for the four branches. This includes adding statistics including total loan amounts, average total loans, and the growth in loans issued at each branch. You are preparing a portfolio review for the 4th quarter, which you plan to issue on December 31.

a. Open IL_EX_3-4.xlsx from the location where you store your Data Files, then save it as **IL_EX_3_Loans**.

b. Use the TODAY function to enter today's date in cell B12. Verify today's date is displayed.

c. Delete the date in cell B12 and replace it with the date 12/31/2025 using the DATE function.

d. Use the Quick Analysis button to enter totals in the range F4:F7 and B8:E8. (*Hint:* You need to use two buttons on the Totals tab to accomplish this.)

e. Enter a formula in cell H4 to find the percentage increase for the total 4th quarter loans over the 3rd quarter total for the Main Street branch. Format the percentage increase using the percent style with two decimal places.

f. Copy the percentage increase formula in cell H4 to the range H5:H7.

g. In cell J4, enter an AND function to determine if the Main Street branch is eligible for a bonus. To be eligible, the 4th quarter percentage increase must be over 10% and the customer ratings must be higher than 85%.

h. Use the fill handle to copy the AND function in cell J4 into the range J5:J7.

i. Enter a function in cell B10 that averages the total 4th quarter loan amounts in column F, then round the average to zero decimal places.

j. In cell B11, enter a function to calculate the number of branches in column A.

k. Create a custom format for the percentages in column H so that the negative values appear in red with parentheses.

l. Format the loan values in the ranges B4:G7, B8:E8, and cell B10 using the Accounting Number Format with no decimals. Widen the columns as necessary to fully display all of the worksheet data.

m. Activate the Documentation tab and use a stacked fraction to document the 4th quarter % increase formula in cell A3.

n. Activate the 4th Quarter Report sheet. Switch to manual calculation for formulas. Change the personal loan amount for the Main Street branch in cell B4 to **1306500**. Calculate the worksheet formula manually. Turn on automatic calculation again.

o. Enter your name in the center footer section.

p. Preview the worksheet. Compare your screen to **FIGURE 3-20**.

q. Save your work, then submit the worksheet to your instructor as directed.

r. Close the workbook and Excel.

FIGURE 3-20

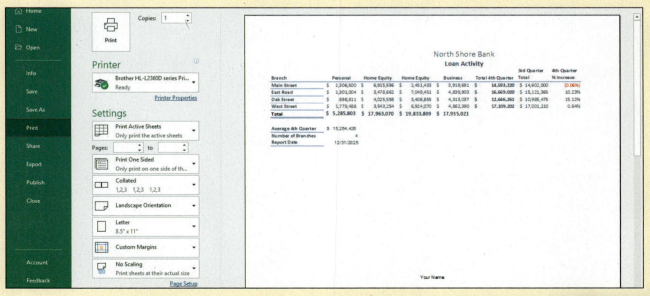

Visual Workshop

Open IL_EX_3-5.xlsx from the location where you store your Data Files, then save it as **IL_EX_3_Freight**. Use the skills you learned in this module to complete the worksheet so it looks like the one shown in FIGURE 3-21. To build the formulas in column G, calculate the percentage increase of the second quarter revenue over the first quarter revenue. (*Hint:* The percentage increases in column G must be calculated before calculating the average increase in cell B10.) To build the formulas in column I, a warning should be issued if the percentage increase is less than the average increase shown in cell B10 AND the on-time delivery is less than 75%. (*Hint:* Remember to use an absolute cell reference where necessary.) When you are finished, enter your name in the center footer section, then submit your work to your instructor as directed.

FIGURE 3-21

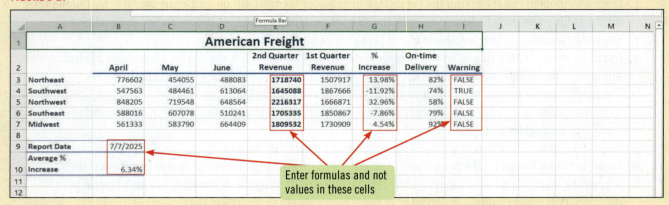

Working with Charts

CASE ▶ At the upcoming annual meeting, Ellie Schwartz, the vice president of finance, wants to review expenses at JCL Talent's U.S. offices. She asks you to create charts showing the expense trends in these offices over the past four quarters.

Module Objectives

After completing this module, you will be able to:

- Plan a chart
- Create a chart
- Move and resize a chart
- Change the chart design
- Change the chart layout

- Format a chart
- Create a pie chart
- Summarize data with sparklines
- Identify data trends

Files You Will Need

IL_EX_4-1.xlsx   IL_EX_4-4.xlsx

IL_EX_4-2.xlsx   IL_EX_4-5.xlsx

IL_EX_4-3.xlsx

Plan a Chart

Learning Outcomes
- Identify chart elements
- Explore common chart types

The process of creating a chart involves deciding which data to use and what type of chart best highlights the trends or patterns that are most important, such as steady increases over time or stellar performance by one sales rep compared to others in the same division. Understanding the parts of a chart makes it easier to evaluate specific elements to make sure the chart effectively illustrates your data. **CASE** ▶ *In preparation for creating the charts for Ellie's presentation, you review the purpose of the charts and decide how to organize the data.*

DETAILS

QUICK TIP

To see the available charts in Excel, select the worksheet data, click the Insert tab on the ribbon, click the Recommended Charts button in the Charts group, then click the All Charts tab.

Use the following guidelines to plan the chart:

- **Determine the purpose of the chart, and identify the data relationships you want to graphically communicate**

  You want to create a chart that shows quarterly expenses for JCL U.S. offices. You also want to illustrate whether the quarterly expenses for each office increased or decreased from quarter to quarter.

- **Determine the results you want to see, and decide which chart type is most appropriate**

  Different chart types display data in distinctive ways. For example, a pie chart compares parts of a whole, whereas a line chart is best for showing trends over time. To choose the best chart type for your data, first decide how you want your data to be interpreted. **FIGURE 4-1** shows the available chart types in Excel, listed by category on the All Charts tab of the Insert Chart dialog box. **TABLE 4-1** describes several of these charts. Because you want to compare JCL expenses in multiple offices over a period of four quarters, you decide to use a column chart.

- **Identify the worksheet data you want the chart to illustrate**

  Sometimes you use all the data in a worksheet to create a chart, while at other times you may need to select a range within the sheet. The worksheet from which you are creating your chart contains expense data for each of the past four quarters and the totals for the past year. To create a column chart, you will need to use all the quarterly data except the quarterly totals.

- **Understand the elements of a chart**

  The chart shown in **FIGURE 4-2** contains basic elements of a chart. In the figure, JCL offices are on the category axis and expense dollar amounts are on the value axis. The **category axis**, also called the *x*-axis, is the horizontal axis in a chart, usually containing the names of data categories. The **value axis**, also called the vertical axis, contains numerical values. In a two-dimensional chart, it is also known as the *y*-axis. (Three-dimensional charts contain a **z-axis**, for comparing data across both categories and values.) The area inside the horizontal and vertical axes that contains the graphical representation of the data series is the **plot area**. **Gridlines**, the horizontal and vertical lines, make a chart easier to read. Each individual piece of data plotted in a chart is a **data point**. In any chart, a **data marker** is a graphical representation of a data point, such as a bar or column. A set of values represented in a chart is a **data series**. In this chart, there are four data series: Quarter 1, Quarter 2, Quarter 3, and Quarter 4. Each is made up of columns of a different color. To differentiate each data series, information called a **legend** or a legend key identifies how the data is represented using colors and/or patterns.

FIGURE 4-1: Insert Chart dialog box lists available charts by category

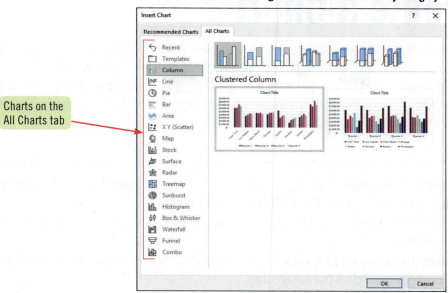

Charts on the
All Charts tab

FIGURE 4-2: Chart elements

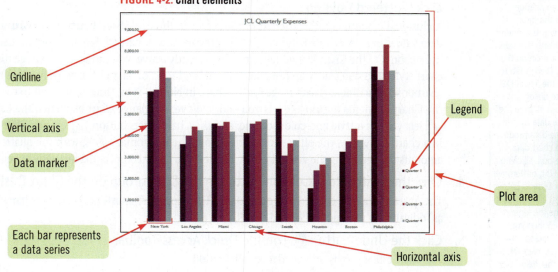

Gridline

Vertical axis

Data marker

Each bar represents
a data series

Legend

Plot area

Horizontal axis

TABLE 4-1: Common chart types

type	description
Column	A chart that displays data values as columns; column height represents its value
Line	A chart or visualization that displays data as separate lines across categories
Pie	A chart in the shape of a circle divided into slices like a pie, which shows data values as percentages of the whole
Bar	A column chart turned on its side so that the length of each bar is based on its value
Area	Shows how individual volume changes over time in relation to total volume
Line with Markers	Compares trends over time by showing data markers that represent worksheet data values

Excel

Working with Charts

EX 4-3

Create a Chart

Learning Outcomes
• Create a chart
• Add a title to a chart

To create a chart in Excel, you first select the worksheet range or ranges containing the data you want to chart. Once you've selected a range, you can use the Quick Analysis tool or the Insert tab on the ribbon to create a chart based on the data in that range. **CASE** ▶ *Using the worksheet containing the quarterly expense data, you create a chart that shows how the expenses in each office varied in relation to each other, across all four quarters of the year.*

STEPS

1. **sam** ↓ **Start Excel, open IL_EX_4-1.xlsx from the location where you store your Data Files, then save it as IL_EX_4_USQuarterlyExpenses**

   You want the chart to include the quarterly office expenses values, as well as quarter and office labels, but not any totals.

2. **Select the range A4:E12, click the Quick Analysis button 📊 in the lower-right corner of the range, then click the Charts tab**

   The Charts tab on the Quick Analysis tool recommends commonly used chart types based on the range you have selected. It also includes a More Charts button for additional chart types.

QUICK TIP
You can change either the data source or the legend by clicking the Select Data button on the Chart Design tab to open the Select Data Source dialog box. You can change the source data by editing the data range in the chart data range box. Clicking Add, Edit, or Remove under Legend Entries (Series) allows you to change the legend labels. When you finish making changes, click OK to close the dialog box.

3. **On the Charts tab, verify that Clustered Column is selected, as shown in FIGURE 4-3, then click Clustered Column**

   A clustered column chart is inserted in the center of the worksheet. **Clustered column charts** display data values in side-by-side columns. Two contextual tabs, Chart Design and Format, become available on the ribbon. On the Chart Design tab, which is currently active, you can quickly change the chart layout and chart style, and you can swap how the columns and rows of data in the worksheet are represented in the chart or select a different data range for the chart. In Normal view, three tools open to the right of the chart: the Chart Elements button ➕ lets you add, remove, or change chart elements; the Chart Styles button 🖌 lets you set a style and color scheme; and the Chart Filters button 🔽 lets you filter the results shown in a chart. Currently, the offices are charted along the horizontal *x*-axis, with the quarterly expense dollar amounts charted along the vertical *y*-axis. This lets you easily compare the quarterly expenses for each office.

4. **Click the Switch Row/Column button in the Data group on the Chart Design tab**

   The quarters are now charted along the x-axis. The expense amounts per office are charted along the y-axis, as indicated by the updated legend. See **FIGURE 4-4**.

5. **Click the Undo button ↺▾ on the Quick Access Toolbar**

   The chart returns to its original data configuration.

6. **Click the Chart Title placeholder, type JCL Quarterly Expenses, click the Enter button ✓, then click anywhere in the chart to deselect the title**

   Adding a title helps identify the chart. The border around the chart, along with the **sizing handles**, the small circles at the corners and the edges, indicates that the chart is selected. See **FIGURE 4-5**. Your chart might be in a different location on the worksheet and may look slightly different; you will move and resize it in the next lesson. Any time a chart is selected, as it is now, a blue border surrounds the worksheet data range on which the chart is based, a purple border surrounds the cells containing the category axis labels, and a red border surrounds the cells containing the data series labels. This chart is known as an **embedded chart** because it is displayed as an object in the worksheet. Embedding a chart in the current sheet is the default selection when creating a chart, but you can also embed a chart on a different sheet in the workbook, or on a newly created chart sheet. A **chart sheet** is a separate sheet in a workbook that contains only a chart that is linked to the workbook data.

7. **Save your work**

FIGURE 4-3: Charts tab in Quick Analysis tool

FIGURE 4-3: Charts tab in Quick Analysis tool

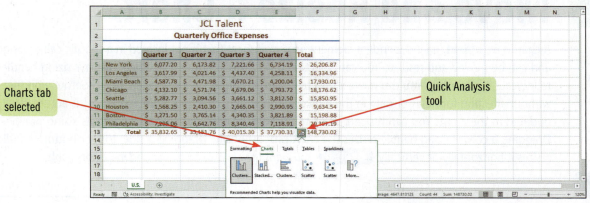

Charts tab selected

Quick Analysis tool

FIGURE 4-4: Clustered Column chart with different configuration of rows and columns

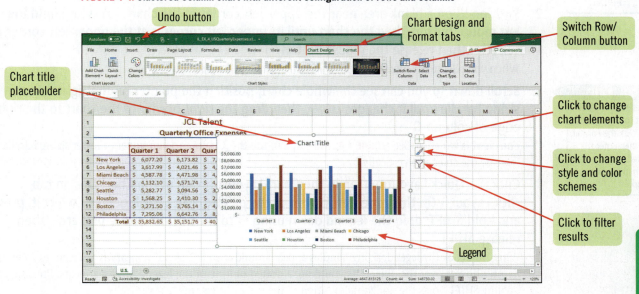

Undo button

Chart Design and Format tabs

Switch Row/Column button

Chart title placeholder

Click to change chart elements

Click to change style and color schemes

Click to filter results

Legend

FIGURE 4-5: Chart with original configuration restored and title added

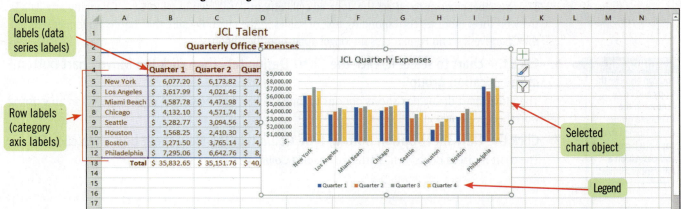

Column labels (data series labels)

Row labels (category axis labels)

Selected chart object

Legend

Excel

Move and Resize a Chart

Learning Outcomes
• Reposition a chart
• Resize a chart

A chart is an **object**, an independent element on a worksheet that is not located in a specific cell or range and can be moved and resized. You can select an object by clicking it; the object displays sizing handles to indicate it is selected. You can move a selected chart anywhere on a worksheet or to another worksheet without affecting formulas or data in the worksheet. Any data changed in the worksheet is automatically updated in the chart. You can resize a chart to improve its appearance by dragging its sizing handles. Dragging a corner sizing handle resizes the chart proportionally. Dragging a side, top, or bottom handle resizes it horizontally or vertically. **CASE** *You want the chart to be bigger and more noticeable.*

STEPS

QUICK TIP
To delete a selected chart, press DEL.

1. **Make sure the chart is still selected, then position the pointer over the chart**

   The pointer shape ⁺ꝅ indicates that you can move the chart.

2. **Position ꝅ on a blank area near the upper-left corner of the chart, press and hold the left mouse button, drag the chart until its upper-left corner is at the upper-left corner of cell A16, then release the mouse button**

   When you release the mouse button, the chart appears in the new location.

QUICK TIP
To resize a selected chart to an exact size, click the Format tab, then enter the desired height and width in the Size group.

3. **Scroll down so you can see the whole chart, position the pointer on the right-middle sizing handle until it changes to ↔, then drag the right border of the chart to the right edge of column G**

   The chart is widened. See **FIGURE 4-6**. You can also use the ↕ pointer on an upper or lower sizing handle to increase the chart size vertically.

4. **Click the Quick Layout button in the Chart Layouts group of the Chart Design tab, click Layout 1 (in the upper-left corner of the palette), click the legend to select it, press and hold SHIFT, drag the legend down using ⁺ꝅ to the bottom of the plot area, then release SHIFT**

   When you click the legend, sizing handles appear around it and "Legend" appears as a ScreenTip when the pointer hovers over the object. As you drag, a dotted outline of the legend border appears. Pressing and holding SHIFT holds the horizontal position of the legend as you move it vertically.

5. **Scroll up if necessary, click cell A7, type Miami, then click the Enter button ✓ on the formula bar**

   The axis label changes to reflect the updated cell contents, as shown in **FIGURE 4-7**. Changing any data in the worksheet modifies corresponding text or values in the chart. Because the chart is no longer selected, the Chart Design and Format tabs no longer appear on the ribbon.

QUICK TIP
You can also use the Copy and Paste buttons in the Clipboard group of the Home tab to copy a selected chart and paste it on a different worksheet.

6. **Click the chart to select it, click the Chart Design tab, then click the Move Chart button in the Location group**

   The Move chart dialog box shows options to move a chart to a new sheet or as an object in an existing worksheet, as shown in **FIGURE 4-8**.

7. **Click the New sheet option button, type Column in the New sheet box, then click OK**

   The chart is placed on its own chart sheet, named Column.

FIGURE 4-6: Moved and resized chart

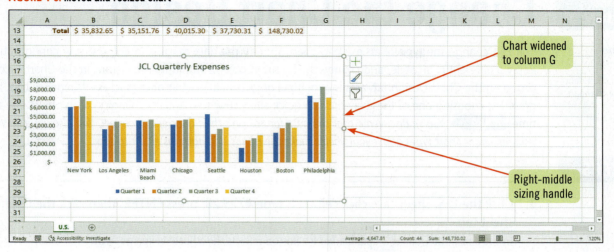

Chart widened to column G

Right-middle sizing handle

FIGURE 4-7: Worksheet with modified legend and label

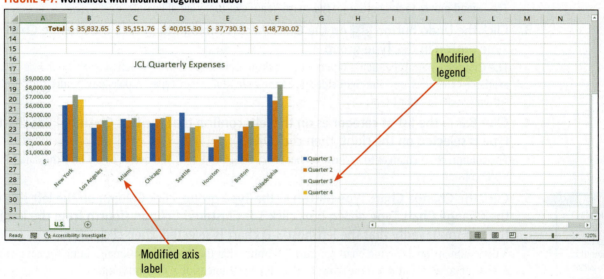

Modified legend

Modified axis label

FIGURE 4-8: Move Chart dialog box

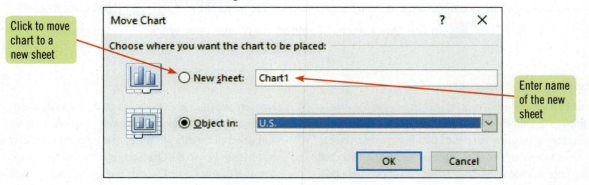

Click to move chart to a new sheet

Enter name of the new sheet

Excel

Change the Chart Design

You can change the type of an existing chart, modify the data range and column/row configuration, apply a different chart style, and change the layout of objects within it. The layouts in the Chart Layouts group on the Chart Design tab arrange multiple objects in a chart at once, such as its legend, title, and gridlines; choosing one of these layouts is a quick alternative to manually changing each object one at a time. **CASE** ▶ *You've discovered that the data for Boston's third quarter is incorrect. You also want to see if using different chart types and layouts helps make the trends and patterns easier to spot.*

STEPS

1. **Click the U.S. sheet tab, click cell D11, type 4775.20, press ENTER, then click the Column sheet tab**

   In the chart, the Quarter 3 data marker for Boston reflects the adjusted expense figure. See **FIGURE 4-9**.

2. **Select the chart, if necessary, by clicking a blank area within the chart border, click the Chart Design tab on the ribbon, click the Quick Layout button in the Chart Layouts group, then click Layout 3**

   The legend moves to the bottom of the chart. You prefer the original layout.

3. **Click the Undo button ↶ ▾ on the Quick Access Toolbar, then click the Change Chart Type button in the Type group**

   The Change Chart Type dialog box opens, as shown in **FIGURE 4-10**. The left side of the dialog box lists available categories, and the right side shows the individual chart types. A pale gray border surrounds the currently selected chart type.

4. **Click Bar in the list of categories on the left, confirm that the first Clustered Bar chart type is selected on the right, then click OK**

   The column chart changes to a Clustered Bar chart. See **FIGURE 4-11**. You decide to see how the data looks in a 3-D column chart.

5. **Click the Change Chart Type button in the Type group, click Column on the left side of the Change Chart Type dialog box, click 3-D Clustered Column (fourth from the left in the top row), verify that the leftmost 3-D chart is selected, then click OK**

   A three-dimensional column chart appears. You notice that the three-dimensional column format gives you a sense of volume, but it is more crowded than the two-dimensional column format.

6. **Click the Change Chart Type button in the Type group, click Clustered Column (first from the left in the top row), then click OK**

7. **Click the Style 3 chart style in the Chart Styles group**

   The columns change to lighter shades of color. You prefer the previous chart style's color scheme.

8. **Click ↶ ▾ on the Quick Access Toolbar, then save your work**

Creating a combo chart

A **combo chart** presents two or more chart types in one—for example, a column chart with a line chart. Combo charts are useful when charting dissimilar but related data. For example, you can create a clustered column–line combination chart based on both home price and home size data, showing home prices in a clustered column chart and related home sizes in a line chart. Here, a secondary axis (such as a vertical axis on the right side of the chart) would supply the scale for the home sizes. To create a combo chart, select all the data you want to plot, click the Insert Combo chart button ▣ ▾ in the Charts group in the Insert tab, click a suggested type or Create Custom Combo Chart, supply additional series information if necessary, then click OK.

FIGURE 4-9: Chart with modified data

Modified data

FIGURE 4-10: Change Chart Type dialog box

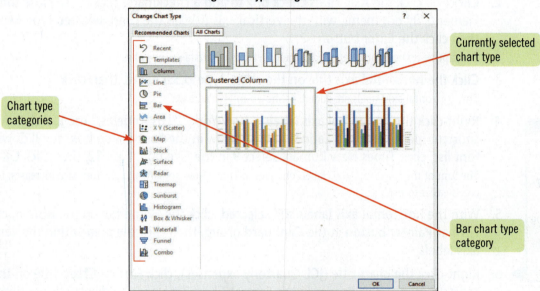

Currently selected chart type

Chart type categories

Bar chart type category

FIGURE 4-11: Column chart changed to bar chart

Click More button to see additional chart styles

Change Chart Type button

Change the Chart Layout

**Learning
Outcomes**
• Change the grid-
lines display
• Add axis titles
• Add a data table

While the Chart Design tab contains preconfigured chart layouts you can apply to a chart, the Chart Elements button makes it easy to add, remove, and modify individual chart objects such as a chart title, gridlines, or legend. Using options on this shortcut menu, you can also add a **data table**, a grid containing the chart data, to the chart. **CASE** ▶ *You want to change the layout of the chart by creating titles for the horizontal and vertical axes. Because the chart is on its own sheet, you also want to add a data table to provide more detailed information.*

STEPS

1. **With the chart still selected, click the Chart Elements button** ⊞ **in the upper-right corner of the chart, click the Gridlines arrow on the Chart Elements fly-out menu, click Primary Major Horizontal to deselect it, then click** ⊞ **to close the menu**
   The gridlines that extend across the chart's plot area are removed, as shown in **FIGURE 4-12**.

2. **Click** ⊞, **click the Axis Titles check box to add a checkmark, click** ⊞ **to close the Chart Elements fly-out menu, with the vertical axis title on the chart selected type Expenses, then click the Enter button** ✓
   Descriptive text on the category axis helps readers understand the chart.

3. **Click the horizontal axis title on the chart, type U.S. Offices, then click** ✓
   The horizontal axis labels are added, as shown in **FIGURE 4-13**.

4. **Right-click the horizontal axis labels ("New York," "Los Angeles," etc.), click Font on the shortcut menu, click the Latin text font arrow in the Font dialog box, scroll down the font list, click Times New Roman, select 9 in the Size box, type 12, then click OK**
   The font of the horizontal axis labels changes to Times New Roman, and the font size increases, making the labels easier to read.

5. **With the horizontal axis labels still selected, click the Home tab on the ribbon, click the Format Painter button in the Clipboard group, then click the area within the vertical axis labels**

6. **Right-click the chart title (JCL Quarterly Expenses), click Format Chart Title on the shortcut menu, click Border in the Format Chart Title pane to display the options if necessary, then click the Solid line option button in the pane**
   A solid border in the default blue color appears around the chart title.

7. **Click the Effects button** 🖼 **in the Format Chart Title pane, click Shadow, click the Presets arrow, click Offset: Bottom Right in the Outer group (first row, first from the left), then close the Format Chart Title pane**
   A border with a drop shadow surrounds the title.

8. **Click** ⊞, **click the Data Table check box to add a data table to the chart, in the list of chart elements click the legend check box to deselect it and remove the original legend, close the Chart Elements menu, then save your work**
   A data table with a legend shows the chart data. Compare your work to **FIGURE 4-14**.

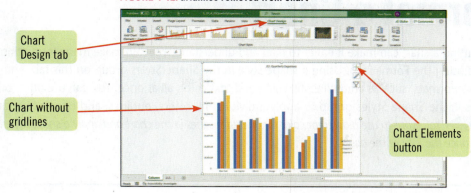

FIGURE 4-12: Gridlines removed from chart

Chart Design tab

Chart without gridlines

Chart Elements button

FIGURE 4-13: Axis titles added to chart

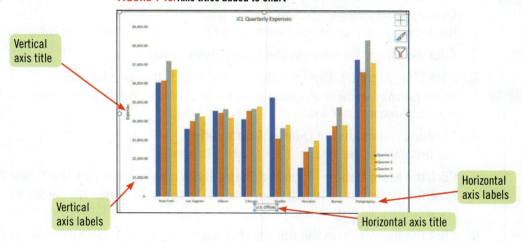

Vertical axis title

Vertical axis labels

Horizontal axis labels

Horizontal axis title

FIGURE 4-14: Enhanced chart

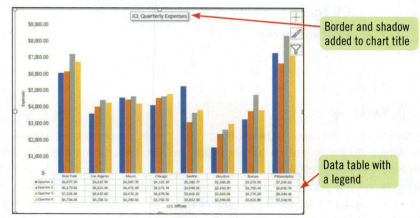

Border and shadow added to chart title

Data table with a legend

Working with chart axes

You can change both the number format and text formatting of a chart's axes. For example, you may want to change the starting and ending values of an axis. You can do this by double-clicking the axis, selecting Format Axis from the shortcut menu, clicking Axis Options in the Format Axis pane if necessary, then entering values in the Minimum and Maximum boxes. To change the number format of the values on an axis, scroll down in the Axis Options, click Number to display the options if necessary, then select from the available number formats. In the Number area, you can also create a number format code by typing a code in the Format Code box and clicking Add. In addition to these axis options, you can work with axis text by clicking the Text Options button at the top of the pane, then clicking the Textbox button. The Text Box group includes options for changing the vertical alignment of the data labels on the axis and the text direction of axis data labels from horizontal to stacked or rotated.

Format a Chart

Learning Outcomes
- Change the fill of a data series
- Apply a style to a data series

Formatting a chart can make it easier to read and understand. You can make many formatting enhancements using the Format tab. Using a shape style in the Shape Styles group on this tab, you can apply multiple formats, such as an outline, fill color, and text color, all at once. You can use other buttons and arrows in the Shape Styles group to apply individual fill colors, outlines, and effects to chart objects. **CASE** ▶ *You want to use a different color for one data series in the chart and apply a shape style to another, to enhance the look of the chart.*

STEPS

1. **With the chart selected, click the Format tab on the ribbon, then click any column in the Quarter 4 data series**

   Handles appear on each column in the Quarter 4 data series, indicating that the entire series is selected.

2. **Click the Shape Fill arrow in the Shape Styles group**

3. **Click Blue, Accent 1, Lighter 80% (second row, fifth from the left)**

   All the columns for the series change to a light shade of blue, and the legend changes to match the new color, as shown in **FIGURE 4-15**.

4. **Click any column in the Quarter 3 data series**

   Handles appear on each column in the Quarter 3 data series.

5. **Click the More button ⬇ on the Shape Styles gallery, then click the Subtle Effect – Gray, Accent 3 (fourth row, fourth from the left) shape style under Theme Styles**

   The style is applied to the data series, as shown in **FIGURE 4-16**.

6. **Click the Insert tab on the ribbon, click the Text button, click the Header & Footer button, click Custom Footer, type your name in the center section, click OK, then click OK again**

7. **Save your work**

Working with WordArt

You can insert WordArt into a worksheet or a chart. To insert WordArt in a worksheet, click the Insert tab on the ribbon, click the Text button in the Text group, click WordArt, then click a style in the gallery. You can change a WordArt style by clicking the WordArt to select it, clicking the WordArt Styles More button ⬇ on the Shape Format tab, then selecting a new WordArt style. You can change the fill color of the WordArt by clicking the Text Fill button in the WordArt Styles group and choosing a fill color, texture, gradient, or picture. You can change the outline of selected WordArt text by clicking the Text Outline button in the WordArt Styles group and choosing an outline color, weight, and/or dashes.

FIGURE 4-15: New shape fill applied to data series

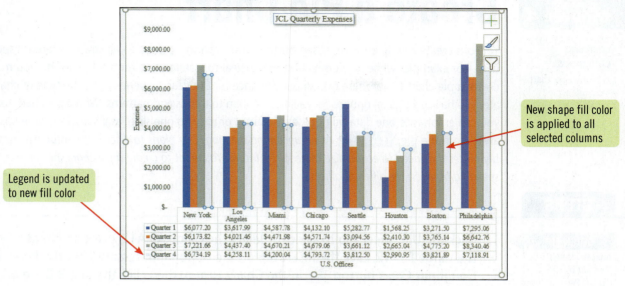

New shape fill color is applied to all selected columns

Legend is updated to new fill color

FIGURE 4-16: Style applied to data series

Shape style applied to selected columns

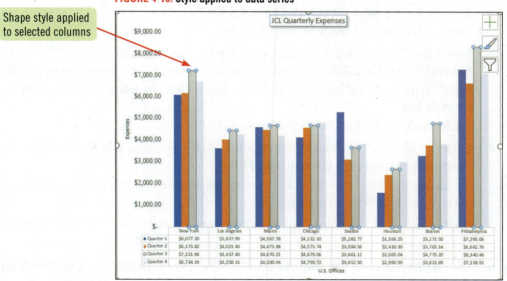

Aligning charts

If you have two or more embedded charts on a worksheet, you can line them up to make them easier to view. First, select the charts by clicking the first chart and holding SHIFT, then click the other chart(s). With the charts selected, click the Shape Format tab, click the Align button in the Arrange group, then choose the alignment position for the charts. The chart shown in **FIGURE 4-17** uses the Align Top option.

FIGURE 4-17: Charts aligned at the top

Aligned charts

Create a Pie Chart

Learning Outcomes
- Create a pie chart
- Explode a pie chart slice

You can create multiple charts based on the same worksheet data, to illustrate different aspects of the data. For example, while a column chart may reveal top performers month by month, you may want to create a pie chart to compare overall performance for the year. Depending on the type of chart you create, you have additional options for calling attention to trends and patterns. With a pie chart, for example, you can emphasize one data point by **exploding**, or moving one slice, as if someone were taking a piece away from the pie. **CASE** ▶ *At an upcoming meeting, Ellie plans to discuss the total expenses and identify offices that need to economize more in the future. You want to create a pie chart she can use to compare spending between the different offices.*

STEPS

1. Click the **U.S. sheet tab** to select it, select the range **A5:A12**, press and hold **CTRL**, select the range **F5:F12**, click the **Insert tab** on the ribbon if necessary, click the **Insert Pie or Doughnut Chart button** 🟠▾ in the Charts group, then click the first **2-D Pie** in the chart gallery

2. Click the **Move Chart button** in the Location group, click the **New sheet option button**, type **Pie** in the New sheet box, then click **OK**

   The chart is placed on a new worksheet named Pie.

3. Select the **Chart Title placeholder**, click the **Format tab**, click the **WordArt Styles More button** ▼, click the **Fill: Gray, Accent Color 3; Sharp Bevel** (second row, first from the right), type **JCL Total Expenses, by Office**, then click the **Enter button** ✓ on the formula bar

   The formatted WordArt title is added, as shown in **FIGURE 4-18**.

4. Click the slice for the **Houston data point**, click it again so it is the only slice selected, right-click it, then click **Format Data Point**

   You can use the Point Explosion slider to control the distance a pie slice moves away from the pie, or you can type a value in the Point Explosion box.

5. Double-click **0** in the Point Explosion box, type **10**, then click the **Close button** ✖

   Compare your chart to **FIGURE 4-19**.

6. Click a blank area of the chart to deselect the slice, click the **Chart Elements button** ➕, click the **Data Labels arrow** ▶, click **Outside End**, click **More Options**, in the Format Data Labels pane click the **Percentage check box** to add a checkmark, click the **Value box** to deselect it, then close the Format Data Labels pane

   The data labels identify the pie slices by percentage.

7. Click ➕, point to **Data Labels**, click ▶, click **Data Callout**, click the **Legend check box** to deselect it, then click ➕

   The data is labeled using percentage callouts, as shown in **FIGURE 4-20**.

8. Click the **Insert tab** on the ribbon, click the **Text button**, click the **Header & Footer button** in the Text group, click the **Custom Footer button**, enter your name in the center section, click **OK**, click **OK** again, then save your work

FIGURE 4-18: Title formatted using WordArt

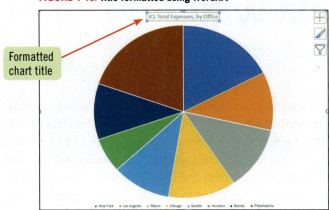

Formatted chart title

FIGURE 4-19: Exploded pie slice

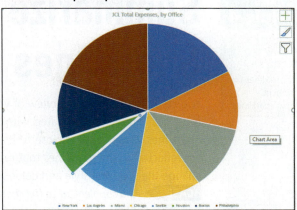

FIGURE 4-20: Pie chart with percentages

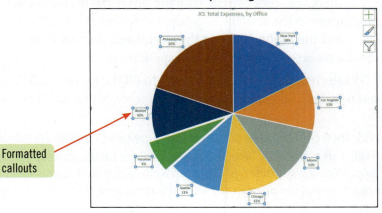

Formatted callouts

Working with other chart types

Excel includes chart types that are useful for illustrating highly specific types of data. These include Waterfall, Histogram, Pareto, Box & Whisker, Treemap, Scatter, and Sunburst. A **treemap chart** is a hierarchy chart in which each category is placed within a rectangle and subcategories are nested as rectangles within those rectangles. A **sunburst chart** is also a hierarchy chart, but it groups categories within a series of concentric rings, with the upper levels of the hierarchy placed in the innermost rings. To insert one of these chart types, click the Insert tab, click the Insert Hierarchy Chart button in the Charts group, then click the chart type. **Waterfall charts** are used to track the addition and subtraction of values within a sum. To insert a Waterfall chart, click the Insert tab, click the Insert Waterfall, Funnel, Stock, Surface, or Radar Chart button in the Charts group, then click Waterfall. A **histogram chart** shows the distribution of data grouped in bins.

These charts look similar to column charts, but each column (or bin) represents a range of values. To insert a histogram chart, click the Insert tab on the ribbon, click the Insert Statistic Chart button in the Charts group, then click the Histogram chart button. You can edit the bins in a histogram chart by double-clicking the x-axis, clicking to expand the Axis Options group on the Format Axis pane, then choosing options under Bins.

A **scatter chart** displays the correlation between two numeric variables. It is a type of **XY scatter chart**, which shows the pattern or relationship between two or more sets of values. Scatter charts look similar to line charts but have two value axes. The data points on a scatter chart show the intersection of the horizontal and vertical axes values. To insert a scatter chart, select the data you want to chart, click the Insert tab, click the Insert Scatter (X,Y) or Bubble Chart button in the Charts group, then choose a scatter chart type.

Summarize Data with Sparklines

You can create a quick overview of your data by adding sparklines to the worksheet cells. A **sparkline** is a small, simple chart located within a worksheet cell that serves as a visual indicator of data trends. Sparklines usually appear close to the data they represent. Any changes that you make to a worksheet are reflected in the sparklines that represent the data. After you add sparklines to a worksheet, you can change the sparkline style and color, and you can format their high and low data points in special colors.

CASE ▸ As a supplement to the charts, Ellie wants the U.S. worksheet to illustrate the expense trends for the year. You decide to add sparklines to tell a quick visual story within the worksheet cells.

STEPS

1. Click the **U.S. sheet tab**, click cell **G5**, click the **Insert tab** on the ribbon if necessary, click the **Column button** in the Sparklines group, verify that the insertion point is in the Data Range box, select the range **B5:E5** on the worksheet, then click **OK**

   Columns showing the expense trend for New York appear in cell G5.

2. With cell G5 selected, drag the **fill handle ✛** to fill the range **G6:G12**

   The sparkline is copied, and column sparklines reflecting the data for each office are added, as shown in **FIGURE 4-21**.

3. Click cell **G5**, then click the **Line button** in the Type group on the Sparkline tab

   When sparklines are copied they become a group, so all the sparklines in this group change to the Line sparkline type. When any sparkline type in a group is changed, the other sparklines in the group change to match the new type. You can ungroup and group sparklines using the Group and Ungroup buttons in the Group group.

4. Click the **Sparkline Color button** in the Style group, then click **Green, Accent 6, Darker 50%** (last row, first color from the right)

5. Click the **More button ▾** in the Style group, then click **Brown, Sparkline Style Accent 2, Darker 50%** (second from the left in the first row)

   The sparkline colors and styles are consistent with the colors on the worksheet.

6. Click the **Marker Color button** in the Style group, point to **High Point**, select **Orange Accent 2, Darker 50%** (sixth from left, sixth row), click the **Marker Color button** in the Style group, point to **Markers**, select **Green, Accent 6** (last in Theme Colors), then click the **Markers check box** in the Show group to add a checkmark if necessary

   Data markers indicate each quarter's expenses, with the highest quarter value in a different color.

7. Click cell **C5**, type **6,742.13**, click the **Enter button ✓**, then compare your screen to **FIGURE 4-22**

   The sparklines update to reflect the new worksheet data.

8. Click the **Insert tab** on the ribbon, click the **Text button**, click the **Header & Footer button** in the Text group, click the **Go to Footer button** in the Navigation group, enter your name in the **center footer section**, click **any cell** on the worksheet, click the **Normal button ▦** on the status bar, then press **CTRL+HOME**

9. Save your changes

FIGURE 4-21: Expense trend sparklines

FIGURE 4-22: Formatted sparklines

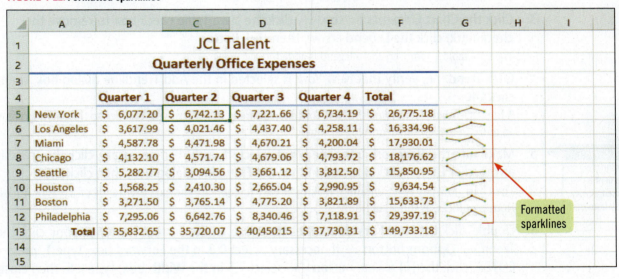

Identify Data Trends

To emphasize trends and patterns that occur over a period of time, you can add one or more trendlines to a chart. A **trendline** is a series of data points on a line that shows data values representing the general direction of a data series. In some business situations, you can use trendlines to project future data based on past trends. **CASE** ▸ *As part of her presentation, Ellie wants to compare the New York and Houston expenses. You decide to use trendlines to highlight spending at these offices over the past year and project expenses for the next six months, if past trends continue.*

STEPS

1. **Right-click the Column sheet tab**, click **Move or Copy** on the shortcut menu, click **(move to end)** in the Before sheet box, click the **Create a copy check box** to add a checkmark, then click **OK**

   The new worksheet Column (2) is a copy of the Column sheet.

2. **Right-click the Column (2) sheet tab**, click **Rename** on the shortcut menu, type **Trends**, click the **chart** to select it, click the **Chart Design tab**, then click the **Switch Row/Column button** in the Data group

   The chart displays quarters, a time measure, on the x-axis.

3. Click the **Chart Elements button** ⊞, click the **Data Table check box** to remove the checkmark, click the **Legend arrow**, then click **Bottom**

   The data table is removed and a legend is added.

4. Click **Trendline**, verify that **New York** is selected in the Add Trendline dialog box, then click **OK**

   A linear trendline identifying the New York expense trend in the past year is added to the chart, along with an entry in the legend identifying the line.

5. Make sure the New York trendline is not selected, click ⊞ if necessary, click the **Trendline arrow**, click **Linear**, click **Houston** in the Add Trendline dialog box, then click **OK**

   The chart now has two trendlines, making it easy to compare the expense trends of the New York and Houston offices, as shown in **FIGURE 4-23**.

6. **Double-click the New York data series trendline**, in the Format Trendline pane click the **Trendline Options button** 📊 if necessary, select **0.0** in the Forward box, type **1**, press **ENTER**, click the **Fill & Line button** 🖍, select **1.5** in the **Width box**, type **2.5**, then close the **Format Trendline pane**

   Trendlines are often used to project future trends. The formatted New York trendline projects an additional quarter of future expenses trends for the office, assuming past trends continue.

7. **Double-click the Houston data series trendline**, select **0.0** in the Forward box, type **1**, press **ENTER**, click 🖍, select **1.5** in the **Width box**, type **2.5**, then close the Format Trendline pane

   The formatted Houston trendline also projects an additional quarter of future expenses, if past trends continue.

8. **sam'↑** Save your work, preview the Trends sheet, compare your chart to **FIGURE 4-24**, close the workbook, submit the workbook to your instructor, then close Excel

FIGURE 4-23: Chart with two trendlines

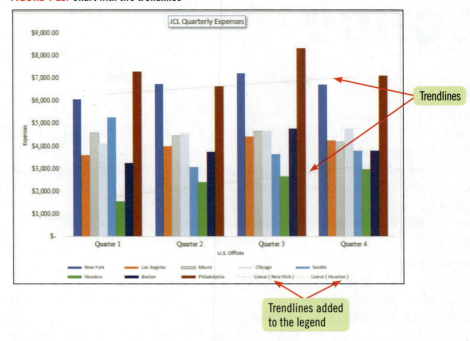

Trendlines

Trendlines added to the legend

FIGURE 4-24: Expense chart with trendlines for New York and Houston data

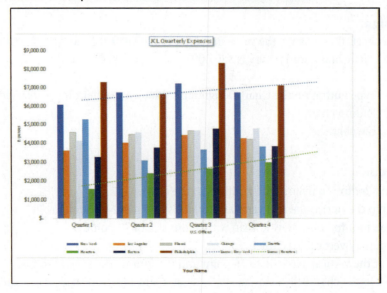

Choosing the right trendline options for your chart

When choosing a trendline, it is important to know which one is best for the information you want to communicate. If the data progression follows a straight line, using a linear trendline helps to emphasize that. If the pattern of a chart's data is linear but the data points don't follow a straight line, you can use a linear forecast trendline to chart a best-fit straight line. When data values increase or decrease in an arc shape, consider using an exponential or power trendline to illustrate this. A two-period moving average smooths out fluctuations in data by averaging the data points.

Practice

Skills Review

1. Create a chart.

a. Start Excel, open IL_EX_4-2.xlsx from the location where you store your Data Files, then save it as **IL_EX_4_FoodServices**.

b. In the worksheet, select the range containing all the sales data and headings. Do not include the totals.

c. Use the Quick Analysis tool to create a Clustered Column chart. Use the first Clustered Column option, placing the months on the x-axis.

d. Add the chart title **Brand Sales, by Month** above the chart.

e. Save your work.

2. Move and resize a chart.

a. Make sure the chart is still selected and close any open panes if necessary.

b. Move the chart beneath the worksheet data so its upper-left corner is at the upper-left corner of cell A11.

c. Widen the chart so it extends to the right edge of column H.

d. Use the Quick Layout button in the Chart Layouts group on the Chart Design tab to move the legend to the right of the charted data. (*Hint:* Use Layout 1.)

e. Move the chart to a new worksheet that you name **Column**.

f. Save your work.

3. Change the chart design.

a. Activate the Q1 & Q2 sheet, then change the value in cell B4 to **80,000.00**. Activate the Column sheet and verify that the value for the Classic brand for January is $80,000.00.

b. Select the chart if necessary.

c. Use the Change Chart Type button on the Chart Design tab to change the chart to a Clustered Bar chart, then change it back to a Clustered Column chart.

d. Apply Chart Style 6 to the chart.

e. Save your work.

4. Change the chart layout.

a. Use the Chart Elements button to remove the gridlines in the chart.

b. Change the font used in the horizontal and vertical axis labels to Times New Roman.

c. Change the chart title's font to Times New Roman with a font size of 20 point.

d. Insert **Sales** as the primary vertical axis title.

e. Change the font size of the vertical axis title to 16 point and the font to Times New Roman.

f. Add a solid line border to the chart title, using the default color and a (preset) shadow of Outer Offset: Bottom Right.

g. Add a data table to the chart with a legend key, then remove the legend from the chart.

h. Save your work.

5. Format a chart.

a. Use the Format tab to change the shape fill of the Classic data series to Olive Green, Accent 3, Darker 50% (last row of the theme colors, seventh from the left).

b. Change the shape style of the Classic data series to Intense Effect – Blue, Accent 1 (sixth row, second from the left), then click the chart area to deselect the Classic data series.

c. Save your work.

Skills Review (continued)

6. Create a pie chart.

    a. Switch to the Q1 & Q2 sheet, then select the range A4:A8 and H4:H8. (*Hint:* Holding CTRL allows you to select multiple nonadjacent ranges.)

    b. Create a 2-D pie chart and move the chart beneath the worksheet data so the upper-left corner is at the upper-left corner of cell A11.

    c. Add data callout labels and do not display the legend.

    d. Change the chart title to **Q1 & Q2 Sales** and format the title using the WordArt style Fill: Blue, Accent color 1, Shadow (second style in the first row).

    e. Explode the Artisan slice from the pie chart at **20%**.

    f. Enter your name in the center footer section of the worksheet, then save your work.

7. Summarize data with sparklines.

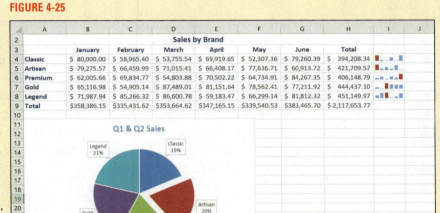

FIGURE 4-25

    a. Add a Line sparkline to cell I4 that represents the data in the range B4:G4.

    b. Copy the sparkline in cell I4 into the range I5:I8.

    c. Change the sparklines to columns.

    d. Apply the Sparkline style Blue Sparkline Style Dark #1 (fifth row, first column) to the group.

    e. Add high point markers with the color of Red, Accent 2 (first row, sixth from the left).

    f. Preview the worksheet and compare it to **FIGURE 4-25**.

    g. Save the workbook.

8. Identify data trends.

    a. Switch to the Column sheet.

    b. Add linear trendlines to the Premium and Gold data series.

    c. Set the forward option to 2 periods for both trendlines.

    d. Change the width of both trendlines to 3, then compare your screen to **FIGURE 4-26**.

    e. Add your name to the center footer section of the Column sheet, save the workbook, close the workbook, then submit the workbook to your instructor.

    f. Close Excel.

FIGURE 4-26

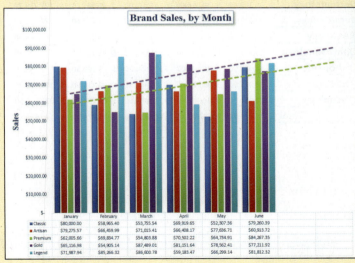

Independent Challenge 1

As an insurance manager for Riverwalk Medical Clinic, you have been asked to review the reimbursements for the clinic's departments. You will create a chart showing the insurance reimbursement over the past four quarters and predict future trends based on this history.

a. Start Excel, open IL_EX_4-3.xlsx from the location where you store your Data Files, then save it as **IL_EX_4_Reimbursements**.

b. Create a Clustered Column chart using the reimbursement amounts for the quarters and departments. (*Hint:* Do not include the totals.)

c. Switch the placement of the rows and columns, if necessary, to place the quarters on the x-axis.

d. Remove the chart gridlines.

e. Change the fill of the Psychology data series to Orange, Accent 6, Darker 50% (last row, last column of the Theme colors).

f. Add the Subtle effect – Red, Accent 2 (fourth row, third from the left) shape style to the Psychology data series.

g. Move the chart so the upper-left corner is at the upper-left corner of cell G2.

h. Change the fourth-quarter psychology reimbursement amount in cell E10 to **60,254.20**.

i. Add the chart title **Reimbursements** and format the title with a solid line blue border from the Standard Colors.

j. Move the bottom chart border to the top of row 20, add a data table, then remove the chart legend.

k. Add trendlines to the cardiology and orthopedics department data forecasting 2 periods ahead.

l. Change the chart to a line chart, apply the Style 12 Chart Style to the chart, then compare your worksheet to FIGURE 4-27.

m. Enter your name in the center section of the worksheet footer, then save your work.

n. Submit your work to your instructor as directed.

o. Close the workbook, then close Excel.

FIGURE 4-27

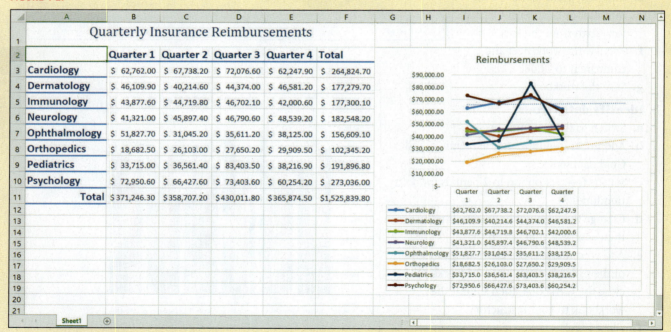

Independent Challenge 2

One of your responsibilities as the director of enrollment at Oceanview College is to present enrollment data to the executive staff at the end of the academic year. Your assistant has organized the college's enrollment data by division in a worksheet. You will review the data and create charts to visually represent the enrollment for the year.

a. Start Excel, open IL_EX_4-4.xlsx from the location where you store your Data Files, then save it as **IL_EX_4_Enrollments**.

b. Create a 3-D Clustered Column chart in the worksheet showing the enrollment data for all four terms. (*Hint:* The divisions, such as STEM, Business, and so forth, should appear on the x-axis.)

c. Add the chart title **Enrollment, by Division**, then format the title with the WordArt style of Fill: Blue, Accent color 1; Shadow (first row, second from left).

d. Move the chart so its upper-left corner is at the upper-left corner of cell H3.

e. On the worksheet, type **Average** in cell F3, then enter a formula in cell F4 to calculate the average STEM enrollment for the year.

f. Copy the average formula in cell F4 to the range F5:F9.

g. Add the average data from column F to the chart. (*Hint:* Use the Select Data button on the Chart Design tab to select the new chart data, including the average data.)

h. Change the chart type to Combo Clustered Column – Line chart (first option of combo charts) with the average data series charted as a line. (*Hint:* After selecting the chart type in the Change Chart Type dialog box, scroll down to make sure the Fall, Spring, Summer, and Intersession series are charted as clustered columns and the Average data series is charted as a line. You may need to change the Intersession chart type. Do not use the secondary axis options.)

i. Using **FIGURE 4-28** as a guide, resize the chart, then add data labels to the Average data series only. (*Hint:* Select the Average data series on the chart before adding data labels.)

j. Save your work.

k. Enter your name in the center footer section of the chart sheet, then preview the worksheet.

l. Submit your work to your instructor as directed, close the workbook, then close Excel.

FIGURE 4-28

Visual Workshop

Open IL_EX_4-5.xlsx from the location where you store your Data Files, then save it as **IL_EX_4_Insurance**. Create, modify, and position charts, including the sparklines, as shown in FIGURE 4-29. (*Hint:* Use the CTRL key as needed to select nonadjacent ranges.) You will need to make formatting, layout, and design changes once you create the charts. (*Hints:* The WordArt Style used in the pie chart title is Fill: Gold, Accent color 4: Soft Bevel. The WordArt Style used in the column chart title is Fill: Blue, Accent color 1: Shadow. The Life data point in the pie chart is exploded 30 degrees.) Enter your name in the center section of the footer, then save and preview the worksheet. Submit your work to your instructor as directed, then close the workbook and close Excel.

FIGURE 4-29

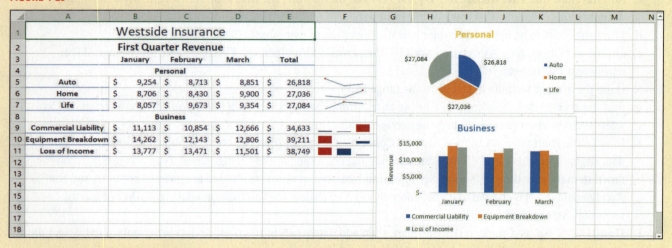

Working with Tables

CASE JCL uses tables to analyze placement data using placement dates, divisions, and commissions. The manager of the Boston office, Cheri McNeil, asks you to help her build and manage a table of information about the office's placements for the year. You will create the table, add information, organize it so it is easy to view, and perform calculations that help Cheri understand how the Boston office performed.

Module Objectives

After completing this module, you will be able to:

- Create and format a table
- Add and delete table data
- Sort table data
- Use formulas in a table
- Filter a table
- Look up values in a table
- Summarize table data
- Validate table data

Files You Will Need

IL_EX_5-1.xlsx   IL_EX_5-4.xlsx

IL_EX_5-2.xlsx   IL_EX_5-5.xlsx

IL_EX_5-3.xlsx

Create and Format a Table

Learning Outcomes
- Create a table
- Format a table

You can analyze and manipulate data in a table structure to take advantage of Excel tools and features designed specifically for tables. An Excel **table** is an organized collection of rows and columns of similarly structured data on a worksheet. Tables offer a convenient way to understand and manage large amounts of information. A table is organized into rows of data called **records**, each of which represents a complete set of field values for a specific person, place, object, event, or idea. A **field** is a column containing a specific property for each record, such as a person's last name or street address. Each field has a field name, which is a column label, such as "Address," that describes its contents. The **header row** is the first row of the table, and it contains the field names. After you create a table you can add preset formatting combinations of fill color, borders, type style, and type color by applying a table style. **CASE** ▶ *You begin building the placement table by creating it using worksheet data and applying a table style.*

STEPS

1. **sam** ⬇ **Start Excel, open IL_EX_5-1.xlsx from the location where you store your Data Files, then save it as IL_EX_5_BostonPlacements**

   QUICK TIP
   You can change a table back to a worksheet range by clicking the Convert to Range button in the Tools group on the Table Design tab.

2. **With cell A1 selected, click the Insert tab on the ribbon, click the Table button in the Tables group, in the Create Table dialog box verify that the range $A$1:$H$65 appears in the Where is the data for your table? box and the My table has headers check box contains a checkmark, as shown in FIGURE 5-1, then click OK**

   The data range is now defined as a table and is selected. **Filter list arrows**, which let you display portions of your data, appear next to each field name in the table. When you create a table, Excel automatically applies a table style. The default table style has a dark blue header row and alternating light and dark blue data rows. The Table Design tab appears, and the Table Styles group displays a gallery of table formatting options.

   QUICK TIP
   To make a table accessible, you can enter a table name in the Table Name text box in the Properties group on the Table Design tab.

3. **Click the Table Styles More button ⬇ on the Table Design tab, scroll and view all of the table styles, then move the pointer over several styles without clicking**

   The Table Styles gallery on the Table Design tab contains three style categories—Light, Medium, and Dark—each of which includes numerous designs. The designs use the current workbook theme colors so the table coordinates with your existing workbook content. If you select a different workbook theme and color scheme in the Themes group on the Page Layout tab, the Table Styles gallery uses those colors.

4. **Click the Green, Table Style Light 14 table style (the first style in the third row under Light), then click cell A1**

5. **Position the pointer in the column heading area for column A until it changes to ⬇, drag to select columns A and B, press CTRL, then drag ⬇ to select the column headings for columns F, G, and H**

   QUICK TIP
   You can remove and display the filter list arrows in a table by clicking the Home tab, clicking the Sort & Filter button in the Editing group, then clicking Filter. You can also use the Filter button in the Sort & Filter group on the Data tab.

6. **Click the Home tab on the ribbon, click the Format button in the Cells group, click Column Width, in the Column Width dialog box type 15.57 in the Column width box, then click OK**

7. **Position the pointer in the column D heading area until it changes to ⬇, drag to select columns D and E, click the Format button in the Cells group, click Column Width, in the Column Width dialog box type 9.43 in the Column width box, then click OK**

8. **Click cell A1, compare your table to FIGURE 5-2, then save your work**

FIGURE 5-1: Create Table dialog box

Verify the table range →

Verify that this check box contains a checkmark →

FIGURE 5-2: Formatted table

Changing table style options

You can change a table's appearance by using the check boxes in the Table Style Options group on the Table Design tab, as shown in **FIGURE 5-3**. You can use the check boxes to turn on or turn off the following options: Header Row, which displays or hides the header row; Total Row, which calculates totals for each column; Banded Rows, which applies or removes **banding**, a type of fill formatting in alternating rows or columns; and First Column and Last Column, which applies or removes special formatting in the first and last columns. You can display or hide the filter arrows on a table using the Filter Button check box; removing the checkmark removes the arrows.

You can also create your own table style by clicking the Table Styles More button, then clicking New Table Style at the bottom of the Table Styles Gallery. In the New Table Style dialog box, enter a name for the style in the Name box, click an item in the Table Element list, then click Format to format the selected element. You can also set a custom style as the default style for your tables by adding a checkmark to the Set as default table style for this document check box. You can remove a table style from the currently selected table by clicking Clear at the bottom of the Table Styles gallery.

FIGURE 5-3: Table Style Options group

Filter list arrows

Table Design tab

Filter button check box

Table Style Options group

Add and Delete Table Data

To keep a table up to date, you need to periodically add and remove records. You also need to check a table for duplicate records so that you can remove unnecessary duplication. You can add records and columns to a table by typing data directly below the last row of the table or directly to the right of the last table column. You can also expand a table by dragging the sizing handle in a table's lower-right corner; drag down to add rows and drag to the right to add columns. **CASE** *A recruiter informs you of an additional placement, so you need to update the table. Cheri also wants the table to display the number of days a placement was posted before it was filled.*

STEPS

1. **Scroll down to the last table row, click cell A66, enter the data shown below, then press [Enter]**

Account #	Employer ID	Division	Posting Date	Filled Date	Position Type	Commission	Preferred Employer
9408	32231	Creative	12/13/2021	12/23/2021	Consultant	$8,125	Yes

   As you scroll down, notice that the table headers are visible at the top of the table as long as the active cell is inside the table. The new placement is now part of the table.

2. **Click cell I1, type Days Posted, press ENTER, then resize the width of column I to 10.00**

   The new field becomes part of the table, and the header formatting extends to the new field name, as shown in **FIGURE 5-4**. The table range is now A1:I66.

3. **Click the inside left edge of cell A3 to select the table row, click the Delete arrow in the Cells group, then click Delete Table Rows**

   The placement in row 3 is deleted, and the placement in row 4 moves up to row 3. You can also delete a table row or a column by right-clicking the row or column, then clicking Delete.

4. **Click the Table Design tab on the ribbon, then click the Remove Duplicates button in the Tools group**

   The table is selected, and the Remove Duplicates dialog box opens, as shown in **FIGURE 5-5**.

5. **Make sure the My data has headers check box contains a checkmark, click Unselect All to deselect all the check boxes, click the Account # check box to add a checkmark, then click OK**

   Excel checks the table for any duplicates in the Account # field. A message box opens, telling you one duplicate record has been found and removed, leaving a total of 64 rows in the table, including the header row.

6. **Click OK, enter your name in the center section of the footer, then save the workbook**

FIGURE 5-4: New table column

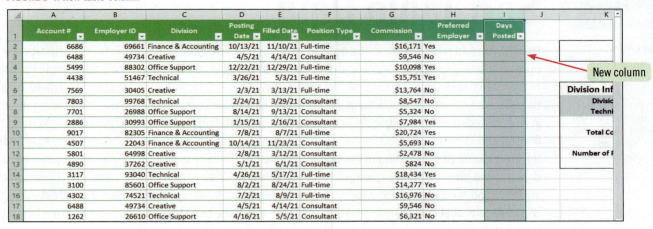

FIGURE 5-5: Remove Duplicates dialog box

Selected columns will be checked for duplicate data

Selecting table elements

When working with tables you often need to select rows, columns, and even the entire table. Clicking to the right of a row number, inside column A, selects the table row. You can select a table column by clicking the top edge of the column. Be careful not to click a column letter or row number, however, because this selects the entire worksheet row or column. You can select the entire table by clicking the upper-left corner of the top-left table cell. When selecting a column or a table, the first click selects only the data in the column or table. If you click a second time, you add the headers to the selection.

Sort Table Data

Learning Outcomes
- Sort a table in ascending order
- Sort a table in descending order
- Sort a table using custom sort options

Usually, you add table records in the order in which you receive information, rather than in alphabetical or numerical order, so new records commonly appear at the bottom of the table. You can change the order of records, or **sort** them, which organizes data in ascending or descending order, based on criteria such as date. Because the data is structured as a table, Excel changes the order of the records while keeping the data in each record, or row, together. You can sort a table in ascending or descending order on a field using the filter list arrows next to the field name, or using the Sort & Filter button on the ribbon. In **ascending order**, the lowest value (the beginning of the alphabet or the earliest date) appears at the top of the table, because data is sorted from lowest to highest, earliest to more recent, or alphabetically from A to Z; in a field containing labels and numbers, numbers appear first in the sorted list. In **descending order**, the highest value (the end of the alphabet or the latest date) appears at the top of the table because data is sorted from highest to lowest, most recent to earliest, or from Z to A; in a field containing labels and numbers, labels appear first. **TABLE 5-1** provides examples of ascending and descending sorts. **CASE** *Cheri wants the table sorted by the date the placement was filled, with placements that were filled the earliest at the top of the table.*

STEPS

1. **Click the Filled Date filter list arrow, then click Sort Oldest to Newest**

   Excel rearranges the records in ascending order by filled date, as shown in **FIGURE 5-6**. The Filled Date filter list arrow displays a small up arrow indicating that an ascending sort in this field has been applied.

2. **Click the Home tab if necessary, click any cell in the Commission column, click the Sort & Filter button in the Editing group, then click Sort Largest to Smallest**

   Excel sorts the table, placing records with higher commissions at the top. The Commission filter list arrow now displays a small down arrow, indicating the descending sort order. You can also rearrange table data using a **multilevel sort**, which reorders records using more than one column or field at a time; each field is considered a different level, based on its importance in the sort. In a two-level sort, for instance, the records are sorted by the first field, and then within each grouping created by that first sort they are sorted by the second field.

3. **Click the Sort & Filter button in the Editing group, then click Custom Sort**

   The Sort dialog box opens, as shown in **FIGURE 5-7**.

4. **Click the Sort by arrow, click Division, click the Order arrow, click A to Z, click Add Level, click the Then by arrow, click Commission, click the second Order arrow, click Smallest to Largest if necessary, then click OK**

   As shown in **FIGURE 5-8**, the table is sorted alphabetically in ascending order (A–Z) by Division and, within each division grouping, in ascending order by the Commission (smallest amount to largest).

5. **Save the workbook**

TABLE 5-1: Sort order options and examples

option	alphabetic	numeric	date	alphanumeric
Ascending	A, B, C	7, 8, 9	1/1, 2/1, 3/1	12A, 99B, DX8, QT7
Descending	C, B, A	9, 8, 7	3/1, 2/1, 1/1	QT7, DX8, 99B, 12A

FIGURE 5-6: Table sorted by filled date

Records are sorted by filled date in ascending order

Up arrow indicates ascending sort in this field

FIGURE 5-7: Sort dialog box

Click to delete sort levels

Click to add additional sort levels

Click to display fields

FIGURE 5-8: Table sorted using two levels

First-level sort arranges records by division

Second-level sort arranges records within each division by commission

Excel

Sorting conditional formatted data

You can emphasize top-ranked or bottom-ranked values in a field or column by applying conditional formatting to the sorted data. To highlight the top or bottom values in a field, select the field data, click the Conditional Formatting button in the Styles group on the Home tab, point to Top/Bottom Rules, click a rule, if necessary modify the percentage or number of cells you want to format, select the desired formatting, then click OK. You can also format your worksheet or table data using color scales based on the cell values. A **color scale** is a formatting scheme that uses a color set or shades of color to convey relative values of data. For example, you could use red fill

to indicate cells that have higher values and green fill to signify lower values. To add a color scale, select a data range, click the Home tab, click the Conditional Formatting button in the Styles group, then point to Color Scales. On the submenu, you can select preformatted color sets or click More Rules to create your own color sets. If conditional formats have been applied to a table or worksheet data, you can sort the table using conditional formatting to arrange the rows. For example, if cells are conditionally formatted with color, you can use the Sort dialog box to sort a field on Cell Color, using the color with the order of On Top or On Bottom in the Sort dialog box.

Specifying a custom sort order

You can identify a custom sort order in the Sort dialog box if the standard alphabetic and numeric sort orders do not meet your needs. For example, you might want to sort records by days of the week (Sun, Mon, Tues, Wed, etc.); an alphabetic sort would not sort these items properly. In the Sort dialog box, first specify

the field you want to sort on, click the Order arrow, then click Custom List. In the Custom Lists dialog box that opens, click an item under Custom lists, view the list entries, then click OK. To build your own custom list, click NEW LIST, click Add, type the desired list under List entries, then click OK.

Use Formulas in a Table

Learning Outcomes
- Build a table formula
- Use calculated columns to display formula results
- Use the table style options to add summary information to a table

The Excel table calculation features help you summarize table data so you can see important patterns and trends. After you enter a single formula into a table cell, the **calculated column** feature automatically fills in the remaining cells in the column with formula results, using the formula you entered. The column continues to fill with the formula results as you enter rows in the table. This makes it easy to update your formulas because you only need to edit the formula once, and the change fills in to the other column cells. These names adjust as you add or delete table fields. An example of a table reference is =[Sales]–[Costs], where Sales and Costs are field names in the table. You can also add a **table total row** to the bottom of a table for calculations on the table data. Clicking a cell in this row displays an arrow you can click to open a list of functions that can be used for the column calculation. The table total row adapts to any changes in the table size. **CASE** ▶ *Cheri asks you to calculate the number of days each placement was posted before being filled. You will also add summary information to the end of the table.*

STEPS

1. **Click cell I2, then type =[**
   A list of the table field names opens, as shown in **FIGURE 5-9**. The **structured reference** feature allows table formulas to refer to table columns by names that are automatically generated when the table is created. You can choose a field name by clicking it and pressing TAB or by double-clicking it.

2. **Double-click @ - This Row, click Filled Date, press TAB, then type]**
   Excel begins the formula, placing [@[Filled Date]] in the cell, in blue, and framing the Filled Date value in cell E2 in a blue border. The @ sign means to use the data in the same row as the formula. The formula uses an extra set of square brackets to enclose a field name that contains a space.

3. **Type -[@, double-click Posting Date, then type]**
   Excel places [@[Posting Date]] in the cell in red and outlines the Posting Date value in cell D2 in a red border.

QUICK TIP
You can undo the calculated column results by clicking Undo Calculated Column in the Auto-Correct Options list. You can turn off the Calculated Columns feature by clicking Stop Automatically Creating Calculated Columns in the AutoCorrect Options list.

4. **Click the Enter button ☑ on the Formula Bar**
   The formula result, 31, is displayed in cell I2. The table column also fills with the formula, displaying the number of days each placement was posted before being filled. The AutoCorrect Options button provides an option to turn off calculated columns. Because the calculated columns option saves time, you decide to leave the feature on.

5. **Click the Table Design tab on the ribbon, then click the Total Row check box in the Table Style Options group to add a checkmark**
   A total row appears at the bottom of the table, and the sum of the number of days posted, 1367, is displayed in cell I65.

6. **Click cell I65, click the cell list arrow on the right side of the cell, click Average, click the Home tab on the ribbon, then click the Decrease Decimal button ⬚ in the Number group five times**

QUICK TIP
The Name Box displays the active cell address. You can use this reference to make sure you selected the correct cell.

7. **Click cell G65 (in the Commission column), click the cell list arrow, then click Sum**
   The total row shows the average of days a placement was posted and the total amount of commissions earned by the office this year.

8. **Click cell A65, press DELETE, click cell F65 (in the Position Type column), type Total Commissions, click ☑, click cell H65, type Average Days, click ☑, widen column F to fully display the label in cell F65, compare your total row to FIGURE 5-10, then save your work**

FIGURE 5-9: Table field names

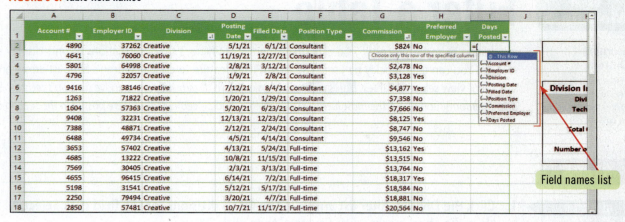

FIGURE 5-10: Table with total row

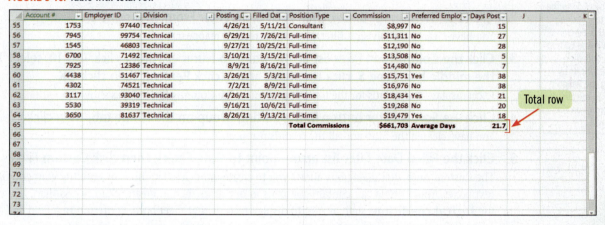

Excel

Filter a Table

Learning Outcomes
- Filter records using AutoFilter
- Filter records using a custom filter

In addition to sorting records, you can **filter** them, specifying a set of restrictions to only display specific records. You can filter quickly by using the **AutoFilter** feature to click a column's filter list arrow and then sort on or view selected values. **CASE** ▶ *Cheri asks you to display only the creative division's records. She also asks for information about the most lucrative placements, and placements that were posted in the second quarter.*

STEPS

QUICK TIP

If you add data to a table where a filter is applied, you can reapply the filter to include the new data either by clicking the Home tab, clicking the Sort & Filter button in the Editing group, and clicking Reapply, or by clicking the Reapply button in the Sort & Filter group on the Data tab.

1. **Click the Division filter list arrow, in the list of divisions for the field click Select All to clear the checkmarks, click Creative, then click OK**

   Only those records containing "Creative" in the Division field appear, as shown in **FIGURE 5-11**. The row numbers for the matching records change to blue, and the list arrow for the filtered field displays a filter icon 🔽. Both indicate that there is a filter in effect and that some of the records are temporarily hidden.

2. **Click the Division list arrow, then click Clear Filter From "Division"**

   You have cleared the Division filter, and all the records reappear.

3. **Click the Commission filter list arrow, point to Number Filters, click Top 10, select 10 in the middle box, type 5, click the Items arrow, click Percent, then click OK**

   Excel displays the records for the top five percent in the Commission field, as shown in **FIGURE 5-12**.

4. **Click the Sort & Filter button in the Editing group on the Home tab, then click Clear**

   You have cleared the filter and all the records reappear.

5. **Click the Filled Date filter list arrow, point to Date Filters, then click Custom Filter**

   The Custom AutoFilter dialog box allows you to create more detailed filters by entering your criteria in the text boxes. Your criteria can contain comparison operators such as greater than or less than. You can also use **logical conditions** such as And to display records that meet both a criterion in a field *and* another criterion in that same field, and you can use Or to display records that meet either criterion in a field.

QUICK TIP

When specifying criteria in the Custom Filter dialog box, you can use the (?) wildcard to represent any single character and the (*) wildcard to represent any series of characters.

6. **Click the left text box arrow on the first line, click is after or equal to, type 4/1/2021 in the right text box on the first line, verify that the And option button is selected, click the left text box arrow on the second line, click is before or equal to, type 6/30/2021 in the right text box on the second line, then click OK**

   Only the placements filled in the second quarter, after 4/1/2021 and before 6/30/2021, appear in the worksheet, as shown in **FIGURE 5-13**.

7. **Click the Filled Date filter list arrow, then click Clear Filter From "Filled Date"**

   You have cleared the filter and all the records reappear.

8. **Save the workbook**

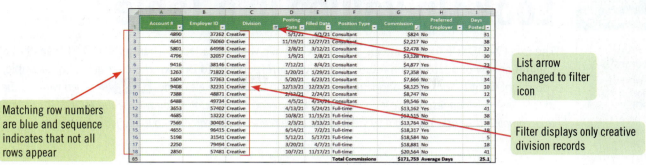

FIGURE 5-11: Table filtered to show Creative placements

Matching row numbers are blue and sequence indicates that not all rows appear

List arrow changed to filter icon

Filter displays only creative division records

FIGURE 5-12: Table filtered with top 5% of commissions

Only records containing the top 5% in commissions appear

FIGURE 5-13: Results of custom filter

Placement dates are between 4/1 and 6/30

Using an advanced filter

When you want to see table data that meets a detailed set of conditions, you can use the Advanced Filter feature. This feature lets you specify data that you want to display from the table using And and Or conditions. Rather than entering the criteria in a dialog box, you enter the criteria in a criteria range on your worksheet. A **criteria range** is a location separate from the table that you use to list specific search specifications. This range is usually a copy of the column labels with at least one additional row beneath the labels that contains the criteria you want to match. Placing all criteria in the same row specifies an **And condition**, which searches only for records where all the entered criteria are matched. Placing criteria in different rows specifies an **Or condition**, which searches for records where at least one entered criterion is matched. To apply an advanced filter, add the criteria range to the worksheet, click any cell in the table, click the Data tab, click the Advanced button in the Sort & Filter group, in the Advanced Filter dialog box verify the table range in the List range box, click the Criteria range text box, select your

criteria range on the worksheet, then click OK. The default setting under Action is to filter the table in its current location ("in-place") rather than copy it to another location. You can move the filtered table data to a different area of the worksheet or to a new worksheet. **FIGURE 5-14** shows a worksheet with the And criteria range located in the range $A$67:$I$68 and the filtered results of consultant positions with commissions greater than $7,000.

FIGURE 5-14: Results of advanced filter

Criteria range

Excel

Look Up Values in a Table

The Excel XLOOKUP function helps you locate specific values in a table or range. XLOOKUP searches a column or row of a table, then returns the value corresponding to the first match it finds. For example, you might want to look up a phone number based on an employee's name. **CASE** *Cheri wants to be able to find a division responsible for a placement by entering the account #. You will use the XLOOKUP function to accomplish this task. You begin by viewing the table name so you can refer to it in a lookup function.*

STEPS

1. **Click the Formulas tab on the ribbon, then click the Name Manager button in the Defined Names group**

   The table name appears in the Name Manager dialog box, as shown in **FIGURE 5-15**. The Excel structured reference feature automatically created the table name of Table1 when the table was created.

2. **Click Close, click cell L2, enter 2850, click cell L3, click the Lookup & Reference button in the Function Library group, then click XLOOKUP**

   The Function Arguments dialog box opens, with boxes for each of the XLOOKUP arguments.

3. **With the insertion point in the Lookup_value text box click cell L2, click the Lookup_array text box, then type Table1[Account '#]**

   Because the value you want to find is in cell L2, L2 is the Lookup_value. The range you want to search, the Account # column in Table1, is the Lookup_array. Be sure to include the apostrophe (') to indicate # is a special character.

4. **Click the Return_array text box, then type Table1[Division]**

   The column containing the information that you want to find and display in cell L3 is the Division column in Table1. The other two arguments are optional. You use the Match_mode argument to set an exact or approximate match. Because an exact match is the default, you do not need to specify this argument. Your completed Function Arguments dialog box should match **FIGURE 5-16**.

5. **Click OK**

   Excel searches down the Account # column of the table until it finds an account # that matches the one in cell L2. It then looks in the Division column of the table and finds the division for that record, Creative, and displays it in cell L3.

6. **Click cell L2, type 6234, then click the Enter button ☑ on the formula bar**

   The XLOOKUP function returns the value of Technical in cell L3. You can use this function to determine the division for other account numbers.

7. **Press CTRL+HOME, then save the workbook**

FIGURE 5-15: Named ranges in the workbook

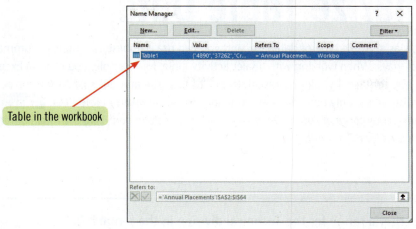

Table in the workbook

FIGURE 5-16: Completed Function Arguments dialog box for XLOOKUP

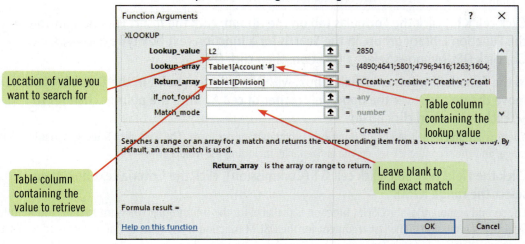

Location of value you want to search for

Table column containing the lookup value

Table column containing the value to retrieve

Leave blank to find exact match

Using other LOOKUP functions

VLOOKUP searches vertically (V) down the far-left column of a table, then reads across the row to find the value you specify. You provide a Lookup_value, the value you want to find, and a Table_array, the table you want to search. The Lookup_value must appear in the far-left column of the table. You set a Col_index_num to identify the column containing the information you want to find and display. For example, a Col_index_num of 3 means the third column from the left in the table range. When your data is arranged horizontally in rows instead of vertically in columns, use the HLOOKUP (Horizontal Lookup) function. HLOOKUP searches horizontally across the upper row of a table until it finds the matching value, then looks down the number of rows you specify. The arguments are identical to those for the VLOOKUP function, except that instead of a Col_index_number, HLOOKUP uses a Row_index_number, which indicates the location of the row you want to search. When you want to know the position of an item in a range, you can use the MATCH function. The MATCH function uses the syntax: MATCH (lookup_value,lookup_array,match_ type)

where the lookup_value is the value you want to match in the lookup_array range. The match_type can be 0 for an exact match, 1 for matching the largest value that is less than or equal to the lookup_value, or –1 for matching the smallest value that is greater than or equal to the lookup_value. The INDEX function is often used with the MATCH function, using the position obtained from the MATCH function and returning a value from a table or range. The syntax for the Index function is: INDEX(range, row_num, column_num). For example, =INDEX(A1:D7, 3, 4) returns the value in the cell located at the intersection of the third row and fourth column in the range A1:D7. The MATCH function can be used to find the row for an INDEX function. For example:

=INDEX(A1:B5,MATCH(3250,E1:E4),2)

Here, the match function searches the database E1:E4 and finds the position of the value 3250. This position becomes the row value for the index function while 2 is the column position in the database A1:B5.

Summarize Table Data

Learning
Outcomes
• Select a database
  for a database
  function
• Summarize table
  data using a
  database function

An Excel table acts as a simple type of database, and you can use database functions to summarize table data in a variety of ways. When working with a sales activity table, for example, you can use Excel to count the number of client contacts by sales representative or to total the amount sold to specific accounts by month. **TABLE 5-2** lists commonly used database functions for summarizing table data. **CASE** *Cheri is reviewing the yearly performance of each division. She needs your help in analyzing the total number of placements and commissions for each division.*

STEPS

1. **Review the criteria range for the Technical division in the range K7:K8**

   The criteria range in K7:K8 tells Excel to summarize records with the entry "Technical" in the Division column.

2. **Click cell K11, click the Formulas tab on the ribbon, click the Insert Function button in the Function Library group, in the Search for a function text box type database, click Go, click DSUM under Select a function, then click OK**

3. **In the Function Arguments dialog box, with the insertion point in the Database text box move the pointer over the upper-left corner of cell A1 until the pointer changes to ↘, click once, then click again**

   The first argument of the DSUM function is the table, or database. The first click selects the table's data range, and the second click selects the entire table, including the header row.

4. **Click the Field text box, click cell G1 (Commission), click the Criteria text box, then select the range K7:K8**

   The second argument of the DSUM function is the label for the column that you want to sum. You want to total the commissions. The last argument for the DSUM function is the criteria that will be used to determine which values to total. Your completed Function Arguments dialog box should match **FIGURE 5-17**.

5. **Click OK, click the Home tab on the ribbon, click the Accounting Number Format button $ in the Number group, then click the Decrease Decimal button ⬚ twice**

   The result in cell K11 is $200,255. Excel totaled the information in the Commission column for those records that meet the criterion of Division equals Technical.

6. **Click cell K13, click the Insert Function button ƒx on the formula bar, in the Search for a function text box type database, click Go, then double-click DCOUNTA in the Select a function list**

   The DCOUNT and the DCOUNTA functions can help you determine the number of records meeting specified criteria in a database field. DCOUNTA counts the number of nonblank cells.

7. **With the insertion point in the Database text box move the pointer over the upper-left corner of cell A1 until it changes to ↘, click once, click again to include the header row, click the Field text box, click cell C1, click the Criteria text box and select the range K7:K8, then click OK**

   The result in cell K13 is 18, and it indicates that the technical division had 18 placements over the past year.

8. **Click cell K8, type Office Support, click the Enter button ✓ on the formula bar, then save your work**

   The formulas in cells K11 and K13 are updated to reflect the new criteria. **FIGURE 5-18** shows that the office support division had 13 placements and commissions of $112,230 over the past year.

Working with Tables

FIGURE 5-17: Completed Function Arguments dialog box for DSUM

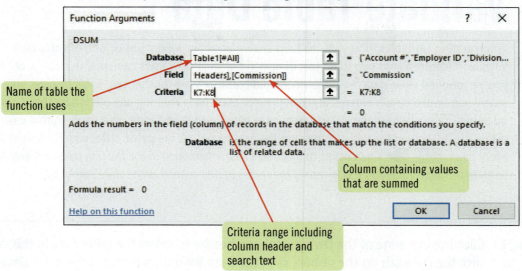

Name of table the function uses

Column containing values that are summed

Criteria range including column header and search text

FIGURE 5-18: Result generated by database functions

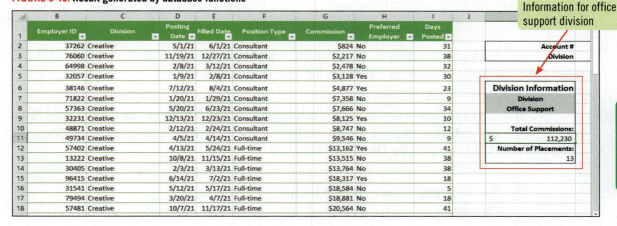

Information for office support division

TABLE 5-2: Common database functions

function	result
DGET	Extracts a single record from a table that matches criteria you specify
DSUM	Totals numbers in a given table column that match criteria you specify
DAVERAGE	Averages numbers in a given table column that match criteria you specify
DCOUNT	Counts the cells that contain numbers in a given table column that match criteria you specify
DCOUNTA	Counts the cells that contain nonblank data in a given table column that match criteria you specify

Excel

Validate Table Data

When setting up tables, you want to help ensure accuracy when you or others enter data. The Data Validation feature allows you to do this by specifying what data users can enter in a range of cells. Once you've specified what data the program should consider valid for that cell, Excel displays an error message when invalid data is entered and can prevent users from entering any other data that it considers to be invalid. When printing tables, you may have more rows than can fit on a page. In that case, you can define the first row of the table (containing the field names) as the **print title**, which prints at the top of every page. **CASE** *Cheri wants to make sure that information in the Division column is entered consistently in the future. She asks you to restrict the entries in that column to the office's divisions.*

STEPS

1. Click the **top edge** of the Division column header to select the table data in this column, click the **Data tab** on the ribbon, click the **Data Validation button** in the Data Tools group, on the Settings tab of the Data Validation dialog box click the **Allow arrow**, click **List**, click the **Source box**, type **Creative, Finance & Accounting, Office Support, Technical**, verify that the **In-cell dropdown check box** contains a checkmark, then click **OK**

2. Click the **Home tab** on the ribbon, click any **cell** in the last table row, click the **Insert arrow** in the Cells group, click **Insert Table Row Below**, click the **Division cell** in this row, then click its **list arrow**

   A list of valid list entries opens, based on the values entered in the Data Validation dialog box, as shown in **FIGURE 5-19**.

3. Click the **list arrow** to close the list, type **Medical**, press **ENTER**, click **Cancel** in the warning dialog box, click the **list arrow**, then click **Creative**

   The cell accepts the valid entry.

4. Click the **Delete arrow** in the Cells group, click **Delete Table Rows**, click the **File tab** on the ribbon, click **Print**, in the Preview window click **No Scaling** under Settings, then click **Fit All Columns on One Page**

   Below the table you see 1 of 2, which indicates you are viewing page 1 of a 2-page document.

5. Click the **Next Page button** in the Preview area

   The rows continue onto page 2, though you cannot see the field names.

6. Return to the worksheet, click the **Page Layout tab** on the ribbon, click the **Print Titles button** in the Page Setup group, click inside the **Rows to repeat at top text box** under Print titles, in the worksheet scroll up to row **1** if necessary, click any **cell** in row 1 of the table, click the **Print Preview button** in the Page Setup dialog box, then click in the preview window to view the second page

   A print title that repeats row 1 shows the field names at the top of each printed page.

7. Return to the worksheet, click the **Insert tab**, click the **Text button**, click the **Header & Footer button**, click the **left header section text box** if necessary, type **2021 Boston Office Placements**, click any **cell** on the worksheet, click the **Normal button** in the status bar, then press **CTRL+HOME**

8. **sam↑** Save the table, preview it, close the workbook, close Excel, then submit the workbook to your instructor

   Compare your printed table with **FIGURE 5-20**.

FIGURE 5-19: Entering data in restricted cells

	Employer ID	Division	Posting D	Filled Dat	Position Type	Commission	Preferred Emplo	Days Post
52	12281	Technical	4/1/21	4/17/21	Consultant	$7,642	No	16
53	99768	Technical	2/24/21	3/29/21	Consultant	$8,547	No	33
54	40627	Technical	1/18/21	2/12/21	Consultant	$8,774	No	25
55	97440	Technical	4/26/21	5/11/21	Consultant	$8,997	No	15
56	99754	Technical	6/29/21	7/26/21	Full-time	$11,311	No	27
57	46803	Technical	9/27/21	10/25/21	Full-time	$12,190	No	28
58	71492	Technical	3/10/21	3/15/21	Full-time	$13,508	No	5
59	12386	Technical	8/9/21	8/16/21	Full-time	$14,480	No	7
60	51467	Technical	3/26/21	5/3/21	Full-time	$15,751	Yes	38
61	74521	Technical	7/2/21	8/9/21	Full-time	$16,976	No	38
62	93040	Technical	4/26/21	5/17/21	Full-time	$18,434	Yes	21
63	39319	Technical	9/16/21	10/6/21	Full-time	$19,268	No	20
64	81637	Technical	8/26/21	9/13/21	Full-time	$19,479	Yes	18
65								0
66	Creative				Total Commissions	$661,703	Average Days	21.4
67	Finance & Accounting							
68	Office Support							
69	Technical							

List →

FIGURE 5-20: Printed table

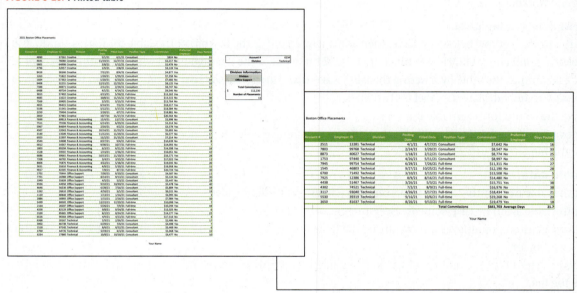

Restricting cell values and data length

In addition to providing an in-cell dropdown list for data entry, you can use data validation to restrict the values that are entered into cells. For example, you might want to restrict cells in a selected range to values less than a certain number, date, or time. To do so, click the Data tab, click the Data Validation button in the Data Tools group, on the Settings tab click the Allow arrow, select Whole number, Decimal, Date, or Time, click the Data arrow, select less than, then in the bottom text box, enter the maximum value. You can also limit the length of data entered into cells by choosing Text length in the Allow list, clicking the Data arrow and selecting less than, then entering the maximum length in the Maximum text box.

Adding input messages and error alerts

You can customize the way data validation works by adding input messages and setting alert styles. To do so, click the Input Message tab in the Data Validation dialog box, enter a message title and message, then click OK. To set an alert style, which controls how a user can proceed when entering invalid data, click the Error Alert tab, then click the Style arrow. The Information style displays your message with the information icon but allows the user to proceed with data entry. The Warning style displays your information with the warning icon and gives the user the option to proceed with data entry or not. The Stop style, which you used in this lesson, is the default; it displays your message and only lets the user retry or cancel data entry for that cell.

Excel

Practice

Skills Review

1. **Create and format a table.**
   a. Start Excel, open IL_EX_5-2.xlsx from the location where you store your Data Files, then save it as **IL_EX_5_Scientific**.
   b. Using the data in the range A1:I17, create a table.
   c. Apply a table style of Red, Table Style Light 14.
   d. Enter your name in the center section of the worksheet footer, enter **EOR Scientific Consulting** in the center section of the header, then activate cell A1.
   e. Save the workbook.

2. **Add and delete table data.**
   a. Insert a worksheet row below the table, then add a new record at the bottom of the table for Carlos Hurdo. Carlos's employee number is 2442. He was hired on 4/2/2021 to work in the Chicago office with a monthly salary of $5,120.
   b. Add a column to the table by entering the label **Annual Compensation** in cell J1. Widen the column as necessary to fully display the label on two lines.
   c. Delete the record for Hank Gole in row 6.
   d. Remove duplicate data in the table by checking for matching employee numbers.
   e. Save the file.

3. **Sort table data.**
   a. Sort the table by Monthly Salary in descending (largest to smallest) order.
   b. Sort the table again by Last Name in ascending (A to Z) order.
   c. Perform a custom, multilevel sort by sorting the table first by Office in A to Z order, and then by Hire Date in Oldest to Newest order.
   d. Review the results of the multilevel sort to make sure the records are sorted first by Office and then by Hire Date.
   e. Save the file.

4. **Use formulas in a table.**
   a. In cell J2, enter a formula, using structured references, to calculate an employee's annual compensation by totaling the annual salary, annual bonus, and annual benefits columns.
   b. Check the table to make sure that the formula from cell J2 filled into the cells in column J, and that the annual compensation is calculated for the cells in the column.
   c. Add a total row to display the total annual compensation for all employees.
   d. Change the function in the total row to display the average annual compensation. Change the label in cell A17 from Total to **Average**.
   e. Save your work.

Skills Review (continued)

5. Filter a table.

   a. Filter the table to list only records for employees in the Dallas branch.

   b. Clear the filter.

   c. Use AutoFilter to list only the three employees with the highest annual compensation. (*Hint:* Find the top three items.)

   d. Redisplay all the records.

   e. Create a Custom AutoFilter showing employees hired in 2020. (*Hint:* Use the criteria after or equal to 1/1/2020 and before or equal to 12/31/2020.)

   f. Redisplay all the records and save your work.

6. Look up values in a table.

   a. Open the Name Manager using a button on the Formulas bar, view named tables in the workbook, then close the Name Manager.

   b. Enter the employee number **1322** in cell B22.

   c. In cell C22, use the XLOOKUP function and enter **B22** as the Lookup_value, **Table1[Employee Number]** as the Lookup_array, and **Table1[Annual Compensation]** as the Return_array; observe the compensation displayed for that employee number, then check it against the table to make sure it is correct.

   d. Replace the existing Employee Number in cell B22 with **1080** and view the annual compensation for that employee.

   e. Format cell C22 with the Accounting format with the $ symbol and no decimal places.

   f. Save the workbook.

7. Summarize table data.

   a. In cell F22, use the DAVERAGE function to find the average benefits for the Dallas office. (*Hint:* Click the upper-left corner of cell A1 twice to select the table and its header row as the Database, select cell I1 for the Field, and select the range E21:E22 for the Criteria.)

   b. Verify that the average Dallas benefit amount is 13,938.

   c. Test the function further by entering the text **Chicago** in cell E22. When the criterion is entered, verify that the average Chicago benefit amount is 11,534.04.

   d. Format cell F22 in the Accounting format with the $ symbol and no decimal places.

   e. Save the workbook.

8. Validate table data.

   a. Select the table data in column E and set a validation criterion specifying that you want to allow a list of valid options.

   b. Enter a list of valid options that restricts the entries to **LA**, **Chicago**, and **Dallas**. Remember to use a comma between each item in the list.

   c. Confirm that the options will appear in an in-cell dropdown list, then close the dialog box.

   d. Add a row to the bottom of the table. Select cell E17, open the dropdown list, then click Chicago.

   e. Complete the new record by adding an Employee Number of **1119**, a First Name of **Cate**, a Last Name of **Smith**, a Hire Date of **10/1/2021**, Office of **Chicago**, and a monthly salary of **$5,000**. Compare your screen to **FIGURE 5-21**.

FIGURE 5-21

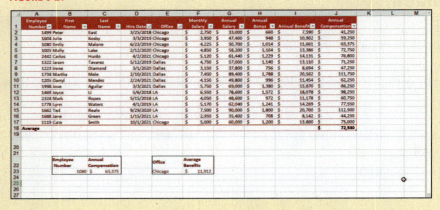

f. Add column A as a print title that repeats at the left of each printed page.

g. Save the worksheet, then preview the worksheet to verify that the employee number column appears on both pages.

h. Submit your workbook to your instructor. Close the workbook, then close Excel.

Independent Challenge 1

As the assistant to the clinic director at Riverwalk Medical Clinic, you have been asked to organize the billing information for the physical therapy department. Using data in an Excel worksheet, you will create a table and analyze the procedure data to help with the January billing.

a. Start Excel, open IL_EX_5-3.xlsx from the location where you store your Data Files, then save it as **IL_EX_5_RiverwalkPT**.

b. Using the data in the range A1:G64 on the January Procedures worksheet, create a table and format the table with the table style Blue-Gray, Table Style Medium 7. Widen the columns as necessary to fully display the field names.

c. Remove the banding of the table rows. (*Hint:* Use the Table Style Options group on the Table Design tab.)

d. Add the record shown below to the end of the table:

Procedure Code	Procedure	Date	Amount Billed	Payment	Provider	Patient ID
601Q	Therap Proc 2	1/15/2021	$65	$30	Rubin	1189

e. Delete the record in row 8 for procedure code 251D.

f. Remove any duplicate records by checking for matching procedure codes.

g. Add a new column to the table by entering a field named **Balance** in cell H1. Calculate the balance for each procedure using structured references to subtract the payment from the amount billed. Format the balance amounts in column H in Accounting format with the $ symbol and no decimal places.

h. Sort the table by Balance in ascending order.

i. Use a custom sort to sort the table first by the procedure in descending order, and then within each procedure by the provider in ascending order.

Independent Challenge 1 (continued)

j. Filter the table to show only Martin's procedures, then copy the filtered records to the Martin Procedures worksheet. Do not copy the field names. Clear the filter from the table on the January Procedures worksheet.

k. Filter the table to show only records where the amount billed is greater than or equal to $80 and less than or equal to $200. Copy the filtered records to the >= 80 <=200 worksheet. Do not copy the field names. Remove the filter from the table on the January Procedures worksheet.

l. On the January Procedures worksheet, enter **467B** in cell J2. Enter an XLOOKUP function in cell J4 to retrieve the procedure based on the procedure code entered in cell J2. Make sure you have an exact match with the procedure code. Test the function by changing the procedure code in cell J2 to **331E**.

m. Use the database function DSUM in cell J10 to total the amount billed for Rubin using the criteria in J7:J8. Format cell J10 in the Accounting format with the $ symbol and no decimal places.

n. Using the criteria in J7:J8, enter a database function in cell J12 to count the number of procedures performed by Rubin. (*Hint:* Use the DCOUNTA function.)

o. Use the Data Validation dialog box to add an in-cell dropdown list to the cells in the provider column that restricts entries to Axel, Martin, and Rubin. Check the list by clicking any cell in column F. Compare your table to **FIGURE 5-22**.

p. Add print titles to repeat the first row at the top of each printed page, enter your name in the center section of the worksheet footer, enter **January Procedures** in the center section of the header, then activate cell A1.

q. Save the workbook, preview it, then submit the workbook to your instructor.

r. Close the workbook, then close Excel.

FIGURE 5-22

Excel

Independent Challenge 2

As the director of development at a small, private independent college, you are responsible for managing alumni donations. The past two years' donation information is organized in a worksheet. You will analyze this information using table features.

a. Start Excel, open IL_EX_5-4.xlsx from the location where you store your Data Files, then save it as **IL_EX_5_Donations**.

b. Using the data in the range A1:E92, create a table and format the table with the table style Blue, Table Style Light 9. Widen the columns, as necessary, to fully display the field names.

c. Delete the record in row 5 for donor #18574. Check the table for duplicates, using the Donor # field, and check to see if there are any duplicate records.

d. Add a field named **% Increase** in cell F1. Widen the columns as necessary to display all field names.

e. Enter a table formula in cell F2 that calculates the percent increase in the donation amount from 2019 to 2020. Check that the formula was filled into the other column cells. Format the values in column F in the Percent Style format with two decimal places. (*Hint:* A % increase is calculated by subtracting the old value from the new value and then dividing that difference by the old value. Remember to use parentheses when calculating the difference between the old and new values.)

f. Use a custom filter for the Class field to find donations from the classes of years 2010 - 2020. Copy the results, including the field names, and paste them on a new sheet named **2010 - 2020 Classes**. Widen the columns as necessary to fully display all of the worksheet data. Return to the 2019 - 2020 Donations sheet and remove the filter from the Class field.

g. Use the Data Validation dialog box to create an in-cell dropdown list that restricts entries in the School column to Business, Arts & Sciences, Engineering, and Health Sciences.

h. Use the Error Alert tab of the Data Validation dialog box to set the alert style to the Warning style with the error message "Data is not valid." Do not include the period after *valid*. Use the Input Message tab to add an input message of "Select the school." Do not include the period after *school*.

i. Add a new row at the end of the table and test the validation in the table with a valid entry. Use the new row to add a record for Donor # 10050, a graduate in the class of 1998 from the Engineering school, who donated $50 in 2019 and $100 in 2020.

j. Test the data validation by entering **Graduate** in cell B92. Verify the correct error message is displayed, then click Cancel to keep the existing valid data.

k. Add a total row to the table to display the total donations for 2019 and 2020. Delete any other total amounts in the row.

l. Apply conditional formatting to the % Increase column to show the values less than 0% in Light Red Fill with Dark Red Text. (*Hint:* Use Highlight Cell Rules with the criteria of Less than 0%.)

Independent Challenge 2 (continued)

m. Sort the records on the % Increase column, to display the Light Red Fill color cells at the top of the column. (*Hint:* Use a custom sort to sort by cell color with fill on top.)

n. Add print titles to repeat the first row at the top of each printed page, enter your name in the center section of the worksheet footer, enter **2019 - 2020 Donations** in the center section of the header, then activate **cell A1**.

o. Save the workbook, preview it, then compare your table to **FIGURE 5-23**.

p. Submit the workbook to your instructor, close the workbook, then close Excel.

FIGURE 5-23

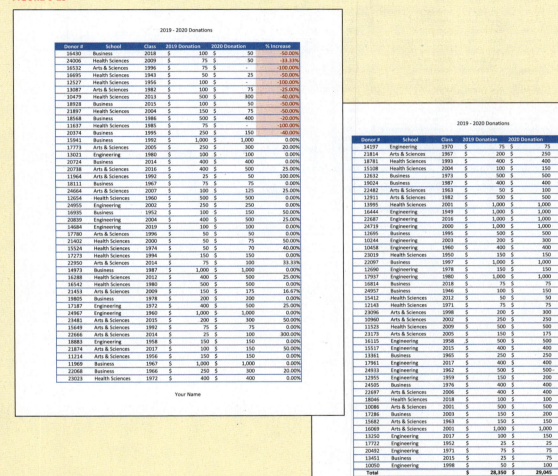

Excel

Visual Workshop

Open IL_EX_5-5.xlsx from the location where you store your Data Files, then save it as **IL_EX_5_Billings**. Create a table with the default table style. Sort, summarize, add a column, build a table formula, and add data validation so that your screen matches the table shown in **FIGURE 5-24**. Enter your name in the center section of the worksheet footer. Save the workbook, preview the table, close the workbook, submit the workbook to your instructor, then close Excel.

FIGURE 5-24

Account #	Attorney	Office	Service	Referral	Billed	Paid	Balance						
1008	Castro	Austin	Real Estate	Friend/Family	$ 1,200	$ 1,000	200					Attorney Billings	
1272	Castro	Austin	Real Estate	Other	$ 300	$ 200	100					Attorney	
1659	Castro	Austin	Real Estate	Chamber of Commerce	$ 1,200	$ -	1200					Castro	
1663	Castro	Austin	Small Business	Friend/Family	$ 250	$ 100	150					Billed	$ 2,950
1762	Rousseau	Dallas	Bankruptcy	Friend/Family	$ 4,500	$ 4,500	0						
1498	Tavarez	Dallas	Bankruptcy	Chamber of Commerce	$ 300	$ 100	200					Referral Billings	
1085	Rousseau	Dallas	Bankruptcy	Online Search	$ 500	$ 400	100					Referral	
1992	Rousseau	Dallas	Civil Litigation	Social Media	$ 500	$ -	500					Chamber of Commerce	
1214	Rousseau	Dallas	Civil Litigation	Social Media	$ 3,000	$ 1,000	2000					Billed	$ 7,800
1153	Rousseau	Dallas	Civil Litigation	Online Search	$ 500	$ 500	0						
1696	Tavarez	Dallas	Real Estate	Other	$ 500	$ 100	400						
1512	Tavarez	Dallas	Real Estate	Other	$ 2,050	$ -	2050						
1035	Rousseau	Dallas	Real Estate	Online Search	$ 1,500	$ 500	1000						
1559	Rousseau	Dallas	Small Business	Online Search	$ 1,500	$ 1,500	0						
1266	Tavarez	Dallas	Small Business	Chamber of Commerce	$ 300	$ 300	0						
1063	Tavarez	Dallas	Small Business	Other	$ 500	$ -	500						
1484	Lewis	Houston	Bankruptcy	Friend/Family	$ 2,050	$ 2,000	50						
1742	Lewis	Houston	Bankruptcy	Social Media	$ 500	$ 500	0						
1134	Lewis	Houston	Civil Litigation	Chamber of Commerce	$ 4,500	$ 1,000	3500						
1300	Lewis	Houston	Estate Planning	Online Search	$ 3,000	$ 3,000	0						
1167	Lewis	Houston	Small Business	Chamber of Commerce	$ 1,500	$ 500	1000						

Friend/Family
Online Search
Chamber of Commerce
Social Media
Other

Managing Workbook Data

CASE ▶ Ellie Schwartz, the vice president of finance at JCL, asks for your help in analyzing yearly sales revenues from the North America and worldwide offices. When the analysis is complete, she will distribute the workbook for office managers to review.

Module Objectives

After completing this module, you will be able to:

- View and arrange worksheets
- Protect worksheets and workbooks
- Save custom views of a worksheet
- Prepare a workbook for distribution

- Insert hyperlinks
- Save a workbook for distribution
- Work with grouped data
- Work with grouped worksheets

Files You Will Need

IL_EX_6-1.xlsx	Support_EX_6-5.xlsx
Support_EX_6-2.xlsx	IL_EX_6-6.xlsx
IL_EX_6-3.xlsx	IL_EX_6-7.xlsx
IL_EX_6-4.xlsx	Support_EX_6-8.xlsx

View and Arrange Worksheets

As you work with workbooks made up of multiple worksheets, you might need to compare data in the various sheets. To do this, you can view each worksheet in its own workbook window, called an **instance**, and display the windows in an arrangement that makes it easy to compare data. When you work with worksheets in separate windows, you are working with different views of the same workbook; the data itself remains in one file. **CASE** *Ellie asks you to compare the monthly revenue totals for the worldwide and North America locations. Because the revenue totals are on different worksheets, you want to arrange the worksheets side by side in separate instances.*

STEPS

1. **sam↓ Start Excel, open IL_EX_6-1.xlsx from the location where you store your Data Files, then save it as IL_EX_6_Revenue**

2. **With the Worldwide sheet active, click the View tab on the ribbon, then click the New Window button in the Window group**

   There are now two instances of the Revenue workbook open, each in their own workbook window.

3. **Point to the Excel icon on the taskbar**

   Two window thumbnails open, IL_EX_6_Revenue - 1 and IL_EX_6_Revenue - 2.

4. **In the current instance, click the North America sheet tab, click the View tab on the ribbon, click the Switch Windows button in the Window group, then click 1 IL_EX_6_Revenue - 1**

   The IL_EX_6_Revenue - 1 instance moves to the front. The Worldwide sheet is active in this instance, and the North America sheet is active in the IL_EX_6_Revenue - 2 instance.

5. **Click the Arrange All button in the Window group**

   The Arrange Windows dialog box, shown in **FIGURE 6-1**, lets you choose how to display the instances. You want to view the workbooks next to each other.

6. **Click the Vertical option button, then click OK**

   The windows are arranged next to each other, as shown in **FIGURE 6-2**. The second instance of the workbook opens at a zoom of 100%, not the 120% zoom of the first instance. You can activate a workbook by clicking one of its cells.

7. **Scroll horizontally to view the data in the IL_EX_6_Revenue - 1 workbook, click anywhere in the IL_EX_6_Revenue - 2 workbook, scroll horizontally and view the data, then click the Hide Window button ⊡ in the Window group**

   When you hide the second instance, only the IL_EX_6_Revenue - 1 workbook is visible.

8. **In the IL_EX_6_Revenue - 1 window, click the Unhide Window button ▢ in the Window group, then with the IL_EX_6_Revenue – 2 worksheet selected in the Unhide dialog box click OK**

9. **Click the Close button ⊠ in the title bar of the IL_EX_6_Revenue - 2 instance, then maximize the IL_EX_6_Revenue.xlsx workbook**

   Closing the IL_EX_6_Revenue – 2 instance leaves only the first instance open. Its name in the title bar returns to IL_EX_6_Revenue. When closing an instance of a workbook, it is important to use the Close button and not the Close command on the File menu, which closes the workbook.

FIGURE 6-1: Arrange Windows dialog box

Window configuration options

FIGURE 6-2: Window instances displayed vertically

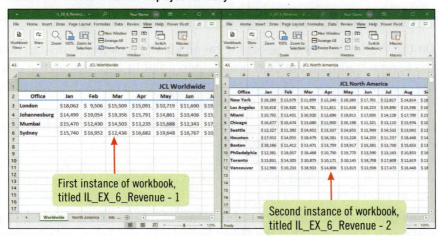

First instance of workbook, titled IL_EX_6_Revenue - 1

Second instance of workbook, titled IL_EX_6_Revenue - 2

Splitting the worksheet into multiple panes

Excel lets you split the worksheet area into vertical and/or horizontal **panes**, or sections of columns and rows. You can then click inside any one pane and scroll to locate information while the other panes remain in place, as shown in **FIGURE 6-3**. To split a worksheet area into multiple panes, click a cell below and to the right of where you want the split to appear, click the View tab on the ribbon, then click the Split button in the Window group. You can also split a worksheet into only two panes by selecting the row or column below or to the right of where you want the split to appear, clicking the View tab on the ribbon, then clicking Split in the Window group. To remove a split, click the View tab, then click Split in the Window group.

FIGURE 6-3: Worksheet split into four panes

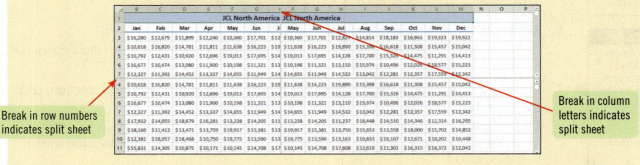

Break in row numbers indicates split sheet

Break in column letters indicates split sheet

Protect Worksheets and Workbooks

Learning Outcomes
- Protect a worksheet
- Create a data entry area on a worksheet by unlocking cells
- Protect a workbook

To protect information, Excel lets you **lock** one or more cells so that other people can view the values and formulas in those cells, but not make changes. Excel locks all cells by default, but this locking does not take effect until you activate the protection feature. A common worksheet protection strategy is to create an unlocked portion of a worksheet where users are able to enter and change data, sometimes called the **data entry area**. Then, when you protect the worksheet, the unlocked areas can still be changed. **CASE** *Because the worldwide revenue figures for January through March have been finalized, Ellie asks you to protect that worksheet area. That way, users cannot change the figures for those months.*

STEPS

QUICK TIP

You can encrypt a file with a password by clicking the File tab on the ribbon, clicking Info, clicking Protect Workbook, clicking Encrypt with Password, then entering a password.

1. **On the Worldwide sheet, select the range E3:M6, click the Home tab on the ribbon, click the Format button in the Cells group, then point to Lock Cell on the menu**

   The lock icon for the Lock Cell option displays a gray box covering a lock, which indicates the cells are currently locked, as shown in **FIGURE 6-4**, so clicking will unlock them.

2. **Click Lock Cell to unlock the cells, click the Review tab on the ribbon, then click the Protect Sheet button in the Protect group**

   The Protect Sheet dialog box opens, as shown in **FIGURE 6-5**. The default options protect the worksheet while allowing users to select locked or unlocked cells only. You can enter a password in the Password to unprotect sheet box.

QUICK TIP

To hide selected formulas, right-click them, click Format Cells on the shortcut menu, in the Format Cells dialog box click the Protection tab, click the Hidden check box to add a checkmark, click OK then protect the worksheet.

3. **Verify that Protect worksheet and contents of locked cells is checked, that the password text box is blank, and that the Select locked cells and Select unlocked cells check boxes contain checkmarks, then click OK**

4. **Click cell B3, type 1 to confirm that locked cells cannot be changed, click OK, click cell F3, type 1, notice that Excel lets you begin the entry, press ESC to cancel the entry, then save your work**

   When you try to change a locked cell on a protected worksheet, a dialog box, shown in **FIGURE 6-6**, reminds you of the protected cell's status and provides instructions to unprotect the worksheet.

QUICK TIP

When you share a protected workbook, the structure of the shared workbook is also protected.

5. **Click the Protect Workbook button in the Protect group, in the Protect Structure and Windows dialog box make sure the Structure check box contains a checkmark, verify that the password text box is blank, then click OK**

   The workbook's structure is protected from changes. If you wanted to provide additional protection to the workbook you could use a password.

6. **Right-click the Worldwide sheet tab**

   The Insert, Delete, Rename, Move or Copy, Tab Color, Hide, and Unhide options on the shortcut menu are not available because the structure is protected.

QUICK TIP

To specify options for protecting a worksheet or workbook, click the File tab on the ribbon, click Info if necessary, then click the Protect Workbook button.

7. **Click the Protect Workbook button in the Protect group to turn off the protection, click the Unprotect Sheet button, then save your changes**

   The Protect Workbook button is a toggle, which means it's like an on/off switch. When it is highlighted, the workbook is protected. Clicking it again removes the highlighting, indicating the protection is removed from the workbook.

FIGURE 6-4: Lock Cell option

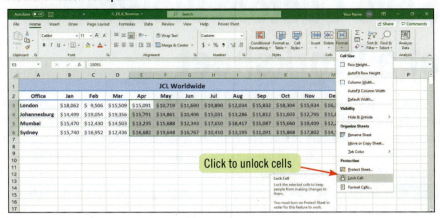

FIGURE 6-5: Protect Sheet dialog box

FIGURE 6-6: Reminder of protected worksheet status

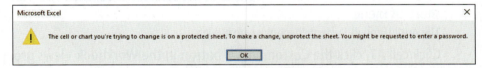

Creating edit ranges

You can allow users to edit certain ranges on a worksheet by selecting the range, clicking the Review tab on the ribbon, clicking the Allow Edit Ranges button in the Protect group, clicking New in the Allow User to Edit Ranges dialog box, entering an optional title for the range and a password to edit it, confirming the password, clicking Protect Sheet, then clicking OK.

Freezing rows and columns

A **pane** is a section of columns and/or rows that you can **freeze**, or set so that they remain visible as you scroll through your worksheet. To freeze panes, click the first cell in the area you want to scroll, click the View tab on the ribbon, click the Freeze Panes button in the Window group, then click Freeze Panes. Excel freezes the columns to the left and the rows above the selected cell, as shown in **FIGURE 6-7**. You can also select Freeze Top Row or Freeze First Column to freeze the top row or left worksheet column. To unfreeze panes, click the View tab, click Freeze Panes, then click Unfreeze Panes.

FIGURE 6-7: Worksheet with top two rows and left column frozen

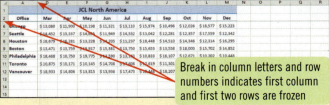

Save Custom Views of a Worksheet

Learning Outcomes
- Create different views of worksheet data using custom views
- Display different views of worksheet data using custom views

A **view** is a set of display and/or print settings that you can name and save, and then access at a later time. By using the Custom Views feature, you can create several different views of a worksheet without having to create separate sheets. For example, if you often hide columns in a worksheet, you can create two views, one that displays all the columns and another with the columns hidden. You set the worksheet display first, then name the view. Then you can open the view whenever you want, using the name. **CASE** ▶ *Because Ellie wants to generate a revenue report from the final revenue data for January through March, she asks you to create a custom view that shows only the first-quarter revenue data.*

STEPS

1. **With the Worldwide sheet active, click cell A1, click the View tab on the ribbon, then click the Custom Views button in the Workbook Views group**

   The Custom Views dialog box opens, as shown in **FIGURE 6-8**. Any previously defined views for the active worksheet appear in the Views box. No views are currently defined for the Worldwide worksheet.

2. **Click Add**

   The Add View dialog box opens. Here, you enter a name for the view and decide whether to include print settings and/or hidden rows, columns, and filter settings. By default, these settings will be included in the new view.

3. **In the Name box type Year Revenue, then click OK**

   You have created a view called Year Revenue that displays all the worksheet columns.

4. **Select columns E through M, right-click the selected area, then click Hide on the shortcut menu**

   The April through December columns are hidden.

> **QUICK TIP**
> Clicking Hide on the shortcut menu will similarly hide selected worksheet rows. To unhide columns and rows, select the columns or rows on both sides of the hidden ones, right-click the selected area, then click Unhide on the shortcut menu.

5. **Click cell A1, click the Custom Views button in the Workbook Views group, click Add, in the Name box type First Quarter, then click OK**

6. **Click the Custom Views button in the Workbook Views group, click Year Revenue in the Views list, then click Show**

   The Year Revenue custom view displays all the months' revenue data.

> **TROUBLE**
> If you receive the message "Some view settings could not be applied," turn off worksheet protection by clicking the Unprotect Sheet button in the Protect group of the Review tab.

7. **Click the Custom Views button in the Workbook Views group, then with First Quarter in the Custom Views dialog box selected, click Show**

   Only the January through March revenue figures appear on the screen, as shown in **FIGURE 6-9**.

8. **Click the Custom Views button, click Year Revenue, click Show, then save your work**

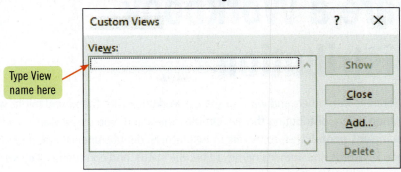

FIGURE 6-8: Custom Views dialog box

Type View name here

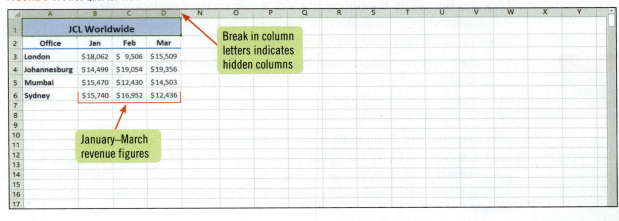

FIGURE 6-9: First Quarter view

Break in column letters indicates hidden columns

January—March revenue figures

Using Page Break Preview

The vertical and horizontal dashed lines in the Normal view of worksheets represent page breaks. Excel automatically inserts a page break when your worksheet data doesn't fit on one page. These page breaks are **dynamic**, which means they adjust automatically when workbook content changes, such as when rows and columns are added, deleted, or resized. Everything to the left of the first vertical dashed line and above the first horizontal dashed line is printed on the first page. You can manually add or remove page breaks by clicking the Page Layout tab on the ribbon, clicking the Breaks button in the Page Setup group, then clicking Insert Page Break, Remove Page Break, or Reset All Page Breaks. Clicking Insert Page Break adds a page break above and to the left of a selected cell, and clicking Remove Page Break removes page breaks above and to the left of a cell. Reset All Page Breaks resets page breaks back to the default setting. You can also view and change page breaks manually by clicking the View tab on the ribbon, then clicking the Page Break Preview button in the Workbook Views group, or by clicking the Page Break Preview button on the status bar. You can drag the blue page break lines to the desired location. Some cells may temporarily display ##### while you are in Page Break Preview. If you drag a page break to the right to include more data on a page, Excel shrinks the type to fit the data on that page. To exit Page Break Preview, click the Normal button in the Workbook Views group.

Prepare a Workbook for Distribution

If you are collaborating with others and want to share a workbook with them, you might want to remove sensitive information before distributing the file. On the other hand, you might want to add details about a file, called **document properties**, to the file to help others identify, understand, and locate it. Properties might include keywords, the author's name, a title, the status, and comments. **Keywords**, also called **tags**, are terms you add to the file's properties that users can use when searching to help them locate your workbook. Properties are also called **metadata**, descriptive information that is used by Microsoft Windows in document searches. In addition, to ensure that others do not make unauthorized changes to your workbook, you can mark a file as final. This makes it a read-only file, which discourages others from making changes to it. **CASE** ▶ *Ellie wants you to protect the workbook and prepare it for distribution.*

STEPS

1. **Click the File tab on the ribbon, then click Info on the navigation bar**

   Backstage view opens and displays the Info pane, which displays information about your file. It also includes tools you can use to check for security issues.

2. **Click the Check for Issues button in the Inspect Workbook area, then click Inspect Document**

   The Document Inspector dialog box opens, as shown in **FIGURE 6-10**. It lists items that Excel can check in the file. All the options are selected by default.

3. **Click Inspect, then scroll to view the inspection results**

   Areas containing data have a red "!" in front of them. If areas are flagged as having data that you can remove from this dialog box, you can click the Remove All button. Some data cannot be removed from this dialog box; for example, hidden names are created by Excel and can't be deleted without running a special program.

4. **Click Close, click the Properties list arrow on the right side of the Info pane, then click Advanced Properties**

   The file's Properties dialog box opens with the Summary tab active, as shown in **FIGURE 6-11**. This tab allows you to enter identifying, and searchable, information for the file.

5. **In the Title text box type Revenue, in the Keywords text box type Worldwide North America Revenue, then in the Comments text box type The first-quarter figures are final., then click OK**

6. **Click the Protect Workbook button on the left side of the Info pane, click Mark as Final, click OK, then click OK again**

   The workbook is marked as final and "Read-Only" appears in the title bar indicating the workbook is saved as a read-only file. A yellow bar also appears below the tabs indicating the workbook is marked as final. The yellow bar also includes an Edit Anyway button.

7. **Click cell B3, type 1 to confirm that the cell cannot be changed, click the Edit Anyway button above the formula bar, then save the workbook**

   By clicking Edit Anyway, you removed the read-only status, making the workbook editable again. Marking a workbook as final is not a strong form of workbook protection because a workbook recipient can remove this Final status.

FIGURE 6-10: Document Inspector dialog box

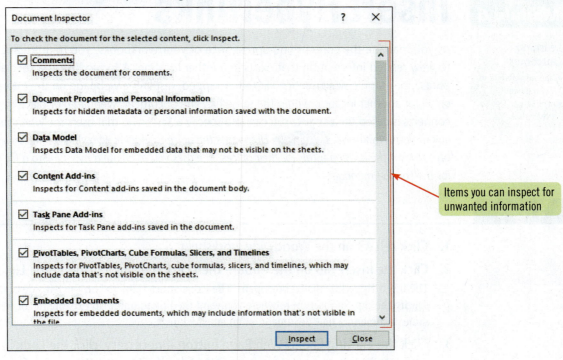

Items you can inspect for unwanted information

FIGURE 6-11: File's Properties dialog box

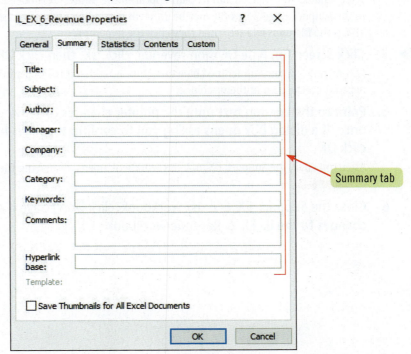

Summary tab

Adding a worksheet background

You can make your Excel data more attractive on the screen by adding a picture to the worksheet background. To add a worksheet background, click the Page Layout tab on the ribbon, click the Background button in the Page Setup group, choose From a file, Bing Image Search, or a OneDrive account in the Insert Pictures dialog box, click the image file in the next dialog boxes, then click Insert. The image appears tiled, repeating as necessary to fill the background behind the worksheet data on the screen. A worksheet background will not print with the worksheet.

Excel

Insert Hyperlinks

As you manage the content and appearance of your workbooks, you might want the workbook user to view related information that exists in another location. A **hyperlink** is a specially formatted word, phrase, or graphic which, when clicked or tapped, displays a webpage on the Internet, another file, an email, or another location within the same file. The document, webpage, or place to which the hyperlink connects is called the **target**. You can also specify a ScreenTip that users see when they point to a hyperlink in your workbook. **CASE** ▶ *Ellie wants the office managers who view the Revenue workbook to also be able to view the division totals for their offices. She asks you to create a hyperlink to a file with this information for the London manager.*

STEPS

1. **Click cell A3 on the Worldwide worksheet**

2. **Click the Insert tab on the ribbon, then click the Link button in the Links group**

   The Insert Hyperlink dialog box opens. The icons under "Link to" on the left side of the dialog box let you specify the type of location to where you want the link to jump: an existing file or webpage, a place in the same document, a new document, or an email address.

3. **Click the Existing File or Web Page button if necessary, click the Look in list arrow, navigate to where you store your Data Files if necessary, then click Support_EX_6-2.xlsx**

   The filename you selected and its path appear in the Address text box, as shown in **FIGURE 6-12**. Your path to the Support_EX_6-2.xlsx file may be different depending on how you set up your files on your computer. This is the file users will see when they click the hyperlink.

4. **Click ScreenTip, type Division revenue, click OK, then click OK again**

   Cell A3 now contains underlined blue text, indicating that it is a hyperlink. The default color of a hyperlink depends on the current theme colors.

5. **Point to the London text until the pointer changes to 🖑, view the ScreenTip, then click once; if a dialog box opens asking you to confirm the file is from a trustworthy source, click OK**

   After you click, the Support_EX_6-2.xlsx workbook opens, displaying the London revenue data, as shown in **FIGURE 6-13**.

6. **Close the Support_EX_6-2.xlsx workbook, click Don't Save if necessary, then save your changes to the IL_EX_6_Revenue workbook**

FIGURE 6-12: Insert Hyperlink dialog box

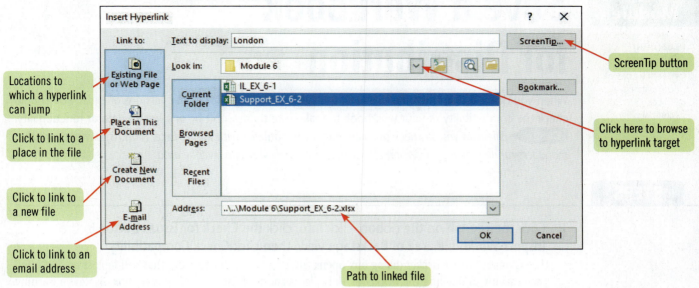

Locations to which a hyperlink can jump

Click to link to a place in the file

Click to link to a new file

Click to link to an email address

ScreenTip button

Click here to browse to hyperlink target

Path to linked file

FIGURE 6-13: Target document

	A	B	C	D	E	F	G	H	I	J	K	L	M	N	O	P	Q	R	S
1						London Revenue													
2		Jan	Feb	Mar	Apr	May	Jun	Jul	Aug	Sep	Oct	Nov	Dec						
3	Finance & Accounting	5947	1545	2930	5320	3570	3410	5297	2897	3362	2971	4964	3481						
4	Technical	4346	1892	3308	3674	2838	2826	3969	2745	4990	5829	4278	5938						
5	Creative	5202	4530	5467	2943	1628	2219	5647	3806	4598	4092	1673	2508						
6	Office Support	2567	1539	3804	3154	2683	3235	4977	2586	2882	5412	5019	4405						
7	Total	$18,062	$9,506	$15,509	$15,091	$10,719	$11,690	$19,890	$12,034	$15,832	$18,304	$15,934	$16,332						
8																			
9																			

Save a Workbook for Distribution

Learning Outcomes
- Check workbook compatibility
- Check compatibility for different Excel versions

When you need to distribute your Excel files to people working with earlier versions of Excel, you should check the compatibility of your workbook to make sure there won't be any loss of data or functionality. **CASE** ▶ *Ellie asks you to check the workbook's compatibility with earlier Excel formats to make sure that managers running an earlier version of Excel can accurately view the revenue data.*

STEPS

1. **Click the File tab on the ribbon, click Info, click the Check for Issues button in the Inspect Workbook area of Backstage view, then click Check Compatibility**

   The Compatibility Checker dialog box opens, alerting you to the features that will be lost or converted when saving or opening the workbook in earlier versions of Excel. The Summary box displays a warning titled "Minor loss of fidelity," indicating that some of the worksheet's formatting either might not be available or might appear differently in earlier versions of Excel. Minor loss of fidelity warnings won't result in lost data or worksheet functionality.

2. **Click the Select versions to show arrow, then click Excel 97-2003 to deselect it**

   The warning in the Summary box is no longer displayed, as shown in **FIGURE 6-14**, because it applies only to 97-2003 versions of Excel.

3. **Click the Select versions to show arrow, click Excel 97-2003 to select it, then click OK**

4. **Click the Home tab on the ribbon, click the Find & Select button in the Editing group, click Go To, type LL1 in the Reference box, click OK, type 1 in cell LL1, then press ENTER**

5. **Click the File tab on the ribbon, click Info, click the Check for Issues button in the Inspect Workbook area of Backstage view, then click Check Compatibility**

   The Compatibility Checker now displays a "Significant loss of functionality warning," as shown in **FIGURE 6-15**. This type of warning indicates a loss of data or functionality when a workbook is opened in an earlier Excel version. The data that was entered in cell LL1 could be lost because column LL is outside the limit of 256 columns in the 97-2003 versions of Excel.

6. **Click OK to close the Compatibility Checker, click cell LL1, press DEL to remove the data from the cell, then press CTRL+HOME**

7. **Click the File tab, click Info, click the Check for Issues button in the Inspect Workbook area of Backstage, click Check Compatibility, verify there is no longer a significant loss of functionality, then click OK**

8. **Save the workbook**

FIGURE 6-14: Compatibility Checker dialog box

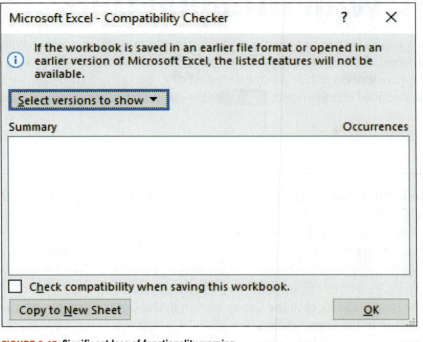

FIGURE 6-15: Significant loss of functionality warning

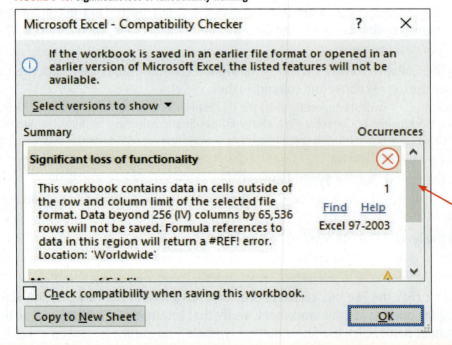

Description of significant compatibility issue

Exporting a workbook to other file types

You can export Excel workbooks to many other different formats. Clicking File, then clicking Export opens the Export pane, where you can either Create a PDF/XPS Document or Change File Type. PDFs and XPS files have the advantage of preserving formatting, fonts, and images, and making it difficult to change the file. These files can be opened and viewed in free viewers available online. To select this option, click Create PDF/XPS in the Create PDF/XPS Document section, choose the file type in the Save as type box, then click Publish. If you click Change File Type in the Export pane you can choose from several file types, including Macro Enabled Workbook, Excel 97-2003 workbook, Template, OpenDocument Spreadsheet (which can be used with OpenOffice), Text, special types of text file such as CSV and Formatted Text, or a Binary workbook that is optimized for fast loading and saving. Click the format you want, click Save As, then click Save in the Save As dialog box.

Work with Grouped Data

You can create groups of rows and columns on a worksheet to manage your data and make it easier to work with and view. The Excel grouping feature displays outline symbols that allow you to easily expand and collapse groups to show or hide selected worksheet data. You can turn off the outline symbols if you are using the condensed data in a report. **CASE** ▶ *Ellie asks you for a report showing the quarterly revenue totals for all JCL offices.*

STEPS

1. **Click the International sheet, select the range C3:E16, click the Data tab on the ribbon, click the Group button in the Outline group, click the Columns option button in the Group dialog box, then click OK**

   The first-quarter data details are grouped. The quarter summary data isn't contained in the group to allow for that summary information to be displayed. The **outline symbols** that let you hide and display details appear over the grouped columns, as shown in **FIGURE 6-16**.

2. **Select the range G3:I16, click the Group button in the Outline group, click the Columns option button in the Group dialog box, click OK, select the range K3:M16, click the Group button in the Outline group, click the Columns option button in the Group dialog box, click OK, select the range O3:Q16, click the Group button in the Outline group, click the Columns option button in the Group dialog box, click OK, then click cell A1**

   All four quarters are grouped.

3. **Click the Collapse Outline button ⊟ above the column F label, then click the Expand Outline button ⊞ above the column F label**

   Clicking the (−) symbol temporarily hides the Q1 detail columns, and the (−) symbol changes to a (+) symbol. Clicking the (+) symbol expands the Q1 details and redisplays the hidden columns. The numbered Outline symbols in the upper-left corner of the worksheet are used to display and hide levels of detail across the entire worksheet.

4. **Click the level 1 Outline Symbol button ☐1**

   All the group details, considered Level 2, collapse, and only the quarter totals, considered Level 1, are displayed.

5. **Click the level 2 Outline Symbol button ☐2**

   You see the quarter details again. Ellie asks you to hide the quarter details and the outline symbols for the summary report.

6. **Click ☐1, click the File tab, click Options, click Advanced in the category list, scroll down to Display options for this worksheet, verify that International is displayed as the worksheet name, click the Show outline symbols if an outline is applied check box to deselect it, then click OK**

   The worksheet displays quarter totals without outline symbols, as shown in **FIGURE 6-17**.

7. **Save the workbook**

FIGURE 6-16: First-quarter data grouped

Outline symbols

Column-level buttons

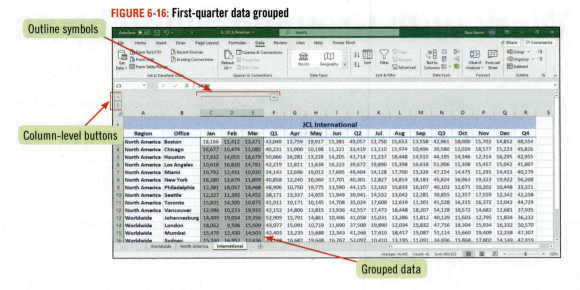

Grouped data

FIGURE 6-17: Quarterly summary

Breaks in column letter sequence indicate data is grouped

Region	Office	Q1	Q2	Q3	Q4
North America	Boston	43,049	49,057	42,961	48,554
North America	Chicago	40,231	33,419	39,580	45,826
North America	Houston	50,666	43,714	44,195	42,955
North America	Los Angeles	42,219	39,672	51,906	41,807
North America	Miami	34,143	49,404	47,154	40,179
North America	New York	40,858	40,301	45,824	56,208
North America	Philadelphia	48,906	44,115	40,103	33,321
North America	Seattle	38,171	39,941	39,855	42,258
North America	Toronto	41,011	35,024	41,528	44,729
North America	Vancouver	42,152	42,557	54,128	37,935
Worldwide	Johannesburg	52,909	41,058	40,129	36,232
Worldwide	London	43,077	37,500	47,756	50,570
Worldwide	Mumbai	42,403	41,266	51,114	47,307
Worldwide	Sydney	45,128	53,097	34,696	47,819

Creating Subtotals

The Excel Subtotals feature provides a quick, easy way to group and summarize a range of data. It lets you create not only subtotals using the SUM function, but other statistics as well, including COUNT, AVERAGE, MAX, and MIN. In order to get meaningful statistics, data must be sorted on the field on which you will group. To create subtotals, first select the range of data you want to subtotal, click the Data tab on the ribbon, click the Subtotal button in the Outline group, click the At each change in arrow in the Subtotal dialog box, select the field by which you want to group the data, such as region, click the Use function arrow, click the function you want to use, select the fields that you want to subtotal in the "Add subtotal to" list, then click OK. **FIGURE 6-18** shows data grouped by region and summed on each quarter.

FIGURE 6-18: Worksheet subtotals and grand total

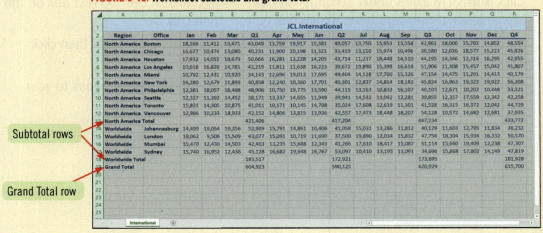

Subtotal rows

Grand Total row

Excel

Work with Grouped Worksheets

**Learning
Outcomes**
• Group worksheets
• Add custom margins to worksheets

You can group worksheets to work on them as a collection. When you enter data into one grouped worksheet, that data is also automatically entered into all the worksheets in the group. This is useful for data that is common to every sheet of a workbook, such as headers and footers, or for column headings that will apply to all worksheets, such as monthly headings in a yearly summary. You can also group worksheets to print them all at one time. **CASE** *Ellie asks you to add text in a new, second row of the Worldwide, North America, and International worksheets. You also need to adjust the margin at the top of these worksheets.*

STEPS

QUICK TIP
You can group non-contiguous worksheets by pressing and holding CTRL while clicking only the sheet tabs you want to include.

1. **Select the Worldwide sheet tab, press and hold SHIFT, click the International sheet tab, then release SHIFT**

   The Worldwide, North America, and International sheets are selected, and the title bar now displays "IL_EX_6_Revenue.xlsx - Group" to indicate that the worksheets are grouped together and this is the first group in the workbook. Now, any changes you make to the Worldwide sheet will also be made to the other sheets.

2. **Select row 2, click the Home tab on the ribbon, click the Insert button in the Cells group, click cell A2, enter Revenue, click the Enter button ✓ on the Formula bar, select the range A2:M2, then click the Merge & Center button in the Alignment group**

   FIGURE 6-19 shows the Worldwide worksheet with the new Revenue row.

3. **Right-click the Worldwide sheet tab, click Ungroup Sheets on the shortcut menu, then verify the revenue label appears on the North America and International sheets**

QUICK TIP
If you want to customize the status bar, right-click it, then click the options that you want.

4. **Select the Worldwide sheet tab, press and hold SHIFT, click the International sheet, release SHIFT, click the Insert tab on the ribbon, click the Header & Footer button in the Text group, enter your name in the center header section, click any cell on the worksheet, click the Normal button ▦ on the status bar, then press CTRL+HOME**

5. **With the worksheets still grouped, click the File tab, click Print, click No Scaling under Settings, click Fit All Columns on One Page, preview the first page, then click the Next Page button ▶ to preview the other two pages**

   Because the worksheets are grouped, all worksheets are ready to print and all pages contain the header with your name.

6. **Click Normal Margins under Settings, click Custom Margins, in the Top text box on the Margins tab of the Page Setup dialog box type .5, then click OK**

7. **Return to the worksheet, right-click the Worldwide worksheet sheet tab, then click Ungroup Sheets**

8. **sam↑ Save and close the workbook, close Excel, then submit the workbook to your instructor**

   The completed worksheets are shown in **FIGURE 6-20**.

FIGURE 6-19: Worldwide worksheet with Revenue label

FIGURE 6-20: Completed worksheets

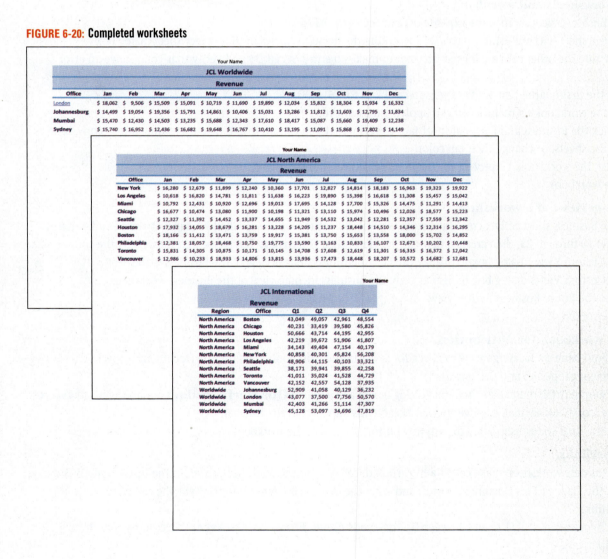

Practice

Skills Review

1. View and arrange worksheets.
  a. Start Excel, open IL_EX_6-3.xlsx from the location where you store your Data Files, then save it as **IL_EX_6_Travel**.
  b. Open a new window that contains another instance of the workbook.
  c. Verify the Business sheet is active in the IL_EX_6_Travel.xlsx - 1 instance of the workbook. Activate the Personal sheet in the IL_EX_6_Travel.xlsx - 2 instance.
  d. Use the Arrange Windows dialog box to view the IL_EX_6_Travel.xlsx - 1 and IL_EX_6_Travel.xlsx - 2 workbook windows tiled horizontally, then compare the workbooks in a vertical arrangement.
  e. Hide the IL_EX_6_Travel.xlsx - 2 instance, then unhide the instance. Close the IL_EX_6_Travel.xlsx - 2 instance, then maximize the IL_EX_6_Travel.xlsx workbook.

2. Protect worksheets and workbooks.
  a. On the Business sheet, unlock the expense data in the range B12:F19.
  b. Protect the sheet without using a password, accepting the default settings in the Protect Sheet dialog box.
  c. To make sure the other cells are locked, attempt to make an entry in cell D4 and verify that you receive an error message.
  d. Change the first-quarter real estate expense in cell B12 to **15,000**.
  e. Protect the workbook's structure without applying a password.
  f. Right-click the Business and Personal sheet tabs to verify that you cannot insert, delete, rename, move, copy, hide or unhide the sheets, or change their tab color.
  g. Unprotect the workbook. Unprotect the Business worksheet.
  h. Save the workbook.

3. Save custom views of a worksheet.
  a. With the Business sheet active, create a custom view of the entire worksheet called **Entire Business Budget**.
  b. Hide rows 10 through 23, then create a new custom view called **Business Income** that shows only the current data.
  c. Use the Custom Views dialog box to display the Entire Business Budget view of the Business worksheet.
  d. Use the Custom Views dialog box to display only the Business Income view of the Business worksheet.
  e. Return to the Entire Business Budget view.
  f. Save the workbook.

4. Prepare a workbook for distribution.
  a. Use the Info pane in Backstage view to check for issues in the workbook, then use the Document Inspector to remove all document properties and personal data.
  b. Use the Summary tab of the file's Properties dialog box to add a title of **Quarterly Budget** and the keyword **travel**.
  c. Mark the workbook as final, then verify that "Read-Only" appears in the title bar.
  d. Remove the final status using the Edit Anyway button, then save the workbook.

5. Insert hyperlinks.
  a. On the Business worksheet, make cell I1 a hyperlink to cell A22 on the worksheet. (*Hint:* In the Insert Hyperlink dialog box, use the Place in This Document button and enter the target cell reference in the Type the cell reference box.)
  b. Test the link.
  c. Edit the hyperlink in cell I1 to add a ScreenTip that reads **Cash Flow by Quarter**, then verify that the ScreenTip opens.
  d. Remove the hyperlink in cell I1, then delete the text in the cell.
  e. Save the workbook.

Skills Review (continued)

6. Save a workbook for distribution.

a. Check the compatibility of the IL_EX_6_Travel.xlsx with all previous versions of Excel.

b. Review the Minor loss of fidelity issue in the Compatibility Checker.

c. Deselect the Excel 97-2003 version in the Select versions to show list, then verify that the Minor loss of fidelity warning no longer appears.

d. Select the Excel 97-2003 version in the Select versions to show list.

e. Save the workbook.

7. Work with grouped data.

a. Activate the Business sheet, then group the income information in the range A5:G9 as rows.

b. Group the expenses information in the range A11:G20 as rows.

c. Collapse the income details in rows 5 through 9.

d. Collapse the expenses details in rows 11 through 20.

e. Expand the income and expenses details.

f. Save the workbook.

8. Work with grouped worksheets.

a. Group the Business and Personal worksheets.

b. Add your name to the center footer section of the grouped worksheets.

c. Add a 1.25" custom margin to the top and bottom of the grouped worksheets.

d. Preview the sheets, then ungroup the sheets.

e. Save the workbook, then compare your Business worksheet to **FIGURE 6-21**.

f. Submit IL_EX_6_Travel.xlsx file to your instructor, close all open files, then close Excel.

FIGURE 6-21

Independent Challenge 1

As the assistant to the CFO at Riverwalk Medical Clinic, you have been asked to analyze the annual insurance reimbursement data for the departments. After you complete your analysis, you will distribute the workbook to the clinic's vice presidents.

a. Start Excel, open IL_EX_6-4.xlsx from the location where you store your Data Files, then save it as **IL_EX_6_RiverwalkReimbursements**.

b. Display each worksheet in its own window, arrange the two sheets horizontally, then compare the data in the two windows.

Excel

Independent Challenge 1 (continued)

c. Hide the window displaying the Acute sheet. Unhide the Acute sheet window, then close this window.

d. Maximize the Elective window. Unlock the data in cells B5:D8.

e. Protect the worksheet without using a password. Verify the protection by trying to edit a locked cell, such as F5. Verify that you can edit the data in an unlocked cell, such as B5, but do not change the data.

f. Unprotect the Elective worksheet.

g. Protect the workbook without using a password.

h. Verify the protection by trying to change the Elective sheet name.

i. Unprotect the workbook.

j. On the Elective sheet, create a custom view called **Annual Reimbursements** that displays all the worksheet data. Hide columns F through Q. Create a custom view displaying the data in A1:E8, named **First Quarter Reimbursements**. Display all the data using a custom view. Display only the first-quarter reimbursement data using a custom view. Use a custom view to view all the reimbursement data for the year.

k. Insert a hyperlink in cell A5 on the Elective worksheet to the file Support_EX_6-5.xlsx. (*Hint:* If necessary, navigate to the location where you store your Data Files to locate and select the target file.) Add a ScreenTip that reads **Reimbursement by Procedure**, then test the hyperlink. Compare your screen to FIGURE 6-22.

FIGURE 6-22

	A	B	C	D	E	F	G	H	I	J	K
1	Ophthalmology										
2	Elective Procedures										
3	Procedure	Reimbursements									
4	CK	$898,812									
5	Lasik	$1,463,456									
6	PRK	$797,425									
7	LTK	$1,023,456									
8	Intacs	$1,005,187									
9											
10											
11											
12											
13											
14											
15											
16											

l. Close the Support_EX_6_5.xlsx file. Change the font of cell A5 to Calibri, to match the worksheet data.

m. Inspect the workbook for issues, then remove all document properties and personal data. Add a title property of **RMC Reimbursements** and keywords **acute** and **elective**. Mark the workbook as final, then remove the final status.

n. Check the compatibility of the workbook with previous Excel versions.

o. On the Elective worksheet, group the reimbursement data by quarters. (*Hint:* Group the monthly data by columns; do not include the quarter totals.) Use the outline buttons to collapse the monthly details and display only the quarter totals.

p. Group the two worksheets, add your name to the center footer section of the worksheets, then add 1.25" custom margins to the top of the worksheets.

q. Preview the worksheets, ungroup the worksheets, then save the workbook.

r. Submit the IL_EX_6_Riverwalk Reimbursements.xlsx file to your instructor, close the workbook, then close Excel.

Independent Challenge 2

As the Director of Finances at LPR Business Services, you need to review the US monthly billings for the regions and industries the company serves. With two months of data in a workbook, you will create formatted monthly worksheets with subtotals for each region. The reports will be distributed to the regional managers.

a. Start Excel, open IL_EX_6-6.xlsx from the location where you store your Data Files, then save it as **IL_EX_6_BusinessServices**.

b. Group the US January and US February worksheets.

c. With the worksheets grouped, add a row at the top of the worksheet with the title **LPR Business Services** merged and centered across columns A through G.

d. Format the title in row 1 using the Title cell style. Format the column headings in row 2 using the Heading 3 cell style. Format the worksheet data with the font color Blue, Accent 1, Darker 50% (the fifth color from the left in the last row of theme colors).

e. Ungroup the worksheets. Arrange the worksheets as necessary to verify that both have the same title row and worksheet formatting. When you are finished, hide any unnecessary instances of the workbook.

f. On the US January worksheet, sort the data in A to Z order on the region field.

g. On this sheet, create subtotals for the billed amount and balance for each region. (*Hint:* In the Subtotals dialog box, select Region in the At each change in list and add subtotals to both the Billed Amount and Balance fields.) Widen column G to fully display the balance totals.

h. Remove the page break from the US January worksheet. (*Hint:* Use Page Break Preview to drag the blue page break line to the bottom of the worksheet data.)

i. Inspect the workbook and remove all document properties and personal information. Add the keywords, or tags, **business** and **consulting** to the workbook's summary properties.

j. Freeze the first two rows of the US January worksheet. Scroll down to row 40 to verify the first two rows appear at the top of the screen. Unfreeze the rows.

k. Check the compatibility of the workbook with earlier versions of Excel.

l. Group the two worksheets. With the worksheets grouped, change the custom top margin to .5".

m. With the worksheets grouped, add a header that includes your name in the left section and the sheet name in the center section. (*Hint:* To add a field that displays the current sheet name, click the Sheet Name button in the Header and Footer Elements group of the Header & Footer tab.)

n. Ungroup the worksheets, then prepare the workbook for distribution by marking as final. Save the workbook, close the workbook, reopen the workbook, and enable editing.

o. Use the outline symbols on the US January worksheet to display only the regional totals and the grand total. Compare your US January worksheet to FIGURE 6-23.

p. Save the workbook, submit the workbook to your instructor, then close Excel.

FIGURE 6-23

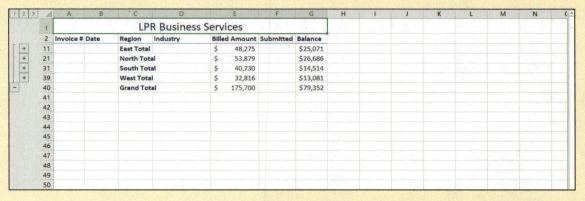

Excel

Visual Workshop

Open IL_EX_6-7.xlsx from the location where you store your Data Files, then save it as
IL_EX_6_BusinessCommunications. Use the skills you learned in this module to complete
the worksheet so it looks like the one shown in **FIGURE 6-24**. The text in cell A6 is a hyperlink to the
Support_EX_6-8.xlsx workbook in the location where you store your Data Files. (*Hint:* You will first need to
add columns and formulas to calculate each quarter's total; you can then group the worksheets and use the
outline symbols to display only the necessary information.) Resize columns as necessary, and adjust merged
and centered data to include any new columns. Enter your name in the center footer section, save the workbook,
submit your work to your instructor as directed, close the workbook, then close Excel.

FIGURE 6-24

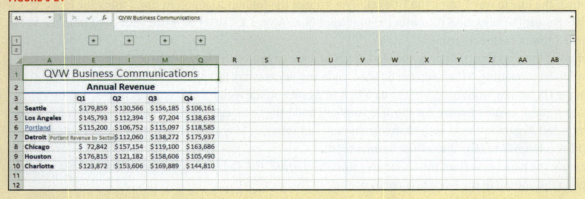

Working with Images and Integrating with Other Programs

CASE Ellie Schwartz, the vice president of finance, is researching the possible purchase of Tech Career Services (TCS), a small company specializing in technology career placements. Ellie needs to review the organization's files and develop a presentation on the feasibility of acquisition. To create the necessary documents, she asks you to create data exchanges between Excel and other programs.

Module Objectives

After completing this module, you will be able to:

- Plan a data exchange
- Import a text file
- Import data from another workbook
- Import a database table
- Link worksheet data to a Word document
- Link an Excel chart to a PowerPoint slide
- Import Excel data into Access
- Insert a graphic file in a worksheet

Files You Will Need

Support_EX_7-1.txt	Support_EX_7-8.txt	Support_EX_7-15.xlsx
Support_EX_7-2.xlsx	Support_EX_7-9.xlsx	Support_EX_7-16.txt
Support_EX_7-3.accdb	Support_EX_7-10.accdb	Support_EX_7-17.accdb
IL_EX_7-4.docx	IL_EX_7-11.docx	Support_EX_7-18.jpg
IL_EX_7-5.pptx	IL_EX_7-12.pptx	Support_EX_7-19.txt
Support_EX_7-6.xlsx	Support_EX_7-13.xlsx	IL_EX_7-20.xlsx
Support_EX_7-7.jpg	Support_EX_7-14.jpg	IL_EX_7-21.pptx

Plan a Data Exchange

Learning Outcomes
- Plan a data exchange between Microsoft 365 apps
- Develop an understanding of data exchange vocabulary

Because the tools available in Microsoft 365 apps are designed to be compatible, exchanging data between Excel and other Microsoft 365 apps is easy. The first step in each data exchange involves planning what you want to accomplish. **CASE** ▶ *Ellie asks you to use the following guidelines to plan data exchanges between Excel and other apps to support her business analysis of Tech Career Services.*

DETAILS

To plan an exchange of data:

- **Identify the data you want to exchange, its file type, and, if possible, the app used to create it**

  Whether the data you want to exchange is a graphics file, database file, worksheet, or simply a text file, it is important to identify its **source program** (the program used to create the data you are linking or embedding) and file type. Once you identify the source program, you can determine options for exchanging the data with Excel. Ellie needs to analyze a text file containing the TCS revenue data. A file that contains data but no formatting is sometimes called an **ASCII file** or a **text file**.

- **Determine the app with which you want to exchange data**

  Besides knowing which program created the data you want to exchange, you must also identify the program that will receive the data, called the **destination program**. This determines the procedure you use to perform the exchange. Ellie received a database table created with the Access database app. You decide to import the database file into Excel so Ellie can analyze it using Excel tools.

- **Determine the method of your data exchange**

  In this module, you use queries to import data into an Excel workbook. A **query** is a request for information from a data source. You can use Excel's Get & Transform tools to import data from other sources. Get & Transform creates a dynamic connection between an Excel workbook and a data source. After connecting to a data source, you can use the **Power Query** tool, which is a BI, or Business Intelligence, tool to query almost any kind of data source in order to transform the data into a more desirable format. For example, you can remove a column, remove a row, split a column, or change a data type in the Query Editor before you manipulate the data in the worksheet window. **FIGURE 7-1** shows data to be imported in the Power Query Editor. You may have multiple queries in a workbook.

  Windows supports a technology called **object linking and embedding (OLE)**, which lets you share information among the Microsoft 365 apps, copying from a source file and pasting, embedding, or linking into a destination file. The data to be exchanged, called an **object**, may consist of text, a worksheet, or any other type of data. You can copy Excel data and paste it in other applications using OLE. The copied data can be linked or embedded in the destination file. When you **embed**, you simply insert a copy of the original object into the destination document; you can later, if necessary, edit this embedded data separately from the source document. You **link** when you want the information you insert to be updated automatically if the data in the source document changes. **FIGURE 7-2** shows an Excel chart that is linked to a PowerPoint slide. You will use object linking when pasting Excel data in other applications so any changes in the Excel data will be updated in the destination files.

FIGURE 7-1: Data to be imported in the Power Query Editor

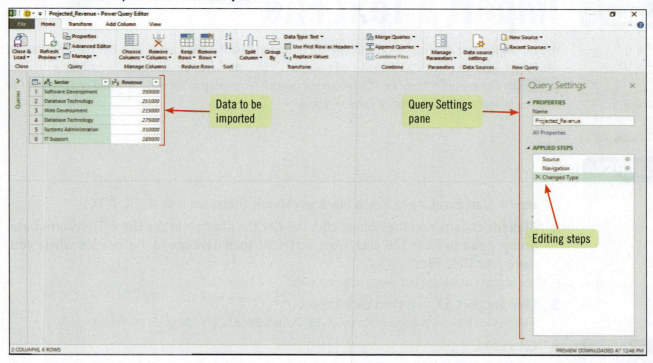

FIGURE 7-2: Excel chart linked to a PowerPoint slide

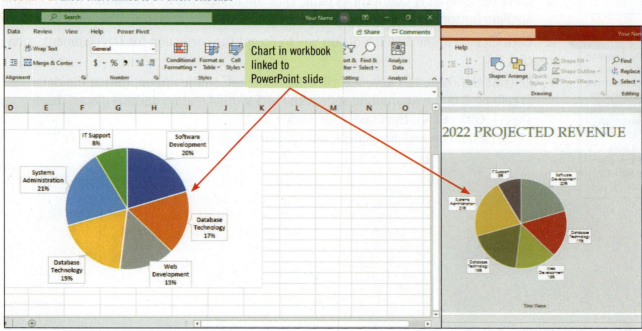

Import a Text File

Learning Outcomes
- Import a text file into an Excel workbook
- Format imported data

You can import text data into Excel and save the imported data in Excel format. Text files use a **delimiter**, which is a separator, such as a space, comma, or semicolon between elements, or columns of data.

CASE ▶ *The annual revenue for TCS broken out by each technology sector was submitted in a text file. Ellie asks you to import that data into an Excel workbook.*

STEPS

1. **sam ⬇** Start Excel, open a new blank workbook, then save it as **IL_EX_7_TCS**

2. Click the **Data tab** on the ribbon, click the **Get Data button** in the Get & Transform Data group, point to **From File**, click **From Text/CSV**, then navigate to the location where you store your Data Files

   The Import Data dialog box shows only text files.

3. Click **Support_EX_7-1**, then click **Import**

   A preview of the data is displayed in the IL_EX_7-1.txt dialog box, as shown in **FIGURE 7-3**.

4. Click **Load**

   The data appears in table format on a new sheet in the workbook. The Queries & Connections pane opens on the right with the Queries tab showing the file name and the number of rows loaded into the worksheet. Because text editors do not have spell-checking functionality, text files are more likely to contain spelling errors.

5. Close the Queries & Connections pane, click the **Review tab** on the ribbon, then click the **Spelling button** in the Proofing group

6. Click **Change** in the Spelling dialog box to accept the correction for **Development**, then click **OK**

7. Rename the sheet **TCS Revenue**, click the **Home tab** on the ribbon, format the data in column **B** in the Accounting style with the $ symbol and no decimal places, delete **Sheet1**, click cell **A1**, then save your work

   FIGURE 7-4 shows the worksheet with the data you imported into Excel.

FIGURE 7-3: Preview of data from text file

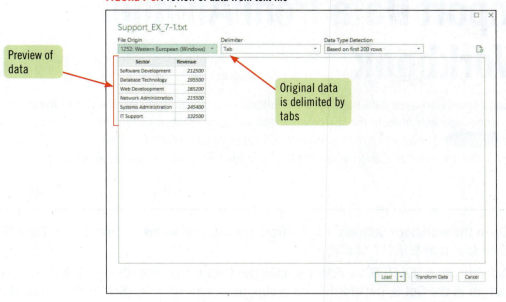

Preview of data

Original data is delimited by tabs

FIGURE 7-4: Worksheet with imported and formatted text file data

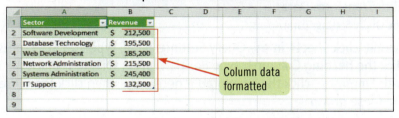

Column data formatted

Importing text files using the Text Import Wizard

Another way to import a text file into Excel is to use the Text Import Wizard. Click the File tab, click Open, then navigate to the location where you store your Data Files. By default, the Open dialog box displays only Excel files. To import a text file, you need to change your view so you see the file you want to open. To do this, click All Excel Files, click Text Files, click the name of the desired text file, then click Open. The Text Import Wizard opens, where you can complete the import by completing each step of the Wizard.

Import Data from Another Workbook

Learning Outcomes
• Import data from another Excel workbook
• Format imported data

You can import worksheet data from another workbook into Excel. If you use the Get & Transform tool, any changes you later make in the source workbook are updated when you refresh the destination workbook. **CASE** ▶ *The human resources office at TCS has provided an Excel file listing the employees and their positions. You will import that information into the workbook containing the revenue information.*

STEPS

1. Open the workbook Support_EX_7-2 from the location where you store your Data Files, then save it as IL_EX_7_Staff

2. Activate the IL_EX_7_TCS workbook, click the Data tab on the ribbon, click the Get Data button in the Get & Transform Data group, point to From File, click From Workbook, then navigate to the location where you store your Data Files

3. Click IL_EX_7_Staff, then click Import

   The Navigator dialog box opens.

4. Click Sheet1 in the Navigator dialog box

   The data in Sheet1 is displayed in the preview area on the right side of the dialog box, as shown in **FIGURE 7-5**.

5. Click Transform Data

   The Query Settings pane opens.

6. Double-click Sheet1 in the Query Settings pane, type TCS Staff, press ENTER, double-click the heading Column1, type Position, press ENTER, replace the Column2 heading with Employee, click the Home tab if necessary, then click the Close & Load button in the Close group

7. Close the Queries & Connections pane

8. Activate the IL_EX_7_Staff workbook, change Ashley McFadden's name in cell B5 to Ashley Elwell, then save and close the IL_EX_7_Staff workbook

9. In the IL_EX_7_TCS workbook click the Data tab, click the Refresh All button in the Queries & Connections group, then save your work

   FIGURE 7-6 shows the worksheet with the updated staff data.

FIGURE 7-5: Preview of worksheet data in dialog box

FIGURE 7-6: Refreshed and updated worksheet data

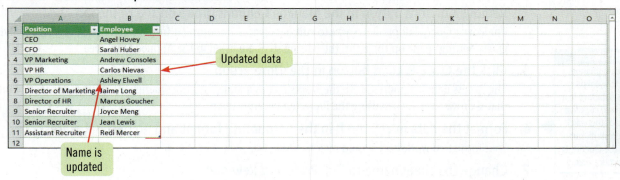

Converting text to columns

You can convert text into columns if, for example, you want to split a column of first and last names into two separate columns. To do so, select the range containing the names, click the Data tab on the ribbon, click the Text to Columns button in the Data Tools group, click the Space check box as the delimiter in the second step of the Convert Text to Columns Wizard dialog box, then click Finish.

Import a Database Table

You can import data from database tables into Excel. A **database table** is a set of data organized using columns and rows, which is created in a database program. A **database program** is an application, such as Microsoft Access, that lets you manage large amounts of data organized in tables. To import data from an Access table into Excel you will use the Get & Transform tool, so that any changes in the Access database can be seen when the workbook is refreshed. **CASE** *Ellie received a database table in Access containing TCS's projected revenue for the year ahead. She asks you to import this table into the Excel workbook containing the TCS revenue and staff data. The data has a column that needs to be removed and Ellie would like you to transform the data before it is imported.*

STEPS

1. **Click the Data tab on the ribbon, click the Get Data button in the Get & Transform Data group, point to From Database, click From Microsoft Access Database, then navigate to the location where you store your Data Files**

2. **Click Support_EX_7-3, then click Import**
   The Navigator dialog box opens, showing the Access file and the Projected Revenue table on the left and a preview window on the right.

3. **Click Projected Revenue in the Navigator dialog box**
   The data in the Projected Revenue table is displayed in the preview area, as shown in **FIGURE 7-7**.

4. **Click Transform Data, then in the Power Query Editor with the ID column selected click the Remove Columns button in the Manage Columns group on the Home tab**
   The Power Query Editor allows you to edit data before importing it into Excel. In the Power Query Editor's Query Settings pane on the right, the editing steps are listed in the Applied Steps area.

5. **Click the Close & Load button in the Close group**
   The Access data is imported into the worksheet as a table, and the Queries & Connections pane confirms that six rows were loaded using the Projected Revenue query.

6. **Format the data in column B in the Accounting format and no decimal places**
   Your formatted worksheet should match **FIGURE 7-8**.

7. **Change the sheet name to TCS Projected Revenue**

8. **Click the TCS Revenue worksheet, hold SHIFT, click the TCS Projected Revenue worksheet, release SHIFT, click the Insert tab on the ribbon, click the Text button, click the Header & Footer button, enter your name in the center header section, click any cell on the worksheet, click the Normal button ⊞ in the status bar, press CTRL+HOME, right-click any worksheet, then click Ungroup Sheets**

9. **Save your work**

FIGURE 7-7: Preview of Access data

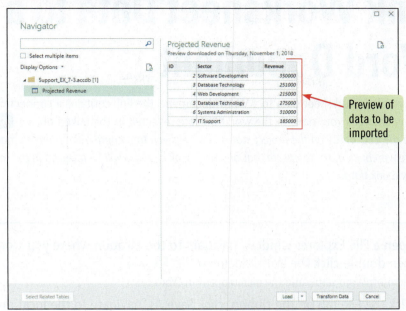

Preview of data to be imported

FIGURE 7-8: Formatted worksheet containing imported data

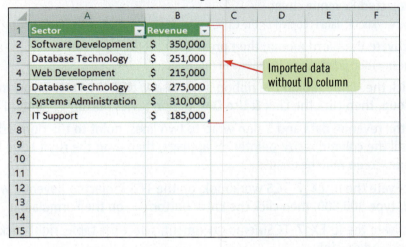

Imported data without ID column

Excel

Link Worksheet Data to a Word Document

When you link worksheet data to a Word document, the link contains a connection to the workbook so that any changes you make to the workbook are reflected in the linked object. **CASE** ▶ *Ellie wants to update the CEO of JCL on the project status. She asks you to prepare a Word memo that includes the projected revenue workbook data. To ensure that any workbook changes will be reflected in the memo, you decide to link the workbook data.*

STEPS

1. **Open a File Explorer window, navigate to the location where you store your Data Files, then double-click the Word document IL_EX_7-4**

   Microsoft Word starts, and the memo opens in Word.

2. **Click the File tab on the ribbon, click Save As, navigate to the location where you store your Data Files, replace the text in the File name text box with IL_EX_7_TCSMemo, then click Save**

3. **Activate the IL_EX_7_TCS workbook, then copy the data in the range A1:B7 on the TCS Projected Revenue sheet**

   The workbook data is copied to the Clipboard.

4. **Activate the Word memo, then press CTRL+END**

   The insertion point moves to the end of the memo.

5. **Click the Home tab on the ribbon if necessary, click the Paste arrow in the Clipboard group, then click the Link & Use Destination Styles button 📋 under Paste Options**

6. **If the revenue data and $ sign wrap to two lines, point to the right edge of the table until the column resize pointer ╫ appears, then drag the right edge to the right, so your screen matches FIGURE 7-9**

7. **Activate the IL_EX_7_TCS workbook, on the TCS Projected Revenue worksheet click cell B2, type 300,000, then click the Enter button ✔ on the Formula Bar**

8. **Activate the IL_EX_7_TCSMemo document, select the table, right-click the table, then click Update Link**

   The table data is updated to reflect the change in the linked Excel workbook, as shown in **FIGURE 7-10**.

9. **Click the Insert tab on the ribbon, click the Header button in the Header & Footer group, click Edit Header, type your name in the Header area, click the Close Header and Footer button in the Close group, save the Word file, close the Word document, then close Word**

FIGURE 7-9: Memo with linked worksheet data

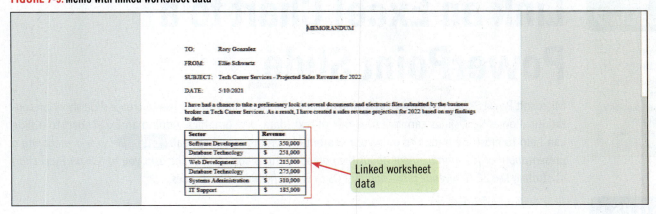

FIGURE 7-10: Memo with updated table data

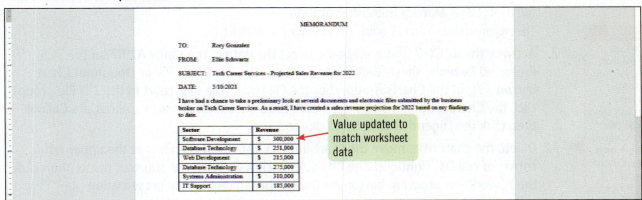

Managing and breaking links

When you open a Word document containing linked data, you are asked if you want to update the linked data. You can manage the updating of links by clicking the File tab on the ribbon, clicking Info, then clicking Edit Links to Files in the right pane. The Links dialog box opens, allowing you to change a link's update method from the default setting of automatic to manual. The Links dialog box also allows you to change the link source, permanently break a link, open the source file, or manually update a link. If you send your linked files to another user, the links will be broken because the linked file path references the local computer where you inserted the links. Because the file path will not be valid on the recipient user's device, the links will no longer be updated when the user opens the destination document. To correct this, recipients who have both the destination and source documents can use the Links dialog box to change the link's source in the destination document to their own device. Then, the links will be automatically updated when they open the destination document in the future. If you are managing links in an Excel workbook you can click the Data tab, then click the Edit Links button in the Queries & Connections group to open the Edit Links dialog box.

Link an Excel Chart to a PowerPoint Slide

Learning Outcomes
• Insert a linked chart in a PowerPoint slide
• Configure automatic links in a PowerPoint file

Microsoft PowerPoint is a **presentation graphics** program that you can use to create slide show presentations. PowerPoint slides can include a mix of text, data, and graphics. Adding an Excel chart to a slide can help to illustrate data and give your presentation more visual appeal. **CASE** ▶ *Ellie is preparing a presentation for JCL management about the potential acquisition of TCS. She asks you to link an Excel chart illustrating the 2022 revenue projection for TCS to one of her PowerPoint slides.*

STEPS

1. Click the **Start button** on the Windows taskbar, begin typing **PowerPoint** in the Search box, click **PowerPoint** in the list that opens, click **Open** on the left side of the Open pane, navigate to where you store your Data Files, double-click **IL_EX_7-5**, then save the file as **IL_EX_7_ManagementPresentation**

   The presentation appears in Normal view, as shown in **FIGURE 7-11**.

2. Activate the **IL_EX_7_TCS workbook**, select the data in the range **A2:B7** on the TCS Projected Revenue sheet, click the **Insert tab**, click the **Insert Pie or Doughnut Chart button** 🥧▾ in the Charts group, click the **Pie chart** (the first chart in the 2-D Pie group), click the **Chart Elements button** ➕, click the **Data Labels arrow** ▶, click **Data Callout**, then click the **Legend check box** to deselect it

3. Delete the **chart title**, move the **chart** until its upper-left corner is at the upper-left corner of cell **D1**, right-click the **Chart Area**, click **Copy** on the shortcut menu, then click the **PowerPoint program button** on the taskbar to display the presentation

4. Click **Slide 2** in the Thumbnails pane, right-click **Slide 2** in the Slide pane, then click the **Use Destination Theme & Link Data button** 📋 in the Paste Options group

   A pie chart illustrating the projected revenue appears in the slide. The chart matches the colors and fonts in the presentation that is the destination document.

5. Click the **File tab** on the ribbon, click **Info**, click **Edit Links to Files** at the bottom of the right pane, in the Links dialog box click the **Automatic Update check box** to add a checkmark, click **Close** in the dialog box, click the **Back button** ◀ at the top of the left pane, then in the presentation click the **Save button** 💾 on the Quick Access Toolbar

   The default setting for updating links in a PowerPoint file is Manual, but you have changed it so that the links will be automatically updated if the Excel file changes.

6. Switch to **Excel**, type **125,000** in cell **B7**, click the **Enter button** ✓ on the Formula bar, then click the **PowerPoint program button** on the taskbar to display the presentation

   The IT Support percentage decreases from 12% to 8%, reflecting the change in the Excel data.

7. Click the **Slide Show button** 🖵 on the status bar

   Slide Show view shows the slide full screen, the way the audience will see it, as shown in **FIGURE 7-12**.

8. Press **ESC** to return to Normal view, with **Slide 2** selected click the **Insert tab** on the ribbon, click the **Header & Footer button** in the Text group, add a checkmark in the **Footer check box**, type your name in the **Footer text box**, click **Apply to All**, save and close the presentation, then close PowerPoint

FIGURE 7-11: Presentation in Normal view

FIGURE 7-12: Completed slide

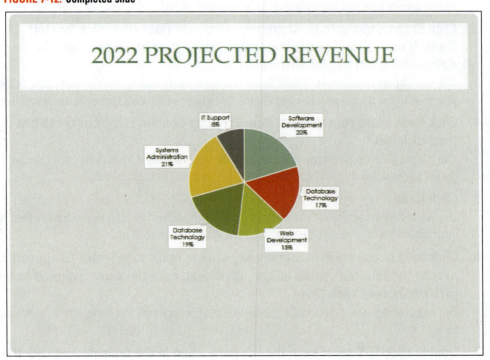

Excel

Import Excel Data into Access

**Learning
Outcomes**
•Import Excel data
 into an Access
 database
•Identify a primary
 key for a database

If you need to manage Excel data using the more extensive tools of a database, you can import it into Microsoft Access. When you import Excel table data into Access, the data becomes an Access table, using the same field names as the Excel table. In the process of importing an Excel table, Access specifies a primary key for the new table. A **primary key** is a field in a database that contains unique information for each record, or set of information. **CASE** ▶ *Rory Gonzales, the CEO of JCL, wants to use the TCS revenue information in an Access database, where he is tracking inventory and other data about the company. This revenue data is in an Excel file, so you need to import it into Microsoft Access.*

STEPS

1. **Start Access, click the Blank database button, edit the filename in the File Name text box to IL_EX_7_TCSRevenue, click the Browse button 📁 next to the filename, navigate to where you store your Data Files, click OK, click Create, then click the Close Table1 button ✕ on the Table1 tab (Do not close Access)**

   The IL_EX_7_Revenue database is created, and Table1 is removed from the database.

2. **Click the External Data tab on the ribbon, click the New Data Source button in the Import & Link group, click From File, then click Excel**

   The Get External Data - Excel Spreadsheet dialog box opens, as shown in **FIGURE 7-13**. This dialog box allows you to specify how you want the data to be stored in Access.

3. **Click Browse, navigate to where you store your Data Files, click Support_EX_7-6, click Open, if necessary click the Import the source data into a new table in the current database. option button, then click OK**

   The first Import Spreadsheet Wizard dialog box opens, with a sample of the sheet data in the lower section. You want to use the column headings in the Excel table as the field names in the Access database.

4. **Click Next, make sure the First Row Contains Column Headings check box is selected, then click Next**

   The Wizard allows you to review and change the field properties by clicking each column in the lower section of the window. You will not make any changes to the field properties.

5. **Click Next**

   The Wizard allows you to choose a primary key for the table. The table's primary key field contains unique information for each record; the Sector ID field is unique for each row.

6. **Click the Choose my own primary key option, make sure Sector ID appears in the box next to the selected option button, click Next, note the name assigned to the new table, click Finish, then click Close**

   The name of the new Access table, TCS Revenue, appears in the left pane, which is called the Navigation pane.

7. **Double-click TCS Revenue in the left pane, then in the table double-click the border between the Sector and the Revenue column headings**

   The Sector column widens. The Access table is shown in **FIGURE 7-14**.

8. **Click in the last row of the table, in the Sector ID column type 9999, press TAB, then type your name in the Sector column**

9. **Click the Save button 💾 on the Quick Access Toolbar, close the file, then close Access**

FIGURE 7-13: Get External Data - Excel Spreadsheet dialog box

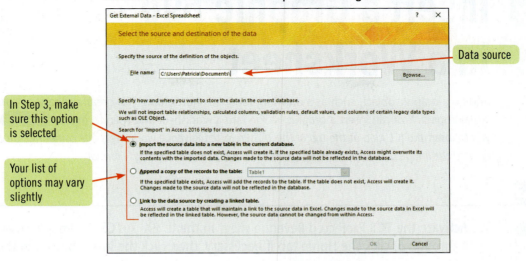

Data source

In Step 3, make sure this option is selected

Your list of options may vary slightly

FIGURE 7-14: Completed Access table with data imported from Excel

Sector ID	Sector	Revenue	Click to Add
1425	Software Development	$212,500	
2654	Database Technology	$195,500	
3125	Web Develooment	$185,200	
4365	Network Administration	$215,500	
5654	Systems Administration	$245,400	
6335	IT Support	$132,500	

TCS Revenue

Access table

Primary key

Adding SmartArt graphics

SmartArt graphics provide another way to visually communicate information on a worksheet. Each SmartArt type communicates a kind of information or relationship, such as a list, process, or hierarchy. Each type has various layouts you can choose. To insert a SmartArt graphic into a worksheet, click the Insert tab, then click the Insert a SmartArt Graphic button in the Illustrations group. In the Choose a SmartArt Graphic dialog box, choose from eight SmartArt types: List, Process, Cycle, Hierarchy, Relationship, Matrix, Pyramid, and Picture. There is also a link for SmartArt available on Office.com. The dialog box describes the type of information that is appropriate for each selected layout. After you choose a layout and click OK, a SmartArt object appears on your worksheet. **FIGURE 7-15** shows examples of SmartArt graphics. You can enter text directly in the placeholders or use the SmartArt text pane. If this pane is in your way, you can close it by clicking the Close button in the upper-right corner of the pane. As you enter text, the font is automatically resized to fit the graphic. You can change the layout by selecting the SmartArt, then clicking a different layout in the Layouts group on the SmartArt Design tab.

FIGURE 7-15: Examples of SmartArt graphics

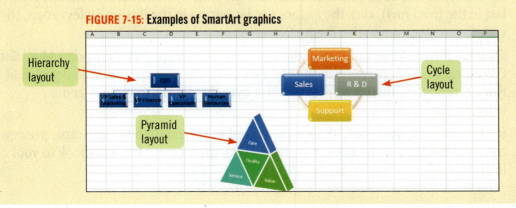

Hierarchy layout

Cycle layout

Pyramid layout

Working with Images and Integrating with Other Programs

Insert a Graphic File in a Worksheet

Learning Outcomes
- Insert an image into an Excel worksheet
- Add a style to an image

Adding a graphic object, such as a drawing, logo, or photograph, can greatly enhance your worksheet's visual impact. You can insert a graphic image into a worksheet and then format it. **CASE** ▸ *Ellie wants you to insert the JCL logo at the top of the TCS Projected Revenue worksheet. The company's graphic designer created the image and saved it in JPG (commonly pronounced "jay-peg") format.*

STEPS

1. **Activate the TCS Projected Revenue sheet in the IL_EX_7_TCS workbook, select rows 1 through 6, click the Home tab if necessary, then click the Insert button in the Cells group**

   Six blank rows appear at the top of the worksheet, leaving space to insert column headings for the workbook data and the logo. If you need to insert multiple rows or columns, it saves time to select the number you need to insert before clicking the Insert button. Six rows were inserted because you selected six rows before clicking the button.

2. **Click cell A6, enter TCS Projected Revenue, click the Enter button ☑ on the Formula bar, click the Cell Styles button in the Styles group, then click Title**

3. **Click cell A1, click the Insert tab on the ribbon, click the Illustrations button in the Illustrations group, click the Pictures button, then click This Device**

   The Insert Picture dialog box opens. Because you specified that you want to insert a picture, the dialog box displays only files that contain graphics file extensions, such as .jpg.

4. **Navigate to where you store your Data Files if necessary, click Support_EX_7-7, then click Insert**

   Excel inserts the image and displays the Picture Format tab. The small circles around the picture's edge are sizing handles. Sizing handles appear when a picture is selected; you use them to change the size of a picture.

5. **Position the pointer over the sizing handle in the logo's lower-right corner until the pointer becomes ⬉, then drag the sizing handle up and to the left so that the logo's outline fits within rows 1 through 5**

   Compare your screen to **FIGURE 7-16**.

6. **With the image selected, click the More button ▦ in the Picture Styles group, point to several styles and observe the effect on the graphic, click the Bevel Rectangle style (the last in the third row), click the Picture Border button in the Picture Styles group, then click Green, Accent 6 in the Theme Colors group**

7. **Click the Picture Effects button in the Picture Styles group, click Glow, click More Glow Colors, click Green, Accent 6 in the Theme Colors group, resize the logo again to fit it in rows 1 through 5, then drag it to center it over the data in columns A and B**

   Compare your worksheet to **FIGURE 7-17**.

8. **sam ↟ Save the workbook, change the worksheet orientation to landscape, preview the worksheet, close the workbook, close Excel, then submit the workbook to your instructor**

FIGURE 7-16: Resized logo

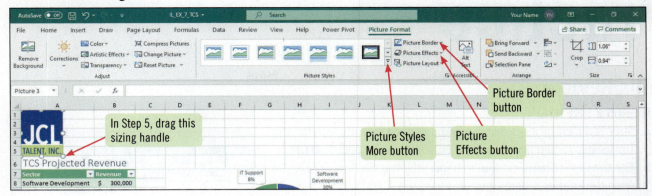

FIGURE 7-17: Worksheet with formatted picture

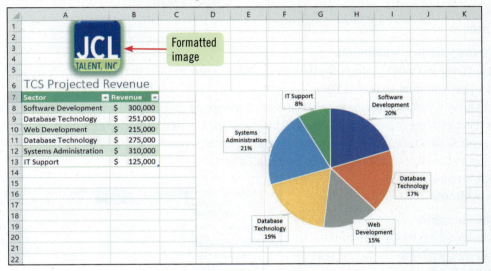

Working with SmartArt graphics

You can add shapes to a SmartArt graphic by selecting the position where the shape will appear, clicking the Add Shape arrow in the Create Graphic group of the SmartArt Design tab, then selecting the desired position. Also in the Create Graphic group are the Promote and Demote buttons, which you can use to increase or decrease the level of a selected shape. The SmartArt Design tab lets you choose color schemes and styles for your SmartArt. You can add shape styles, fills, outlines, and other shape effects to SmartArt graphics using choices on the Format tab. Clicking the Shape Fill button in the Shape Styles group of this tab, then clicking Picture inserts a picture in a shape. You can also add fills, outlines, and other effects to text using this tab. You can change the size of a SmartArt shape by selecting the shape, then clicking the Larger button or the Smaller button in the Shapes group on the Format tab. You can resize an entire SmartArt graphic by clicking it and dragging a resizing handle. To resize a graphic proportionally, drag any corner sizing handle. If you drag an edge sizing handle instead, the graphic will be resized nonproportionally. You can align multiple SmartArt graphics at once by selecting them, clicking Align in the Arrange group on the Shape Format tab, then selecting the alignment option. (This also aligns other objects on a worksheet.)

Practice

Skills Review

1. Import a text file.

FIGURE 7-18

a. Start Excel, create a new blank workbook, then save the workbook in the location where you store your Data Files as **IL_EX_7_OLP**.

b. Use the Get & Transform tool to import the text file Support_EX_7-8 from the location where you store your Data Files. The data is delimited using tabs.

	A	B	C
1	Category	Expenses	
2	Compensation	$ 323,060	
3	Facility	$ 317,638	
4	Supplies	$ 251,461	
5	Equipment	$ 271,334	
6	Total	$ 1,163,493	
7			
8			

c. Format the data in column B using the Accounting style and no decimal places.

d. Rename the sheet tab **May**, then delete Sheet1.

e. Add a table total row to show the total expenses, as shown in **FIGURE 7-18**.

f. Save the workbook.

2. Import data from another workbook.

a. Use the Get & Transform tool to import the data on the April Expenses sheet in the Excel file Support_EX_7-9 from the location where you store your Data Files.

b. In the Power Query Editor, change the column labels to **Category** and **Expenses**. Close and load the edits.

c. Rename the sheet with the imported data **April**, then close the Queries & Connections pane.

d. Format the expense data using the Accounting style and no decimal places.

e. Add a total row to the table to display the sum of the expense amounts.

f. Save the workbook.

FIGURE 7-19

3. Import a database table.

a. Use the Get & Transform tool to import the data on the Expenses table in the Access Data File Support_EX_7-10 from the location where you store your Data Files.

b. Rename the sheet with the imported data **May Details**.

c. Format the amount data in column D using the Accounting style and no decimal places.

d. Add a total row to the table to display the sum of the expense amounts. Autofit column D if necessary to display all the data.

e. Scroll down to see the entire table, save the workbook, then compare your screen to **FIGURE 7-19**.

	A	B	C	D	E
1	Category	Item	Month	Amount	
2	Compensation	Benefits	May	$ 50,000	
3	Compensation	Bonuses	May	$ 40,000	
4	Compensation	Commissions	May	$ 35,000	
5	Compensation	Conferences	May	$ 42,000	
6	Compensation	Promotions	May	$ 65,048	
7	Compensation	Payroll Taxes	May	$ 18,954	
8	Compensation	Salaries	May	$ 63,514	
9	Compensation	Training	May	$ 8,544	
10	Facility	Lease	May	$ 42,184	
11	Facility	Maintenance	May	$ 63,214	
12	Facility	Other	May	$ 11,478	
13	Facility	Rent	May	$ 80,214	
14	Facility	Telephone	May	$ 62,584	
15	Facility	Utilities	May	$ 57,964	
16	Supplies	Food	May	$ 61,775	
17	Supplies	Computer	May	$ 43,217	
18	Supplies	General Office	May	$ 47,854	
19	Supplies	Other	May	$ 56,741	
20	Supplies	Outside Services	May	$ 41,874	
21	Equipment	Computer	May	$ 49,874	
22	Equipment	Other	May	$ 43,547	
23	Equipment	Cash Registers	May	$ 55,987	
24	Equipment	Software	May	$ 63,147	
25	Equipment	Telecommunications	May	$ 58,779	
26	Total			$1,163,493	

Skills Review (continued)

4. Link worksheet data to a Word document.

  a. With the May Details sheet active, copy the range A1:D26.

  b. Open a File Explorer window, then double-click the Word file IL_EX_7-11 from the location where you store your Data Files. When the file opens in Word, save it as **IL_EX_7_OLPMemo**.

  c. At the end of the memo body, use the Paste menu to paste the copied worksheet data by linking it and using the destination styles. Widen the Amount column if necessary to display the values on one line.

  d. Note that the first compensation value in the memo is currently $50,000. Switch to Excel, activate the May Details worksheet in the IL_EX_7_OLP workbook, press ESC to deactivate the copied range, then change the value in cell D2 to **$35,000**.

  e. Activate the IL_EX_7_OLPMemo document in Word, update the linked data, then verify that the first compensation value has changed to $35,000, as shown in **FIGURE 7-20**. (*Hint:* To update the link, right-click the table in the memo, then click Update Link.)

  f. Use a tool on the Insert tab of the ribbon to edit the header, enter your name in the header, save your changes to the IL_EX_7_OLPMemo document, preview the memo, close the document, then close Word.

FIGURE 7-20

Category	Item	Month	Amount
Compensation	Benefits	May	$ 35,000
Compensation	Bonuses	May	$ 40,000
Compensation	Commissions	May	$ 35,000
Compensation	Conferences	May	$ 42,000
Compensation	Promotions	May	$ 65,048
Compensation	Payroll Taxes	May	$ 18,954
Compensation	Salaries	May	$ 63,514
Compensation	Training	May	$ 8,544
Facility	Lease	May	$ 42,184
Facility	Maintenance	May	$ 63,214
Facility	Other	May	$ 11,478
Facility	Rent	May	$ 80,214
Facility	Telephone	May	$ 62,584
Facility	Utilities	May	$ 57,964
Supplies	Food	May	$ 61,775
Supplies	Computer	May	$ 43,217
Supplies	General Office	May	$ 47,854
Supplies	Other	May	$ 56,741
Supplies	Outside Services	May	$ 41,874
Equipment	Computer	May	$ 49,874
Equipment	Other	May	$ 43,547
Equipment	Cash Registers	May	$ 55,987
Equipment	Software	May	$ 63,147
Equipment	Telecommunications	May	$ 58,779
Total			$ 1,148,493

Excel

5. Link an Excel chart to a PowerPoint slide.

  a. Start PowerPoint, open the presentation IL_EX_7-12 from the location where you store your Data Files, then save it as **IL_EX_7_OLPPresentation**.

  b. Switch to Excel, activate the May worksheet in the IL_EX_7_OLP workbook, then using the data in the range A2:B5, create a 2-D pie chart. Delete the chart title, add data callouts, then delete the chart legend. Move the chart so its upper-left corner is at the upper-left corner of cell D1.

  c. Copy the chart, activate the PowerPoint file, then display Slide 6, May Expenses. (*Hint:* Click slide 6 in the Thumbnails pane.)

  d. Link the copied chart to Slide 6, using the theme of the destination file. Notice that Compensation is currently 28% of total expenses.

Skills Review (continued)

e. Open the Info pane on the File tab, then edit the file's links to automatically update. Return to the presentation.

f. Switch to Excel, then change the compensation amount in cell B2 of the May worksheet to **$500,000**. Notice in the pie chart that Compensation is now 37% of total expenses.

g. Activate the IL_EX_7_OLPPresentation file, then verify the Compensation percentage in the chart on Slide 6 changed to 37%.

h. Enlarge the chart and re-center it if necessary under the title, so it matches **FIGURE 7-21**.

i. Use a tool on the Insert tab to add a footer containing your name to all of the slides.

j. Save the presentation, close the presentation, then close PowerPoint.

FIGURE 7-21

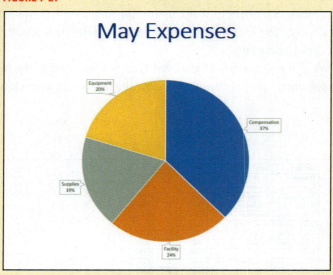

6. **Import Excel data into Access.**

a. Start Access, then create a blank database named **IL_EX_7_RevisedMay** in the location where you store your Data Files. Close Table1.

b. Use the External Data tab to import the Excel table in the Support_EX_7-13 file from the location where you store your Data Files. In the Get External Data dialog box, choose the first option to import the source data into a new Access table. Step through the Import Spreadsheet Wizard, making sure the First Row Contains Column Headings check box is selected, and accepting the default assignment of field names. Identify a primary key by letting Access add one. Accept the default table name, and do not save the import steps.

c. Open the Revised May Expenses table in Access, then compare your screen to **FIGURE 7-22**.

d. Enter your name in the Category column of row 5 in the table, save the database file, then close Access.

FIGURE 7-22

Revised May Expenses			
ID ▾	Category ▾	Expenses ▾	Click to Add ▾
1	Compensation	$312,500	
2	Facility	$307,851	
3	Supplies	$235,487	
4	Equipment	$251,487	
* (New)			

Skills Review (continued)

7. Insert a graphic file in a worksheet.

   a. Activate the April worksheet in the IL_EX_7_OLP file. Select rows 1 through 4, then use a tool on the Home tab of the ribbon to insert four blank rows above row 1 to create space for an image.

   b. In rows 1 through 4, insert the picture file Support_EX_7-14.jpg from the location where you store your Data Files.

   c. Resize and reposition the logo as necessary to make it fit in rows 1 through 4.

   d. Apply the Beveled Matte, White Picture Style, then change the picture border color to Green, Accent 6 in the Theme colors.

   e. Resize the picture to fit the image and the border in the first four rows. Move the picture to center it between columns A and B. Compare your worksheet to **FIGURE 7-23**.

   f. Group the worksheets, change the orientation of the worksheets to landscape, add your name to the center section of the footer, preview the workbook, ungroup the worksheets, save and close the workbook, then submit the workbook to your instructor.

FIGURE 7-23

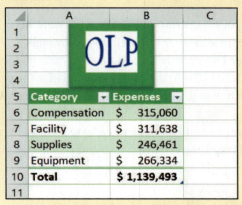

Excel

Independent Challenge 1

You have started a new position managing the respiratory therapy clinic at Riverwalk Medical Center. The previous manager left important data for the first quarter of the year in various text, workbook, and database files. You need to bring the data from all these sources into an Excel workbook, so you can analyze it together.

a. Start Excel, create a new workbook, then save it as **IL_EX_7_RiverwalkQ1** in the location where you store your Data Files.

b. Use the Get & Transform tool to import the data from Sheet1 of the Excel workbook file Support_EX_7-15. Rename the worksheet **Jan**, then delete Sheet1.

c. Format the billing data in column B using the Accounting number format and no decimal places.

d. Use the Get & Transform tool to import the data from the tab delimited text file Support_EX_7-16. Rename the worksheet **Feb**.

e. Format the billing data in column B using the Accounting number format and no decimal places.

f. Use the Get & Transform tool to import the data from the March Billings table in the Access file Support_EX_7-17. Rename the worksheet **Mar**, then close the Queries & Connections pane.

g. Delete column A in the Mar worksheet, then format the Billings data in column B as Accounting with no decimal places.

h. Activate the Jan worksheet. Insert four blank rows at the top of the worksheet.

i. Insert the Support_EX_7-18 image file and resize it to fit in rows 1 through 4.

j. Apply the Center Shadow Rectangle Picture Style (second row, second from the right), then change the picture border color to Green, Accent 6, Darker 50% in the Theme colors. Resize the picture to fit the image and the border in the first four rows. Move the picture so it appears centered above the range A1:C1.

k. Compare your Jan worksheet to **FIGURE 7-24**.

l. Group the worksheets, add the sheet name to the center header section, add your name to the center section of the footer, preview the workbook, ungroup the worksheets, save and close the workbook, then submit the workbook to your instructor.

FIGURE 7-24

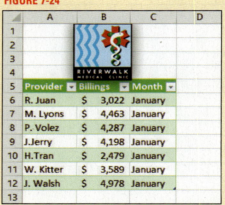

Independent Challenge 2

You are the executive assistant for the CEO of a national credit institution. The CEO has asked for an organizational chart of the company's upper management. The employee data is stored in a text file that you will import into Excel.

a. Start Excel, create a new workbook, then save it as **IL_EX_7_OrgChart** in the location where you store your Data Files.

b. Use the Get & Transform tool to import the data from the Support_EX_7-19 text file.

Independent Challenge 2 (continued)

c. Delete Sheet1, then rename the sheet with the imported data **Hierarchy**.

d. Use the Edit button in the Edit group of the Query tab to open the Power Query Editor, then rename the first column header **Employee** and the second column header **Position**.

e. Click any cell outside the data, then insert a SmartArt graphic, choosing the first Organization Chart in the Hierarchy category. (*Hint:* Click the Insert tab on the ribbon, then click the SmartArt button in the Illustrations group.)

f. Close the Queries & Connections pane, then move the SmartArt graphic to line up the upper-left corner with the upper-left corner of cell C1.

g. Referring to the imported data, enter the employee name, **Seth Werthen**, and the position, **CEO**, in the top shape of the SmartArt graphic, with the name appearing in the first line and the position in the second line. (*Hint:* Press ENTER to move to the next line in a shape.)

h. In the shape on the second level, enter Julie Hadley's information using the same format of name on the first line and position on the second line.

i. In the leftmost box on the third level, enter the information for Justin Phillips using the same format used for the previous shapes.

j. In the middle box on the third level, enter the information for Katelyn Wolff using the same format used for the previous shapes.

k. In the box farthest to the right on the third level, enter the information for Connor Ogah using the same format used for the previous shapes.

l. Add a shape below Justin Phillips, then enter Lucille Fischer's information in the new shape. (*Hint:* You can add a shape below a selected shape by clicking the Add Shape arrow and clicking Add Shape Below.)

m. Add a shape below Katelyn Wolff, then enter Christine Hassan's information in the new shape. Add a shape below Connor Ogah, then enter Huiwei Phillip's information in the new shape.

n. Change the SmartArt style to Subtle Effect.

o. Change the SmartArt colors to Gradient Loop – Accent 6. (*Hint:* Use the Change Colors tool on the SmartArt Design tab.)

p. Resize the SmartArt graphic proportionally to line up the lower-right corner with the lower-right corner of cell J16, then compare your worksheet to FIGURE 7-25.

q. Enter your name in the worksheet footer, change the orientation to landscape, preview the workbook, save and close the workbook, then submit the workbook to your instructor.

Excel

FIGURE 7-25

Visual Workshop

Open IL_EX_7-20.xlsx from the location where your Data Files are stored, then save it as **IL_EX_7_Systems**. Start PowerPoint, open the presentation IL_EX_7-21.pptx from the location where your Data Files are stored, then save it as **IL_EX_7_Northern**. Edit the Annual Revenue slide to match FIGURE 7-26 by creating the pie chart in the IL_EX_7_Systems file, showing data labels with the category names and percentages on the outside end of the data series and linking the chart on slide 2 of the IL_EX_7_Northern file. (*Hint:* The chart links to the Excel file and uses the destination theme.) Add a footer of your name to all the slides, save the worksheet and presentation, close the presentation and workbook, then close PowerPoint and Excel. Submit the PowerPoint file to your instructor.

FIGURE 7-26

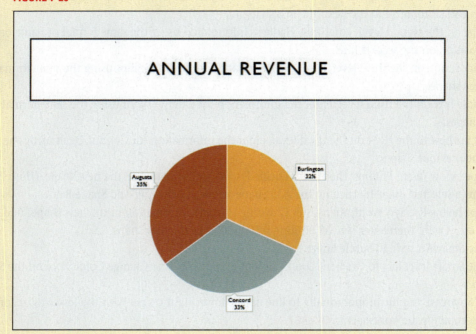

Analyzing Data with PivotTables

> **CASE** ▶ JCL uses PivotTables to analyze revenue data. Ellie Schwartz is preparing for the annual directors' meeting and asks you to analyze revenue in JCL's Northeast offices over the past year. You will create a PivotTable to summarize last year's revenue data by quarter, position, office, and division. You will also illustrate the information using a PivotChart.

Module Objectives

After completing this module, you will be able to:

- Plan and design a PivotTable report
- Create a PivotTable report
- Change a PivotTable's summary function and design
- Filter PivotTable data
- Explore PivotTable Data Relationships
- Create a PivotChart report
- Update a PivotTable report
- Use the GETPIVOTDATA function

Files You Will Need

IL_EX_8-1.xlsx   IL_EX_8-4.xlsx

IL_EX_8-2.xlsx   IL_EX_8-5.xlsx

IL_EX_8-3.xlsx

Learning Outcomes
• Develop guidelines for a PivotTable
• Develop an understanding of Pivot-Table vocabulary

Plan and Design a PivotTable Report

The PivotTable Report feature lets you summarize large amounts of worksheet data in a compact table format. Then you can freely rearrange, or "pivot," PivotTable rows and columns to explore the relationships within your data. Before you begin creating a PivotTable report (often called a PivotTable), you need to review the data and consider how a PivotTable can best summarize it. **CASE** *Ellie asks you to design a PivotTable to display JCL's revenue information for its offices in the Northeast. You begin by reviewing guidelines for creating PivotTables.*

DETAILS

Before you create a PivotTable, think about the following guidelines:

• **Review the source data**

Before you can effectively summarize data in a PivotTable, you need to understand the source data's scope and structure. The source data does not have to be defined as a table, but it should be in a table-like format; that is, it should have column headings and the same type of data in each column, and it should not have any blank rows or columns. To create a meaningful PivotTable, make sure that at least one of the fields has repeated information so that the PivotTable can effectively group it. Also, be sure to include numeric data that the PivotTable can total for each group. The data columns represent categories of data, which are called fields, just as in a table. You are working with revenue information that Ellie received from JCL's Northeastern office managers, shown in **FIGURE 8-1**. Information is repeated in the Position ID, Division, Office, and Quarter Columns, and numeric information is displayed in the revenue column, so you will be able to summarize this data effectively in a PivotTable.

• **Determine the purpose of the PivotTable**

The purpose of your PivotTable is to summarize revenue information by quarter across various offices.

• **Identify the fields you want to include**

You want your PivotTable to summarize the data in the Position ID, Division, Office, Quarter, and Revenue columns, so you need to include those fields in your PivotTable.

• **Determine which field contains the data you want to summarize and which summary function you want to use**

The JCL offices are organized into divisions, such as Technical, Finance & Accounting, Creative, and Office Support. You want to summarize revenue information by summing that field for each division in an office by quarter. You'll do this by using the Sum function.

• **Decide how you want to arrange the data**

The PivotTable layout you choose determines the information you want to communicate. Position ID values will appear in the PivotTable columns, office and quarter numbers will appear in rows, and the PivotTable will summarize revenue figures, as shown in **FIGURE 8-2**.

• **Determine the location of the PivotTable**

You can place a PivotTable in any worksheet of any workbook. Placing a PivotTable on a separate worksheet makes it easier to locate and prevents you from accidentally overwriting parts of an existing sheet. You decide to create the PivotTable as a new worksheet in the current workbook.

FIGURE 8-1: Revenue data

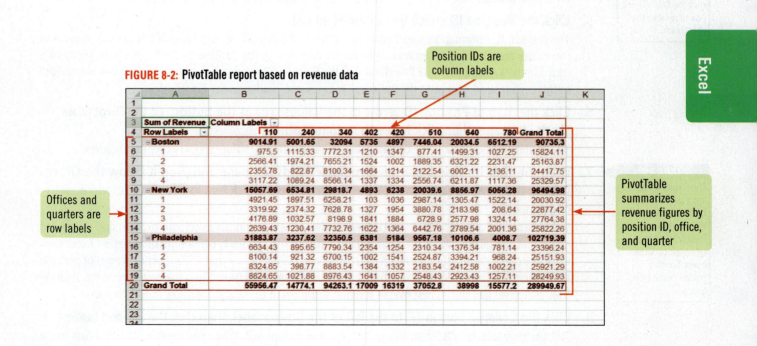

	A	B	C	D	E
1		JCL Revenue			
2	Position ID	Division	Office	Quarter	Revenue
3	240	Finance & Accounting	Boston	1	$ 1,115.33
4	240	Finance & Accounting	Boston	2	$ 1,974.21
5	240	Finance & Accounting	Boston	3	$ 822.87
6	240	Finance & Accounting	Boston	4	$ 1,089.24
7	110	Technical	Boston	1	$ 975.50
8	110	Technical	Boston	2	$ 2,566.41
9	110	Technical	Boston	3	$ 2,355.78
10	110	Technical	Boston	4	$ 3,117.22
11	340	Creative	Boston	1	$ 7,772.31
12	340	Creative	Boston	2	$ 7,655.21
13	340	Creative	Boston	3	$ 8,100.34
14	340	Creative	Boston	4	$ 8,566.14
15	402	Office Support	Boston	1	$ 1,210.00
16	402	Office Support	Boston	2	$ 1,524.00
17	402	Office Support	Boston	3	$ 1,664.00
18	402	Office Support	Boston	4	$ 1,337.00
19	780	Finance & Accounting	Boston	1	$ 1,027.25
20	780	Finance & Accounting	Boston	2	$ 2,231.47
21	780	Finance & Accounting	Boston	3	$ 2,136.11
22	780	Finance & Accounting	Boston	4	$ 1,117.36
23	640	Technical	Boston	1	$ 1,499.31

Northeast

Ready   120%

Data with repeated information

Numeric data

FIGURE 8-2: PivotTable report based on revenue data

Position IDs are column labels

Offices and quarters are row labels

PivotTable summarizes revenue figures by position ID, office, and quarter

	A	B	C	D	E	F	G	H	I	J
1										
2										
3	Sum of Revenue	Column Labels ▾								
4	Row Labels ▾	110	240	340	402	420	510	640	780	Grand Total
5	⊟ Boston	9014.91	5001.65	32094	5735	4897	7446.04	20034.5	6512.19	90735.3
6	1	975.5	1115.33	7772.31	1210	1347	877.41	1499.31	1027.25	15824.11
7	2	2566.41	1974.21	7655.21	1524	1002	1889.35	6321.22	2231.47	25163.87
8	3	2355.78	822.87	8100.34	1664	1214	2122.54	6002.11	2136.11	24417.75
9	4	3117.22	1089.24	8566.14	1337	1334	2556.74	6211.87	1117.36	25329.57
10	⊟ New York	15057.69	6534.81	29818.7	4893	6238	20039.6	8856.97	5056.28	96494.98
11	1	4921.45	1897.51	6258.21	103	1036	2987.14	1305.47	1522.14	20030.92
12	2	3319.92	2374.32	7628.78	1327	1954	3880.78	2183.98	208.64	22877.42
13	3	4176.89	1032.57	8198.9	1841	1884	6728.9	2577.98	1324.14	27764.38
14	4	2639.43	1230.41	7732.76	1622	1364	6442.76	2789.54	2001.36	25822.26
15	⊟ Philadelphia	31883.87	3237.62	32350.5	6381	5184	9567.18	10106.6	4008.7	102719.39
16	1	6634.43	895.65	7790.34	2354	1254	2310.34	1376.34	781.14	23396.24
17	2	8100.14	921.32	6700.15	1002	1541	2524.87	3394.21	968.24	25151.93
18	3	8324.65	398.77	8883.54	1384	1332	2183.54	2412.58	1002.21	25921.29
19	4	8824.65	1021.88	8976.43	1641	1057	2548.43	2923.43	1257.11	28249.93
20	Grand Total	55956.47	14774.1	94263.1	17009	16319	37052.8	38998	15577.2	289949.67

Excel

Create a PivotTable Report

Once you've planned and designed your PivotTable report, you are ready to create it. Then, you can **populate** it by adding fields to areas in the PivotTable. A PivotTable has four areas: the Report Filter, which is the field by which you want to filter the PivotTable; the Row Labels, which contain the fields whose labels will describe the values in the rows; the Column Labels, which appear above the PivotTable values and describe the columns; and the Values, which summarize the numeric data. **CASE** *With the planning and design stage complete, you are ready to create a PivotTable that summarizes revenue information.*

STEPS

1. **sam** ↓ Start Excel, open **IL_EX_8-1.xlsx** from the location where you store your Data Files, then save it as **IL_EX_8_NERevenue**

2. Click the **Insert tab** on the ribbon, click the **Recommended PivotTables button** in the Tables group, then click each **layout** in the dialog box, scrolling as necessary

   The Recommended PivotTables dialog box displays recommended layouts, as shown in **FIGURE 8-3**.

3. Click **Blank PivotTable** at the bottom of the dialog box

   A new, blank PivotTable appears on the left side of the worksheet and the PivotTable Fields List appears in a pane on the right, as shown in **FIGURE 8-4**. To populate the PivotTable, you can click field check boxes in the PivotTable Fields List pane, often simply called the Field List. The diagram area at the bottom of the pane represents the main PivotTable areas and helps you track field locations as you populate the PivotTable. You can also drag fields among the diagram areas to change the PivotTable layout.

4. Click the **Office field check box** in the Field List

   Because the office field is a text, rather than a numeric, field, Excel adds the offices to the Rows area of the PivotTable and adds the Office field name to the Rows area in the PivotTable Fields pane.

5. Click the **Position ID check box** in the Field List

   The Position ID information is automatically added to the PivotTable, and "Sum of Position ID" appears in the Values area in the diagram area. Because the data type of the Position ID field is numeric, the field is added to the Values area of the PivotTable and the Position ID values are summed, which is not meaningful in this case. Instead, you want the Position IDs as column headers in the PivotTable.

6. Click the **Sum of Position ID arrow** in the Values area at the bottom of the PivotTable Fields List pane, then click **Move to Column Labels**

   The Position ID field becomes a column label, so the Position ID values appear as column headers.

7. Drag the **Quarter field** from the PivotTable Fields List pane and drop it below the **Office field** in the Rows area, then click the **Revenue field check box** in the pane to add a checkmark

   You have created a PivotTable that totals revenue, with the position IDs as column headers, and offices and quarters as row labels. Sum is the Excel default function for data fields containing numbers, so Excel automatically calculates the sum of the revenue. The PivotTable tells you that Philadelphia revenue of position #110 (Technical) was twice the New York revenue and more than three times the Boston revenue. Position #340 (Creative) had the highest overall revenue, as shown in the Grand Total row in **FIGURE 8-5**.

8. Click the **Collapse button** ⊟ to the left of the **Boston** label, then click the **Expand button** ⊞

   The quarterly total details for Boston are hidden, then redisplayed. When you have two levels of data in the rows or columns area, you can drill down and drill up in the data to expand or collapse the second-level field details below the top field.

FIGURE 8-3: Recommended PivotTables dialog box

Examples of recommended PivotTables

Preview of selected layout

FIGURE 8-4: Empty PivotTable ready to receive field data

Empty PivotTable

Click a check box to add field to the PivotTable

Diagram of PivotTable areas

FIGURE 8-5: New PivotTable with fields in place

Sum of Revenue	Column Labels									
Row Labels	110	240	340	402	420	510	640	780	Grand Total
⊟ Boston	9014.91	5001.65	32094	5735	4897	7446.04	20034.5	6512.19	90735.3
1	975.5	1115.33	7772.31	1210	1347	877.41	1499.31	1027.25	15824.11
2	2566.41	1974.21	7655.21	1524	1002	1889.35	6321.22	2231.47	25163.87
3	2355.78	822.87	8100.34	1664	1214	2122.54	6002.11	2136.11	24417.75
4	3117.22	1089.24	8566.14	1337	1334	2556.74	6211.87	1117.36	25329.57
⊟ New York	15057.69	6534.81	29818.7	4893	6238	20039.6	8856.97	5056.28	96494.98
1	4921.45	1897.51	6258.21	103	1036	2987.14	1305.47	1522.14	20030.92
2	3319.92	2374.32	7628.78	1327	1954	3880.78	2183.98	208.64	22877.42
3	4176.89	1032.57	8198.9	1841	1884	6728.9	2577.98	1324.14	27764.38
4	2639.43	1230.41	7732.76	1622	1364	6442.76	2789.54	2001.36	25822.26
⊟ Philadelphia	31883.87	3237.62	32350.5	6381	5184	9567.18	10106.6	4008.7	102719.39
1	6634.43	895.65	7790.34	2354	1254	2310.34	1376.34	781.14	23396.24
2	8100.14	921.32	6700.15	1002	1541	2524.87	3394.21	968.24	25151.93
3	8324.65	398.77	8883.54	1384	1332	2183.54	2412.58	1002.21	25921.29
4	8824.65	1021.88	8976.43	1641	1057	2548.43	2923.43	1257.11	28249.93
Grand Total	55956.47	14774.1	94263.1	17009	16319	37052.8	38998	15577.2	289949.67

Philadelphia revenue for position 110 is twice as high as New York and three times Boston's revenue

Position 340 shows highest overall revenue

Changing a PivotTable layout

The default layout for PivotTables is the compact form; the row labels are displayed in a single column, and the second-level field items (such as the quarters in the JCL example) are indented for readability. You can change the layout of your PivotTable by clicking the Design tab, clicking the Report Layout button in the Layout group, then clicking either Show in Outline Form or Show in Tabular Form. The tabular form and the outline form show each row label in its own column. The tabular and outline layouts take up more space on a worksheet than the compact layout.

Excel

Change a PivotTable's Summary Function and Design

A PivotTable's **summary function** determines what type of calculation Excel applies, or uses to summarize the table data. Unless you specify otherwise, Excel applies the Sum function to numeric data and the Count function to data fields containing text. However, you can easily change the default summary functions. **CASE** *Ellie wants you to explore using the average function to summarize the revenue for the Northeast offices. She would like you to improve the appearance of the PivotTable for her presentation.*

STEPS

1. **Right-click cell A3, then point to Summarize Values By in the shortcut menu**
   The shortcut menu shows that the Sum function is selected by default, as shown in **FIGURE 8-6**.

2. **Click Average**
   The data area of the PivotTable shows the average revenue for each position by office and quarter, and cell A3 now contains "Average of Revenue."

3. **Click the Design tab on the ribbon, click the Subtotals button in the Layout group, then click Do Not Show Subtotals**
   The subtotals are removed from the PivotTable. After reviewing the data, you decide that it would be more useful to sum the revenue information than to average it, and to see subtotals.

4. **Right-click cell A3, point to Summarize Values By on the shortcut menu, then click Sum**
   Excel recalculates the PivotTable, now summing the revenue data instead of averaging it.

5. **Click the Design tab on the ribbon if necessary, click the Subtotals button in the Layout group, then click Show all Subtotals at Top of Group**
   Just as Excel tables have styles that let you quickly format them, PivotTables have a gallery of styles from which to choose.

6. **Click the More button ▼ in the PivotTable Styles gallery, then click White, Pivot Style Light 3**

7. **Click the PivotTable Analyze tab on the ribbon, then click the Field Headers button in the Show group to deselect it**
   The unnecessary headers "Column Labels" and "Row Labels" are removed.

8. **Click any revenue value in the PivotTable, click the Field Settings button in the Active Field group, click Number Format in the Value Field Settings dialog box, click Currency in the Category list, make sure Decimal places is 2 and Symbol is $, click OK, click OK again, AutoFit any columns if necessary to display all the data, then compare your PivotTable to FIGURE 8-7**
   The revenue values are formatted as currency.

9. **Rename Sheet1 PivotTable, add your name to the worksheet footer, then save the workbook**

FIGURE 8-6: Shortcut menu showing Sum function selected

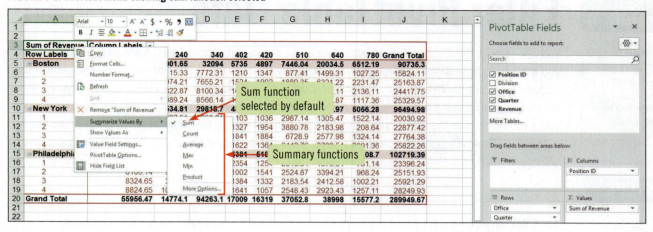

Sum function selected by default

Summary functions

FIGURE 8-7: Formatted PivotTable

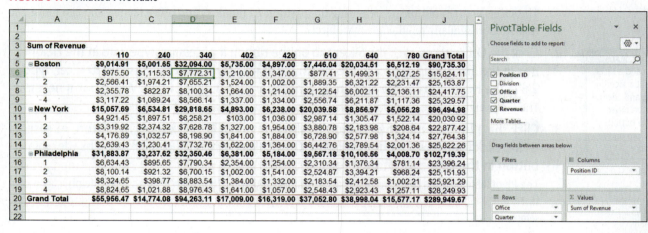

	A	110	240	340	402	420	510	640	780	Grand Total
5	⊟Boston	$9,014.91	$5,001.65	$32,094.00	$5,735.00	$4,897.00	$7,446.04	$20,034.51	$6,512.19	$90,735.30
6	1	$975.50	$1,115.33	$7,772.31	$1,210.00	$1,347.00	$877.41	$1,499.31	$1,027.25	$15,824.11
7	2	$2,566.41	$1,974.21	$7,655.21	$1,524.00	$1,002.00	$1,889.35	$6,321.22	$2,231.47	$25,163.87
8	3	$2,355.78	$822.87	$8,100.34	$1,664.00	$1,214.00	$2,122.54	$6,002.11	$2,136.11	$24,417.75
9	4	$3,117.22	$1,089.24	$8,566.14	$1,337.00	$1,334.00	$2,556.74	$6,211.87	$1,117.36	$25,329.57
10	⊟New York	$15,057.69	$6,534.81	$29,818.65	$4,893.00	$6,238.00	$20,039.58	$8,856.97	$5,056.28	$96,494.98
11	1	$4,921.45	$1,897.51	$6,258.21	$103.00	$1,036.00	$2,987.14	$1,305.47	$1,522.14	$20,030.92
12	2	$3,319.92	$2,374.32	$7,628.78	$1,327.00	$1,954.00	$3,880.78	$2,183.98	$208.64	$22,877.42
13	3	$4,176.89	$1,032.57	$8,198.90	$1,841.00	$1,884.00	$6,728.90	$2,577.98	$1,324.14	$27,764.38
14	4	$2,639.43	$1,230.41	$7,732.76	$1,622.00	$1,364.00	$6,442.76	$2,789.54	$2,001.36	$25,822.26
15	⊟Philadelphia	$31,883.87	$3,237.62	$32,350.46	$6,381.00	$5,184.00	$9,567.18	$10,106.56	$4,008.70	$102,719.39
16	1	$6,634.43	$895.65	$7,790.34	$2,354.00	$1,254.00	$2,310.34	$1,376.34	$781.14	$23,396.24
17	2	$8,100.14	$921.32	$6,700.15	$1,002.00	$1,541.00	$2,524.87	$3,394.21	$968.24	$25,151.93
18	3	$8,324.65	$398.77	$8,883.54	$1,384.00	$1,332.00	$2,183.54	$2,412.58	$1,002.21	$25,921.29
19	4	$8,824.65	$1,021.88	$8,976.43	$1,641.00	$1,057.00	$2,548.43	$2,923.43	$1,257.11	$28,249.93
20	Grand Total	$55,956.47	$14,774.08	$94,263.11	$17,009.00	$16,319.00	$37,052.80	$38,998.04	$15,577.17	$289,949.67

Using the Show buttons

To display and hide PivotTable elements, you can use the toggle buttons in the Show group on the PivotTable Analyze tab. For example, clicking the Field List button hides or displays the PivotTable Fields List pane. Clicking the +/- button hides or displays the Expand and Collapse Outline buttons, and clicking the Field Headers button hides or displays the Row and Column Label headers on the PivotTable.

Excel

Filter PivotTable Data

You can restrict the display of PivotTable data using slicers and report filters. A **slicer** is a graphic object you can use to filter data in a PivotTable, to show only the data you need. For example, you can use slicer buttons to show only data about a specific product. You can also filter a PivotTable using a **report filter**, which lets you filter the data to show data for one or more fields, using a list arrow. For example, if you add a month field to the Filters area, you can filter a PivotTable so that only January revenue data appears in the PivotTable. **CASE** ▶ *Ellie wants to compare revenue data about specific positions across specific offices and quarters.*

STEPS

1. **Click any cell in the PivotTable, click the PivotTable Analyze tab on the ribbon if necessary, click the Insert Slicer button in the Filter group, in the Insert Slicers dialog box click the Position ID check box and the Office check box to add checkmarks to both fields, click OK, then drag both slicers to the right of the PivotTable**

   The slicers contain buttons representing the position ID numbers and office names. You can move and resize a slicer similarly to other graphic objects.

2. **Click the Office slicer, click the Slicer tab on the ribbon if necessary, type 1.18 in the Height box in the Size group, type 2 in the Width box if necessary, click the Position ID slicer, type 2.6 in the Height box in the Size group if necessary, then type 2 in the Width box if necessary**

   The slicers are just large enough to display a button for each value, as shown in **FIGURE 8-8**.

3. **Click the 110 button in the Position ID slicer, press CTRL, click the 510 button, release CTRL, click the New York button in the Office slicer, press CTRL, click the Philadelphia button in the Office slicer, then release CTRL**

   The PivotTable displays only the data for position IDs 110 and 510 in New York and Philadelphia, as shown in **FIGURE 8-9**. In the slicers, the Filter symbol changes, indicating the PivotTable is filtered to display the selected fields.

4. **Click the Clear Filter button ⧩ in the Position ID slicer, click ⧩ in the Office slicer, click the top of the Office slicer, press CTRL, click the top of the Position ID slicer, release CTRL, right-click the Position ID slicer, then click Remove Slicers on the shortcut menu**

   The filters are cleared and the slicers are removed.

5. **In the PivotTable Fields List pane, click the Quarter field arrow in the Rows area, then click Move to Report Filter in the list that opens**

   The Quarter field moves to cell A1, and a list arrow and the word "(All)" appears in cell B1. The list arrow lets you filter the data in the PivotTable by Quarter. "(All)" indicates that the PivotTable currently shows data for all quarters.

6. **Click the cell B1 list arrow, click 4, click OK, then save your work**

   The PivotTable filters the revenue data to display the fourth quarter only, as shown in **FIGURE 8-10**. The Quarter field list arrow changes to a filter symbol. A filter symbol also appears to the right of the Quarter field in the PivotTable Fields List pane, indicating that the PivotTable is filtered and summarizes only a portion of the PivotTable data.

FIGURE 8-8: Slicers for Position ID and Office fields

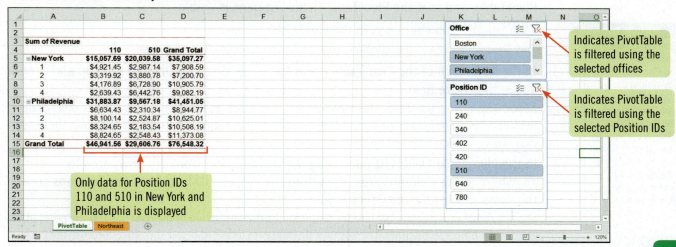

FIGURE 8-9: PivotTable filtered by Position ID and Office

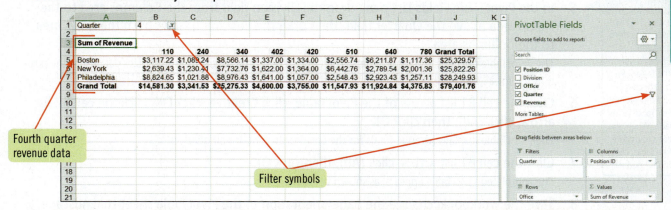

FIGURE 8-10: PivotTable filtered by fourth quarter

Filtering PivotTables using multiple values

Instead of using slicers to display multiple values when filtering a PivotTable report, you can use a report filter. After clicking a field's report filter list arrow in the top section of the PivotTable Fields List pane or in cell B1 on the PivotTable itself, click the Select Multiple Items check box at the bottom of the filter selections. You can then select multiple values for the filter. For example, selecting quarters 1 and 2 as the report filter in a PivotTable

with quarters displays all the data for those quarters. You can also select multiple values for the row and column labels by clicking the PivotTable Analyze tab, clicking the Field Headers button in the Show group, clicking the Row Labels list arrow or the Column Labels list arrow in cells A4 and B3 on the PivotTable, then selecting the data items that you want to display.

Explore PivotTable Data Relationships

Learning Outcomes
- Change a PivotTable's organization
- Add fields to a PivotTable

What makes a PivotTable such a powerful analysis tool is the ability to change the way data is organized in the report. By moving fields to different positions in the report, you can explore relationships and trends that you might not see in the original report structure. **CASE** ▸ *Ellie asks you to include division information in the revenue report. She is also interested in viewing the PivotTable in different arrangements to find the best organization of data for her presentation.*

STEPS

1. **Make sure that the PivotTable sheet is active, that the active cell is anywhere inside the PivotTable, and that the PivotTable Fields List pane is visible**

2. **Click the Division check box in the Field List**

    The Division data is added to the Rows area below the corresponding office data.

3. **In the Rows area of the PivotTable Fields List pane, drag the Division field up and drop it above the Office field**

    As you drag, a green bar shows where the field will be inserted. The division field is now the outer or upper field, and the office field is the inner or lower field. The PivotTable is restructured to display the revenue data first by division and then by office, as shown in **FIGURE 8-11**.

4. **In the PivotTable Fields List pane drag the Division field from the Rows area to anywhere in the Columns area, then drag the Position ID field from the Columns area to the Rows area below the Office field**

    The PivotTable now displays the revenue data with the division values in the columns and the position IDs grouped by offices in the rows. The Position ID values are indented below the offices because the Position ID field is the inner row label.

5. **In the PivotTable Fields List pane drag the Division field from the Columns area to the Filters area above the Quarter field, then drag the Position ID field from the Rows area to the Columns area**

    The PivotTable now has two report filters. The upper report filter, Division, summarizes data using the position IDs for all four divisions.

6. **Click the cell B1 list arrow of the PivotTable, click Creative, click OK, click the cell B2 list arrow, click (All), then click OK**

    The PivotTable displays revenue totals for the creative division for all quarters.

7. **Click the cell B1 list arrow, click (All), then click OK**

    The completed PivotTable appears, as shown in **FIGURE 8-12**.

8. **Save the workbook, change the page orientation of the PivotTable sheet to landscape, then preview the PivotTable**

FIGURE 8-11: PivotTable structured by offices within divisions

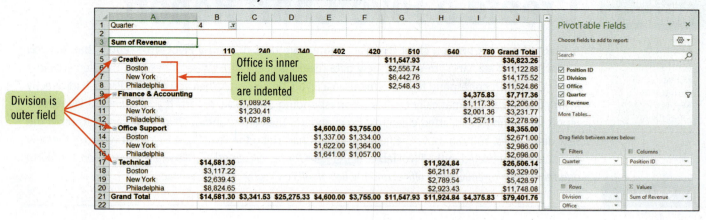

Division is outer field

Office is inner field and values are indented

FIGURE 8-12: Completed PivotTable report

	A	B	C	D	E	F	G	H	I	J
1	Division	(All)								
2	Quarter	(All)								
3										
4	Sum of Revenue									
5		110	240	340	402	420	510	640	780	Grand Total
6	Boston	$9,014.91	$5,001.65	$32,094.00	$5,735.00	$4,897.00	$7,446.04	$20,034.51	$6,512.19	$90,735.30
7	New York	$15,057.69	$6,534.81	$29,818.65	$4,893.00	$6,238.00	$20,039.58	$8,856.97	$5,056.28	$96,494.98
8	Philadelphia	$31,883.87	$3,237.62	$32,350.46	$6,381.00	$5,184.00	$9,567.18	$10,106.56	$4,008.70	$102,719.39
9	Grand Total	$55,956.47	$14,774.08	$94,263.11	$17,009.00	$16,319.00	$37,052.80	$38,998.04	$15,577.17	$289,949.67

Grouping PivotTable data

You can group PivotTable data to analyze specific values in a field as a unit. For example, you may want to group revenue data for quarters 1 and 2 to analyze the first half of the year. To group PivotTable data, first select the Rows and Columns that you want to group, click the PivotTable Analyze tab, then click the Group Selection button in the Group group. The default group name of Group1 can be edited by entering the new name in the cell with the default name. Once data is grouped, it can be expanded or collapsed to show the grouped details using the Collapse button [–] or the Expand button [+] next to the group name. **FIGURE 8-13** shows a PivotTable grouped by quarters with the first two quarters expanded and the last two quarters collapsed. To ungroup data, select the Group name in the PivotTable, then click the Ungroup button in the Group group.

FIGURE 8-13: Grouped PivotTable data

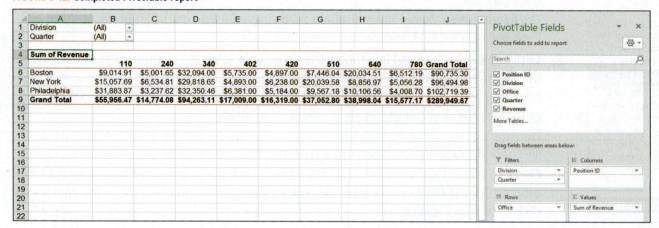

First two quarters grouping is expanded

Grouping for quarters 3 and 4 is collapsed

Excel

Create a PivotChart Report

A **PivotChart report** is a chart that you create from data or from a PivotTable report that lets you summarize and rearrange to explore new data relationships. **TABLE 8-1** describes how the elements in a PivotTable report correspond to the elements in a PivotChart report. When you create a PivotChart directly from data, Excel automatically creates a corresponding PivotTable report. If you change a PivotChart report by filtering the charted elements, Excel updates the corresponding PivotTable report to show the new data values. You can move the fields of a PivotChart using the PivotChart Fields List window; the new layout will be reflected in the PivotTable. **CASE** *For her presentation, Ellie wants you to chart the fourth quarter creative revenue for all offices and the Boston office's yearly creative revenue.*

STEPS

1. **Click the cell B1 list arrow, click Creative, click OK, click the Quarter list arrow, click 4, then click OK**

   The fourth quarter creative revenue information appears in the PivotTable. You want to create the PivotChart from the PivotTable information you have displayed.

2. **Click any cell in the PivotTable, click the PivotTable Analyze tab on the ribbon, then click the PivotChart button in the Tools group**

   The Insert Chart dialog box opens and shows a gallery of chart types.

   QUICK TIP
   You can change a PivotChart's type by clicking the Change Chart Type button in the Type group on the Design tab.

3. **Click the Clustered Column chart if necessary, then click OK**

   The PivotChart appears on the worksheet, as shown in **FIGURE 8-14**. The chart has field buttons that let you filter a PivotChart in the same way you do a PivotTable. You can also add a slicer to filter a PivotChart.

4. **Click the PivotChart Analyze tab on the ribbon, click the Insert Slicer button in the Filter group, click the Office check box, click OK, move the slicer to the right of the chart, then click Boston in the slicer**

   Only the Boston revenue data is shown in the chart.

   QUICK TIP
   You can add a chart style to a PivotChart by clicking a style in the Chart Styles group on the Design tab.

5. **Click the PivotChart to select it, click the Design tab on the ribbon, click the Move Chart button in the Location group, click the New sheet option button, type PivotChart in the text box, then click OK**

6. **Click the Quarter field button at the top of the PivotChart, click All, then click OK**

   The chart now represents the Boston office's creative revenue for the year, as shown in **FIGURE 8-15**.

   QUICK TIP
   If you have more than one field in the Axis area, you can drill up or down in a PivotChart using the Collapse button ⊟ to hide the details of the second field and the Expand button ⊞ to display the second field details. If the buttons are not visible, click the Field Buttons button in the Show/Hide group on the PivotChart Analyze tab.

7. **Click the Design tab, click the Quick Layout button in the Chart Layouts group, click Layout 3, click the Chart Title element to select it, type Annual Creative Revenue, then press ENTER**

   You are finished filtering the chart data.

8. **Click the PivotChart Analyze tab, then click the Field Buttons button in the Show/Hide group**

   Removing the field buttons improves the chart's appearance.

9. **Enter your name in the center section of the PivotChart sheet footer, save the workbook, then preview the PivotChart report**

   The final PivotChart report displaying Boston's creative revenue for the year is shown in **FIGURE 8-16**.

FIGURE 8-14: PivotChart with fourth quarter creative revenue

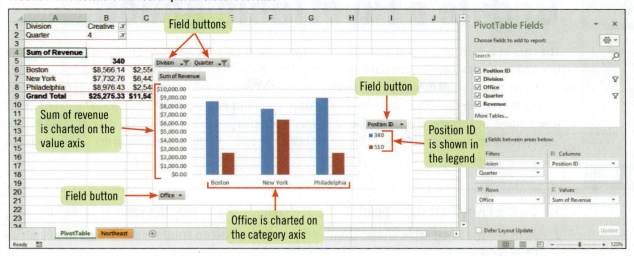

FIGURE 8-15: PivotChart displaying Boston's creative revenue for the year

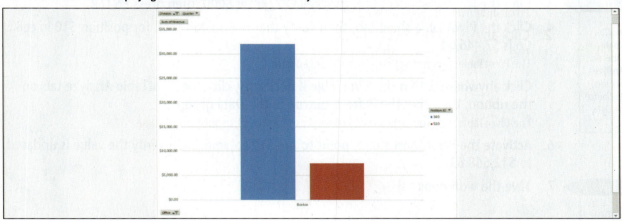

FIGURE 8-16: Completed PivotChart report

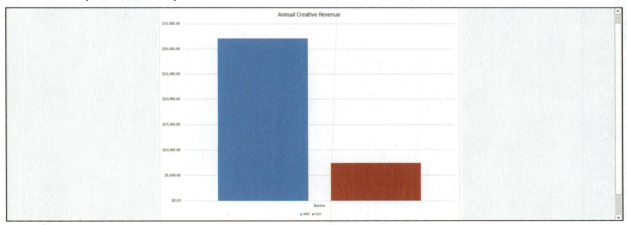

TABLE 8-1: PivotTable and PivotChart elements

PivotTable items	PivotChart items
Row labels	Axis fields
Column labels	Legend fields
Report Filters	Report Filters

Update a PivotTable Report

The data in a PivotTable report looks like typical worksheet data. However, because the PivotTable data is linked to a **data source** (the data you used to create the PivotTable), the results it displays are read-only. That means you cannot move or modify a part of a PivotTable by inserting or deleting rows, editing results, or moving cells. To change PivotTable data, you must edit the items directly in the data source, then update, or **refresh**, the PivotTable so it reflects the changes to the underlying data. **CASE** ▶ *Ellie just learned that there was an error in the Boston office's creative revenue information for the first quarter. She asks you to fix this error.*

STEPS

1. On the PivotChart sheet point to the **510 column**, then verify the value is **$7,446.04**

2. Activate the **PivotTable sheet**, then verify that the Boston total for position 510 in cell **C6** is **$7,446.04**

QUICK TIP

If you want to change a PivotTable's source data range, click the PivotTable Analyze tab, then click the Change Data Source button in the Data group.

3. Click the **Northeast sheet tab**, click cell **E27**, enter **6000**, then press **ENTER**

4. Click the **PivotTable sheet tab**, then verify that the Boston total for position 510 in cell **C6** is **$7,446.04**

   The PivotTable does not yet reflect the changed data.

5. **Click anywhere within the PivotTable if necessary, click the PivotTable Analyze tab on the ribbon, then click the Refresh button in the Data group**

   The PivotTable now shows Boston's 510 total as $12,568.63, as shown in **FIGURE 8-17**.

6. **Activate the PivotChart sheet, point to the 510 column, then verify the value is updated to $12,568.63**

QUICK TIP

If you want Excel to refresh a PivotTable or PivotChart report automatically when you open a workbook, click the PivotTable/ PivotChart Analyze tab on the ribbon, click the Options button in the PivotTable/ PivotChart group, click the Data tab in the PivotTable Options dialog box, click the Refresh data when opening the file check box, then click OK.

7. **Save the workbook**

Analyzing Data with PivotTables

FIGURE 8-17: Updated PivotTable report

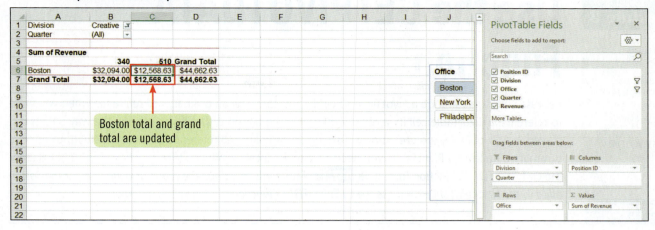

Adding a calculated field to a PivotTable and a PivotChart

You can use formulas to analyze PivotTable and PivotChart data in a field by adding a calculated field. A calculated field appears in the PivotTable's or PivotChart's Field List and can be manipulated like other PivotTable fields. To add a calculated field, click any cell in the PivotTable, click the PivotTable Analyze tab, click the Fields, Items, & Sets button in the Calculations group, then click Calculated Field. The Insert Calculated Field dialog box opens. Enter the field name in the Name text box, click in the Formula text box, click a field name in the Field list that you want to use in the formula, and click Insert Field. Use standard arithmetic operators to enter the formula you want to use. For example, you can enter a formula such as =Revenue*1.2 to increase the revenue data by 20 percent. After entering the formula in the Insert Calculated Field dialog box, click Add, then click OK. The new field with the formula results appears in the PivotTable and the PivotChart, and the field is added to the PivotTable and PivotChart Fields List pane. **FIGURE 8-18** shows a calculated field added to a PivotTable.

FIGURE 8-18: PivotTable with calculated field

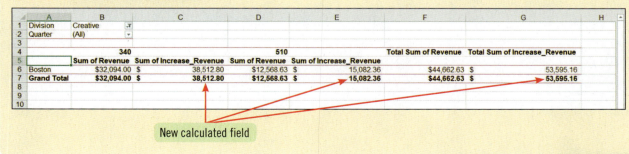

Use the GETPIVOTDATA Function

Learning Outcomes
- Analyze the GETPIVOTDATA function
- Retrieve information using the GETPIVOTDATA function

Because you can rearrange a PivotTable so easily, you can't use an ordinary cell reference when you want to reference a PivotTable cell in another worksheet. The reason is that if you change the way data is displayed in a PivotTable, the data moves, making an ordinary cell reference incorrect. Instead, to retrieve summary data from a PivotTable, you need to use the Excel GETPIVOTDATA function. See **FIGURE 8-19** for the GETPIVOTDATA function format. **CASE** ▸ *Ellie wants to include the yearly revenue total for the Boston office in the Northeast sheet. You use the GETPIVOTDATA function to retrieve this information.*

STEPS

1. **Activate the PivotTable sheet**

   The revenue figures in the PivotTable are filtered to show only the creative positions.

2. **Click the Division filter arrow in cell B1, click (All), then click OK**

   The PivotChart report displays revenue information for all Boston positions.

3. **Activate the Northeast sheet, click cell G1, type Total Boston Revenue, click the Enter button ✓ on the formula bar, click the Home tab on the ribbon if necessary, click the Align Right button ≡ in the Alignment group, click the Bold button B in the Font group, then adjust the width of column G to display the new label**

4. **Click cell G2, type =, click the PivotTable sheet tab, click cell J6 on the PivotTable, then click ✓**

   Cell J6 on the PivotTable contains the data you want to display on the Northeast sheet. The GETPIVOT-DATA function, along with its arguments, is inserted into cell G2 of the Northeast sheet. You want to format the revenue total.

5. **Click the Accounting Number Format button $ in the Number group**

   The current revenue total for the Boston office is $95,857.89 as shown in **FIGURE 8-20**. This is the same value displayed in cell J6 of the PivotTable.

6. **Add your name to the Northeast sheet custom footer, save the workbook, then preview the Northeast worksheet**

7. **sam✦ Close the file, close Excel, then submit the workbook to your instructor**

   The Northeast worksheet is shown in **FIGURE 8-21**.

FIGURE 8-19: Format of GETPIVOTDATA function

=GETPIVOTDATA("Revenue",PivotTable!$A$4,"Office","Boston")

Field where data is extracted from

PivotTable name and cell in the report that contains the data you want to retrieve

Field and value pair that describe the data you want to retrieve

FIGURE 8-20: GETPIVOTDATA function in the Northeast sheet

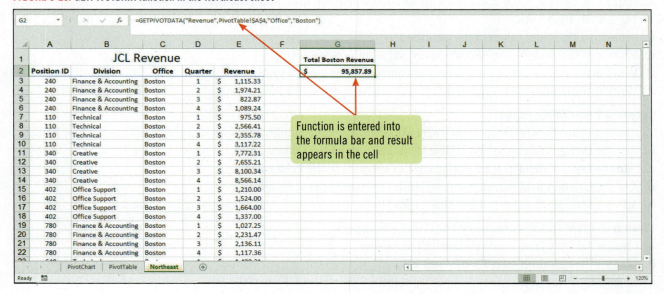

FIGURE 8-21: Completed Northeast worksheet showing total Boston revenue

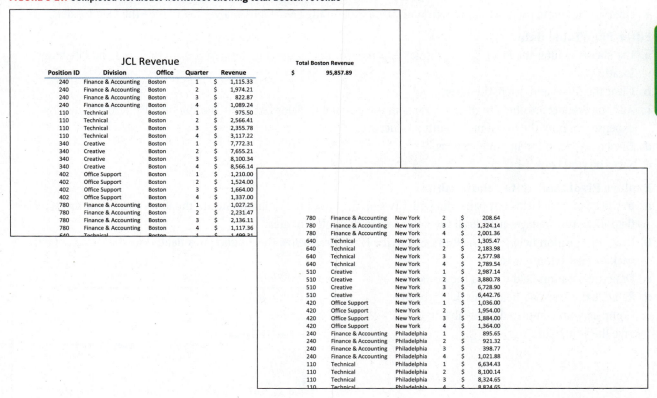

Practice

Skills Review

1. Plan and design a PivotTable report.

  a. Start Excel, open IL_EX_8-2.xlsx from the location where you store your Data Files, then save it as **IL_EX_8_Pharma**.

  b. Review the fields and values in the worksheet.

  c. Verify that the worksheet contains repeated values in one or more fields.

  d. Verify that there are not any blank rows or columns in the range A1:E25.

  e. Verify that the worksheet contains a field that can be summed in a PivotTable.

2. Create a PivotTable report.

  a. Create a blank PivotTable report on a new worksheet using the January Expenses worksheet data in the range A1:E25.

  b. Add the Division field in the PivotTable Fields List pane to the Columns area.

  c. Add the Expenses field in the PivotTable Fields List pane to the Values area.

  d. Add the Location field in the PivotTable Fields List pane to the Rows area.

  e. Add the Manager field in the PivotTable Fields List pane to the Rows area below the Location field.

3. Change a PivotTable's summary function and design.

  a. Change the PivotTable summary function to Average.

  b. Rename the new sheet **Jan Expenses PT**.

  c. Change the PivotTable Style to Light Orange, Pivot Style Light 14. Format the expense values in the PivotTable as currency with a $ symbol and no decimal places.

  d. Enter your name in the center section of the PivotTable report footer, then save the workbook.

  e. Change the summary function back to Sum. Use a tool on the PivotTable Analyze tab to hide the field headers.

4. Filter PivotTable data.

  a. Use slicers to filter the PivotTable to display expenses for the production division only in the Basel and Pittsburgh locations.

  b. Clear the filters and delete the slicer.

  c. Add the Product area field to the Filters area in the PivotTable Fields List pane. Use the filter list arrow to display expenses for only the Consumer Health product area.

  d. Display expenses for all product areas.

  e. Save the workbook.

5. Explore PivotTable data relationships.

  a. In the PivotTable Fields List pane, drag the Division field from the Columns area to the Rows area below the Manager field. Drag the Manager field from the Rows area to the Columns area.

  b. Drag the Location field from the Rows area to the Filters area below the Product Area field. Drag the Division field back to the Columns area.

  c. Drag the Location field back to the Rows area.

  d. Remove the Manager field from the PivotTable.

  e. Compare your completed PivotTable to **FIGURE 8-22**, then save the workbook.

FIGURE 8-22

	A	B	C	D	E	F
1						
2	Product Area	(All)				
3						
4	Sum of Expenses					
5		Production	R & D	Support	Grand Total	
6	Basel	$60,986	$57,453	$41,629	$160,068	
7	Pittsburgh	$51,709	$60,550	$29,597	$141,856	
8	Seattle	$53,466	$58,527	$38,355	$150,348	
9	Singapore	$35,170	$54,153	$30,461	$119,784	
10	Grand Total	$201,331	$230,683	$140,042	$572,056	
11						
12						

Analyzing Data with PivotTables

Skills Review (continued)

6. Create a PivotChart report.

  a. Use the existing PivotTable data to create a Clustered Column PivotChart report.

  b. Move the PivotChart to a new worksheet, then name the sheet **PivotChart**.

  c. Apply the Quick Layout, Layout 1, to the PivotChart. Add the title **January Expenses** to the chart.

  d. Filter the chart to display only expense data for the Crop Science product area. Display the expense data for all product areas. Hide the field buttons.

  e. Add your name to the center section of the PivotChart custom sheet footer. Compare your PivotChart with **FIGURE 8-23**, then save the workbook.

FIGURE 8-23

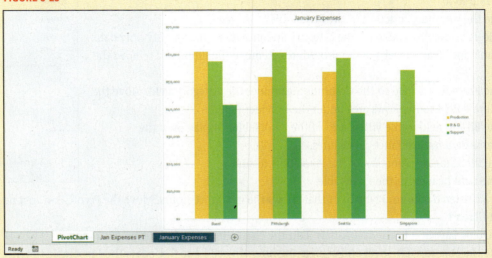

7. Update a PivotTable report.

  a. Activate the Jan Expenses PT sheet, then note the Seattle total for production.

  b. Activate the January Expenses sheet and change the Expenses value in cell D14 to **$30,000**.

  c. Refresh the PivotTable so it reflects the new value.

  d. Verify that the Seattle total for production increased to $60,287 on both the PivotTable and the PivotChart.

  e. Save the workbook.

8. Use the GETPIVOTDATA function.

  a. In cell D27 of the January Expenses sheet type **=**, click the Jan Expenses PT sheet, click the cell that contains the grand total for Pittsburgh, then press ENTER.

  b. Review the GETPIVOTDATA function that was entered in cell D27, then format the value in cell D27 in Accounting Number format and no decimal places.

  c. Enter your name in the January Expenses sheet footer, compare your January Expenses sheet to **FIGURE 8-24**, save the workbook, then preview the January Expenses worksheet.

  d. Close the workbook, then close Excel.

  e. Submit the workbook to your instructor.

FIGURE 8-24

	A	B	C	D	E	F
1	**Division**	**Product Area**	**Location**	**Expenses**	**Manager**	
2	Production	Consumer Health	Basel	$ 29,518	C. Berwick	
3	R & D	Consumer Health	Basel	$ 30,234	C. Berwick	
4	Support	Consumer Health	Basel	$ 23,971	C. Berwick	
5	Production	Crop Science	Basel	$ 31,468	J. Allen	
6	R & D	Crop Science	Basel	$ 27,219	J. Allen	
7	Support	Crop Science	Basel	$ 17,658	J. Allen	
8	Production	Consumer Health	Pittsburgh	$ 22,075	D. Macey	
9	R & D	Consumer Health	Pittsburgh	$ 31,355	D. Macey	
10	Support	Consumer Health	Pittsburgh	$ 15,940	D. Macey	
11	Production	Crop Science	Pittsburgh	$ 29,634	T. Holland	
12	R & D	Crop Science	Pittsburgh	$ 29,195	T. Holland	
13	Support	Crop Science	Pittsburgh	$ 13,657	T. Holland	
14	Production	Consumer Health	Seattle	$ 30,000	L. Bartlet	
15	R & D	Consumer Health	Seattle	$ 32,443	L. Bartlet	
16	Support	Consumer Health	Seattle	$ 26,603	L. Bartlet	
17	Production	Crop Science	Seattle	$ 30,287	S. Simpson	
18	R & D	Crop Science	Seattle	$ 26,084	S. Simpson	
19	Support	Crop Science	Seattle	$ 11,752	S. Simpson	
20	Production	Consumer Health	Singapore	$ 13,056	P. Lee	
21	R & D	Consumer Health	Singapore	$ 24,883	P. Lee	
22	Support	Consumer Health	Singapore	$ 16,957	P. Lee	
23	Production	Crop Science	Singapore	$ 22,114	L. Williams	
24	R & D	Crop Science	Singapore	$ 29,270	L. Williams	
25	Support	Crop Science	Singapore	$ 13,504	L. Williams	
26						
27		**Pittsburgh Expenses for January:**		$ 141,856		
28						

Independent Challenge 1

As the office manager for the occupational therapy clinic at the Riverwalk Medical Clinic, you have been asked to review the billings for the month of February. The CFO of the clinic has asked you to analyze the hours being spent on the various categories of occupational therapy and how the services are paid.

FIGURE 8-25

a. Start Excel, open IL_EX_8-3.xlsx from the location where you store your Data Files, then save it as **IL_EX_8_RiverwalkOT**.

b. Create a blank PivotTable on a separate worksheet that sums hours by Provider and Division, using **FIGURE 8-25** as a guide.

c. Name the new sheet **PivotTable**, and apply the White, Pivot Style Light 5 PivotTable style.

d. Change the summary function of the PivotTable to average.

e. Add slicers to the PivotTable for the category and provider data. Display only data for Jolan's and Ryan's level 1 and 2 procedures. Remove the filters and remove the slicers.

f. Add the Procedure # field to the Columns area under the Category field. Move the Procedure # field to the Rows area under the Provider field.

g. Add the Billing field to the Filters area of the PivotTable. Display only the PivotTable data for insurance procedures.

h. Change the summary function of the PivotTable to sum.

i. Hide the field headers in the PivotTable.

j. Create a clustered column PivotChart that shows the insurance hours. Move the PivotChart to a new sheet named **PivotChart**.

k. Apply Quick Layout 3 to the PivotChart. Edit the chart title to **Insurance Hours**.

l. Activate the February OT sheet and change the hours in cell E4 to 2. Update the PivotTable to reflect this change.

m. Activate the February OT sheet, then use the GETPIVOTDATA function to display the total number of insurance hours in cell A29.

n. Add your name to the center section of the three worksheet footers, then save the workbook. Preview the three worksheets, comparing them to **FIGURE 8-26**.

o. Close the workbook, then close Excel. Submit the workbook to your instructor.

FIGURE 8-26

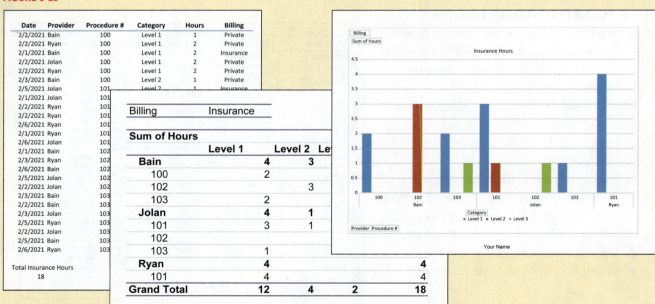

Analyzing Data with PivotTables

Independent Challenge 2

You are the assistant to the CFO of an international hotel group with properties in North America, Europe, and Asia. The properties in your collection cater to both business and leisure travelers. You want to create a PivotTable to analyze and graph the revenue in each quarter by purpose and region.

a. Start Excel, open IL_EX_8-4.xlsx from the location where you store your Data Files, then save it as **IL_EX_8_Accommodations**.

FIGURE 8-27

b. Create a PivotTable on a new worksheet named **PivotTable** that sums the revenue amount for each region across the rows and each purpose down the columns. Add the quarter field as an inner row label. Use **FIGURE 8-27** as a guide.

c. Widen column C of the PivotTable if necessary to fully display the grand total value for that column.

d. Group the first two quarters (*Hint:* Select the first two quarter cells in any region, then click the Group Selection button in the Group group on the PivotTable Analyze tab.)

e. Rename the Group1 label **First Half**. (*Hint:* Enter the new name in any cell with the Group1 label.)

f. Group the third and fourth quarters, then name this new group **Last Half**.

g. Collapse both the First Half and Last Half groups.

h. Turn off the grand totals for the Columns. (*Hint:* Click the Grand Totals button in the Layout group on the Design tab, then click On for Rows Only.)

i. Format the revenue values using the Currency format with the $ symbol and no decimal places.

j. On the Revenue worksheet, change the North America Quarter 1 Business Revenue value in cell D2 to **$50,000,000**. Update the PivotTable to reflect this increase in revenue.

k. Create a stacked column PivotChart report for the revenue data for all three regions. (*Hint:* Choose the first Stacked Column Chart type in the dialog box.)

l. Move the PivotChart to a new sheet, and name the chart sheet **PivotChart**.

m. Apply a quick layout of Layout 4 to the PivotChart.

n. Use the Region field button at the bottom of the PivotChart to filter the chart to display only Europe and North America properties.

o. Add a Quarter 2 slicer to the PivotTable. Use the slicer to display the revenue for the first half of the year only.

p. Check the PivotChart to be sure it displays only the filtered data.

q. On the PivotTable sheet, change the slicer caption to **Grouped Quarters**. (*Hint:* Use the Slicer group on the Slicer tab.)

r. Add a slicer style of Light Blue, Slicer Style Dark 1, then move the slicer below the Pivot Table.

s. Using **FIGURE 8-28** as a guide, configure the slicer so the buttons appear side by side and there is space above and below the text in each button. Resize the slicer if necessary. (Hint: Use the Buttons and Size groups on the Slicer tab.)

t. Add your name to the center section of the three worksheet footers, save the workbook, then preview the PivotTable and the PivotChart. Close the workbook and close Excel. Submit the workbook to your instructor.

FIGURE 8-28

Excel

Visual Workshop

Open IL_EX_8-5.xlsx from the location where you store your Data Files, then save it as **IL_EX_8_Insurance**. Using the data on the First Quarter worksheet, create the PivotTable and slicer shown in **FIGURE 8-29** on a new worksheet named **PivotTable**. Format the table, slicer, and data as necessary to match the figure. (*Hint:* The PivotTable has been formatted using the Ice Blue, Pivot Style Medium 9 Pivot Style.) Add your name to the PivotTable footer, then preview the PivotTable. Save the workbook, close the workbook, close Excel, then submit the workbook to your instructor.

FIGURE 8-29

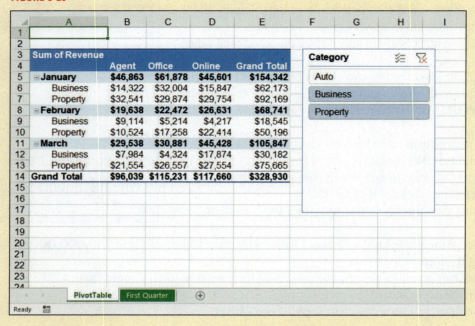

Analyzing Data with PivotTables

Automating Worksheet Tasks

CASE ▶ Cheri McNeil, manager of the Boston office at JCL, is in the process of reviewing the annual revenue generated by each recruiter in the office. She created a worksheet with test data that will act as a form for the collection of data for each recruiter. Cheri asks you to create macros to calculate the annual revenue total and evaluate whether quotas for bonus payments are met.

Module Objectives

After completing this module, you will be able to:

- Plan a macro
- Enable a macro
- Record a macro
- Run a macro
- Edit a macro
- Assign a macro to a button
- Assign a macro to a command button
- Assign a macro to a form control

Files You Will Need

IL_EX_9-1.xlsx
IL_EX_9-2.xlsx
IL_EX_9-3.xlsx
IL_EX_9-4.xlsx
IL_EX_9-5.xlsx

Plan a Macro

**Learning
Outcomes**
• Plan a macro
• Determine the
storage location
for a macro

A **macro** is a named set of instructions, written in the Visual Basic programming language, that perform tasks automatically in a specified order. You can create macros to automate Excel tasks that you perform frequently. You don't need to know the Visual Basic programming language to create a macro, because instead of writing code you can simply record a series of actions using the macro recorder built into Excel. When recording a macro, the sequence of actions in a macro is important, so you need to plan the macro carefully before you begin recording. **CASE** *You need to create a macro to calculate the total revenue for the Boston office. You work with Cheri to plan the macro.*

DETAILS

To plan a macro, use the following guidelines:

- ### Assign the macro a descriptive name

    The first character of a macro name must be a letter; the remaining characters can be letters, numbers, or underscores. Letters can be uppercase or lowercase. Spaces are not allowed in macro names; use underscores instead. You can press SHIFT+HYPHEN (-) to enter an underscore character. You decide to name the macro AddTotal. See **TABLE 9-1** for a list of macros that could be created to automate other common tasks in JCL spreadsheets.

- ### Write out the steps the macro will perform

    This planning helps eliminate careless errors. After a discussion with Cheri, you write down a description of the new AddTotal macro, as shown in **FIGURE 9-1**.

- ### Decide how you will perform the actions you want to record

    You can use the mouse, the keyboard, or a combination of the two. For the new AddTotal macro, you want to use both the mouse and the keyboard.

- ### Practice the steps you want Excel to record, and write them down

    During your meeting with Cheri, you write down the sequence of actions to include in the macro.

- ### Decide where to store the description of the macro and the macro itself

    Macros can be stored in an active workbook, in a new workbook, or in the **Personal Macro Workbook**, a special workbook that can contain macros that are available to any open workbook; it opens whenever you start Excel to make macros available at any time but is hidden by default. You decide to store the macro in the active workbook.

FIGURE 9-1: Handwritten description of planned macro

Macro to calculate the annual revenue total

Name: AddTotal

Description: Calculates the annual revenue

Steps: 1. Select cell A9
                2. Enter Total
                3. Click the Enter button
                4. Select cell B9
                5. Click the AutoSum button
                6. Click the Enter button

TABLE 9-1: Possible macros and their descriptive names

description of macro	descriptive name
Enter a frequently used division, such as Technology	TechDiv
Enter a frequently used company name, such as JCL	Company_Name
Print the active worksheet on a single page, in landscape orientation	FitToLand
Add a footer to a worksheet	FooterStamp
Add a total to a worksheet	AddTotal

Enable a Macro

Learning Outcomes
- Create a macro-enabled workbook
- Enable macros by changing a work-book's security level

Because a macro may contain a virus, a destructive type of computer program that can damage your computer files, the default security setting in Excel disables macros from running. Although a workbook containing a macro will open, if macros are disabled they will not function. You can manually change the Excel security setting to allow macros to run if you know a macro came from a trusted source. When saving a workbook with a macro, you need to save it as a macro-enabled workbook with the extension .xlsm.

CASE ▶ *Cheri asks you to change the security level to enable all macros. For your security, as well as that of others who are sharing your computer, you will change the security level back to the default setting after you create and run your macros.*

STEPS

1. **sam** ⬇ **Start Excel, open IL_EX_9-1xlsx from the location where you store your Data Files, click the File tab, click Save As, navigate to where you store your Data Files, in the Save As dialog box click the Save as type list arrow, click Excel Macro-Enabled Workbook (*.xlsm), in the File name text box type IL_EX_9_Bonus, then click Save**

   The security settings that enable macros are available on the Developer tab on the ribbon. The Developer tab does not appear by default.

QUICK TIP
If the Developer tab is already displayed on your Ribbon, skip Steps 2 and 3.

2. **Click the File tab on the ribbon, click Options, then click Customize Ribbon in the category list**

   The Customize the Ribbon options open in the Excel Options dialog box, as shown in **FIGURE 9-2**.

3. **Click the Developer check box in the Main Tabs area on the right side of the screen to add a checkmark if necessary, then click OK**

   The Developer tab appears on the Ribbon. You are ready to change the security settings.

QUICK TIP
For increased security, you can click the security setting "Disable all macros with notification" instead. If you are using that setting, you need to click Enable Content to run macros in an .xlsm file.

4. **Click the Developer tab on the ribbon, then click the Macro Security button in the Code group**

   The Trust Center dialog box opens.

5. **Click Macro Settings in the category list if necessary, click the Enable VBA macros (not recommended; potentially dangerous code can run) option button to select it, as shown in FIGURE 9-3, then click OK**

   The dialog box closes. Macros will remain enabled until you disable them by deselecting the Enable all macros option. As you work with Excel, you should disable macros when you are not working with them.

Adding security to your macro projects

To add security to your projects, you can add a digital signature to the project. A **digital signature** is an electronic attachment not visible in the file that verifies the authenticity of the author or the version of the file by comparing the digital signature to a digital certificate. In Excel, it guarantees your project hasn't been altered since it was signed. Sign macros only after you have tested them and are ready to distribute them. If the code in a digitally signed macro project is changed in any way, its digital signature is removed. To add a digital signature to a Visual Basic project, select the project that you want to sign in the Visual Basic Project Explorer window, click the Tools menu in the Visual Basic Editor, click Digital Signature, click Choose, select the certificate, then click OK twice. If there aren't any certificates available, you will be directed to contact your administrator or insert a smart card. Digital certificates and smart cards, which store digital certificates, can be issued by your administrator. There are also third-party certification authorities that issue certificates that are trusted by Microsoft. When you add a digital signature to a project, the macro project is automatically re-signed whenever it is saved on your computer.

FIGURE 9-2: Excel Options dialog box

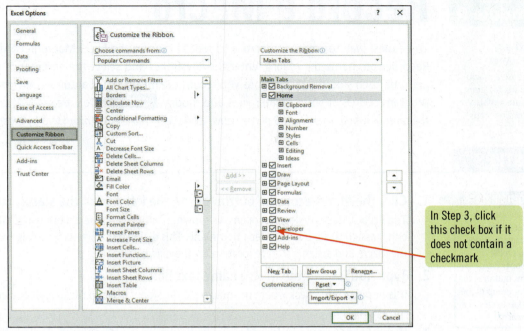

In Step 3, click this check box if it does not contain a checkmark

FIGURE 9-3: Trust Center dialog box

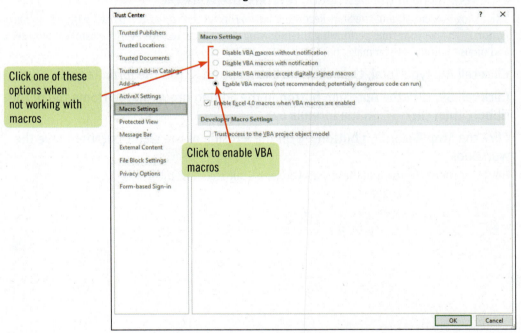

Click one of these options when not working with macros

Click to enable VBA macros

Disabling macros

To prevent viruses from running on your computer, you should disable all macros when you are not working with them. To disable macros, click the Developer tab, then click the Macro Security button in the Code group. Clicking any of the first three options disables macros. The first option disables all macros without notifying you. The second option notifies you when macros are disabled, and the third option allows only digitally signed macros to run.

Record a Macro

Learning Outcomes
- Choose a macro storage location
- Create a macro by recording steps

The easiest way to create a macro is to record it using the Excel Macro Recorder. You turn the Macro Recorder on, name the macro, enter the keystrokes and select the commands you want the macro to perform, then stop the recorder. As you record the macro, Excel automatically translates each action into program code that you can later view and modify. **CASE** *You are ready to create a macro that totals the revenue values in column B of the active worksheet. You create this macro by recording your actions.*

STEPS

QUICK TIP
You can also click the Record Macro button in the Code group on the Developer tab or the Macros button in the Macros group of the View tab to record a new macro.

1. **Click the Start Recording button 🖺 on the left side of the status bar**

   The Record Macro dialog box opens, as shown in **FIGURE 9-4**. The default name Macro1 is selected. You can either assign this name or enter a new name. This dialog box also lets you assign a shortcut key for running the macro and assign a storage location for the macro.

2. **Type AddTotal in the Macro name text box**

   It is important to check where the macro will be stored because the default choice is the last location that was selected.

3. **If the Store macro in box does not display "This Workbook," click the Store macro in list arrow, then click This Workbook**

4. **Type your name in the Description text box, then click OK**

   The dialog box closes, and the Start Recording button on the status bar is replaced with a Stop Recording button 🔲. Take your time performing the following steps. Excel records every keystroke, menu selection, and mouse action that you make, not the amount of time you take to record them.

5. **Click cell A9, type Total, then click the Enter button ✓ on the formula bar**

6. **Click cell B9, click the AutoSum button in the Editing group on the Home tab of the ribbon, then click ✓ on the formula bar**

QUICK TIP
You can also click the Stop Recording button in the Code group on the Developer tab to stop recording a macro.

7. **Click the Stop Recording button 🔲 on the left side of the status bar, then save the workbook**

   FIGURE 9-5 shows the result of the actions you took while recording the macro.

FIGURE 9-4: Record Macro dialog box

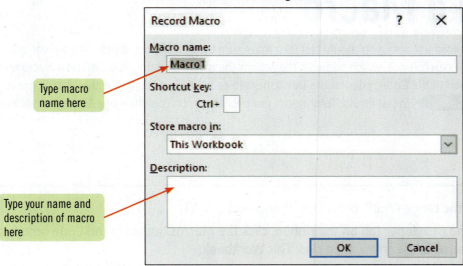

Type macro name here

Type your name and description of macro here

FIGURE 9-5: Worksheet with new data and formula

Run a Macro

Learning Outcomes
- Display selected macros
- Run a macro using the Macro dialog box

Once you record a macro, you should test it to make sure that the actions it performs are correct. To test a macro, you **run** (play) it, which performs the actions the macro contains. You can run a macro using the Macros button in the Code group of the Developer tab or the Macros button in the Macros group of the View tab. **CASE** ▸ *To test the AddTotal macro, you clear the contents of the range A9:B9 and add test data.*

STEPS

QUICK TIP

To delete a macro, click the macro name in the Macro dialog box, click Delete, then click Yes to confirm the deletion.

1. **Select the range A9:B9, press DEL, then select cell A1**

2. **Click the Developer tab on the ribbon, click the Macros button in the Code group, click the Macros in list arrow, then click This Workbook**

   The Macro dialog box, shown in **FIGURE 9-6**, displays all the macros contained in the current workbook.

3. **Click AddTotal in the Macro name list if necessary, then click Run**

   The macro quickly plays back the steps you recorded in the previous lesson. When the macro is finished, your screen should look like **FIGURE 9-7**.

4. **Select the range A9:B9, press DEL, then select cell A1**

   The total label and the total value are deleted to test the macro again.

QUICK TIP

To create a button on the Quick Access Toolbar that runs a macro, click the Customize Quick Access Toolbar button ⬇, click More Commands, click the Choose commands from list arrow, click Macros, click the desired macro in the list, click Add, then click OK.

5. **Click the View tab on the ribbon, then click the Macros button in the Macros group**

6. **Verify that This Workbook appears in the Macros in box, click AddTotal in the Macro name list if necessary, click Run, then save your work**

Running a macro automatically

You can create a macro that automatically performs certain tasks when the workbook in which it is saved opens. This is useful for actions you want to do every time you open a workbook. For example, you may always import data from an external data source into a workbook or format the worksheet data in a certain way. To create a macro that automatically runs when you open the workbook, you need to name the macro Auto_Open and save it in that workbook.

FIGURE 9-6: Macro dialog box

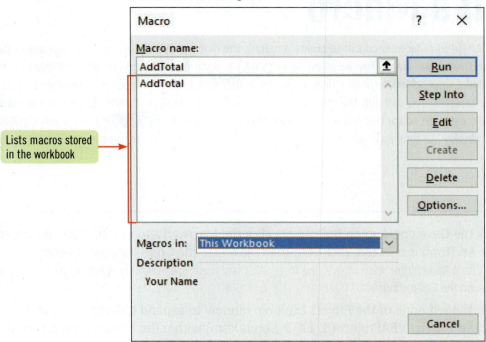

Lists macros stored in the workbook

FIGURE 9-7: Result of running AddTotal macro

Total label and total revenue in row 9

Creating a main procedure

A sequence of VBA statements is called a procedure. For this reason, macros are often referred to as procedures. When you routinely need to run several macros one after another, you can save time by executing them in one procedure. This type of procedure, which contains multiple procedures that run sequentially, is referred to as the **main procedure**. To create a main procedure, you type a **Call statement**, a Visual Basic statement that retrieves a procedure, using the format Call *procedurename*, where *procedurename* is the name of the procedure, or macro, you want to run. For example, Call AddTotal in a main procedure would run the AddTotal macro.

Edit a Macro

When you use the Macro Recorder to create a macro, the macro instructions, called **program code**, are written in the **Visual Basic for Applications (VBA)** programming language, and the macro is stored as a **module**, or program code container, attached to the workbook. After you record a macro, you might need to change it. You can edit the macro code, also called a procedure, directly using the **Visual Basic Editor**, a full-screen editor that lets you display and edit lines of code. **CASE** ▶ *Cheri wants the AddTotal macro to display the total label aligned right in the cell. This is a small change you can easily make by editing the macro code.*

STEPS

TROUBLE

If the Properties window does not appear in the lower-left portion of your screen, click the Properties Window button 🖼 on the Visual Basic toolbar, then resize it as shown in the figure if necessary.

1. **Click the Developer tab on the ribbon, click the Macros button in the Code group, make sure AddTotal is selected, click Edit, then maximize the Code window, if necessary**

   The Visual Basic Editor starts, displaying three windows: the Project Explorer window, the Properties window, and the Code window.

2. **Drag the left edge of the Project Explorer window to expand it if necessary, click Module 1 in the VBAProject (IL_EX_9_Bonus.xlsm) within the Project Explorer window if it's not already selected, then examine the steps in the macro**

   Compare your screen to **FIGURE 9-8**. Excel has translated your keystrokes and commands into macro code. For example, the line Range("A9").Select was generated when you selected cell A9. In the first line of the macro code, the keyword Sub indicates that this is a Sub procedure, a series of Visual Basic statements that perform an action. The code lines in green, beginning with an apostrophe, are comments that help explain the procedure. Items that appear in blue are keywords, which are words Excel recognizes as part of the VBA programming language. Notice that twice in the procedure, a line of code (or statement) selects a range, and then subsequent lines act on that selection. The lines that begin with ActiveCell.Formula insert the information enclosed in quotation marks into the active, selected, cell. The last line, End Sub, indicates the end of the Sub procedure.

QUICK TIP

You can also open the Editor by clicking the Developer tab, then clicking the Visual Basic button in the Code group.

3. **Click at the end of the line Range("A9").Select, press ENTER, then type With Selection**

   You have entered the first line of code in a With Selection/End With block, which allows you to change all properties within the block at once.

QUICK TIP

Comments are used to document VBA code. To enter a comment, you must type an apostrophe (') before the comment text so the program doesn't interpret the statement as a command. Comments appear in green after you press ENTER.

4. **Click at the end of the line ActiveCell.FormulaR1C1 = "Total", press ENTER, type .HorizontalAlignment = xlRight, press ENTER, type End With, then compare your work with the code shown in FIGURE 9-9**

   You have added a With Selection/End With block to the procedure, so that you only need to refer to the selection once, rather than multiple times.

5. **Click File on the menu bar, then click Close and Return to Microsoft Excel**

   You want to rerun the AddTotal macro to make sure the macro reflects the change you made using the Visual Basic Editor.

QUICK TIP

You can return to Excel without closing the module by clicking the View Microsoft Excel button 🖼 on the Visual Basic Editor toolbar.

6. **Select the range A9:B9, press DEL, then activate cell A1**

7. **Click the Macros button in the Code group on the Developer tab, make sure AddTotal is selected, then click Run**

   The Total label is right-aligned in the cell, as shown in **FIGURE 9-10**.

8. **Save the workbook**

FIGURE 9-8: Visual Basic Editor

Properties window button

Comments appear in green

Project Explorer window with Module1 selected

Properties window showing properties for Module1

Code window

FIGURE 9-9: Edited Visual Basic code

```
Sub AddTotal()
'
' AddTotal Macro
' Your Name
'
'
    Range("A9").Select
    With Selection
    ActiveCell.FormulaR1C1 = "Total"
    .HorizontalAlignment = xlRight
    End With
    Range("B9").Select
    ActiveCell.FormulaR1C1 = "=SUM(R[-4]C:R[-1]C)"
End Sub
```

FIGURE 9-10: Result of running the edited AddTotal macro

	A	B	C	D	E	F	G	H	I	J
1	JCL		Recruiter #							
2	**Annual Bonus Report**		Bonus Status:							
3	Quota:		Quota Status:							
4	**Quarter**	**Revenue**								
5	Q1	$1,000.00								
6	Q2	$2,000.00								
7	Q3	$3,000.00								
8	Q4	$4,000.00								
9	Total	$10,000.00								
10										
11										

Total label is aligned right

Using relative referencing when creating a macro

By default, Excel records absolute cell references in macros, but you can record a macro's actions based on the relative position of the active cell by clicking the Use Relative References button in the Code group prior to recording the action. For example, when you create a macro using the default setting of absolute referencing, bolding the range A1:A3 will always bold that range when the macro is run. However, if you click the Use Relative References button when recording the macro before bolding the range, then running the macro will not necessarily result in bolding the range A1:A3. The range that is bolded will depend on the location of the active cell when the macro is run. If the active cell is F1, then the range F1:F3 will be bolded. Selecting the Use Relative References button highlights the button name, indicating it is active, and it remains active until you click it again to deselect it.

Assign a Macro to a Button

**Learning
Outcomes**
• Create a button
shape in a
worksheet
• Assign a macro to
a button

When you create macros for others who will use your workbook, you might want to make the macros more visible so they're easier to use. You can create a button object on your worksheet and then assign the button to a macro, so that when users click the button the macro runs. **CASE** ▶ *To make it easier for Cheri to run the AddTotal macro, you decide to assign it to a button on the workbook. You begin by creating the button.*

STEPS

QUICK TIP
To format a macro
button using 3-D
effects, clip art,
photographs, fills,
and shadows, right-
click it, select Format
Shape from the
shortcut menu, then
select the desired
options in the
Format Shape pane.

1. **Select the range A9:B9, then press DEL**

2. **Click the Insert tab on the ribbon, click the Shapes button in the Illustrations group, then click the first rectangle shape under Rectangles**
   The mouse pointer changes to a ╋ symbol.

3. **Click at the upper-left corner of cell A10, then drag ╋ to the lower-right corner of cell A11**
   Compare your screen to **FIGURE 9-11**.

4. **Type Add Total, click the Home tab on the ribbon, click the Center button ☰ in the Alignment group, then click the Middle Align button ☰ in the Alignment group**
   Now that you have created the button and added a text label, you are ready to assign the macro to it.

5. **Right-click the new button, then on the shortcut menu click Assign Macro**
   The Assign Macro dialog box opens.

6. **Click AddTotal under Macro name, then click OK**
   You have assigned the AddTotal macro to the button.

7. **Click any cell to deselect the button, then click the button**
   The AddTotal macro runs, and the total label and value appear in the range A9:B9, as shown in **FIGURE 9-12**.

8. **Save the workbook**

QUICK TIP
You can move a
shape button by
placing the cursor
on the shape and
dragging it to a
new location on the
worksheet.

FIGURE 9-11: Button shape

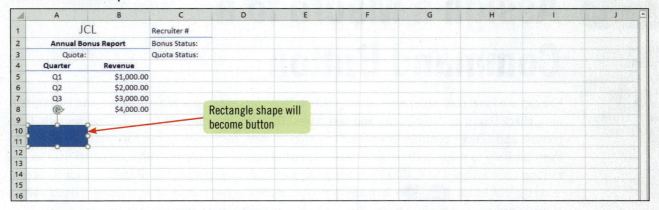

Rectangle shape will become button

FIGURE 9-12: Result of clicking the macro button

Excel

Assign a Macro to a Command Button

You can use Excel controls to run macros. Controls help users enter data in a worksheet, and include buttons, check boxes, option buttons, and text boxes. There are two different types of Excel controls: form controls and ActiveX controls. In addition to collecting data, form controls can have macros assigned to them, similarly to shape buttons. An ActiveX command button contains the VBA code rather than having existing code assigned to it. When you use an ActiveX command button, the procedure code is entered using the VBA Editor. **CASE** ▶ *Recruiters in the Boston office receive bonuses when they meet annual revenue quotas. Cheri asks you to add a button that can be used to determine if a recruiter's annual quota is met.*

STEPS

1. **Click the Developer tab** on the ribbon, click the **Insert button** in the Controls group, then click the **Command Button (ActiveX Control) icon** ▢

2. **Click at the upper-left corner of cell A13**, then drag ╋ to the **lower-right corner of cell A14**

   An ActiveX control named CommandButton1 is displayed on the worksheet. The button name isn't fully displayed because the button isn't large enough. The Design Mode button in the Controls group is selected, indicating you are working in Design Mode, where properties can be changed.

   QUICK TIP
   If you want a caption on the selected control to wrap to the next line, set the WordWrap property to True.

3. **Click the Properties button** in the Controls group, on the Alphabetic tab in the Properties pane double-click the **(Name) box**, enter **QuotaButton**, double-click the **Caption box**, enter **Check Quota**, click the **BackColor box**, click the **arrow**, scroll if necessary and click **Active Title Bar** on the System tab, click the **Font box**, click the **... button**, scroll to and click **Times New Roman** in the Font dialog box, click **OK**, compare your Properties pane to **FIGURE 9-13**, then close the Properties pane

   The name of the command button is used internally to reference it. The caption name is displayed as a label for the button.

4. **Click the View Code button** in the Controls group

   The Visual Basic Editor opens. You will enter the code for the button in the Code window. This button will compare the revenue total in cell B9 with the quota in cell B3. If the total revenue is less than the quota, the text "Missed Quota" will be entered in cell D3; otherwise "Met Quota" will be entered. To specify an action based on certain conditions, you will use an If...Then...Else conditional statement.

   QUICK TIP
   You can add a form control button to a worksheet and assign a macro to it. Click the Developer tab, click the Insert button in the Controls group, then click the Button (Form Control) ▢ in the first row. After drawing a button, the Assign Macro dialog box opens where you can select a macro for the button, then click OK.

5. **Click the General arrow** at the top of the Code window, click **QuotaButton**, then type the procedure code between the Private Sub and End Sub lines exactly as shown in **FIGURE 9-14**, making sure not to duplicate the Private Sub and End Sub lines

6. **Click File** on the menu bar, click **Close and Return to Microsoft Excel**, then click the **Design Mode button** in the Controls group

   Design Mode is turned off. This mode allows you to change the properties and enter Visual Basic Code for a command button, but for a button to function, it needs to be off.

7. **Click cell B3**, type **11000**, press **ENTER**, then click the **Check Quota button**

   You need to enter a quota value to test the macro. The text *Missed Quota* is entered in cell D3.

8. **Click cell B3**, enter **8000**, click the **Check Quota button**, then save the workbook

   The new test quota data checks the message entered when the quota is met. The text *Met Quota* is entered in cell D3.

FIGURE 9-13: Properties pane

Name

BackColor

Caption

Font

FIGURE 9-14: Code for ActiveX command button

```
Private Sub QuotaButton_Click()

'If the total revenue is less than B3 then
    'insert "Missed Quota" in cell D3

    If Range("B9") <= Range("B3") Then

        Range("D3").Select
        ActiveCell.Formula = "Missed Quota"

    'otherwise, insert "Met Quota" in cell D3

    Else
        Range("D3").Select
        ActiveCell.Formula = "Met Quota"

    End If

    Range("A1").Select

End Sub
```

Working with ActiveX text boxes

To add an ActiveX text box into a worksheet, click the Developer tab on the ribbon, click the Insert button in the Controls group, then click the Text Box (ActiveX Control) button abl under ActiveX Controls. Click the upper-left corner of the cell where you want to locate the text box, then drag ┼ to draw the desired shape.

To edit the text box's properties, switch to Design Mode if necessary, then click the Properties button in the Controls group. In the LinkedCell box, enter the cell where you want the text box data to be displayed. The Shadow property provides the options True for a shadow and False for no shadow. **FIGURE 9-15** shows the properties for a text box with the name Notes in the range A1:D2. Because the LinkedCell in the properties is Quarter1!A9, text entered in the text box will appear on the Quarter1 worksheet in cell A9.

FIGURE 9-15: ActiveX text box properties

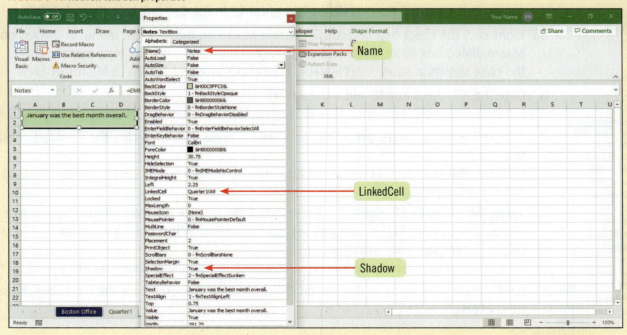

Name

LinkedCell

Shadow

Excel

Assign a Macro to a Form Control

Learning Outcomes
- Create a Check Box form control
- Assign a cell link to a check box control

Form controls such as check boxes and option buttons are often used on a worksheet to help with data entry. To perform an action based on entered data, you assign a macro to a form control. **CASE** ▶ *JCL recruiters who meet their revenue quotas receive bonuses. Although revenue and quota data are tracked for contract workers as a consideration for future contracts, contract workers are not eligible for bonuses. To make it easier for Cheri to determine if a recruiter should receive a bonus, you will add check boxes to the worksheet form and enter macros for each check box.*

STEPS

QUICK TIP

In addition to changing a check box caption, you can change the internal name of the check box object by right-clicking the check box object, then entering the object name in the Name Box.

1. Click the **Developer tab** on the ribbon if necessary, click the **Insert button** in the Controls group, click the **Check Box (Form Control) button shape** ☑ in the first row, click the **upper-left corner of cell A16**, drag ╋ to the **lower-right corner of that cell**, select the **text label** for the control, then type **JCL**

2. Click the **Properties button** in the Controls group, in the Format Control dialog box click the **Control tab** if necessary, enter **E1** in the Cell link box, then click **OK**

   The cell entered in the Cell link box will display TRUE if the check box contains a checkmark.

3. **Right-click** the **check box object**, click **Assign Macro** on the shortcut menu, in the Assign Macro dialog box type **JCL** in the Macro name box, click **New**, enter the code shown in **FIGURE 9-16**, click **File**, then click **Close and Return to Microsoft Excel**

4. Click any cell outside the check box object to deselect it, click the **Insert button** in the Controls group, click the **Check Box (Form Control) button** ☑ in the first row, click at the **upper-left corner** of cell **B16**, drag ╋ to the lower-right corner of the cell, select the **text label** for the object, enter **Contract**, click the **Properties button** in the Controls group, in the Format Control dialog box enter **E2** in the Cell link box, then click **OK**

5. **Right-click** the **check box object**, click **Assign Macro** on the shortcut menu, in the Assign Macro dialog box enter **Contract** in the Macro name box, click the **New button**, enter the code shown in **FIGURE 9-17**, click **File**, then click **Close and Return to Microsoft Excel**

6. Click the **JCL check box** to add a checkmark

   Cell E1, the linked cell, displays the value TRUE and Annual Bonus is entered into cell D2.

7. Click cell **D2** if necessary, press **DEL**, click cell **E1**, press **DEL**, then click the **Contract check box**

   Cell E2, the linked cell for the Contract check box, displays the value "TRUE" and the message "No Annual Bonus" is entered into cell D2.

QUICK TIP

When you finish working with macros you should disable all macros by clicking the Developer tab, clicking the Macro Security button in the Code group, clicking Macro Settings if necessary, clicking the Disable all macros with notification option button to select it, then clicking OK.

8. Select the range **E1:E2**, right-click the selected range, click **Format Cells** on the shortcut menu, click **Custom** in the Category list, select **General** in the Type: box, enter **;;;**, click **OK**, then compare your worksheet to **FIGURE 9-18**

   The custom number format ;;; improves the appearance of the worksheet by hiding the values in cells.

9. **sam** ⬆ Enter your name in the Boston Office worksheet footer, save the workbook, then close Excel

FIGURE 9-16: Code for JCL check box

```
Sub JCL()

If Range("E1") = True And Range("D3") = "Met Quota" Then

        Range("D2").Select
        ActiveCell.Formula = "Annual Bonus"

    Else

    If Range("E1") = True And Range("D3") = "Missed Quota" Then

        Range("D2").Select
        ActiveCell.Formula = "No Annual Bonus"

    End If
    End If

End Sub
```

FIGURE 9-17: Code for Contract check box control

```
Sub Contract()

If Range("E2") = True Then

        Range("D2").Select
        ActiveCell.Formula = "No Annual Bonus"

End If

End Sub
```

FIGURE 9-18: Worksheet with check boxes

Working with option buttons

You can add option button form controls to a worksheet to allow users to select from a list of available options. To add an option button to a worksheet, click the Developer tab, click the Insert button in the Controls group, then click the Option Button Form Control ◉ in the first row and drag ➕ to draw the option button. After adding the desired option buttons, right-click an option button, click Format Control on the shortcut menu, then enter the desired linked cell in the Cell link box in the Format Control dialog box. The clicked option button position will be entered in the linked cell. For example, if you click the second option button, the number *2* will be entered in the linked cell.

You can use an index list (a range to which an Index function refers) with this type of form control to facilitate data entry using option buttons. The index list range consists of all the options, in the order they appear on the worksheet, as option buttons. Then, an Index formula is added to the worksheet with the syntax @INDEX(range, row) where *range* equals the list of options corresponding to the option buttons and *row* is the linked cell that holds the number of the clicked option. The result of this

Index function is that the range value, at the given row position, is placed in the cell with the Index function. For example, **FIGURE 9-19** shows option buttons for the four divisions at JCL. The cell link for the option buttons is B1 and the Index formula in cell D1 references the range named Divisions, which is F1:F4 on the worksheet. The named range can be located on a different worksheet. Clicking the Technical option button places the number *2* (the second option button) in cell B1 (the linked cell), and the index function returns the second entry in the range list.

FIGURE 9-19: Worksheet with option buttons

Practice

Skills Review

1. Plan and enable a macro.
a. You need to plan a macro that enters a Total label in cell D17 and a formula in cell E17 that totals the managed assets in the range E3:E16.
b. Write out the steps the macro will perform, and plan to store the macro in the workbook where you will use it.
c. Start Excel, open IL_EX_9-2.xlsx from the location where you store your Data Files, then save it as a macro-enabled workbook named **IL_EX_9_Assets**. (*Hint*: The file will have the file extension .xlsm.)
d. Use the Excel Options feature to display the Developer tab if it does not appear on the Ribbon.
e. Using the Trust Center dialog box, enable all macros.

2. Record a macro.
a. Open the Record Macro dialog box.
b. Name the new macro **Total**, store it in the current workbook, and enter your name in the Description text box.
c. Record the macro, entering the label **Total** in cell D17.
d. Right-align the label in cell D17.
e. Add bold formatting to the label in cell D17.
f. Use AutoSum to enter a function in cell E17 that totals the range E3:E16.
g. Stop the recorder, then save the workbook.

3. Run a macro.
a. Delete the contents of the range D17:E17.
b. Run the Total macro.
c. Confirm that the total text is right-aligned and bolded in cell D17.
d. Confirm that the total assets appear in cell E17.
e. Clear the cell entries generated by running the Total macro.
f. Save the workbook.

4. Edit a macro.
a. Open the Macros dialog box, then open the Total macro for editing.
b. In the Visual Basic window, change the line of code Selection.Font.Bold = True to **Selection.Font.Bold = False**.
c. Use the Close and Return to Microsoft Excel command on the File menu to return to Excel.
d. Test the Total macro, verifying that the Total label is not bold.
e. Save the workbook.

5. Assign a macro to a button.
a. Clear the cell entries generated by running the Total macro.
b. Using the first rectangle shape under Rectangles on the Shapes palette, draw a rectangle in cell A17.
c. Label the button with the text **Total Assets**, then center and middle align the text.
d. Assign the Total macro to the button, then test the button.
e. Verify that the Total label and the total assets are entered in the range D17:E17.

Skills Review (continued)

6. Assign a macro to a command button.

  a. Add an ActiveX command button control in the range A18:B19.

  b. Add a caption to the button with the text **Target** and change the BackColor property to System Active Title Bar.

  c. Enter the macro code shown in **FIGURE 9-20** in the Visual Basic code window. (*Hint*: Remember to use the list arrow at the upper left of the VBA Editor to select the command object.)

  d. Save the macro code and test the Target button. (*Hint*: Remember to deselect the Design Mode button before testing the button.)

  e. Verify that "Met Target" is displayed in cell F2.

FIGURE 9-20

```
Private Sub CommandButton1_Click()

If Range("E17") <= Range("G1") Then

        Range("F2").Select
        ActiveCell.Formula = "Missed Target"

    Else
        Range("F2").Select
        ActiveCell.Formula = "Met Target"

    End If

    Range("A1").Select

End Sub
```

7. Assign a macro to a form control.

  a. Add a form control check box in the range A21:B21.

  b. Change the name of the check box to **Jill Hurley**.

  c. Format the check box to enter the cell link of J1.

  d. Assign a new macro to the check box by opening the Visual Basic code window for the object and entering the code shown in **FIGURE 9-21**.

FIGURE 9-21

```
Sub CheckBox2_Click()

If Range("J1") = True Then

        Range("I1").Select
        ActiveCell.Formula = "Boston Office Manager"


End If

End Sub
```

  e. Save the macro code, close the VBA window, deselect the check box, then select it.

  f. Widen column I to fully display the text in cell I1 and verify that the text "Boston Office Manager" is displayed in that cell. Verify that "True" is displayed in cell J1.

  g. Format the text in cell J1 to hide the value. (*Hint*: Switch to Design Mode to make this change.)

  h. Add your name to the Texas Office footer, then save the workbook.

  i. Disable all macros with notification if you are finished working with macros.

  j. Close the workbook, then close Excel.

Excel

Independent Challenge 1

As the office manager of Riverwalk Medical Clinic, you want to develop macros to help work more efficiently with the weekly time sheets. You will modify a worksheet that can be used as a form to collect time sheet data for therapists from the OT and PT departments. You will enter sample data in the form, add macros within the workbook to format the worksheet, calculate the total weekly hours, and determine whether there are overtime hours for the week.

    a. Start Excel, open IL_EX_9-3.xlsx from where you store your Data Files, then save it as a macro-enabled workbook called **IL_EX_9_Timesheet**.

    b. Check your macro security setting on the Developer tab to be sure that all macros are enabled.

    c. Enter the data shown in **FIGURE 9-22**.

FIGURE 9-22

    d. Create a macro named **Format_Total**, enter your name in the macro description, then save it in the current workbook. Record the macro using the following instructions:
- Add a row to the top of the worksheet.
- Add the text **Riverwalk Medical Clinic** to the inserted top row and format the text using the Title cell style.
- Merge and Center the Riverwalk Medical Clinic text over the range A1:D1.
- In cell B11 enter a function to total the range B5:B10. (*Hint*: Ignore the formula warning that the date isn't included in the summed cells.)
- End the macro recording.

    e. Create a button using the first Rectangle shape tool in the range A12:B13. Label the button **Format & Total**. Center and middle align the button label.

    f. Assign the Format_Total macro to the new button.

    g. Delete the first row of the worksheet and the total in cell B10, then test the Format_Total macro using the Format & Total button.

    h. Insert an ActiveX command button in the range A15:B16. Using the properties panel, change the caption of the button to **Check Overtime**.

    i. Enter the ActiveX command button code shown in **FIGURE 9-23**. (*Hint*: Don't forget to select the Command button in the VBA window by clicking the list arrow at the top of the code window.)

Independent Challenge 1 (continued)

FIGURE 9-23

```
Private Sub CommandButton1_Click()


  If Range("B11") <= "40" Then

        Range("D2").Select
        ActiveCell.Formula = "No Overtime"


    Else
        Range("D2").Select
        ActiveCell.Formula = Range("B11") - "40"

    End If

End Sub
```

j. Click the Check Overtime button to display overtime hours. (*Hint*: Don't forget to deselect Design Mode before using the button.)

k. In cells A18 and B18, create two form control check boxes, the first named **PT** and the second named **OT**. Assign cell E1 as the cell link for the first check box and cell E2 as the cell link for the second check box.

l. Enter the check box code shown in FIGURE 9-24 for the first check box.

m. Enter the check box code for the second check box by copying the code for the first check box and pasting it in the code window for the second check box.

n. Make sure both check boxes aren't checked, exit Design Mode, then check the PT check box. Verify that "PT" is shown in the worksheet header. Delete True from cell E1, then click the OT check box. Verify that "OT" is shown in the worksheet header.

o. Format the range E1:E2 to hide the values.

p. Enter your name in the worksheet footer. Save the file, disable all macros with notification if you are finished working with macros, close the workbook, then close Excel.

FIGURE 9-24

```
Sub CheckBox2_Click()

If Range("E1") = "True" Then

  ActiveWindow.View = xlPageLayoutView
    With ActiveSheet.PageSetup
     .CenterHeader = "PT"
    End With
    Range("A1").Select
    Application.Wait (Now + TimeValue("0:00:02"))
    ActiveWindow.View = xlNormalView

Else

If Range("E2") = "True" Then
ActiveWindow.View = xlPageLayoutView
    With ActiveSheet.PageSetup
     .CenterHeader = "OT"
    End With
    Range("A1").Select
    Application.Wait (Now + TimeValue("0:00:02"))
    ActiveWindow.View = xlNormalView

End If
End If
End Sub
```

Excel

Independent Challenge 2

You are an assistant to the CFO at a national real estate firm. As part of your work, you analyze royalty payments for different offices of the company. The company is planning to expand and offer multiple offices in regions of the country and will begin noting the office's region as documentation on each worksheet. You will create option button form controls to look up the region for an office. You will also create a macro to total royalty payments. (*Note:* Remember to disable all macros when you are finished working with them.)

a. Start Excel, open IL_EX_9-4.xlsx from the location where you store your Data Files, then save it as a macro-enabled workbook called **IL_EX_9_Region**.

b. Check your macro security settings to confirm that macros are enabled.

c. With the Payments sheet active, record a macro with the name **Totals**. Store the macro in this workbook, add your name to the description, and assign the macro a shortcut key combination of CTRL+SHIFT+F (or a different combination if necessary) and store it in the current workbook. (*Hint*: Use the Shortcut key combination in the Record Macro dialog box.)

The macro should do the following:

- Total the residential, commercial, and rental payments in column F.
- Total the Q1, Q2, Q3, Q4, and Total columns in row 6.
- Change the page orientation to landscape.

d. After you finish recording the macro, change the page orientation to Portrait, then delete the totals in the ranges B6:F6 and F3:F5. Test the macro using the shortcut key combination you set in Step B. Verify the macro results are correct.

e. Edit the Totals macro to insert an instruction that formats the totals as bold. To do this, add the following code lines before the End Sub line:

Range("F3:F6").Select
Selection.Font.Bold = True
Range("B6:E6").Select
Selection.Font.Bold = True

f. Change the page orientation to Portrait, delete the totals in the range B6:F6 and F3:F5. Test the macro to verify that it runs correctly and that the totals appear in bold format.

g. Create four option button form controls in the range A9:D9. (*Hint*: To insert each button, click the Insert button in the Controls group, then click the Option Button [Form Control].)

h. Label the first button **Boston**, the second button **Chicago**, the third button **Miami**, and the fourth button **Los Angeles.**

i. Align the tops of the buttons. (*Hints*: Right-click one of the buttons, hold CTRL, then right-click each remaining button. With the buttons selected, click the Align button in the Arrange group on the Shape Format tab, then click Align Top.)

j. Format one of the buttons to enter the cell link of cell I1. (*Hint*: Right-click a button, click Format Control, then enter I1 in the Cell link box in the Format Control dialog box. The cell link is the same for all option buttons, so you only need to enter it for one button.)

k. Test the cell link by clicking each option button. The first option button should enter 1 in cell I1, the second should enter 2, and the third and fourth should enter 3 and 4, respectively.

l. Activate the Regions sheet, then select the range A1:A4 and verify the range name in the Name box is Region.

Independent Challenge 2 (continued)

m. Activate the Payments sheet, then enter an Index function in cell H2 that looks up the Region range on the Regions sheet using the value in cell I1 for its position. (*Hint*: The Index formula =@INDEX(Region,I1) should be entered in cell H2.)

n. Test each option button to verify the correct region appears in cell H2 for each office.

o. Apply a custom format so the value in cell I1 is hidden, click the Boston button, then compare your worksheet to **FIGURE 9-25**.

FIGURE 9-25

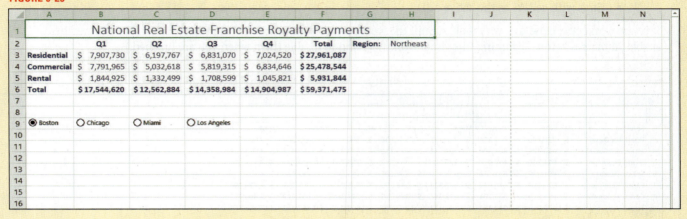

p. Enter your name in the worksheet footer, save the workbook, close the workbook, close Excel, then submit the workbook to your instructor.

Visual Workshop

Start Excel, open IL_EX_9-5.xlsx from the location where you store your Data Files, then save it as a macro-enabled workbook named **IL_EX_9_Services**. Modify and format the worksheet to match FIGURE 9-26. The button named Format & Total runs a macro named Format_Total stored in the workbook that does the following:

- Adds a row at the top of the worksheet
- Inserts a label of MES Commercial Engineering in cell A1, formatted with the Title cell style and merged and centered across columns A through H
- Adds totals in row 9 and column H
- Applies the Accounting format with zero decimal places to the range B3:H9
- Autofits the widths of columns A through H
- Ends with cell A1 as the active cell

Save the workbook, close the workbook, submit the workbook to your instructor, then close Excel. (*Note:* Remember to enable all macros before beginning this visual workshop, and to disable them when you are finished.)

FIGURE 9-26

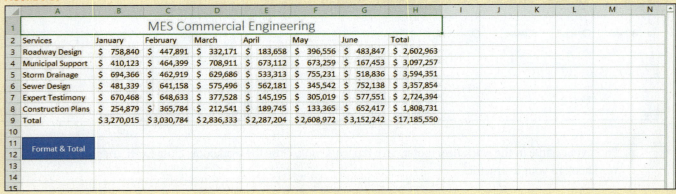

Automating Worksheet Tasks

Advanced Worksheet Management

CASE ▶ Ellie Schwartz, JCL's vice president of Finance, wants to facilitate future tracking of expenses at JCL Talent's U.S. offices. She asks you to use Excel tools and options to help her staff work quickly and efficiently in a customized environment.

Module Objectives

After completing this module, you will be able to:

- Create and apply a template
- Import HTML data
- Create a custom AutoFill list
- Work with themes

- Work with cell comments
- Customize an Excel workbook
- Encrypt a workbook with a password
- Work with the Analyze Data feature

Files You Will Need

IL_EX_10-1.xlsx	Support_EX_10-6.htm
Support_EX_10-2.htm	IL_EX_10-7.xlsx
IL_EX_10-3.xlsx	Support_EX_10-8.htm
Support_EX_10-4.htm	IL_EX_10-9.xlsx
IL_EX_10-5.xlsx	Support_EX_10-10.htm

Excel Module 10

Create and Apply a Template

Learning Outcomes
• Create a template
• Apply a template

A template is a workbook with an .xltx file extension that contains text, formulas, and formatting that you use repeatedly. When you save a workbook as a template, you can then use it to a create new workbook without having to reenter the repetitive data and formatting. To use a template, you apply it, which means you create a workbook *based on* the template. A workbook based on a template contains the same content, formulas, and formatting contained in the template, but is saved in the .xlsx format. The template file itself remains unchanged. **CASE** *Ellie has a workbook that contains formulas, styles, and labels for tracking this year's expenses at JCL. She asks you to use the workbook to create a template that will allow her to quickly create new workbooks for tracking expenses in future years.*

STEPS

1. **sam↓ Start Excel, then open IL_EX_10-1.xlsx from the location where you store your Data Files**

   The U.S. worksheet contains formulas that analyze this year's expenses for the U.S. offices and is formatted to be easy to read. You can reuse some of this formatting and content in workbooks you create to track future expenses.

QUICK TIP
The "#DIV/0!" or divide-by-zero error messages in column H are temporary and will no longer appear once you open a document based on the template and enter next year's data.

2. **Click the File tab on the ribbon, click Save As, in Backstage view click Browse, click the Save as type list arrow, click Excel Template (*.xltx), navigate to where you store your Data Files, type IL_EX_10_Expenses in the File name box, then click Save**

   Excel saves the file as a template, with the .xltx extension.

3. **Select the range C5:F12, press DEL, then click cell A1**

   The data specific to this worksheet is not needed for future worksheets. The reusable information and formatting remain to serve as the basis for future yearly worksheets, as shown in **FIGURE 10-1**.

4. **Save the template, then close the template**

   The completed template IL_EX_10_Expenses is now available to use in creating new workbooks.

QUICK TIP
If you want to edit the template itself, open the template (the .xltx file) using the Open dialog box in Excel. After making changes, save the template under the same name in the same location. Your changes are applied only to new documents you create based on the template from this point forward.

5. **Open File Explorer, navigate to the location where you store your Data Files, then double-click IL_EX_10_Expenses.xltx**

   A new workbook is created and has the default name IL_EX_10_Expenses1, as shown in **FIGURE 10-2**. The "1" at the end of the name identifies it as a new workbook based on the IL_EX_10_Expenses template, just as "1" at the end of "Book1" identifies a new workbook based on the blank Excel template.

6. **Click cell C5, enter 200, click cell C6, enter 300, select the range C5:C6, then use the fill handle to fill the range C7:C12 with this series**

   You are entering test data to make sure the template contains accurate formulas.

7. **Copy the range C5:C12, paste it into the range D5:F12, then compare your workbook to FIGURE 10-3**

   The totals and percentages appear to be correct.

8. **Close the workbook without saving it**

   Because you created this workbook only to test the template's formulas and formatting, you don't need to save it for future use.

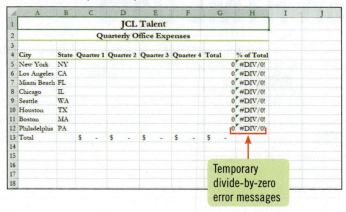

FIGURE 10-1: Completed template

Temporary
divide-by-zero
error messages

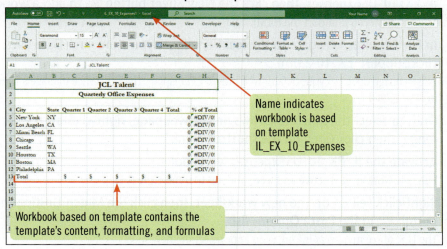

FIGURE 10-2: New workbook based on Expenses template

Name indicates
workbook is based
on template
IL_EX_10_Expenses

Workbook based on template contains the
template's content, formatting, and formulas

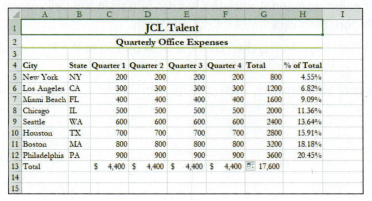

FIGURE 10-3: Test data entered in new workbook

	City	State	Quarter 1	Quarter 2	Quarter 3	Quarter 4	Total	% of Total
5	New York	NY	200	200	200	200	800	4.55%
6	Los Angeles	CA	300	300	300	300	1200	6.82%
7	Miami Beach	FL	400	400	400	400	1600	9.09%
8	Chicago	IL	500	500	500	500	2000	11.36%
9	Seattle	WA	600	600	600	600	2400	13.64%
10	Houston	TX	700	700	700	700	2800	15.91%
11	Boston	MA	800	800	800	800	3200	18.18%
12	Philadelphia	PA	900	900	900	900	3600	20.45%
13	Total		$ 4,400	$ 4,400	$ 4,400	$ 4,400	17,600	

(JCL Talent — Quarterly Office Expenses)

Creating a new workbook using a template

In addition to creating your own templates, you can use one of the many templates Excel offers for common documents such as balance sheets, budgets, or time cards. To create a workbook using an Excel template, click the File tab on the ribbon, then click New on the navigation bar. The New place in Backstage view displays thumbnails of some of the many templates available. The Blank workbook template is selected by default; when you create a new, blank workbook with no content or special formatting, this is the template the workbook is based on. To select a different template, click one of the selections in the New place, view the preview, then click Create.

Import HTML Data

When you need data available on a webpage, you can import the data into Excel in a few ways. You can open an HTML file directly in Excel if it's stored on an accessible drive, but often the information is published on the web and is not available as a file. In this situation, you can import the HTML data by copying the data on the webpage and pasting it into an Excel worksheet. This allows you to import only the information you need. Once the HTML data is in your worksheet, you can analyze it using Excel features. **CASE** ▶ *A list of the U.S. office managers is published on JCL's website. Ellie asks you to import this data into a new worksheet in the workbook.*

STEPS

1. **Open IL_EX_10-1.xlsx from the location where you store your Data Files, save it as IL_EX_10_USExpenses, then click the New Sheet button ⊕ to add a worksheet**
   This is where you'll import the HTML data.

2. **In File Explorer, navigate to the location where you store your Data Files, then double-click Support_EX_10-2.htm**
   The webpage opens in your default web browser. It displays the U.S. office managers information, as shown in **FIGURE 10-4**.

3. **Drag to select the nine table rows on the webpage, right-click any cell in the selected range, then click Copy on the shortcut menu**

4. **Activate the IL_EX_10_USExpenses workbook**
   The new worksheet is active and ready for you to import the data.

5. **Right-click cell A1 on the new worksheet, then click the Match Destination Formatting button 📋 in the Paste Options list**
   The U.S. office managers information appears on the new sheet.

6. **Double-click the Sheet1 sheet tab, type Managers, then press ENTER**

7. **Select columns A and B, click the Format button in the Cells group on the Home tab of the ribbon, then click AutoFit Column Width**

8. **Select the range A1:B1, then click the Bold button in the Font group**
   Compare your worksheet to **FIGURE 10-5**.

9. **Close your web browser, then save the workbook**

Importing XML data

Excel allows you to import and export XML data, a format often used for storing and exchanging data. To import XML data, click the Developer tab on the ribbon, click the Import button in the XML group, in the Import XML dialog box navigate to the xml file, click Import, then click OK twice. If you wish to specify a schema, or a map that describes the incoming data, before importing it, click the Source button in the XML group, in the XML Source pane click XML Maps, click Add in the XML Maps dialog box, navigate to a schema file in the Select XML source dialog box, click Open, then click OK.

FIGURE 10-4: Webpage listing JCL U.S. office managers

U.S. Managers

Office	Manager
New York	Nyack Afolayan
Los Angeles	Shavonn Rudd
Miami	Rosella Leigh
Chicago	Gary Jaeger
Seattle	Sophie Tan
Houston	Max Gallardo
Boston	Cheri McNeil
Philadelphia	Chris Wang

Data displayed in a browser

FIGURE 10-5: Imported and formatted HTML data

	A	B	C	D	E
1	**Office**	**Manager**			
2	New York	Nyack Afolayan			
3	Los Angeles	Shavonn Rudd			
4	Miami	Rosella Leigh			
5	Chicago	Gary Jaeger			
6	Seattle	Sophie Tan			
7	Houston	Max Gallardo			
8	Boston	Cheri McNeil			
9	Philadelphia	Chris Wang			
10					
11					

U.S. office managers' imported data

Importing HTML files directly into Excel

If you have an Internet connection, you can import data from a webpage online into an Excel worksheet by clicking the Data tab, clicking the From Web button in the Get & Transform group, verifying the Basic option is selected, entering the web address in the URL box of the From Web dialog box, clicking OK, selecting the items you wish to import in the Display Options section of the Navigator dialog box, selecting the Web View or Table view tab, then clicking Load. If you wish to use this method to import html data from a file stored locally on your computer, enter the path to the webpage file in the URL box rather than a web address. If you receive an Unable to Connect error regarding the file path, click Edit, click Browse, navigate to the file, click Import in the Import Data dialog box, click OK, select the data you wish to import and either Web or Table view in the Navigator dialog box, then click Load.

You can also import a locally stored HTML file directly into an Excel workbook by clicking the File tab, clicking Open, clicking Browse, selecting All Files in the Open dialog box, browsing to the HTML file, then clicking Open.

Create a Custom AutoFill List

Whenever you need to type a list of words regularly, you can save time by creating a custom list. Then you can simply enter the first value in a blank cell and drag the fill handle. Excel AutoFills the range, entering the rest of the information for you. **FIGURE 10-6** shows examples of custom lists that are built into Excel. **CASE** *JCL's offices are identified by the city where they are located. Ellie often has to enter a list of JCL's U.S. offices in her worksheets. She asks you to create a custom list to save having to manually enter the information each time she needs it.*

STEPS

1. Click the **U.S. sheet**, then select the range **A5:A12**

2. Click the **File tab** on the ribbon, click **Options**, click the **Advanced** category, scroll down to the **General section**, then click **Edit Custom Lists**

    The Custom Lists dialog box displays all existing custom lists, including those already built into Excel, as shown in **FIGURE 10-7**. The Import list from cells text box contains the range you selected before opening the dialog box.

3. Click **Import**

    The list of offices is highlighted in the Custom lists box and appears in the List entries box.

4. Click **OK** to confirm the list, then click **OK** again

5. Click the **New Sheet button** ⊕, double-click the **Sheet2** worksheet tab, type **Offices**, then press **ENTER**

6. With the Offices sheet active, type **New York** in cell **A1**, click the **Enter button** ✓ on the formula bar, then drag the **fill handle** to AutoFill the range **A2:A8**

    The highlighted range now contains the custom list of offices you created, as shown in **FIGURE 10-8**.

7. Click cell **A1**, click the **File tab** on the ribbon, click **Options**, click **Advanced** in the Excel Options list, scroll down to the **General section**, click **Edit Custom Lists**, click the list beginning with New York in the Custom lists box, click **Delete**, click **OK** to confirm the deletion, then click **OK** two more times

    If you share a computer with others, it is best to delete any custom lists you create after you are finished using them.

8. Save the workbook

FIGURE 10-6: Examples of custom lists

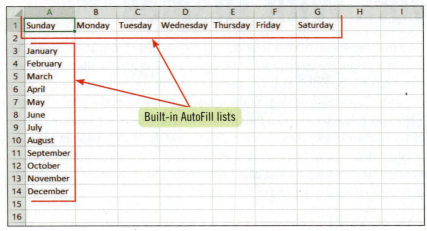

FIGURE 10-7: Custom Lists dialog box

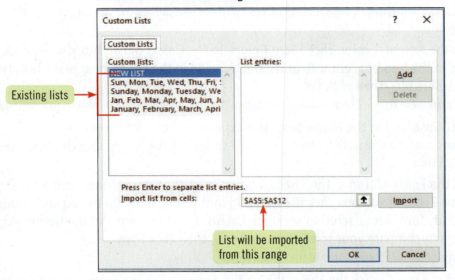

FIGURE 10-8: Custom list of offices

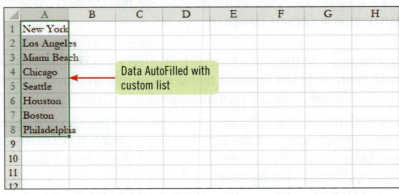

Work with Themes

You have used workbook themes to apply a predefined set of formats to a workbook. Formatting choices included in a theme are colors, fonts, cell styles, and line and fill effects. You can create custom theme fonts and color sets, which you can then use in any theme, and you can create custom themes to reflect current formatting settings under a new name, so that the original theme remains unchanged. **CASE** ▸ *Ellie asks you to create a theme that will be used for all JCL future workbooks. The preselected colors and fonts of the workbook's current theme, Organic, are displayed in galleries when you select colors and fonts for worksheet data. You will explore changes to these theme fonts and colors to create a custom theme that will provide a consistent look across all JCL workbooks. (To preserve the settings on shared computers, these changes will be removed at the end of the lesson.)*

STEPS

1. **Click the U.S. sheet tab, click cell A1, click the Page Layout tab on the ribbon, click the Colors button in the Themes group, then click Customize Colors**

   The Create New Theme Colors dialog box opens, where you can see the current colors in this theme and change them.

2. **Click the Accent 1 color, click More Colors, in the Colors dialog box double-click the value in the Red box, enter 0, press TAB, type 84 in the Green box, press TAB, type 166 in the Blue box, then click OK**

   The Create New Theme Colors dialog box displays the new Accent 1 color, as shown in **FIGURE 10-9**.

3. **Select Custom 1 in the Name box, type Expenses, then click Save**

   You have created a new set of theme colors called Expenses. The worksheet colors change to reflect the new Accent 1 color.

4. **Click the Fonts button in the Themes group, click Customize Fonts, in the Create New Theme Fonts dialog box click the Heading font arrow, scroll up to and click Calibri, click the Body font arrow, scroll to and click Calibri, select Custom 1 in the Name box, type Expenses, compare your screen to FIGURE 10-10, then click Save**

   The worksheet data is formatted in the Calibri font.

5. **Select column G, click the Home tab on the ribbon, click the Format button in the Cells group, click AutoFit Column Width, then click cell A1**

   The column fully displays the data in the Calibri font.

6. **Click the Page Layout tab on the ribbon, click the Themes button in the Themes group, then click Save Current Theme**

   The Document Themes folder opens. This is the location where themes are stored for Office files.

7. **Enter Expenses in the Name box, click Save, click the Themes button in the Themes group, then verify the Expenses theme is available, as shown in FIGURE 10-11**

   User-created themes are listed in the Custom themes section, above Office themes.

8. **Right-click the Expenses theme, click Delete, click Yes, click the Colors button in the Themes group, right-click the Expenses custom color, click Delete, click Yes, click the Fonts button in the Themes group, right-click the Expenses custom font, click Delete, click Yes, then save the workbook**

   It is best to remove custom fonts, colors, and themes from Office if you are sharing a computer with other people.

FIGURE 10-9: Create New Theme Colors dialog box

FIGURE 10-10: Create New Theme Fonts dialog box

FIGURE 10-11: Workbook themes

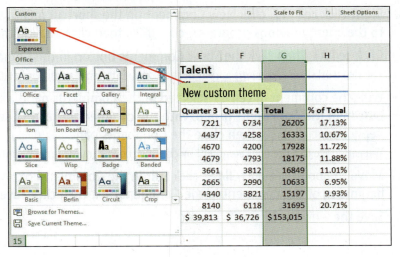

Work with Cell Comments

Learning Outcomes
- Insert a new comment
- Show worksheet comments
- Edit a comment

If you plan to share a workbook with others, it's a good idea to **document**, or make notes about the basic assumptions, complex formulas, or questionable data it contains. By reading your documentation, a coworker can quickly become familiar with your workbook. The easiest way to document a workbook is to use **cell comments**, which are notes you add to individual worksheet cells; the comment appears when you place the pointer over a cell. These are threaded so that you can reply directly below the original comment. When you sort or copy and paste cells, any comments attached to them move to the new location. In PivotTable reports, however, the comments do not move with the worksheet data.

CASE ▶ *You think one of the quarterly expense values in the worksheet may be incorrect, so you decide to add a comment about it. You also want to add a question for Ellie about a quarterly expense value that is significantly lower than the expenses for the other quarters. You will be able to see Ellie's reply to the comment when she sends the workbook back to you.*

STEPS

1. **Click the File tab on the ribbon if necessary, click Options, click Advanced in the Excel Options list, scroll to the Display section, click the Indicators only, and comments and notes on hover option button to select it in the For cells with comments, show: section if necessary, then click OK**

   The other options in the "For cells with comments, show:" area allow you to display the comment and its indicator or no comments.

2. **On the U.S. sheet click cell C9, click the Review tab on the ribbon, then click the New Comment button in the Comments group**

   The Comment box opens, as shown in **FIGURE 10-12**. Excel automatically includes the current username at the beginning of the comment; this is the name of the user currently logged in to Windows, and appears in the User name box of the Excel Options dialog box.

3. **Type Is this figure correct? It looks high to me., click the Post button 🖅, then click outside the Comment box**

   A pink triangle appears in the upper-right corner of cell C9, indicating that a comment is attached to the cell.

4. **Place the pointer over cell C9**

   The comment appears next to the cell. When you move the pointer or click outside cell C9, the comment disappears.

5. **Right-click cell F12, click New Comment on the shortcut menu, type Is this decrease due to the energy-savings program?, click 🖅, then click outside the Comment box**

6. **Click cell A1, then click the Show Comments button in the Comments group**

   The two worksheet comments appear in the Comments pane, as shown in **FIGURE 10-13**.

7. **With the comment in cell C9 selected in the Comments pane, click the Next Comment button in the Comments group, with the comment in cell F12 selected, type Yes in the Reply box, click 🖅, then close the Comments pane**

   You can move to a previous comment by clicking the Previous Comment button in the Comments group.

8. **Move the pointer over cell C9, click Edit in the Comment box, type Ellie - at the beginning of the comment in the Comment box, then click Save**

9. **Save the workbook**

FIGURE 10-12: Comment box

FIGURE 10-13: Comments pane

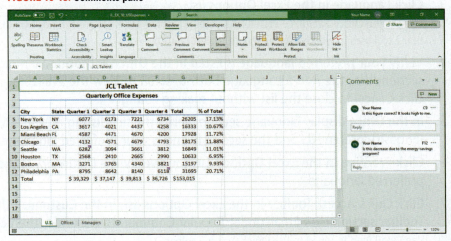

Sharing Excel workbooks

If you have a subscription to Office 365, you can coauthor a workbook with others to collaboratively add and edit data. When you coauthor, you can see the changes made by people with whom you have shared a workbook, and they can see yours. To share your workbook, click the Share button in the upper-right corner of the screen, upload your workbook to a OneDrive account, and provide a name for the workbook. The Send link dialog box allows you to enter the email addresses of your coauthors. You can also select email addresses from your address book. Clicking the Can edit arrow allows you to choose whether the recipients will be able to view or edit the workbook. After entering an optional message, click Send to email a link to

the workbook on OneDrive. When a recipient clicks the link, the workbook opens in Excel Online.

You can also use the Send link dialog box to share a workbook by clicking Send a copy, then choosing options in the Send link dialog box. For instance, you can click Copy link to create a shareable link to the file that you can then paste to an email message or other document.

When a file is saved to OneDrive, AutoSave is enabled so the workbook is automatically saved as you and other people make changes. When working with a shared workbook, you will see the names of the people with whom you are working in the title bar.

Customize an Excel Workbook

The Excel default settings for editing and viewing a worksheet are designed to meet the needs of most Excel users. You may find, however, that you want to change some of these settings. You have already used the Advanced category in the Excel Options dialog box to create custom lists and the Formulas category to switch to manual calculation. The most commonly used categories of the Excel Options are explained in more detail in **TABLE 10-1**. **CASE** *Ellie is interested in working more efficiently. She asks you to customize the workbook and check on other workbook settings to increase efficiency in Excel.*

STEPS

1. **Click the File tab on the ribbon, then click Options**
   The General category of the Excel Options list displays default options that Excel uses in new workbooks, as shown in **FIGURE 10-14**.

2. **In the Personalize your copy of Microsoft Office section, verify that the correct name appears in the User name box, then scroll down to view the other settings for the workbook**

3. **Click Language in the Excel Options list**
   The Set the Office Language Preferences category of the Excel Options dialog box displays default options that Excel uses in workbooks, as shown in **FIGURE 10-15**.

4. **Verify your preferred language is listed in the Office authoring languages and proofing section, click the Add a Language button, scroll to view the available languages, then click Cancel to close the list without making changes**

5. **In the Office display language section, verify the first listing is Match Microsoft Windows [English]<preferred> and the second listing is your preferred language**

6. **Click Proofing in the Excel Options list, then verify the Dictionary language shows your preferred language**

7. **Click Quick Access Toolbar in the Excel Options list, in the Customize the Quick Access Toolbar section click Email under Popular Commands, click Add, then click OK**
   The Email icon is added to the Quick Access Toolbar.

8. **Click File, click Options, click Quick Access Toolbar in the Excel Options list, click Reset, click Reset only Quick Access Toolbar, click Yes, then click OK**
   If you are working on a shared computer, you should restore the original settings to remove customizations.

Tracking changes in a workbook

You can track modifications to a workbook when you want to show what changes are being made to it from the present point onward. To use this feature, you can add the Track Changes button to the ribbon. To do so, right-click the ribbon, click Customize the Ribbon, right-click Review, click Add New Group, click the Choose Commands from arrow, click Commands Not in the Ribbon, click Track changes (Legacy) in the list of commands, click Add, then click OK. You can use the Highlight Changes command to specify what types of changes to track. Note that this legacy feature is not compatible with newer features in Excel, such as uploading to OneDrive.

FIGURE 10-14: General category of Excel options

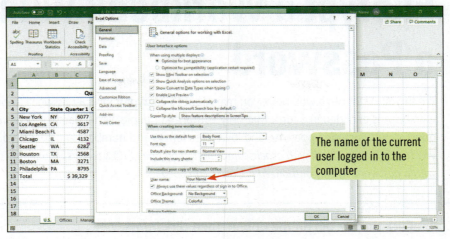

The name of the current user logged in to the computer

FIGURE 10-15: Language category of Excel Options dialog box

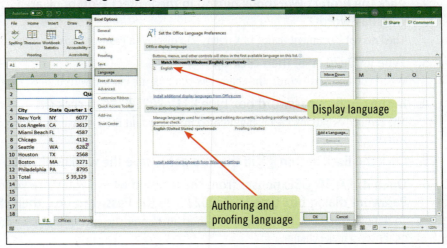

Display language

Authoring and proofing language

TABLE 10-1: Categories of Excel options you can change

category	allows you to
General	Change the username, customize default settings of new workbooks, enable LinkedIn features, and customize the user interface
Formulas	Control how the worksheet is calculated, how formulas appear, and error-checking settings and rules
Data	Control how data is analyzed and imported
Proofing	Control AutoCorrect and spell-checking options
Save	Select a default format and location for saving files, and customize AutoRecover settings
Language	Control the languages displayed and add additional languages and proofing tools
Ease of Access	Specify options to make Excel more accessible, such as changing the document display font size
Advanced	Set options for pen settings, create custom lists, and customize editing and display options
Customize Ribbon	Add commands, tabs, and groups to the Ribbon
Quick Access Toolbar	Add commands to the Quick Access Toolbar
Add-Ins	Install Excel Add-in programs such as Solver and Analysis ToolPak
Trust Center	Change Trust Center settings to protect your Excel files and your computer

Excel

Encrypt a Workbook with a Password

Learning Outcomes
- Use a password to encrypt a workbook
- Delete a password on an encrypted workbook

When you distribute a workbook you may want to encrypt it with a password to protect it. An encrypted workbook is encoded in a form that only authorized people with a password can read. For security, it is a good idea to include uppercase and lowercase letters and numbers in a password. **CASE** ▶ *Ellie wants you to put the workbook with expense information on one of JCL's servers. You decide to encrypt the workbook with a password so only authorized JCL users can open it.*

STEPS

1. **Click the File tab on the ribbon, then click Info**

   The Info pane displays information about your file. It also includes tools you can use to check for security issues.

2. **Click the Protect Workbook button in the Protect Workbook area, then click Encrypt with Password**

   The Encrypt Document dialog box opens and displays a Password box, as shown in **FIGURE 10-16**.

3. **Type JcLQe2021%, then click OK**

   When you enter passwords, the characters you type are masked with bullets (• • •) for security purposes.

4. **In the Confirm password box type JcLQe2021%, then click OK**

   The Protect Workbook area is highlighted in yellow and the message "A password is required to open this workbook" appears.

5. **Click the Back button ⬅ in the Info pane, save the workbook, then close the workbook**

6. **Open IL_EX_10_USExpenses from the location where you store your Data Files, in the Password dialog box type JcLQe2021% in the Password box, then click OK**

   To remove workbook encryption, you must first enter the encryption password, to verify that you are qualified to make changes.

7. **Click the File tab on the ribbon, click Info, click the Protect Workbook button in the Protect Workbook area, then click Encrypt with Password**

   The Encrypt Document dialog is displayed with the masked password, as shown in **FIGURE 10-17**.

8. **In the Password box select the masked password, press DEL, then click OK**

   The password is removed from the Workbook, and encryption is turned off.

9. **Click ⬅, then save the workbook**

FIGURE 10-16: Encrypt Document dialog box

FIGURE 10-17: Masked password

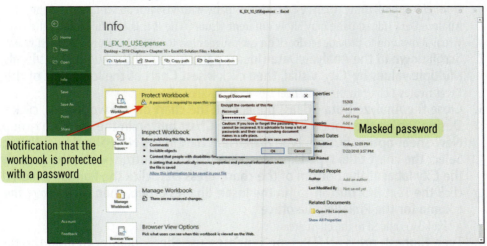

Working with a previous version of an Excel workbook

When you save your Excel files on OneDrive, AutoSave is automatically turned on to save versions of your workbook while you make changes. The older saved versions can be restored if you make errors in newer versions using Version history by clicking the File tab on the ribbon, clicking Info, clicking Version History in the Version History area, then clicking the desired version in the Version History pane. **FIGURE 10-18** shows two versions of a workbook. After your desired version opens, you can click the Restore button above the formula bar to save the file.

FIGURE 10-18: Version History pane

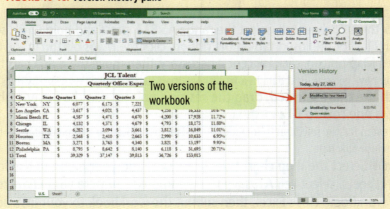

Work with the Analyze Data Feature

Learning Outcomes
- Create a chart using Ideas
- Add alternative text to a chart

The Analyze Data feature in Excel identifies patterns in data and creates charts summarizing different data groups. Usually these are charts of various types, but depending on the selected data they may also include sparklines, trendlines, PivotCharts, and other useful visuals. If you insert a suggested chart, you should consider adding alternative text, also called alt text, to help people using screen readers understand what the chart represents. This feature requires an Internet connection. **CASE** ▶ *Ellie asks you to chart the expenses for the U.S. offices. You will explore the Analyze Data feature to see the suggested charts.*

STEPS

TROUBLE

If this is the first time the Analyze Data feature is used, click Turn on to activate Office Intelligent Services. If you are using an earlier version of Excel the Analyze Data button might appear as the Ideas button.

1. **With the U.S. sheet active, select the range A4:F12, click the Home tab on the ribbon, then click the Analyze Data button in the Analysis group**
   FIGURE 10-19 shows the Analyze Data (Ideas) pane with visual representations of the selected data. Your Analyze Data (Ideas) pane may show different visuals. The Is this helpful? link at the lower right of each visual allows you to provide feedback on each suggestion to improve future suggested visuals.

2. **Scroll down in the Analyze Data (Ideas) pane to see all the suggested visuals, click the Multiple values by 'City' visual, then click Insert Chart at the lower left of the visual**
   Excel creates a chart in the worksheet based on this Idea.

3. **Close the Analyze Data (Ideas) pane, click the chart on the worksheet, click the Chart Design tab on the ribbon, click the Move Chart button in the Location group, click the New Sheet option button, type Expenses Chart in the New Sheet box, then click OK**

QUICK TIP

You can use the Search pane to access additional online resources for the currently selected data. Click the Review tab, click the Smart Lookup button in the Insights group, then review the search results for your selected data.

4. **Select the chart title, type Expenses, click the Enter button ✔ on the formula bar, select the City label at the bottom of the chart, press DEL, click the Format tab on the ribbon, click the Text Box button 🄰 in the Insert Shapes group, then click above the quarter 1 column for the Philadelphia office**
   A text box is added to the chart area.

5. **Type Highest, press ENTER, type Expenses, use the ↖ pointer to drag the text box corners to resize the text box so the text is fully displayed if necessary, then use the ⇧ pointer to move the text box above the Philadelphia Quarter 1 column**
   The text box clarifies the information in the column.

6. **Right-click a blank area of the chart, click Edit Alt Text on the shortcut menu, click inside the text box in the Alt Text pane, select any text inside the text box, type Chart showing expenses for U.S. offices by quarter., then close the Alt Text pane**
   The alt text describes the chart to a person with visual impairments. If you have an object that is decorative and not informational, for example a border, you can add a checkmark to the Mark as decorative check box. Because this object is informational, you leave this check box unchecked.

QUICK TIP

You can add an additional data series to a chart by clicking anywhere in the chart, then dragging the sizing handles to include the new data.

7. **Click the U.S. sheet tab, select the range A5:B11, press and hold CTRL, select the range H5:H11, click the Insert tab on the ribbon, click the Maps button in the Chart group, click the Filled Map button, click I accept if necessary, then move the map chart to the range I2:N15**
   If you have geographical data in a worksheet, map charts display associated values over the region.

8. **With the chart selected, drag the resizing pointer ↘ in the lower-right corner of cell B11 down one row to B12**
   You extended the selection to include the Philadelphia location and percentage data, and the chart updated to include this data.

9. **sam↑ Select the map chart title, press DEL, add your name to the footers of all four worksheets, select cell A1, save the workbook, compare your chart to FIGURE 10-20, close the workbook, close Excel, then submit the workbook to your instructor**

FIGURE 10-19: Analyze Data (Ideas) pane

FIGURE 10-20: Map chart

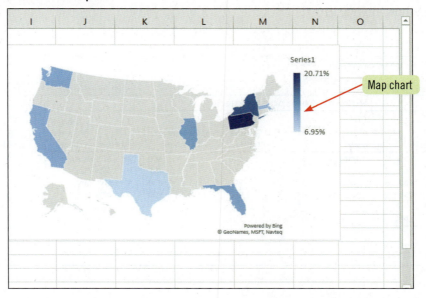

Working with Funnel charts

You can use a funnel chart to show values at different stages of a process. They are most useful when you want to illustrate data values decreasing, so that the resulting chart resembles a funnel. **FIGURE 10-21** shows an example of a funnel chart illustrating the number of hours decreasing with each stage in a process.

FIGURE 10-21: Funnel chart

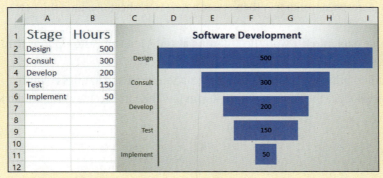

Excel

Practice

Skills Review

1. Create and apply a template.

a. Start Excel, then open IL_EX_10-3.xlsx from the location where you store your Data Files.

b. Save the workbook as a template in the location where you store your Data Files with the name **IL_EX_10_FirstQuarter.xltx**.

c. Delete the values in ranges B3:D6 and F3:F6. Leave the worksheet formulas intact.

d. Save and close the template, then open a new workbook based on the template.

e. In the new IL_EX_10_FirstQuarter1 workbook, test the template by entering the data in ranges B3:D6 and F3:F6, shown in **FIGURE 10-22**.

FIGURE 10-22

	A	B	C	D	E	F	G	H
					National Aerospace Materials			
1								
2	Location	January	February	March	First Quarter Revenue	Previous Quarter Revenue	% Increase	Quarter Revenue Target
3	Houston	$ 100	$ 200	$ 300	$ 600	$ 550	9.09%	Missed
4	New York	$ 150	$ 250	$ 350	$ 750	$ 725	3.45%	Missed
5	San Diego	$ 200	$ 300	$ 400	$ 900	$ 800	12.50%	Met
6	Phoenix	$ 250	$ 350	$ 450	$ 1,050	$ 900	16.67%	Met
7	Target % increase	10%						
8	Average Quarter Revenue	$ 825						
9								

Cell reference: A1 — National Aerospace Materials

f. After verifying that the formulas and formatting in the workbook appear to work correctly, close the workbook without saving it.

2. Import HTML data.

a. Re-open IL_EX_10-3.xlsx from the location where you store your Data Files, then save the workbook as **IL_EX_10_Aerospace**.

b. Open File Explorer, navigate to the location where you store your Data Files, then open the webpage Support_EX_10-4.htm in your web browser. Copy the data in the five rows of the webpage table, including the column headings.

c. Activate the IL_EX_10_Aerospace workbook, then create a new worksheet. Rename the new sheet **Quality Ratings**.

d. Paste the copied webpage data into the worksheet starting at cell A1, using Paste Options to match the destination formatting.

e. Autofit columns A and B to fully display the Location data and narrow the Ratings column.

f. Activate your web browser, close the Support_EX_10-4.htm file, then in Excel save the workbook.

Advanced Worksheet Management

3. Create a custom AutoFill list.

a. Activate the First Quarter sheet, then select the range A3:A6.

b. Open the Custom Lists dialog box, then import the selected data.

c. Close the dialog box.

d. Add a worksheet to the workbook. Rename the new worksheet **Locations** and move it so it is the last worksheet in the workbook. On the Locations worksheet, enter **Houston** in cell A1.

e. Use the fill handle to enter the custom list through cell A4, then widen column A to fully display the locations.

f. Open the Custom Lists dialog box again, delete the custom list you just created, then save the workbook.

4. Work with themes.

a. Activate the First Quarter sheet and use the Create New Theme Colors dialog box to change the Accent 1 color to a custom color with the RGB values Red: **0**, Green: **138**, and Blue: **135**.

b. Name the new theme color palette **FQ** and save it.

c. Use the Create New Theme Fonts dialog box to change both the heading and body fonts to Calibri. Save the new theme font set as **FQ**.

d. Save the current theme as **FQ**, then compare your worksheet to **FIGURE 10-23**.

FIGURE 10-23

	A	B	C	D	E	F	G	H	I
				Ja	National Aerospace Materials				
1				National Aerospace Materials					
2	Location	January	February	March	First Quarter Revenue	Previous Quarter Revenue	% Increase	Quarter Revenue Target	
3	Houston	$ 59,529	$ 58,017	$ 74,193	$ 191,739	$ 162,571	17.94%	Met	
4	New York	$ 68,008	$ 74,471	$ 74,691	$ 217,170	$ 166,545	30.40%	Met	
5	San Diego	$ 65,909	$ 72,444	$ 67,841	$ 206,194	$ 179,852	14.65%	Met	
6	Phoenix	$ 52,146	$ 56,734	$ 58,770	$ 167,650	$ 176,645	(5.09%)	Missed	
7	Target % increase	10%							
8	Average Quarter Revenue	$ 195,688							
9									

e. Verify that the custom FQ color palette is listed in the Theme Colors list, the FQ font set is listed in the Theme Fonts list, and theme is listed the Themes list, then delete each custom setting.

f. Save the workbook.

5. Work with cell comments.

a. Insert a comment in cell E2 that reads **Are these final values?**. (*Hint*: Don't type the period.)

b. Click anywhere outside the Comment box to close it.

c. Insert a comment in cell G4 that reads **Nice Increase!**.

d. Edit the comment in cell E2 to read **Are these final revenue values?**.

e. Add a reply to the comment in cell G4 that reads **Thanks.**.

f. Display all worksheet comments. Hide all worksheet comments.

g. Delete the comment in cell E2.

h. Save the workbook.

Excel

Skills Review (continued)

6. Customize an Excel workbook.

   a. Use the General category of the Excel Options dialog box to verify the correct username appears.

   b. Use the Language category of the Excel Options dialog box to verify the editing, display, and help languages are set correctly for your Excel workbook.

   c. Use the Proofing category of the Excel Options dialog box to verify the dictionary language setting is correct for your Excel workbook.

   d. Use the Quick Access Toolbar category of the Excel Options dialog box to add the Open button to the Quick Access Toolbar.

   e. Reset all customizations of the workbook to the defaults.

7. Encrypt a workbook with a password.

   a. Encrypt the workbook with the password **FjfmQpin8!**.

   b. Save and close the workbook.

   c. Open the workbook using the password.

   d. Delete the password.

   e. Save the workbook.

8. Work with The Analyze Data feature.

   a. Select the range A2:D6 and use the Analyze Data feature to see suggested visuals for analyzing the selected data.

   b. Insert the first suggested visual, a chart, from the Analyze Data (Ideas) pane, then close the pane.

   c. Move and resize the chart to fit in the range C7:H18.

   d. Edit the chart title to **Q1 Revenue**.

   e. Add the alternative text: **January, February, and March revenue for Houston, New York, San Diego, and Phoenix**.

   f. Close the Alt Text pane.

   g. Compare your First Quarter worksheet to **FIGURE 10-24**. Note that your chart may not match the one in **FIGURE 10-24** if your Analyze Data (Ideas) pane displayed a different first visual.

FIGURE 10-24

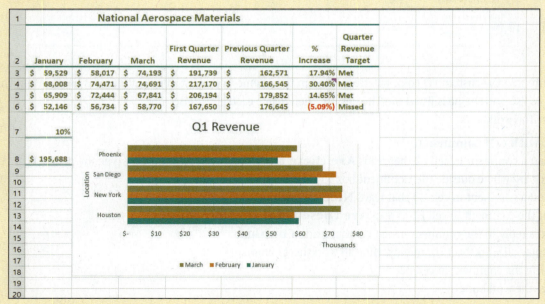

   h. Group the worksheets, add your name to the center footer section of the sheets, save the workbook, close the workbook, then submit the workbook to your instructor.

   i. Close Excel.

    Advanced Worksheet Management

Independent Challenge 1

The manager at Riverwalk Medical Clinic has hired you to increase efficiency at an affiliated local imaging facility. You decide to create a template to speed up the facility's monthly billing process, and to use Excel features to make the billing easier to manage each month.

a. Open IL_EX_10-5.xlsx from the location where you store your Data Files.

b. Delete the billing and insurance data in columns B and C, leaving the total formulas. Save the workbook as a template with the name **IL_EX_10_MonthlyBilling.xltx** in the location where you store your Data Files, then close the template.

c. Open a new workbook based on the IL_EX_10_MonthlyBilling template. Enter test data of your choosing for billing and insurance, then check the results to verify the template is calculating the balance correctly. Close the IL_EX_10_MonthlyBilling1 workbook without saving it.

d. Re-open IL_EX_10-5.xlsx from the location where you store your Data Files, then save it as **IL_EX_10_Billing**. Create a new worksheet in the workbook named **NH Locations**. Open the webpage Support_EX_10-6.htm in your web browser from the location where you store your Data Files. Copy the data in the four rows of the webpage table, excluding the column heading. Paste the copied data to the range A1:A4 in the NH Locations worksheet. Match the destination formatting and Autofit column A to fully display the locations. Close the webpage file Support_EX_10-6.htm, then save the workbook.

e. Activate the Jan sheet, then create a custom list based on the locations in the range A3:A9. Test the custom AutoFill list on a new worksheet in the workbook named **Locations**. Position the Locations sheet between the Jan and NH Locations sheets. Use the Custom Lists dialog box to delete the custom list from your computer. Do not delete the list of locations on the Locations sheet.

f. In the Jan sheet, add a comment to cell D5 that reads: **High Balance**.

g. Add a comment to cell A9 that reads: **Is this facility merging with Beverly?**.

h. Use the Next and Previous buttons in the Comments group of the Review tab to move between comments on the worksheet.

i. Edit the comment in cell D5 so it reads **High Balance – any ideas why?**. Show the worksheet comments and compare your Jan worksheet to **FIGURE 10-25**. Delete the comment in cell A9, then hide the worksheet comments.

FIGURE 10-25

j. Use the Excel Options dialog box to review the user name as well as languages for editing, display, help, and the dictionary.

k. Add the Spelling command to the Quick Access Toolbar. Test the new button, then reset all customizations of the workbook to the defaults.

Independent Challenge 1 (continued)

l. Encrypt the workbook with the password **BilLne367$**. Test the password by saving the workbook, closing the workbook, and then opening the workbook. Remove encryption from the workbook.

m. Add your name to the center section of all the worksheet footers, then save the workbook.

n. Close the workbook, exit Excel, then submit the workbook to your instructor.

Independent Challenge 2

As the senior loan officer at South Shore Bank, one of your responsibilities is reviewing the quarterly loan portfolios for the four branches. This analysis is completed every quarter, so creating a template will simplify this process. You will also use Excel features to help with this quarterly analysis.

a. Start Excel, then open IL_EX_10-7.xlsx from the location where you store your Data Files.

b. Delete the values in the ranges B4:D7 and F4:F7. Change the label in cell F3 to **Previous Quarter Total**, change the label in cell E3 to **Total for Quarter**, change the label in cell G3 to **Quarter % Increase**, change the label in cell A10 to **Quarter Average**, then change the sheet tab name to **Quarter Report**. Save the workbook as a template with the name **IL_EX_10_QuarterAnalysis** in the location where you store your Data Files, then close the template.

c. Open a new workbook based on the template, verify the template is calculating the formulas correctly by entering test data, then close the IL_EX_10_QuarterAnalysis1 workbook without saving it.

d. Reopen IL_EX_10-7.xlsx from the location where you store your Data Files, then save it as **IL_EX_10_SecondQuarter**. Open the webpage Support_EX_10-8.htm in your browser from the location where you store your Data Files. Copy the data in the four rows of the webpage table, excluding the column heading. Activate the workbook, paste the copied data starting in cell H4 of the worksheet, matching the destination formatting. Delete column H. Enter the label **Survey Positive Rating** in cell H3. Format the new data font in the range H4:H7 as 11 point and bold so that it matches the other worksheet values. Close your web browser.

e. Create a new set of theme colors with a custom Accent 1 color with the RGB settings of Red: **128**, Green: **157**, and Blue: **209**. Save the new theme custom colors with the name **QBlue**. Create a new set of theme fonts with both the heading and body fonts of Arial. Save the new theme font set as **QFont**. Widen the worksheet columns as necessary to display all worksheet data in the new font. Save the custom colors and fonts in a custom theme named **QTheme**. Verify the custom color palette, font set, and theme are available, then delete each custom setting.

f. Review the spelling correction settings in the Proofing category of the Excel Options dialog box. Click the AutoCorrect Options button, then review the entries in the Replace and With columns in the AutoCorrect dialog box. Close the AutoCorrect dialog box without making any changes. Review the AutoRecover save time setting in the Save category of the Excel Options, then enter the save time in the left section of the worksheet footer.

g. Use the Analyze Data feature to see visuals that chart data in the range A3:D7. Insert the first suggested column chart into the worksheet. Move and resize the chart to fit in the range C10:G26. Delete the Branch label at the bottom of the chart. Change the chart title to **Second Quarter**. Add the alternative text **Second quarter personal, home equity, and business loans for branches**.

Advanced Worksheet Management

Independent Challenge 2 (continued)

h. Compare your worksheet to **FIGURE 10-26**. Note that your chart may not match the one shown here if your Analyze Data (Ideas) pane displayed a different first column chart.

FIGURE 10-26

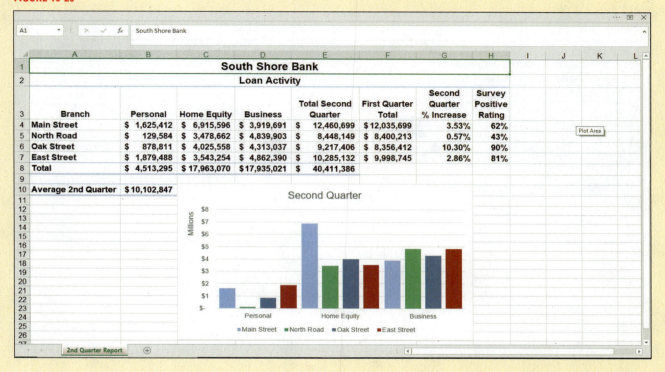

i. Add your name to the center section of the worksheet footer, then save the workbook.

j. Close the workbook, close Excel, then submit your workbook to your instructor.

Excel

Visual Workshop

Open IL_EX_10-9.xlsx from the location where you store your Data Files, then save it as **IL_EX_10_Hotels**. Import and add content as necessary so your screen matches **FIGURE 10-27**. (*Hint*: The file Support_EX_10-10.htm contains the data you need to import.) Add your name to the center section of the worksheet footer, then save the workbook. Close the workbook, close Excel, then submit the workbook to your instructor.

FIGURE 10-27

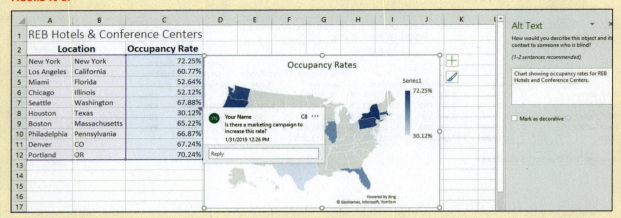

Advanced Formulas and Functions

CASE ▶ Ellie Schwartz, JCL's vice president of finance, uses Excel formulas and functions to analyze and consolidate data for the company's regions and divisions. Because management is considering adding a new regional office in the Northeast, Ellie asks you to format and summarize data from the current Northeast offices. You will compare commissions and placements in the Northeast offices and consolidate this data by division and office. Ellie also asks you to estimate the loan costs for the potential new office.

Module Objectives

After completing this module, you will be able to:

- Separate data using Flash Fill
- Format data using text functions
- Sum a data range based on conditions
- Find values based on conditions
- Construct formulas using named ranges

- Consolidate worksheet data
- Audit a worksheet
- Calculate payments with the PMT function

Files You Will Need

IL_EX_11-1.xlsx   IL_EX_11-4.xlsx

IL_EX_11-2.xlsx   IL_EX_11-5.xlsx

IL_EX_11-3.xlsx

Separate Data Using Flash Fill

Often, you need to import data into Excel from an outside source, such as another program or the Internet. Sometimes multiple data fields are imported in a single column. You can easily break the fields into separate columns using the Flash Fill feature. **CASE** ▶ *Ellie requested data from the Human Resources Department on recruiters who expressed interest in working at the new office and the divisions in which they specialize, so she can assess future hiring needs. After importing this data into Excel, you notice that the position and division fields were mistakenly combined into one column.*

STEPS

1. **sam**↓ **Start Excel, open IL_EX_11-1.xlsx from the location where you store your Data Files, then save it as IL_EX_11_NE**

2. **On the Recruiters sheet click cell D2, type Technical, press TAB, in cell E2 type Senior Recruiter, then click the Enter button** ☑ **in the formula bar**
   You manually separated the data in cell C2 into the adjacent cells, as shown in **FIGURE 11-1**, by entering the correct data in each cell. Completing this task provides an example for Flash Fill to use to complete the rows below. **Flash Fill** looks for patterns in the data you enter and automatically fills or formats data in remaining cells based on those patterns.

3. **With cell E2 selected click Fill in the Editing group on the ribbon, then click Flash Fill**
   The positions from column C are copied into the range E3:E13.

4. **Select cell D2, click Fill in the Editing group, then click Flash Fill**
   The divisions from Column C are copied into the range D3:D13.

5. **Move the Position label from cell D1 to cell E1, click cell D1, type Division, then press ENTER**

6. **Widen columns D and E to fully display the data, then compare your work to FIGURE 11-2**

7. **Save your work**

FIGURE 11-1: Worksheet with data separated into columns

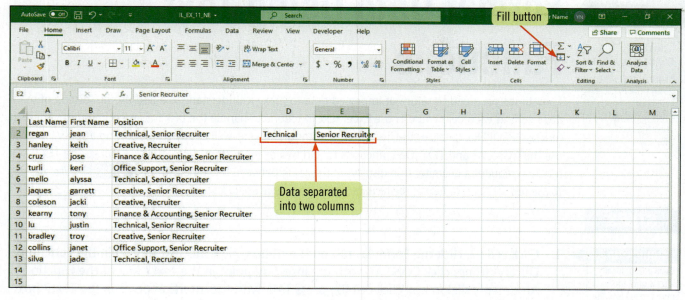

FIGURE 11-2: Worksheet with data formatted in columns

	A	B	C	D	E	F
1	Last Name	First Name	Position	Division	Position	
2	regan	jean	Technical, Senior Recruiter	Technical	Senior Recruiter	
3	hanley	keith	Creative, Recruiter	Creative	Recruiter	
4	cruz	jose	Finance & Accounting, Senior Recruiter	Finance & Accounting	Senior Recruiter	
5	turli	keri	Office Support, Senior Recruiter	Office Support	Senior Recruiter	
6	mello	alyssa	Technical, Senior Recruiter	Technical	Senior Recruiter	
7	jaques	garrett	Creative, Senior Recruiter	Creative	Senior Recruiter	
8	coleson	jacki	Creative, Recruiter	Creative	Recruiter	
9	kearny	tony	Finance & Accounting, Senior Recruiter	Finance & Accounting	Senior Recruiter	
10	lu	justin	Technical, Senior Recruiter	Technical	Senior Recruiter	
11	bradley	troy	Creative, Senior Recruiter	Creative	Senior Recruiter	
12	collins	janet	Office Support, Senior Recruiter	Office Support	Senior Recruiter	
13	silva	jade	Technical, Recruiter	Technical	Recruiter	
14						

Working with Excel series

You can use Excel fill series to generate worksheet data based on linear or growth trends. For example, if you want to review payments for a range of interest rates between 4% and 5%, you can fill a worksheet series with interest rates increasing by a desired amount. To fill the series, enter the starting percentage in a cell, click the Home tab on the ribbon, click the Fill button in the Editing group, click Series, in the Series dialog box select the Rows or Columns option button indicating where the results will be placed, verify the Linear option button is selected in the Type category, in the Step value box enter the increase amount for each subsequent value, in the Stop value box enter the final amount, then click OK. In a situation where you need values to increase by a certain percentage each year, you need to use an exponential growth series, also called a growth trend. To create a growth trend, select the Growth option button in the Type category of the Series dialog box, enter the growth amount in the Step value box, then click OK. For example if you wanted a sales target to increase by 20 percent each year, you would enter 1.2 in the Step value box. If the Stop value is blank the values are calculated using the step value as the growth trend.

Excel

Format Data Using Text Functions

Learning Outcomes
- Format text data using the PROPER function
- Join text data using a text function

Sometimes you need to reformat imported data to make it understandable and useful. Instead of manually editing each cell, you can use Excel text functions to handle the task for an entire range. The text function PROPER capitalizes the first letter in a string of text as well as any text following a space. You can use the CONCAT and TEXTJOIN functions to join two or more strings into one text string. The TEXTJOIN function requires a delimiter that displays in the result between the joined strings. **CASE** ▶ *Ellie asks you to use text formulas to format the recruiter data into a more useful layout.*

STEPS

QUICK TIP

Excel automatically inserts quotation marks to enclose the space.

1. Click cell **F2**, click the **Formulas tab** on the ribbon, click the **Text button** in the Function Library group, click **CONCAT**, with the insertion point in the Text1 box of the Function Arguments dialog box click cell **B2**, press **TAB**, with the insertion point in the Text2 box press **SPACEBAR**, press **TAB**, with the insertion point in the Text3 box click cell **A2**, then click **OK**

QUICK TIP

The CONCAT function replaces CONCATENATE from earlier versions of Excel. CONCATENATE remains available in Excel for compatibility purposes.

2. Drag the **fill handle** ➕ to copy the formula in cell **F2** into the range **F3:F13**, then widen column **F** to fully display the data in the column

3. Click cell **G2**, click the **Text button** in the Function Library group, click **PROPER**, with the insertion point in the Text box of the Function Arguments dialog box click cell **F2**, click **OK**, then compare your worksheet to **FIGURE 11-3**

   The name is copied from cell F2 to cell G2 with the correct uppercase letters for proper names.

4. Copy the formula in cell **G2** into the range **G3:G13**, then widen column **G** to fully display the data in the column

5. Click cell **H2**, click the **Text button** in the Function Library group, click **TEXTJOIN**, with the insertion point in the Delimiter box of the Function Arguments dialog box press **SPACEBAR**, press **TAB**, with the insertion point in the Ignore_empty box press **TAB** to accept the default, with the insertion point in the Text1 box click cell **D2**, press **TAB**, with the insertion point in the Text2 box type **Careers**, then click **OK**

   Like CONCAT, the TEXTJOIN function joins strings of text; however, you enter the delimiter in the Delimiter box of the Function Arguments dialog box rather than in the Text box.

6. Copy the formula in cell **H2** into the range **H3:H13**, then widen column **H** to fully display the data in the column

7. Select the range **G2:H13**, click the **Home tab**, click the **Copy button** 📋 in the Clipboard group, click cell **I1**, click the **Paste button arrow** in the Clipboard group, click **Values button** 📋 in the Paste Values category, then press **ESC**

8. Select columns **A** through **H**, click the **Delete button** in the Cells group, then widen columns **A** and **B** to fully display the data

   Compare your worksheet to **FIGURE 11-4**.

9. Save your work

FIGURE 11-3: Names with Proper formatting

	A	B	C	D	E	F	G	H	I
1	Last Name	First Name	Position	Division	Position				
2	regan	jean	Technical, Senior Recruiter	Technical	Senior Recruiter	jean regan	Jean Regan		
3	hanley	keith	Creative, Recruiter	Creative	Recruiter	keith hanley			
4	cruz	jose	Finance & Accounting, Senior Recruiter	Finance & Accounting	Senior Recruiter	jose cruz			
5	turli	keri	Office Support, Senior Recruiter	Office Support	Senior Recruiter	keri turli			
6	mello	alyssa	Technical, Senior Recruiter	Technical	Senior Recruiter	alyssa mello			
7	jaques	garrett	Creative, Senior Recruiter	Creative	Senior Recruiter	garrett jaqu			
8	coleson	jacki	Creative, Recruiter	Creative	Recruiter	jacki coleso			
9	kearny	tony	Finance & Accounting, Senior Recruiter	Finance & Accounting	Senior Recruiter	tony kearny			
10	lu	justin	Technical, Senior Recruiter	Technical	Senior Recruiter	justin lu			
11	bradley	troy	Creative, Senior Recruiter	Creative	Senior Recruiter	troy bradley			
12	collins	janet	Office Support, Senior Recruiter	Office Support	Senior Recruiter	janet collins			
13	silva	jade	Technical, Recruiter	Technical	Recruiter	jade silva			
14									

Name in Proper format

FIGURE 11-4: Worksheet with data formatted using Text functions

	A	B	C	D	E	F	G	H	I	J	K	L
1	Jean Regan	Technical Careers										
2	Keith Hanley	Creative Careers										
3	Jose Cruz	Finance & Accounting Careers										
4	Keri Turli	Office Support Careers										
5	Alyssa Mello	Technical Careers										
6	Garrett Jaques	Creative Careers										
7	Jacki Coleson	Creative Careers										
8	Tony Kearny	Finance & Accounting Careers										
9	Justin Lu	Technical Careers										
10	Troy Bradley	Creative Careers										
11	Janet Collins	Office Support Careers										
12	Jade Silva	Technical Careers										
13												

Working with other text functions

Other useful text functions include UPPER, LOWER, SUBSTITUTE, LEN, RIGHT, LEFT, and MID. UPPER converts text to all uppercase letters, LOWER converts text to all lowercase letters, SUBSTITUTE replaces text in a text string, and LEN displays the number of characters in a string of text. For example, if cell A1 contains the text string "Today is Wednesday", then =LOWER(A1) would produce "today is wednesday"; =UPPER(A1) would produce "TODAY IS WEDNESDAY"; =SUBSTITUTE(A1, "Wednesday", "Tuesday") would result in "Today is Tuesday"; and =LEN(A1) would result in 18. You can also use functions to display one or more characters at certain locations within a string. Use RIGHT to find the last characters with the syntax =RIGHT(string, # characters), where # is the number of characters you want to display, such as the last 3. Similarly, use LEFT to find the first characters with the syntax =LEFT(string, # characters), or MID to display the middle characters with the syntax =MID(string, starting character, # characters).

Sum a Data Range Based on Conditions

**Learning
Outcomes**
• Total data using
the SUMIF
function
• Summarize data
using the AVER-
AGEIF function

You can use Excel functions to sum and average data in a range based on criteria, or conditions, you set. The SUMIF function totals only the cells in a range that meet given criteria. The AVERAGEIF function averages values in a range based on a specified condition. The format for the SUMIF function appears in **FIGURE 11-5**. **CASE** ▶ *Ellie asks you to analyze the Boston office's placement data to provide her with information about each division, including the commission for the technical divisions.*

STEPS

1. **Click the Boston sheet tab, click cell I2, click the Formulas tab on the ribbon, click the Math & Trig button in the Function Library group, scroll down the list of functions, then click SUMIF**

   The Function Arguments dialog box opens.

2. **With the insertion point in the Range box select the range C2:C65, press F4, press TAB, with the insertion point in the Criteria box click cell H2, press TAB, with the insertion point in the Sum_range box select the range E2:E65, press F4, then click OK**

   Your formula, as shown in the formula bar in **FIGURE 11-6**, asks Excel to search the range C2:C65, and where it finds the value in cell H2, Technical, to add the corresponding amount from column E. The result, the total commission for the technical divisions, appears in cell I2.

3. **Click cell J2, click the More Functions button in the Function Library group, point to Statistical, then click AVERAGEIF**

4. **With the insertion point in the Range box select the range C2:C65, press F4, press TAB, with the insertion point in the Criteria box click cell H2, press TAB, with the insertion point in the Average_range box select the range E2:E65, press F4, then click OK**

   The average commission for the technical division placements, 4736.39, appears in cell J2.

5. **Select the range I2:J2, then drag the fill handle ➕ to fill the range I3:J5**

6. **Click cell I6, click the Math & Trig button in the Function Library group, scroll down the list of functions, then click SUMIFS**

   The SUMIFS function allows you to sum ranges with multiple criteria.

7. **With the insertion point in the Sum_range box select the range E2:E65, press F4, press TAB, with the insertion point in the Criteria_range1 box select the range C2:C65, press F4, press TAB, with the insertion point in the Criteria1 box, type Technical, press TAB, with the insertion point in the Criteria_range2 box select the range D2:D65, press F4, press TAB, with the insertion point in the Criteria2 box type Full-time, then click OK**

   The total commissions for the Technical division's full-time placements, 26397, appears in cell I6.

8. **With cell I6 selected, drag the fill handle ➕ to cell J6, click cell J6, verify that cell I6 is no longer selected, select SUM in the SUMIFS formula displayed in the formula bar, type AVERAGE, then click the Enter button ✓ in the formula bar**

   After copying the formula from cell I6, you edited it to contain the AVERAGEIFS function, which averages ranges with multiple criteria. Cell J2 displays the average commission for the Technical division's full-time placements, as shown in **FIGURE 11-7**.

9. **Save your work**

FIGURE 11-5: Format of SUMIF function

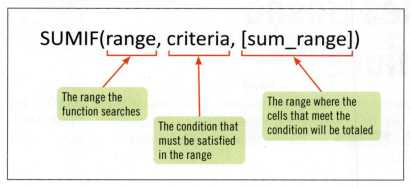

SUMIF(range, criteria, [sum_range])

The range the function searches

The condition that must be satisfied in the range

The range where the cells that meet the condition will be totaled

FIGURE 11-6: SUMIF function in the formula bar

I2   =SUMIF($C$2:$C$65,H2,$E$2:$E$65) ← Formula for SUMIF function

	A	B	C	D	E	F	G	H	I	J
1	Account #	Employer ID	Division	Position Type	Commission	Preferred Employer			Commission Totals	Commission Averages
2	6686	69661	Finance & Accounting	Full-time	$1,171	Yes		Technical	85255	
3	6488	49734	Creative	Consultant	$4,546	No		Creative		
4	5499	88302	Office Support	Full-time	$1,098	Yes		Office Support		
5	4438	51467	Technical	Full-time	$5,751	Yes		Finance & Accounting		
6	7569	30405	Creative	Full-time	$3,764	No		Technical Full-tim		
7	7803	99768	Technical	Consultant	$8,547	No				
8	7701	26988	Office Support	Consultant	$5,324	No		Lowest Technical ...-		

Total commission for the technical divisions

FIGURE 11-7: AVERAGEIFS function

J6   =AVERAGEIFS($E$2:$E$65,$C$2:$C$65,"Technical",$D$2:$D$65,"Full-time") ← Formula for AVERAGEIFS function

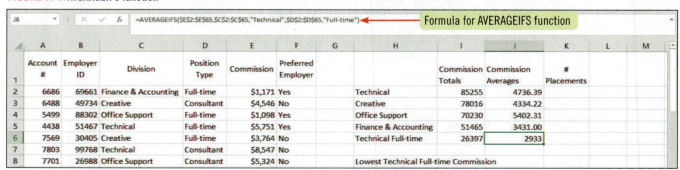

	A	B	C	D	E	F	G	H	I	J	K	L	M
1	Account #	Employer ID	Division	Position Type	Commission	Preferred Employer			Commission Totals	Commission Averages	# Placements		
2	6686	69661	Finance & Accounting	Full-time	$1,171	Yes		Technical	85255	4736.39			
3	6488	49734	Creative	Consultant	$4,546	No		Creative	78016	4334.22			
4	5499	88302	Office Support	Full-time	$1,098	Yes		Office Support	70230	5402.31			
5	4438	51467	Technical	Full-time	$5,751	Yes		Finance & Accounting	51465	3431.00			
6	7569	30405	Creative	Full-time	$3,764	No		Technical Full-time	26397	2933			
7	7803	99768	Technical	Consultant	$8,547	No							
8	7701	26988	Office Support	Consultant	$5,324	No		Lowest Technical Full-time Commission					

Excel

Advanced Formulas and Functions

Find Values Based on Conditions

You can use Excel functions to find the minimum and maximum values in a range that meets multiple criteria. The MINIFS function finds the smallest value that meets a given set of conditions and the MAXIFS function finds the largest value. **CASE** ▶ *Ellie asks you to find the lowest and highest commissions for full-time technical positions in the Boston office.*

STEPS

1. **Click cell H9, click the Insert Function button in the Function Library group, in the Insert Function dialog box type MINIFS in the Search for a function box, click Go, in the Select a function box verify that MINIFS is selected, then click OK**

2. **With the insertion point in the Min_range box select the range E2:E65, press F4, press TAB, with the insertion point in the Criteria_range1 box select the range C2:C65, press F4, press TAB, with the insertion point in the Criteria1 box type Technical, press TAB, with the insertion point in the Criteria_range2 box select the range D2:D65, press F4, press TAB, with the insertion point in the Criteria2 box type Full-time, then click OK**

   The lowest commission for the technical division's full-time placements, 1311, appears in cell H9. Your formula, as shown in the formula bar in **FIGURE 11-8**, asks Excel to search the range C2:C65 for the value Technical and the range D2:D65 for the value Full-time, and when both of those conditions are met to return the lowest value in the range E2:E65.

3. **With cell H9 selected click the Home tab on the ribbon, click the Copy button ⬚ in the Clipboard group, click cell H11, click the Paste button arrow in the Clipboard group, then click the Formulas button ⬚ in the Paste category**

   The MINIFS formula is pasted in cell H11 and appears in the formula bar.

4. **Press ESC, verify cell H11 is selected, select MIN in the MINIFS formula in the formula bar, type MAX, then click the Enter button ☑ in the formula bar**

   The formula is edited to find the maximum value in the commission range for the technical division's full-time placements rather than the minimum, and the result, 9268, appears in cell H11.

5. **Select the range I2:J6, press and hold CTRL, click cell H9, then click cell H11**

6. **Click the Accounting Number Format button ⬚ in the Number group, then widen column I if necessary to fully display the commission values**

7. **Compare your worksheet to FIGURE 11-9, then save your work**

FIGURE 11-8: MINIFS function

FIGURE 11-9: Formatted commissions

Working with logical functions

IF functions such as MINIFS and MAXIFS are in the logical category in the function library. Other logical functions include IFS and SWITCH. You can use IFS when you are using nested IF functions, to check a condition or conditions and display the value shown for the first true condition. For example, in **FIGURE 11-10**, the IFS function in cell B2 displays the letter grade that corresponds to the numeric grade in cell A2. The SWITCH function looks for a matching value and displays text to switch with it. In the example shown here, the formula in cell C2 is =SWITCH(B2,"A","Excellent","B","Good","C","Fair", "D","Poor","F","Failing"). This function looks at the letter grade in cell B2 and displays the corresponding value.

FIGURE 11-10: Logical functions

	A	B	C
1	Average	Grade	Evaluation
2	82	B	Good

Formula for IFS function: =IFS(A2>=90,"A",A2>=80,"B",A2>=70,"C",A2>=60,"D",A2<60,"F")

Result of IFS function

B corresponds to Good in SWITCH formula

Construct Formulas Using Named Ranges

Learning Outcomes
- Assign names to cell ranges
- Build formulas using names

To make your worksheet easier to follow, you can assign names to cells and ranges. Then you can use the names in formulas to make them easier to build and to reduce formula errors. Cell and range names can use uppercase or lowercase letters as well as digits but cannot have spaces. After you name a cell or range, you can define its **scope**, or the location in a worksheet where you want the range to be recognized. When defining a name's scope, you can limit its use to a worksheet or make it available to the entire workbook. When used in formulas, names become absolute cell references by default. **CASE** ▸ *Ellie asks you to calculate the number of placements for each division. You will use range names to construct the formula.*

STEPS

1. **On the Boston sheet select the range C2:C65, click the Formulas tab on the ribbon, then click the Define Name button in the Defined Names group**

   The New Name dialog box opens, as shown in **FIGURE 11-11**.

2. **Type Division in the Name box, click the Scope list arrow, click Boston, then click OK**

   The name assigned to the selected range appears in the Name Box. The scope is limited to the Boston sheet because the New York and Philadelphia sheets also contain division data.

3. **Select the range D1:D65, click the Create from Selection button in the Defined Names group, in the Create Names from Selection dialog box, verify the Top row check box is selected, then click OK**

   The range D2:D65 is assigned a name from the top row of the selection, Position Type.

4. **Click the Name Manager button in the Defined Names group**

   The two names that have been assigned Division and Position_Type are listed in the Name Manager dialog box, as shown in **FIGURE 11-12**. Excel added an underscore (_) between *Position* and *Type* because range names cannot contain spaces. The Name Manager can be used to create, delete, and edit names in a workbook.

5. **Click Close, click cell K2, click the More Functions button in the Function Library group, point to Statistical, scroll down the list of functions if necessary, then click COUNTIF**

   Like SUMIF and AVERAGEIF, the COUNTIF function allows you to specify conditions. COUNTIF counts cells based on those specified conditions.

6. **With the insertion point in the Range box type Division, press TAB, with the insertion point in the Criteria box click cell H2, then click OK**

   Your formula asks Excel to search the range named Division, and where it finds the value shown in cell H2, "Technical," to add one to the total count. The number of technical placements, 18, appears in cell K2.

7. **With cell K2 selected, drag the fill handle to fill the range K3:K5**

8. **Click cell K6, type =COUNT, in the list of functions double-click COUNTIFS, click the Use in Formula button in the Defined Names group, click Division, type , "Technical",, click the Use in Formula button, click Position_Type, type , "Full-time"), then click the Enter button ☑ in the formula bar**

   The number of technical full-time placements, 9, appears in cell K6, as shown in **FIGURE 11-13**.

9. **Save the workbook**

Advanced Formulas and Functions

FIGURE 11-11: New Name dialog box

FIGURE 11-12: Name Manager dialog box

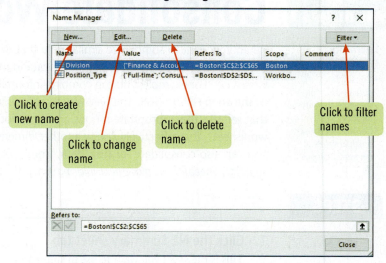

FIGURE 11-13: Worksheet with placement information

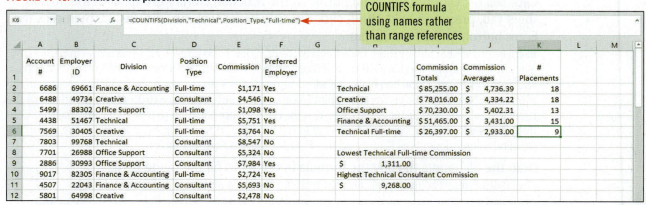

Using formulas to conditionally format data

You can use a formula to format worksheet data by entering it in a conditional formatting rule. To create a conditional formatting rule with a formula, select the cells you want to format, click the Home tab on the ribbon, click the Conditional Formatting button in the Styles group, then click New Rule. In the New Formatting Rule dialog box, click Use a formula to determine which cells to format, enter the formula in the Format values where this formula is true box, click the Format button, choose a format, then click OK. For example, applying the formatting rule shown in **FIGURE 11-14** formats the selected range E2:E17 using blue fill.

FIGURE 11-14: Conditional formatting rule with formula

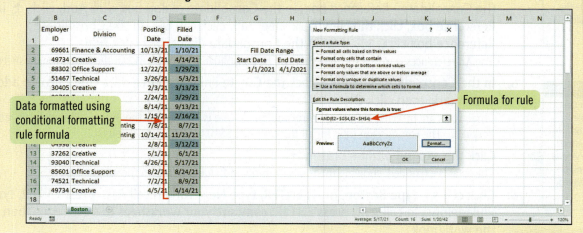

Advanced Formulas and Functions

Consolidate Worksheet Data

Learning Outcomes
- Consolidate data on multiple sheets in the same location
- Consolidate data on multiple sheets in different locations

When you want to summarize similar data that exists in different sheets or workbooks, you can consolidate it. **Consolidating data** combines data in multiple worksheets and displays the results on another worksheet. For example, you can combine information from three different sheets on one summary sheet, as shown in **FIGURE 11-15**. The best way to consolidate data is to add cell references in the summary sheet that refer to the appropriate ranges on the various sheets. Because these references span two or more worksheets, they effectively create another dimension in the workbook and are called **3-D references**. You can also consolidate, or **link** data, from separate workbooks. **CASE** *Ellie asks you to prepare a summary sheet for the placement information in the three Northeast offices.*

STEPS

1. **Click the NE Summary sheet tab**

   This is the sheet you want to use to summarize the placement data contained in the other sheets.

2. **Click cell B4, click the AutoSum button in the Function Library group, click the Boston sheet tab, press and hold SHIFT, click the New York sheet tab, click cell I2, then click the Enter button in the formula bar**

   In cell B4 of the NE Summary sheet, the formula bar reads =SUM('Boston:New York'!I2), as shown in **FIGURE 11-16**. 'Boston:New York' indicates Boston is the first sheet and New York is the last in the group of Boston, Philadelphia, and New York sheets. Quotation marks are added automatically when a sheet name includes a space as in the sheet name New York. The exclamation point (!) is an **external reference indicator**, indicating that the referenced cells are outside the active sheet; I2 is the cell reference you want to total in the external sheets. All three sheets reference the same cell. The result in cell B4 of the NE Summary sheet, 153488, is the sum of the technical commissions in cell I2 of the Boston, Philadelphia, and New York sheets.

3. **Drag the fill handle to copy the formula in cell B4 to fill the range B5:B7**

   The copied formula adjusts to calculate the totals for the other divisions.

4. **Click cell B9, click the Data tab on the ribbon, click the Consolidate button ▤ in the Data Tools group, in the Consolidate dialog box verify Sum is selected in the Function box, click the Collapse dialog box button ⬆ in the Reference box, click the Boston sheet tab, click cell E66, click the Expand dialog box button ⬇ in the Consolidate - Reference box, then click Add in the Consolidate dialog box**

   The Consolidate dialog box offers an alternative to using the formula bar to enter external references and consolidates worksheet data located in different ranges of a workbook. The Boston sheet reference to cell E66 is added to the All references box.

QUICK TIP

Entering the formula =SUM(Boston!E66+ Philadelphia!E61+ 'New York'!E63) in cell B12 of the NE Summary worksheet to consolidate the data will result in the same total.

5. **Click ⬆ in the Reference box, click the Philadelphia sheet tab, click cell E61, click ⬇ in the Consolidate - Reference box, in the Consolidate dialog box click Add, click ⬆ in the Reference box, click the New York sheet tab, click cell E63, in the Consolidate - Reference box click ⬇, then in the Consolidate dialog box click Add**

   The All references box lists the data that will be consolidated into cell B12 in the NE Summary sheet.

6. **In the Consolidate dialog box click the Create links to source data check box to add a checkmark, then click OK**

   Three rows are inserted above row nine and an outline is created for the Boston, Philadelphia, and New York data. The commission total for all three offices, $510,618, appears in cell B12.

QUICK TIP

You can click the level 2 Outline Symbol button 2 to display the total details and the level 1 Outline Symbol button 1 to hide the details.

7. **Click the expand outline button ⊞**

   The total is expanded, showing the totals from the individual offices in the range B9:B11.

8. **Click cell A9, type Boston, press ENTER, type New York in cell A10, press ENTER, type Philadelphia in cell A11, press ENTER, compare your worksheet to FIGURE 11-17, then save the workbook**

FIGURE 11-15: Consolidating data from three worksheets

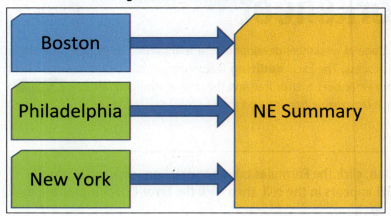

FIGURE 11-16: 3-D reference in formula

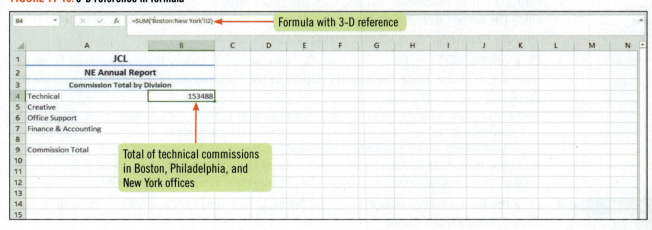

Formula with 3-D reference

Total of technical commissions in Boston, Philadelphia, and New York offices

FIGURE 11-17: NE Summary worksheet with totals

Expanded outline shows commissions from individual offices

Audit a Worksheet

Because errors can occur at any stage of worksheet development, it is important to include auditing as part of your workbook-building process. The Excel **auditing** feature helps you track errors and check worksheet logic to make sure your worksheet is error free and the data is arranged sensibly. **CASE** *Ellie asks you to help identify errors in the expense-tracking worksheet.*

STEPS

QUICK TIP

You can use the IFERROR function to display a message that you specify if there is an error in a formula; for example, if editing the formula in cell N7 to =IFERROR(N3+N4+N5+N6, "Error in Formula") displays "Error in Formula" in cell N7 rather than #VALUE!.

1. **Click the Expenses sheet tab, click the Formulas tab on the ribbon, click cell N7, verify the error message #VALUE! appears in the cell, then click the Error Checking button in the Formula Auditing group**

   The Error Checking dialog box opens and alerts you to a data type error. This error is a result of cell N3, which contains text, having been included in the formula, as shown in **FIGURE 11-18**.

2. **Click Edit in Formula Bar in the Error Checking dialog box, edit the formula in the formula bar to read =N4+N5+N6, click the Enter button ✓ in the formula bar, then close the Error Checking dialog box**

   The edited formula produces the correct result, $132,192 in cell N7.

3. **Click cell N5, click the Error Checking Options button ⚠, view the Inconsistent Formula warning, click the Trace Precedents button in the Formula Auditing group, then click the Trace Dependents button**

   Blue arrows point from the cells referenced by the formula to the active cell, and to cells in which the formula is referenced, as shown in **FIGURE 11-19**. These **tracer arrows** help you determine which cells might have caused the error and whether any additional errors might be present. Tracing the precedents shows you that cell B5, the January total, isn't included in the Philadelphia annual total formula. Tracing the dependents indicates that this formula error affects the formulas in cells N7 and O5.

QUICK TIP

You can use the Trace Error tool to highlight the cells used to calculate a formula by clicking the Formulas tab on the Ribbon, clicking the Error Checking button arrow in the Formula Auditing group, then clicking Trace Error.

4. **Click the Remove Arrows button in the Formula Auditing group, click ⚠, then click Copy Formula from Above**

   The Philadelphia total changes to $37,898.

5. **Click cell O5, click the Evaluate Formula button in the Formula Auditing group, click Evaluate, verify that 37898 was substituted for N5 in the Evaluation box, click Evaluate again, verify that 0 was substituted for N8, click Evaluate again, verify that #DIV/0! appears in the Evaluation box, then click Close**

   The source of the error lies in the reference to cell N8 in the denominator, which has a value of zero, rather than the total in cell N7. The formula in cell O4 uses a relative reference to cell N7, and when the formula was copied the denominator changed to N8.

6. **Click cell O4, click to the left of N7 in the formula bar, press F4, click ✓ in the formula bar, drag the fill handle ✚ to fill the range O5:O6, click cell A1, click the Error Checking button in the Formula Auditing group, verify there aren't any additional errors, as shown in FIGURE 11-20, click OK, then save the workbook**

Watching formulas

As you edit your worksheet, you can watch the effect that cell changes have on selected worksheet formulas. Select the cell or cells that you want to watch, click the Formulas tab on the ribbon, click the Watch Window button in the Formula Auditing group, click Add Watch in the Watch Window, then click Add. The Watch Window lists the workbook name, worksheet name, the cell address you want to watch, the current cell value, and its formula. As cell values that "feed into" the formula change, the resulting formula value in the Watch Window changes. To delete a watch, select the cell information in the Watch Window, click Delete Watch, then close the Watch Window.

FIGURE 11-18: Error Checking dialog box

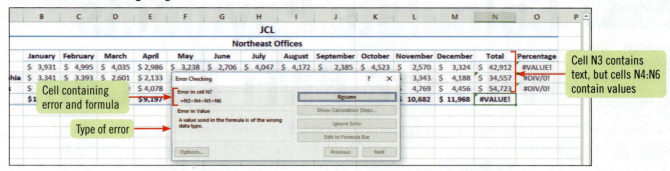

Cell N3 contains text, but cells N4:N6 contain values

Cell containing error and formula

Type of error

FIGURE 11-19: Worksheet with tracer arrows

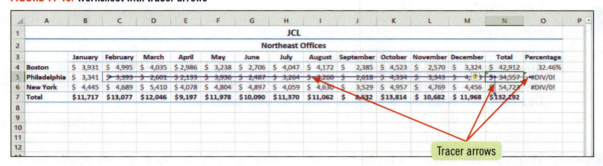

Tracer arrows

FIGURE 11-20: Final error check results

Confirmation the sheet has been checked for errors

Circling invalid data

If you enter data validation criteria to your worksheet data, you can locate data that doesn't satisfy that criteria by clicking the Data tab on the ribbon, clicking the Data Validation arrow, then clicking Circle Invalid Data. Red circles appear around cells that are not consistent with data validation criteria, as shown in **FIGURE 11-21**. To clear the circles on the worksheet, click, then click Clear Validation Circles.

FIGURE 11-21: Circled invalid data

Data that doesn't meet the data validation criteria

Maximum value for selected range

Calculate Payments with the PMT Function

**Learning
Outcomes**
• Calculate monthly
  payments using
  the PMT function
• Edit the PMT
  function to display
  payments as a
  positive value

PMT is a financial function that calculates the periodic payment amount for money borrowed. **FIGURE 11-22** illustrates a PMT function that calculates the monthly payment for a $20,000 car loan at 6.5% interest over 5 years. **CASE** *JCL's Northeast region is considering opening a new branch in Providence. Ellie has obtained loan quotes from a commercial bank, a venture capitalist, and a private lender. She wants you to summarize the loan information.*

STEPS

1. Click the **Loan** sheet tab, click cell **F4**, click the **Financial button** in the Function Library group, scroll down the list of functions, click **PMT**, with the insertion point in the Rate box click cell **D4** on the worksheet, type **/12**, then press **TAB**

   You must divide the annual interest by 12 because you are calculating monthly, not annual, payments. You need to be consistent about the units you use for rate and nper.

2. With the insertion point in the Nper box click cell **E4**, click the **Pv box**, click cell **B4**, then click **OK**

   The payment of ($5,193.98) in cell F4 appears in red, indicating that it is a negative amount. Excel displays the result of a PMT function as a negative value to reflect the negative cash flow the loan represents to the borrower.

   QUICK TIP
   The Fv and Type
   arguments are
   optional: Fv is the
   future value, or the
   total amount you
   want to obtain after
   all payments. If you
   omit it, Excel assumes
   you want to pay off
   the loan completely,
   so the default Fv is 0.
   Type indicates when
   the payments are
   made; 0 is the end of
   the period, and 1 is
   the beginning of the
   period. The default is
   the end of the period.

3. Double-click cell **F4**, edit **B4** in the formula bar to **-B4**, then click the **Enter button** ☑ in the formula bar

   The monthly payment displays a positive number as shown in **FIGURE 11-23**.

4. With cell **F4** selected, drag the **fill handle** to fill the range **F5:F6**

   A monthly payment of $9,401.29 for the venture capitalist loan appears in cell F5. A monthly payment of $15,019.15 for the private lender loan appears in cell F6.

5. Click cell **G4**, type **=**, click cell **E4**, type *****, click cell **F4**, press **TAB**, in cell H4 type **=**, click cell **G4**, type **–**, click cell **B4**, click ☑, copy cells **G4:H4** into the range **G5:H6**, click cell **A1**, then compare your worksheet to **FIGURE 11-24**

6. **sam↑** Group all the worksheets, add your name to the center section of the grouped footer, ungroup the worksheets, save the workbook, submit the workbook to your instructor, close the workbook, then close Excel

FIGURE 11-22: Example of PMT function for car loan

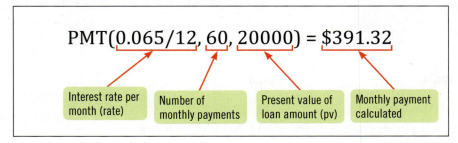

FIGURE 11-23: PMT function calculating monthly loan payment

FIGURE 11-24: Completed worksheet

	A	B	C	D	E	F	G	H	I	J	K
1					JCL						
2				Expansion Loan Summary							
3	Lender	Loan Amount	Term (Years)	Interest Rate	Term (Months)	Monthly Payment	Total Payments	Total Interest			
4	Commercial Bank	$ 500,000	10	4.55%	120	$5,193.98	$ 623,277.60	$ 123,277.60			
5	Venture Capitalist	$ 500,000	5	4.85%	60	$9,401.29	$ 564,077.68	$ 64,077.68			
6	Private Lender	$ 500,000	3	5.15%	36	$15,019.15	$ 540,689.22	$ 40,689.22			
7											

Working with other financial functions

You can use the FV (Future Value) function to determine the amount of money a given monthly investment will amount to, at a given interest rate, after a given number of payment periods. The syntax is FV(rate,nper,pmt,pv,type), where *rate* is the interest paid by the financial institution, *nper* is the number of periods, and *pmt* is the amount you deposit. For example, suppose you want to invest $1,000 every month for the next 12 months into an account that pays 2% a year. You can enter the function FV(.02/12,12,-1000) and Excel returns the value $12,110.61 as the future value of your investment.

You can use the NPER function to determine the number of payment periods required for a loan or investment. For example, if you want to take out a loan for $20,000 at an interest rate of 6% with payments of $400 monthly, you can enter =NPER(6%/12,400,-20000) and Excel returns the value 57.68. You can use the PV function to find the present value of a loan or an investment. For example, if you have an investment that will pay you an amount of $200 for 10% per month over 30 years, you can enter =PV(10%/12,12*30,200) and Excel returns a value of $22,790.16.

Practice

Skills Review

1. **Separate data using Flash Fill.**
   a. Start Excel, open IL_EX_11-2.xlsx from the location where you store your Data Files, then save it as **IL_EX_11_LegalServices**.
   b. On the Managers worksheet, insert two new columns to the left of column B.
   c. Enter **Jay** in cell B1 and **Sears** in cell C1.
   d. Use Flash Fill to enter all first names in column B and all last names in column C.
   e. Save your work.

2. **Format data using text functions.**
   a. In cell E1, use a text function to convert the first letter of the department in cell D1 to uppercase, then copy the formula in cell E1 into the range E2:E8.
   b. In cell F1, use the CONCAT text function to display the first and last names together, with a space between them.
   c. Copy the formula in cell F1 into the range F2:F8, then widen column F to fully display the full names.
   d. In cell G1, use the TEXTJOIN text function to combine the department name in cell E1 with the text **Department**, using a space as a delimiter.
   e. Copy the formula in cell G1 into the range G2:G8, then widen column G to fully display the department names.
   f. Copy the range F1:G8, then paste the copied data as values starting in cell H1.
   g. Delete columns A through G, widen columns A and B to fully display the names and departments, then save your work. Compare your worksheet to **FIGURE 11-25**.

FIGURE 11-25

	A	B	C	D	E	F	G	H	I	J	K	L	M	N	O
1	Jay Sears	Civil Department													
2	Carol Trull	Land Department													
3	Lucy Knoll	Operations Department													
4	Mia Meng	Land Department													
5	Robert Dally	Civil Department													
6	Carey Degual	Land Department													
7	Jody Wolls	Civil Department													
8	Mary Alworth	Operations Department													
9															
10															

3. **Sum a data range based on conditions.**
   a. Activate the Partners worksheet.
   b. In cell B15, use the AVERAGEIF function to average the salaries and bonuses of those with a review of 5.
   c. In cell B16, use the SUMIF function to total the salaries of employees with a review of 5.
   d. Format cells B15 and B16 with the Accounting Number format using two decimals.
   e. Save your work.

4. **Find values based on conditions.**
   a. In cell B20, use the MAXIFS function to find the highest salary of employees with a rating of 5 and professional development hours of 10 or more. Use absolute cell references for the ranges in the formula.
   b. In cell B21, use the MINIFS function to find the lowest salary of employees with a rating of 5 and professional development hours of 10 or more. (*Hint:* You can copy the formula in cell B20 and edit it for MINIFS.)
   c. Format cells B20 and B21 with the Accounting Number format using two decimals.
   d. Save your work.

Skills Review (continued)

5. Construct formulas using named ranges.

a. On the Partners sheet, name the range C3:C11 **Review**, and limit the scope of the name to the Partners worksheet.

b. In cell B17, use the COUNTIF function to count the number of employees with a review of 5 using the named range.

c. Use the Name Manager to add a comment of **Scale of 1 to 5** to the review name. (*Hint:* In the Name Manager dialog box, click the Review name, then click Edit to enter the comment.)

d. Save your work.

e. Compare your worksheet to **FIGURE 11-26**.

FIGURE 11-26

6. Consolidate data using a formula.

a. Activate the Summary sheet.

b. In cell B3, use the AutoSum function to total cell D12 on the Partners and Associates sheets.

c. Format cell B3 with the Accounting Number format with two decimal places.

d. In cell B4, use the Consolidate dialog box to total cell B16 on the Partners sheets and cell G5 on the Associates sheet, creating links to the source data.

e. Expand the outlined data, then enter **Associates** in cell A4 and **Partners** in cell A5.

f. Compare your worksheet to **FIGURE 11-27**.

FIGURE 11-27

Skills Review (continued)

7. Audit a worksheet.

  a. Activate the Profit worksheet.

  b. Select cell B15, then use the Trace Precedents button to find the cells on which that figure is based. Use the Trace Dependents button to find cells that use the value in cell B15. Remove all tracer arrows.

  c. Correct the formula in cell B15. (*Hint:* It should subtract Total Expenses from Total Income.)

  d. Select cell G5 and use the Error Checking button to review a description of the error. Evaluate the formula in cell G5 to locate the error, then fix the error.

  e. Use the Error Checking button to check the worksheet for any other errors. Compare your worksheet to **FIGURE 11-28**, then save the workbook.

FIGURE 11-28

	A	B	C	D	E	F	G	H	I	J	K	L
1				TWP Legal Services								
2		Q1	Q2	Q3	Q4	Total	% of Total					
3	Income											
4	Civil	$ 1,552,263	$ 1,505,095	$ 2,084,056	$ 1,648,297	$ 6,789,711	47.46%					
5	Land	$ 1,514,954	$ 2,414,730	$ 2,063,992	$ 1,524,199	$ 7,517,875	52.54%					
6	Total Income	$ 3,067,217	$ 3,919,825	$ 4,148,048	$ 3,172,496	$ 14,307,586						
7												
8	Expenses											
9	Salaries & Bonuses	$ 950,158	$ 928,751	$ 940,582	$ 912,544	$ 3,732,035	95.06%					
10	Rent	$ 25,000	$ 25,000	$ 25,000	$ 25,000	$ 100,000	2.55%					
11	Advertising	$ 3,900	$ 18,200	$ 18,500	$ 2,300	$ 42,900	1.09%					
12	Cleaning	$ 2,100	$ 2,100	$ 2,800	$ 1,900	$ 8,900	0.23%					
13	Insurance	$ 10,542	$ 10,542	$ 10,542	$ 10,542	$ 42,168	1.07%					
14	Total Expenses	$ 991,700	$ 984,593	$ 997,424	$ 952,286	$ 3,926,003	100.00%					
15	Net Profit	$ 2,075,517	$ 2,935,232	$ 3,150,624	$ 2,220,210	$ 10,381,583						
16												

8. Calculate payments with the PMT function.

  a. Activate the Loan sheet.

  b. In cell B8, determine the monthly payment using the loan information shown. (*Hint:* Use the Function Arguments dialog box to enter the formula **=PMT(B4/12,B5,-B3)**.)

  c. In cell B9, enter a formula that multiplies the total number of payments by the monthly payment.

  d. In cell B10, enter the formula that subtracts the loan amount from the total payment amount, if necessary format cell B10 as currency, then compare your results to **FIGURE 11-29**.

  e. Group the six worksheets, enter your name in the grouped worksheet footer, ungroup the worksheets, save the workbook, then submit your workbook to your instructor.

  f. Close the workbook, then close Excel.

FIGURE 11-29

	A	B	C	D	E	F	G	H	I	J	K	L	M	N	O
1		TWP Legal Services													
2		New Office Loan													
3	Loan Amount	$ 775,000													
4	Interest Rate	4.75%													
5	Term in Months	48													
6															
7															
8	Monthly Payment:	$17,760.07													
9	Total Payments:	$852,483.31													
10	Total Interest:	$77,483.31													
11															
12															
13															
14															

Independent Challenge 1

Tony Sanchez, RM's office manager, uses Excel formulas and functions to analyze insurance reimbursement data for the Northeast imaging facilities. You will help Tony analyze and consolidate imaging data and estimate loan costs for a new imaging center.

a. Start Excel, open IL_EX_11-3.xlsx from the location where you store your Data Files, then save it as **IL_EX_11_Imaging**.

b. On the Technicians sheet, enter **troy silva** in cell B4, enter **boston** in cell C4, then enter **5** in cell D4.

c. Using the data you entered as an example, use Flash Fill to enter the names, offices, and years in columns B, C, and D.

d. In cell E4, use the PROPER function to display the name from cell B4 with the correct capitalization for proper names.

e. Use the fill handle to copy the formula in cell E4 to cell F4, then copy the formulas in cells E4:F4 to the range E5:F15.

f. In cell G4, use the TEXTJOIN function to join the text in cell D4 with the text **Years**, using a space as a delimiter.

g. Copy the formula in cell G4 into the range G5:G15. Copy the data in the range E1:G15, then paste the selection as values in the range that begins in cell H1. Delete columns A through G.

h. On the Boston sheet, name the range A4:A22 **Procedure**, and give the name a scope of the workbook. (*Hint:* Select the range A3:A22, then use the top row to create the Procedure name from the selection.)

i. In cell F5, use the COUNTIF function, the named range Procedure, and the value in cell E5 to determine the number of MRI procedures, then copy the formula into the range F6:F8.

j. Assign the name **Insurance_Payment** to the range B4:B22, using the scope of the workbook. In cell G5, use the SUMIF function, the named ranges Procedure and Insurance_Payment, and the value in cell E5 to determine the total insurance payments for MRI procedures, then copy the formula into the range G6:G8.

k. In cell H5, use the AVERAGEIF function, the named ranges Procedure and Insurance_Payment, and the value in cell E5 to determine the average payment for MRI procedures, then copy the formula into the range H6:H8.

l. In cell B4 on the NE Summary sheet, enter a formula that uses 3-D references to total the number of MRI procedures in cell F5 on the Boston and Newton sheets. Copy the formula in cell B4 to cell C4, then copy the formulas in the range B4:C4 to the range B5:C7.

m. In cell F4, use the Consolidate dialog box to total the insurance payments in cell B23 of the Boston sheet and cell B24 of the Newton sheet. Link the total to the source data.

n. Format the value in cell D6 as a percentage with two decimal places. Use error checking to find a description of the error in cell D7. Evaluate the formula in cell D7 to troubleshoot and resolve the error. Use tracer arrows to find cells referenced in the formula, then delete the arrows.

o. Edit the formula in cell D6 so it reads = C6/$F$6, then copy the formula in cell D6 to the range D7:D9.

p. In cell F4 on the Loan sheet, use the PMT function to calculate the monthly payment using the loan amount in cell B4, the interest rate in cell D4, and the term in cell E4. (*Hint:* Divide the rate by 12 to enter a monthly rate.)

Independent Challenge 1 (continued)

q. Widen column F to fully display the monthly payment, then edit the formula in cell F4 to display the payment as a positive number.

r. In cell G4 enter a formula that calculates the total payments by multiplying the monthly payment by the number of months. In cell H4, enter a formula to calculate the total interest by subtracting the loan amount from the total payments, then widen column H to fully display the total interest.

s. Copy the formulas in the range F4:H4 into the range F5:H6, then compare your worksheet to FIGURE 11-30.

t. Group the worksheets, add your name to the center section of the grouped worksheet footers, ungroup the worksheets, save the workbook, then submit the workbook to your instructor.

u. Close the workbook, then close Excel.

FIGURE 11-30

	A	B	C	D	E	F	G	H	I	J
1				Riverwalk Clinic						
2				Imaging Center Loan Summary						
3	Lender	Loan Amount	Term (Years)	Interest Rate	Term (Months)	Monthly Payment	Total Payments	Total Interest		
4	Commercial Bank	$400,000	5	5.15%	60	$7,576.01	$454,560.78	$54,560.78		
5	Venture Capitalist	$400,000	3	5.05%	36	$11,997.34	$431,904.26	$31,904.26		
6	Investment Banker	$400,000	2	4.75%	24	$17,503.81	$420,091.34	$20,091.34		
7										
8										
9										
10										

Independent Challenge 2

As an accountant working in RSJ Advertising, you have been asked to analyze revenue in the Texas offices. The firm plans to open a new office in the state, and you will examine the options for a loan to finance this expansion.

a. Start Excel, open IL_EX_11-4.xlsx from the location where you store your Data Files, then save it as **IL_EX_11_Revenue**.

b. Name the range containing the company's offices **Office** with a scope of the workbook, name the range containing the revenue data **Revenue** with a scope of the workbook, then name the range containing the type data **Type** with a scope of the workbook.

c. In cell G4, use the SUMIF function and named ranges to calculate the total revenue for print advertising. Use a relative reference to cell F4 for the criteria.

d. In cell H4, use the AVERAGEIF function and named ranges to calculate the average revenue for print advertising. Use a relative reference to cell F4 for the criteria.

e. In cell I4, use the COUNTIF function and a named range to calculate the total number of print ads. Use a relative reference to cell F4 for the criteria.

f. Copy the formulas in G4:I4 into the range G5:I7.

g. In cell G8, use the SUMIFS function and named ranges to calculate the total revenue for Houston broadcast media advertising.

h. In cell H8, use the AVERAGEIFS function and named ranges to calculate the average revenue for Houston broadcast media advertising.

i. In cell I8, use the COUNTIFS function and named ranges to calculate the total number of Houston broadcast media ads.

j. In cell G11, use the MINIFS function and named ranges to calculate the lowest revenue Houston broadcast media ad.

k. In cell G12, use the MAXIFS function and named ranges to calculate the highest revenue Houston broadcast media ad.

l. In cell C3 of the Loan sheet, use the NPER function to find the number of months required to pay off a $500,000 loan with monthly payments of $8000 at an interest rate of 5.15%. (*Hint:* The present value, pv, is in cell A3, the rate needs to be divided by 12 for a monthly rate, and a - needs to be typed before the pv value so the month is displayed as a positive value.)

m. Copy the loan amount in cell A3 into the range A4:A10, then copy the monthly payment in cell D3 into the range D4:D10.

n. Select cell B3, then use **FIGURE 11-31** to enter interest rates in the range B4:B10 by increasing the rate by .25% until a rate of 7% is met. (*Hint:* To open the dialog box click the Home tab, click the Fill button in the Editing group, then click Series.)

o. Copy the formula in cell C3 into the range C4:C10.

p. Group the two worksheets, enter your name in the worksheet footer, ungroup the worksheets, save the workbook, then submit it to your instructor.

q. Close the workbook, then close Excel.

FIGURE 11-31

Visual Workshop

Open IL_EX_11-5.xlsx from the location where you store your Data Files, then save it as **IL_EX_11_Enrollment**. Use the data in the Fall, Spring, and Summer worksheets to create summary information on the Annual worksheet shown in **FIGURE 11-32**. The enrollment data are in the same location on all three worksheets. The number of graduates for each session appears in different locations on the three worksheets. Enter your name in the Annual worksheet footer, save the workbook, submit it to your instructor, then close Excel.

FIGURE 11-32

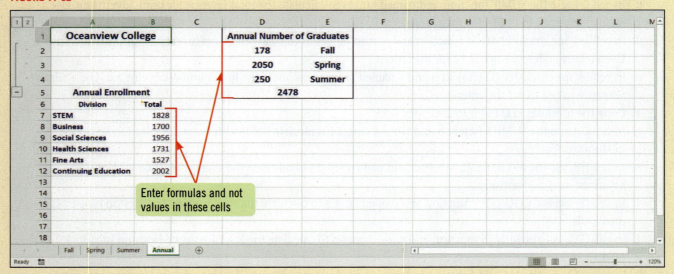

Advanced Formulas and Functions

Performing What-If Analysis

CASE ▸ Ellie Schwartz, JCL's vice president of finance, uses what-if analysis to analyze regional data and forecast possible outcomes. You will help Ellie using the data analysis tools and add-ins in Excel.

Module Objectives

After completing this module, you will be able to:

- Define what-if analysis
- Track what-if analysis with Scenario Manager
- Generate a scenario summary
- Project figures using a data table

- Use Goal Seek
- Find solutions using Solver
- Manage data using a data model
- Analyze data using Power Pivot

Files You Will Need

IL_EX_12-1.xlsx	IL_EX_12-5.xlsx
IL_EX_12-2.xlsx	IL_EX_12-6.xlsx
IL_EX_12-3.xlsx	IL_EX_12-7.xlsx
IL_EX_12-4.xlsx	

Define What-If Analysis

Learning Outcomes
- Develop guidelines for performing what-if analysis
- Define what-if analysis terminology

By performing what-if analysis in a worksheet, you can get immediate answers to questions such as, "What happens to profits if we sell 25 percent more of a certain product?" or, "What happens to monthly payments if interest rates rise or fall?" A worksheet you use to perform what-if analysis is often called a **model** because it acts as the basis for multiple outcomes or sets of results. To perform what-if analysis in a worksheet, you change the value in one or more **input cells** (cells that contain data instead of formulas), then observe the effects on dependent cells. A **dependent cell** usually contains a formula whose resulting value changes depending on the values in the input cells. For more advanced data analysis, you can use Power Pivot, an Excel add-in, to create a PivotTable from multiple tables to obtain answers to what-if questions. **CASE** ▸ *Ellie has received projected revenue, budget, and placement data from the Northeast office managers. She has created a worksheet model to perform an initial what-if analysis, as shown in* **FIGURE 12-1**. *She thinks the Boston revenue projections for the month of January should be higher. You first review the guidelines for performing what-if analysis.*

DETAILS

When performing what-if analysis, use the following guidelines:

- **Understand and state the purpose of the worksheet model**

  Identify what you want to accomplish with the model. What problem are you trying to solve? What questions do you want the model to answer for you? Ellie's worksheet model is designed to total JCL revenue projections for the four offices during the first half of the year and to calculate the percentage of total revenue for each office. It also calculates total revenues and percentages for each month within that period.

- **Determine the data input value(s) that, if changed, affect(s) dependent cell results**

  In what-if analysis, changes in the data input cells produce varying results in the output cells. You will use the model to work with one data input value: the January value for the Boston office, in cell B3.

- **Identify the dependent cell(s) that will contain results**

  The dependent cells usually contain formulas, and the formula results adjust as you enter different values in the input cells. The results of two dependent cell formulas appear in cells H3 (the Total for Boston) and I3 (the Percent of Total Revenue for Boston). Cell B6 (the Total for January) is also a dependent cell, as is cell B7 (the Percent of Total Revenue for January).

- **Formulate questions you want what-if analysis to answer and perform what-if analysis**

  It is important that you know the questions you want your model to answer before performing a what-if analysis. In the JCL model, one of the questions you want to answer is: What January Boston revenue target is required to bring the overall January revenue percentage to 18 percent?

- **Determine when to use advanced what-if analysis**

  If the answers to your what-if questions require data from multiple tables, you can use Power Pivot. Power Pivot enables you to create PivotTables using fields from multiple tables. **FIGURE 12-2** shows a PivotTable created with fields from two tables.

FIGURE 12-1: Worksheet model for a what-if analysis

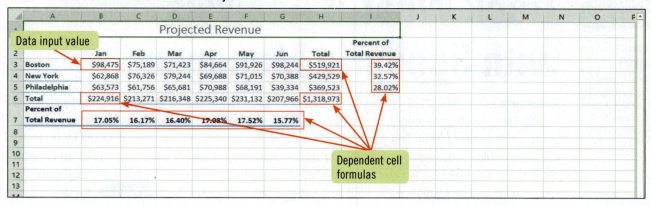

FIGURE 12-2: PivotTable using fields from two tables

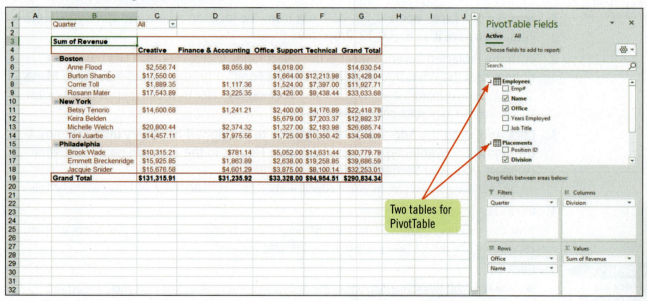

Track What-If Analysis with Scenario Manager

A **scenario** is a named set of values you use in a what-if analysis to store and observe different worksheet results. For example, you might plan to sell 100 of a particular item, at a price of $5 per item, producing revenue results of $500. But what if you reduced the price to $4 or increased it to $6? Each of these scenarios would produce different revenue results. A changing input value, such as the price in this example, is called a **variable**. The Excel Scenario Manager simplifies the process of what-if analysis by allowing you to name and save multiple scenarios with variable values in a worksheet. **CASE** *You decide to use Scenario Manager to create scenarios showing how a Boston revenue increase can affect total JCL revenue over the three-month period of February through April.*

STEPS

1. **sam↓** **Start Excel, open IL_EX_12-1.xlsx from the location where you store your Data Files, then save it as IL_EX_12_Projection**

2. **With the Projected Revenue sheet active select range C3:E3, click the Data tab on the ribbon, click the What-If Analysis button in the Forecast group, then click Scenario Manager**

   The first step in defining a scenario is choosing the **changing cells**, those that contain the values that will change in order to produce multiple sets of results.

3. **Click Add, drag the Add Scenario dialog box to the right if necessary until columns A through G are visible, type Original Revenue Figures in the Scenario name box, then compare your Add Scenario dialog box to FIGURE 12-3**

   You want to be able to easily return to your original worksheet values, so this first scenario contains those figures.

4. **Click OK**

   Now that you have confirmed the scenario range, the Scenario Values dialog box opens, as shown in FIGURE 12-4. The current values appear in the changing cell boxes.

5. **Click OK**

   Because you want this scenario to reflect the current worksheet values, you leave these unchanged.

6. **Click Add, in the Scenario name box type Increase Feb, Mar, Apr by 4000, verify that the Changing cells box reads C3:E3, click OK, in the Scenario Values dialog box change the value in the $C$3 box to 79189, change the value in the $D$3 box to 75423, change the value in the $E$3 box to 88664, then click Add**

   The second scenario shows the effects of increasing revenue by $4,000 in February, March, and April.

7. **In the Scenario name box type Increase Feb, Mar, Apr by 10000, click OK, in the Scenario Values dialog box change the value in the $C$3 box to 85189, change the value in the $D$3 box to 81423, change the value in the $E$3 box to 94664, then click OK**

   The Scenario Manager dialog box lists the three scenarios, as shown in FIGURE 12-5.

8. **Click the Increase Feb, Mar, Apr by 10000 scenario, click Show, notice that the percent of Boston revenue in cell I3 changes to 40.77%, click the Increase Feb, Mar, Apr by 4000 scenario, click Show, notice that the Boston revenue percent is now 39.96%, click Original Revenue Figures, click Show, then click Close**

9. **Save the workbook**

FIGURE 12-3: Add Scenario dialog box

Cell range containing value that you will change

Your username and date will be different

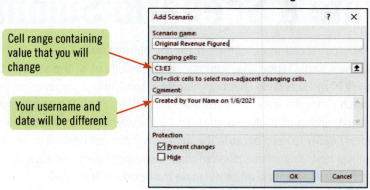

FIGURE 12-4: Scenario Values dialog box

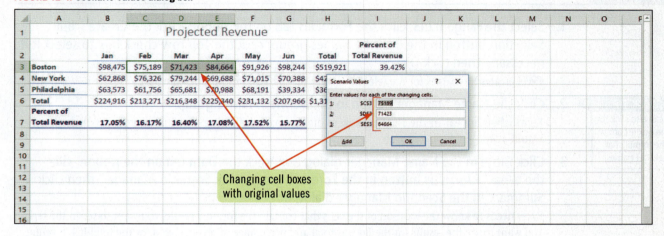

Changing cell boxes with original values

FIGURE 12-5: Scenario Manager dialog box with three scenarios listed

Scenarios

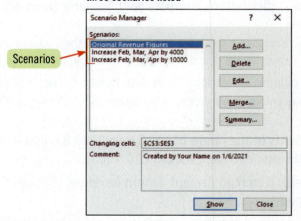

Merging scenarios

Excel stores scenarios on the worksheet of the workbook in which you created them. To apply scenarios from another worksheet or workbook into the current worksheet, click the Merge button in the Scenario Manager dialog box. The Merge Scenarios dialog box opens, letting you select scenarios from other locations. When you click a sheet name in the sheet list, a message under the sheet list tells you how many scenarios exist on that sheet.

To merge scenarios from another workbook, such as those sent to you in a workbook from a coworker, open the other workbook file, click the Book list arrow in the Merge Scenarios dialog box, then click the workbook name. When you merge workbook scenarios, it's best if the workbooks have the same structure, so that there is no confusion of cell values.

Generate a Scenario Summary

When comparing different scenario outcomes, it can be cumbersome to view each one separately. You might prefer to see a single report that summarizes the results of all the scenarios in a worksheet. A **scenario summary** is an Excel table that compiles data from various scenarios so that you can view the results next to each other, for easy comparison. For example, you can use a scenario summary to compare the best, worst, and most likely scenarios for a particular set of circumstances. Using cell naming makes the summary easier to read because the names, not the cell references, appear in the report. **CASE** ▶ *Now that you have defined multiple scenarios, you want to generate a scenario summary report. You begin by creating selected cell names, which will make the report easier to read.*

STEPS

1. **Select the range B2:I3, click the Formulas tab on the ribbon, click the Create from Selection button in the Defined Names group, click the Top row check box to select it if necessary, then click OK**

   Excel creates the names for the selected data in row 3 based on the labels in row 2.

2. **Click the Name Manager button in the Defined Names group**

   Eight labels appear in the Name Manager dialog box, confirming that they were created, as shown in **FIGURE 12-6**.

3. **Click Close in the Name Manager dialog box, click the Data tab on the ribbon, click the What-If Analysis button in the Forecast group, click Scenario Manager, then click Summary in the Scenario Manager dialog box**

   Excel needs to know the location of the cells that contain the formula results you want to see in the report. You want to see the results for the Boston total and percentage of revenue, and for the total JCL revenue.

4. **With the contents of the Result cells box selected click cell H3 on the worksheet, type „ click cell I3, type „ click cell H6, compare your Scenario Summary dialog box to FIGURE 12-7, then click OK**

   A summary of the worksheet's scenarios appears on a new sheet named Scenario Summary. The report shows outline buttons to the left of and above the worksheet so that you can hide or show report details.

5. **Right-click the column D heading, then click Delete in the shortcut menu**

   The Current Values column isn't necessary because it shows the same values as the Original Revenue Figures column.

6. **Delete the contents of the range B13:B15, select cell B2, edit it to read Scenario Summary for Boston Revenue, click cell C10, then edit it to read Total Boston Revenue**

7. **Click cell C11, edit it to read Percent Boston Revenue, click cell C12, then edit it to read Total JCL Revenue**

8. **Right-click the column A heading, click Delete in the shortcut menu, right-click the row 1 heading, click Delete in the shortcut menu, change the page orientation to landscape, then save the workbook**

   The scenario summary is now easier to read and understand, as shown in **FIGURE 12-8**.

FIGURE 12-6: Name Manager dialog box displaying names

FIGURE 12-7: Scenario Summary dialog box

Default report type

Cells to be recalculated when a new scenario is applied

FIGURE 12-8: Completed Scenario Summary report

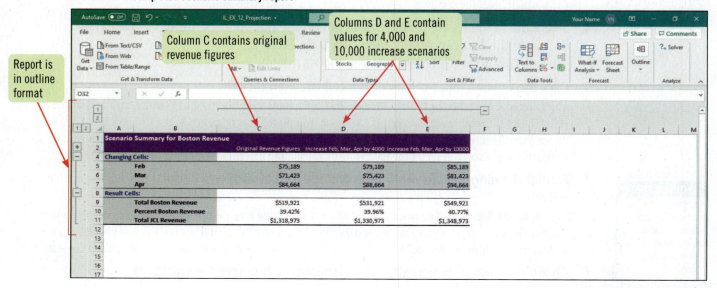

Column C contains original revenue figures

Columns D and E contain values for 4,000 and 10,000 increase scenarios

Report is in outline format

Project Figures Using a Data Table

Learning
Outcomes
• Develop a data
table structure
• Analyze options
using a data table

Another way to answer what-if questions in a worksheet is by using a data table. A **data table** is a range of cells that shows the resulting values when you change one or more input values in a formula. A **one-input data table** is a range of cells that shows the result of varying one input value. **CASE** ▶ *You want to find out how the Boston revenue percentage would change if the Boston total revenue increased. You begin by entering a set of possible values, in $50,000 increments, for the Boston total.*

STEPS

1. **Click the Projected Revenue sheet tab, enter Total Boston Revenue in cell K1, widen column K to fit the label, in cell K2 enter 419921, select the range K2:K6, click the Home tab on the ribbon, click the Fill button in the Editing group, click Series, in the Series dialog box make sure the Columns and Linear option buttons are selected, type 50000 in the Step value box, click OK, then format the selected range using the Accounting number format with no decimal places**

   You set up your data table by entering Boston revenue values lower and higher than the current projection in cell H3. Because the revenue values varied by a constant number, you used a linear series to quickly fill in the amounts. These possible revenue values constitute the **input values** in the data table.

2. **Click cell L1, type =, click cell I3, click the Enter button ✓ on the formula bar, then format cell L1 using the Percentage format with two decimal places**

   The value in cell I3, 39.42%, appears in cell L1, and the cell name =Percent_of_Total_Revenue appears in the formula bar, as shown in **FIGURE 12-9**. The percent formula in cell I3 will be used to create the data table by calculating the percentages (called the **output values**) in column L.

3. **With cell L1 selected click the Format button in the Cells group on the Home tab, click Format Cells, click the Number tab in the Format Cells dialog box if necessary, click Custom under Category, select the contents of the Type box, type ;;;, then click OK**

   Because it isn't necessary for users of the data table to see the value in cell L1, although the formula it references will be used in generating the data table, you applied the custom cell format of three semicolons (;;;), which hides the contents.

4. **Select the range K1:L6, click the Data tab on the ribbon, click the What-If Analysis button in the Forecast group, then click Data Table**

   The Data Table dialog box opens, as shown in **FIGURE 12-10**.

5. **Click the Column input cell box, click cell H3, then click OK**

   You entered a reference to cell H3 because the percentage formula in cell I3 (which you referenced in cell L1) uses the total revenue in cell H3 as input. You placed this reference in the Column input cell box rather than the Row input cell box because the varying input values are arranged in a column in your data table structure. Excel completes the data table by calculating percentages for each revenue amount.

6. **Format the range L2:L6 with the Percentage format with two decimal places, then click cell A1**

   The formatted data table is shown in **FIGURE 12-11**. It shows the revenue percentages for each of the possible levels of Boston revenue. By looking at the data table, Ellie determines that if she can increase total Boston revenue to $619,921, the Boston office will then comprise over 43% of total revenue for the first half of the year.

7. **Change the worksheet orientation to landscape, then save the workbook**

FIGURE 12-9: One-input data table structure

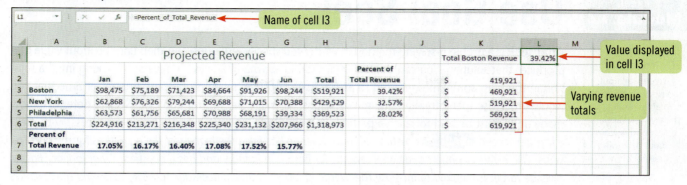

FIGURE 12-10: Data Table dialog box

Enter reference to total Boston revenue here →

FIGURE 12-11: Completed data table with resulting values

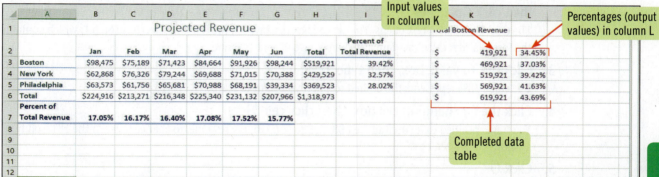

Creating a two-input data table

A **two-input data table** is a table in which you can vary the results in two cells and see the recalculated results. You could, for example, use a two-input data table to calculate your monthly car payment based on both varying interest rates and varying loan terms, as shown in **FIGURE 12-12**. In a two-input data table, different values of one input cell appear across the top row of the table, while different values of a second input cell are listed down the left column. You create a two-input data table the same way that you create a one-input data table, except you enter both a row and a column input cell. In the example, the two-input data table structure was created by first entering the number of payments in the range B6:D6 and the rates in the range A7:A15. Next, the data table values were created by selecting the range A6:D15, clicking the Data tab, clicking the What-If Analysis button in the Forecast group, then clicking Data Table. In the Data Table dialog box, the row input value is the term in cell B3. The column input value is the interest rate in cell B2. You can check the accuracy of these

values by cross-referencing the values in the data table with those in the range B1:B4, where you can see that an interest rate of 3.75% for 60 months has a monthly payment of $302.01.

FIGURE 12-12: Two-input data table

	A	B	C	D	E
1	Loan Amount	$16,500.00			
2	Annual Interest Rate	3.75%			
3	Term in Months	60			
4	Monthly Payment:	$302.01			
5					
6			36	48	60
7		3.00%	$479.84	$365.22	$296.48
8		3.25%	$481.66	$367.04	$298.32
9		3.50%	$483.48	$368.87	$300.16
10		3.75%	$485.31	$370.71	$302.01
11		4.00%	$487.15	$372.55	$303.87
12		4.25%	$488.98	$374.40	$305.74
13		4.50%	$490.82	$376.26	$307.61
14		4.75%	$492.67	$378.12	$309.49
15		5.00%	$494.52	$379.98	$311.38
16					
17					
18					
19					
20					
21					

Use Goal Seek

Goal seek is a problem-solving method in which you specify a solution and then find the input value that produces that solution. You can think of goal seeking as what-if analysis in reverse. "Backing into" a solution in this way, sometimes referred to as **backsolving**, can save a significant amount of time that you would otherwise spend trying many sets of values. For example, you can use Goal Seek to determine how many units must be sold to reach a particular revenue goal or what expense levels are necessary to meet a budget target. **CASE** ▶ *Boston's January revenue has been the highest of the JCL offices for the past few years. Ellie wants to project additional revenue for Boston in January and has a question: What January Boston revenue target is required to increase the overall January revenue percentage to 18%, assuming the revenues for the other offices don't change?*

STEPS

1. **Click cell B7**

   The first step in using Goal Seek is to select a goal cell. A **goal cell** contains a formula in which you can substitute values to find a specific value, or goal. You use cell B7 as the goal cell because it contains the January percent of total revenue formula.

2. **Click the Data tab on the ribbon, click the What-If Analysis button in the Forecast group, then click Goal Seek**

   The Goal Seek dialog box opens. The Set cell box displays B7, the cell you selected in Step 1, which contains the formula that calculates January's percentage of total revenue.

3. **Click the To value box, then type 18%**

   The value 18% represents the desired solution you want to reach.

4. **Click the By changing cell box, then click cell B3**

   You have specified that you want cell B3, the Boston January revenue, to change to reach the 18% solution, as shown in **FIGURE 12-13**.

5. **Click OK**

   The Goal Seek Status dialog box opens and displays the message, "Goal Seeking with Cell B7 found a solution." Cell B3 now displays the amount $113,671, the revenue necessary to achieve a January percentage of 18%.

6. **Click OK, then click cell A1**

   Changing the revenue amount in cell B3 changes the other dependent values in the worksheet (B6, H3, I3, and H6), as shown in **FIGURE 12-14**. The overall revenues increase as a result of increasing the Boston January percentage.

7. **Save the workbook**

FIGURE 12-13: Completed Goal Seek dialog box

FIGURE 12-14: Worksheet with Goal Seek solution

	A	B	C	D	E	F	G	H	I	J	K	L	M	N
1				Projected Revenue							Total Boston Revenue			
2		Jan	Feb	Mar	Apr	May	Jun	Total	Percent of Total Revenue		$	419,921	34.45%	
3	Boston	$113,671	$75,189	$71,423	$84,664	$91,926	$98,244	$535,117	40.11%		$	469,921	37.03%	
4	New York	$62,868	$76,326	$79,244	$69,688	$71,015	$70,388	$429,529	32.19%		$	519,921	39.42%	
5	Philadelphia	$63,573	$61,756	$65,681	$70,988	$68,191	$39,334	$369,523	27.70%		$	569,921	41.63%	
6	Total	$240,112	$213,271	$216,348	$225,340	$231,132	$207,966	$1,334,169			$	619,921	43.69%	
7	Percent of Total Revenue	18.00%	15.99%	16.22%	16.89%	17.32%	15.59%							
8														

Predicting data trends with Forecast Sheet

Forecast Sheet is a tool you can use when you have historical time-based data, to project future data based on past trends. You can forecast the future of your data related to a timeline by selecting the data, clicking the Data tab, then clicking the Forecast Sheet button in the Forecast group. The Create Forecast Worksheet dialog box opens, where you enter your Forecast End date, then click Create. The new chart displays your values along with the forecasted values and related confidence levels. A data table is also added to the worksheet, showing the new projected data for the chart. If your data lacks a valid pattern or seasonality, you can manually set this by expanding the Options area, then choosing the Set Manually option button, lowering the Confidence Interval percentage, or clicking the Fill Missing Points Using list arrow and selecting Zeros. Forecasting sheet functions can also be used to predict future values based on historical data. For example, Forecast.ETS() returns the projected value for a specific future target date. You can also use Forecast.ETS.Confint() and Forecast.ETS.Seasonality() to find confidence intervals and the repetitive pattern length of data.

Find Solutions Using Solver

The Excel Solver is an **add-in**, software that adds features and commands to Excel or another Office app. It must be installed before you can use it. Solver finds the best solution to a problem that has several inputs. The cell containing the formula is called the **target cell**, or **objective**. Solver is helpful when you need to perform a complex what-if analysis involving multiple input values or when the input values must conform to specific limitations, called **constraints**. **CASE** ▶ *JCL's CEO directed Ellie to limit the budget total for JCL's Northeast offices to $2,000,000. Ellie is willing to adjust some budget items to meet this overall amount, but not others. You use Solver to help her find the best possible allocation.*

STEPS

1. **Click the Budget sheet tab**

   The budget constraints appear in the range A7:C11, as shown in **FIGURE 12-15**. The minimum office total budget, maximum salaries budget, minimum communication budget, and total budget requirements are shown in this range.

2. **Click the Data tab on the ribbon if necessary, then click the Solver button in the Analysis group**

   In the Solver Parameters dialog box, you indicate the target cell with its objective, the changing cells, and the constraints under which you want Solver to work.

3. **With the insertion point in the Set Objective box click cell I6 in the worksheet if necessary, click the Value Of option button if necessary, double-click the Value Of box, then type 2,000,000**

   You have specified an objective of $2,000,000 for the total budget.

4. **Click the By Changing Variable Cells box, select the range B3:B5, press and hold CTRL, then select the range E3:E5**

   You have told Excel which cells to vary to reach the goal of a $2,000,000 total budget.

5. **Click Add, with the insertion point in the Cell Reference box in the Add Constraint dialog box select the range I3:I5 in the worksheet, click the list arrow displaying <= in the dialog box, click >=, then with the insertion point in the Constraint box click cell C8**

   These settings specify that the values in the range I3:I5, the total office budget amounts, should be greater than or equal to the value in cell C8, the minimum total office budget.

6. **Click Add, with the insertion point in the Cell Reference box select the range E3:E5, verify that <= is selected, click in the Constraint box, then click cell C9**

   You added the constraint that the budgeted salary amounts should be less than or equal to $400,000.

7. **Click Add, with the insertion point in the Cell Reference box select the range B3:B5, click the list arrow displaying <=, click >=, with the insertion point in the Constraint box click cell C10, click OK, then click Solve**

   After you specified a constraint for all communications budgets to be a minimum of $65,000 and ran the Solver, Solver found a solution as indicated in the Solver Results dialog box.

8. **sam↑ With the Keep Solver Solution option selected, click OK, compare your results to FIGURE 12-16, change the worksheet orientation to landscape, group the worksheets, add your name to the footers of the grouped worksheets, ungroup the worksheets, save and close the workbook, then submit the workbook to your instructor as directed**

FIGURE 12-15: Worksheet with constraints

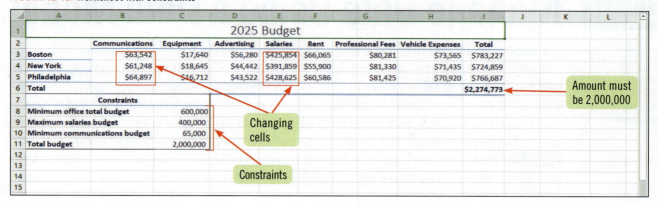

FIGURE 12-16: Solver solution

	A	B	C	D	E	F	G	H	I
1					2025 Budget				
2		Communications	Equipment	Advertising	Salaries	Rent	Professional Fees	Vehicle Expenses	Total
3	Boston	$65,000	$17,640	$56,280	$324,798	$66,065	$80,281	$73,565	$683,629
4	New York	$65,000	$18,645	$44,442	$316,657	$55,900	$81,330	$71,435	$653,409
5	Philadelphia	$65,000	$16,712	$43,522	$324,798	$60,586	$81,425	$70,920	$662,963
6	Total								$2,000,000
7		Constraints							
8	Minimum office total budget	600,000							
9	Maximum salaries budget	400,000							
10	Minimum communications budget	65,000							
11	Total budget	2,000,000							
12									
13									

Analyzing data using the Analysis ToolPak

The Analysis ToolPak is an Excel add-in that contains many statistical analysis tools. You can use one of these tools by clicking the Data tab, clicking the Data Analysis button in the Analysis group, selecting the desired analysis tool in the Data Analysis dialog box, clicking OK, entering the input range and other relevant specifications in the data tool's dialog box, then clicking OK. For example, clicking the Descriptive Statistics tool in the Data Analysis dialog box and selecting Summary statistics generates a statistical report including mean, median, mode, minimum, maximum, and sum for an input range you specify on your worksheet.

Creating an Answer Report

After solver finds a solution, you can generate an Answer Report summarizing the target cell information, the adjustable cells, and the constraints by selecting Answer from three types of reports in the Solver Results window, then clicking OK. The report appears as a separate worksheet named Answer Report 1 with three sections. The top section has the target cell information; it compares the original value of the target cell with the final value. The middle section of the report contains information about the adjustable cells. It lists the original and final values for all cells that were changed to reach the target value.

The last report section has information about the constraints. Each constraint you added into Solver is listed in the Formula column, along with the cell address and a description of the cell data. The Cell Value column contains the Solver solution values for the cells. The Status column contains information on whether the constraints were binding or not binding in reaching the solution. Binding constraints indicate all of the allocated resource was used or the constraint was pushed to its limit. Non-binding constraints indicate there was extra resource available after the constraint was met.

Excel

Manage Data Using a Data Model

The **data model** is part of an Excel workbook that documents processes and events to capture and translate complex data into easy-to-understand information. It describes the structure of data tables and how they interact. You can use Power Pivot to add existing workbook data to a data model. Power Pivot is one of the Component Object Model (COM) add-ins that extend the functionality of Excel. It displays the workbook's data model and provides more advanced data analysis tools to work with data in different sources. Once data is included in the workbook data model, it can be used in PivotTables and PivotCharts.

CASE ▶ *Ellie has placement and employee data in separate tables in a workbook. She asks you to analyze the data in both workbooks. You will add the data from both tables to the data model to begin your analysis.*

STEPS

1. Open **IL_EX_12-2.xlsx** from the location where you store your Data Files, save it as **IL_EX_12_Placements**, click the **File tab** on the ribbon, click **Options** in Backstage view, click **Add-ins** in the Excel Options dialog box menu, click the **Manage arrow** at the bottom of the dialog box, select **COM Add-ins**, click **Go**, in the COM Add-ins dialog box click the **Microsoft Power Pivot for Excel check box** to select it, then click **OK**

2. With the Placements sheet active click the **Power Pivot tab** on the ribbon, click the **Add to Data Model button** in the Tables group, then in the Create Table dialog box click **OK**
   This method of adding data to a data model is referred to as adding a query. After you add the query, the Power Pivot window opens, as shown in **FIGURE 12-17**. The top pane in Power Pivot displays the table, and the bottom pane is the calculation area.

3. Click the **Switch to Workbook button** 📇 on the Quick Access Toolbar, click the **Employees sheet tab**, click cell **A1**, click the **Power Pivot tab**, click the **Add to Data Model button** in the Tables group, then click **OK**
   The two tables are now part of the data model.

4. Double-click the **Table1 sheet tab** in Power Pivot, type **Placements**, press **ENTER**, double-click the **Table2 sheet tab**, type **Employees**, then press **ENTER**

5. Click the **Design tab** on the ribbon, then click the **Create Relationship button** in the Relationships group, in the Create Relationship dialog box click the **first list arrow** if necessary and click **Employees**, select the **Emp# field** if it is not already highlighted, click the **second list arrow** and click **Placements**, click the **Recruiter ID field** to highlight it, then click **OK**
   Creating a relationship between tables allows you to access corresponding data from both tables.

6. Click the **Home tab**, then click the **Diagram View button** in the View group
   The two tables and their relationship are shown in **FIGURE 12-18**. This is a one-to-many relationship because each Emp# value can be associated with multiple RecruiterID rows in the Placements table.

7. Click the **Switch to Workbook button** 📇 on the Quick Access Toolbar, click the **Employees sheet tab** if necessary, click cell **B2**, edit the name Anne Chard to **Anne Flood**, click the **Power Pivot tab**, click the **Manage button** in the Data Model group, click the **Data View button** in the View group, then click the **Refresh button**
   The Data Refresh dialog box shows that the data was successfully updated.

8. Click **Close** in the Data Refresh dialog box, widen the **Name column** to fully display the Employees' names, verify that Anne's last name in row 1 is Flood, then save your work

FIGURE 12-17: Power Pivot window

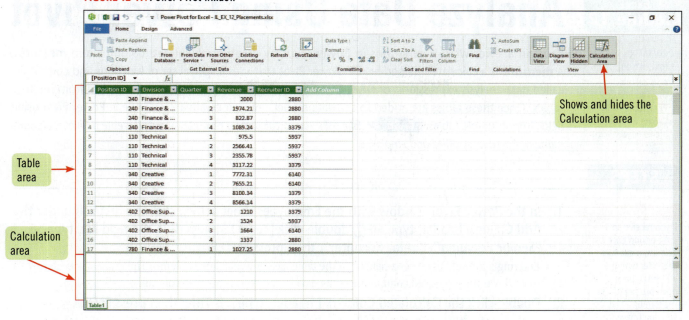

Table area

Calculation area

Shows and hides the Calculation area

FIGURE 12-18: Diagram of the relationship between tables

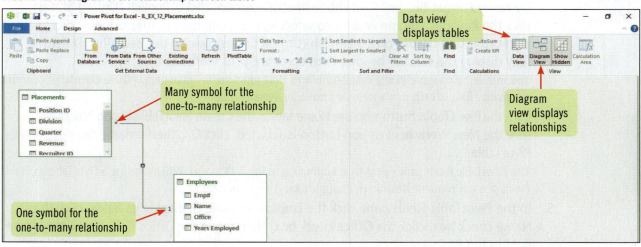

Data view displays tables

Many symbol for the one-to-many relationship

One symbol for the one-to-many relationship

Diagram view displays relationships

Excel

Analyze Data Using Power Pivot

**Learning
Outcomes**
- Add calcula-
tions to Power
PivotTables
- Create a PivotTa-
ble in Power Pivot

You can answer what-if questions in Power Pivot by creating calculated columns and measures. A **measure** is a calculated named field in Power Pivot that uses a special set of functions and commands called data analysis expressions, or DAX. Often answering what-if questions requires data from multiple tables. Once these tables are added to the data model, you can create a PivotTable in Power Pivot using fields from multiple tables. **CASE** ▶ *Ellie asks you to calculate a revenue total and create a PivotTable summarizing revenue by office and employee.*

STEPS

TROUBLE

If you receive an error or don't see the field list, make sure that after typing =IF(you type an open bracket ([ ) in the formula. Also, you don't have to type the closing parenthesis [ )] at the end of the for-mula because Excel adds it for you.

1. **In the Power Pivot window with the Employees sheet active, click the first cell under the Add Column header, type =IF([, double-click [Years Employed] in the field list, type >6, "Senior Recruiter","Junior Recruiter", then press ENTER**
   Entering a formula that uses a field from the table creates a calculated column. The results for each row are filled down the calculated column using the data in the Years Employed column.

2. **Double-click the Calculated Column 1 header, type Job Title, then press ENTER**

3. **Activate the Placements table in the Power Pivot window, click the first cell in the Calculation area below the Revenue data, click the AutoSum button in the Calculations group, widen the Revenue column to fully display the Sum of Revenue, click the Apply Currency Format button $ in the Formatting group, click $ English (United States), click the Revenue column header to select the revenue data in that column, click $ in the Formatting group, click $ English (United States), widen the Recruiter ID field to fully display the column header, then compare your work to FIGURE 12-19**
   You inserted a measure in the calculation area that sums the revenue data. Where calculated columns summarize data in each row, a measure creates an overall summary.

4. **Click the PivotTable button on the Home tab, in the Create PivotTable dialog box make sure the New Worksheet option button is selected, click OK, then rename the new sheet PivotTable**
   The PivotTable Fields pane opens with both tables in the data model. When creating a PivotTable in Power Pivot, you can combine fields from multiple tables in a PivotTable.

5. **In the PivotTable Fields pane click the Employees table to display its fields, click the Name check box, click the Office check box, then move the Office field above the Name field in the Rows area**
   The data from the Name and Office fields are placed in the PivotTable rows.

6. **In the PivotTable Fields pane scroll down, click the Placements table to expand its fields, click the Division check box, move the Division field from the Rows area to the Columns area, click the Quarter check box, move the Quarter field to the Filters area, then click the Revenue check box**
   The PivotTable summarizes data from both tables and can answer questions about revenue from the Place-ments table related to the JCL offices in the Employee table.

7. **Click the PivotTable Analyze tab on the ribbon, click the Field Headers button in the Show group to deselect it, close the PivotTable Fields pane, change the worksheet orientation to landscape, then compare your PivotTable to FIGURE 12-20**

8. **sam'↑ Group the worksheets, add your name to the grouped footers, ungroup the sheets, save the workbook, close the workbook, close Excel, then submit the workbook to your instructor as directed**

FIGURE 12-19: Calculation area with measure

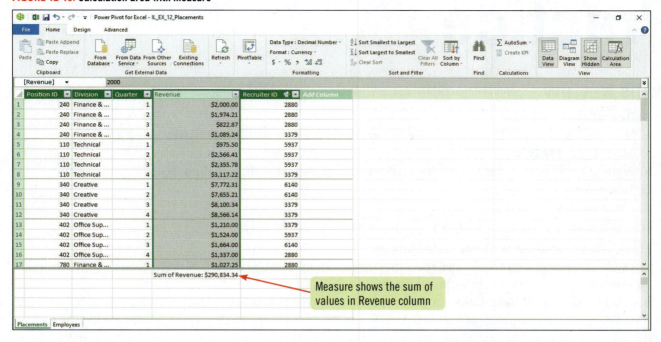

Measure shows the sum of
values in Revenue column

FIGURE 12-20: PivotTable created in Power Pivot

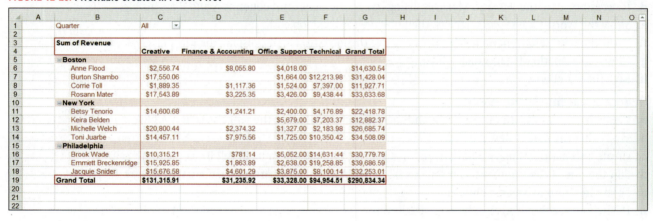

Using the Excel 3D Maps tool

Power Map, also called 3D Maps, is an Excel COM add-in that helps to visualize worksheet data in 3-D formats. To insert a Power Map into a worksheet, click the Insert tab, then click 3D Map in the Tours group. Data should be organized in a table for mapping. The 3D Maps window opens with its own ribbon containing a Home tab, a Tour pane on the left showing Tour 1, an automatically created Tour with a single scene, a Field List showing the fields available to map, and a Layer pane on the right with areas for map locations, height, category, and time. A tour is a list of maps in the 3D Map and each map is a scene. Most often 3D Maps contain several scenes that make up an animation offering different points of focus of the data. You can create a new scene by clicking the New Scene button in the Scene group, then dragging fields from the Field List to the desired areas on the Layer pane. Fields with location data can be dragged to the Location area, fields with values should be placed in the height area, the category area holds fields for different markers, and the time area shows the map changes over time. When you save your workbook, 3D Map tours and scenes are saved.

Practice

Skills Review

1. **Define what-if analysis.**
   a. Start Excel, open IL_EX_12-3.xlsx from the location where you store your Data Files, then save it as **IL_EX_12_Freight**.
   b. Examine the Equipment Repair worksheet to determine the purpose of the worksheet model.
   c. Locate the data input cells.
   d. Locate any dependent cells.
   e. Examine the worksheet to determine problems the worksheet model can solve.

2. **Track what-if analysis with Scenario Manager.**
   a. On the Equipment Repair worksheet, select the range B3:B5, then use the Scenario Manager to set up a scenario called **Most Likely** that includes the current data input values.
   b. Add a scenario called **Best Case** using the same changing cells, but change the Labor cost per hour in the $B$3 box to **85**, change the Parts cost per job in the $B$4 box to **75**, then change the Hours per job value in cell $B$5 to **3**.
   c. Add a scenario called **Worst Case**. For this scenario, change the Labor cost per hour in the $B$3 box to **95**, change the Parts cost per job in the $B$4 box to **85**, then change the Hours per job in the $B$5 box to **4**.
   d. If necessary, drag the Scenario Manager dialog box to the right until columns A and B are visible.
   e. Show the Worst Case scenario results, then observe the total job cost.
   f. Show the Best Case scenario results, then observe the job cost. Finally, display the Most Likely scenario results.
   g. Close the Scenario Manager dialog box.
   h. Save the workbook.

3. **Generate a scenario summary.**
   a. Create names for the input value cells and the dependent cell using the range selection A3:B7.
   b. Verify that the names were created.
   c. Create a scenario summary report, using the Cost to complete job value in cell B7 as the result cell.
   d. Edit the title of the Summary report in cell B2 to **Scenario Summary for Equipment Repair**.
   e. Delete the Current Values column.
   f. Delete row 1, column A, and the notes beginning in cell B11. Compare your worksheet to **FIGURE 12-21**.
   g. Add your name in the center section of the Scenario Summary sheet footer, then save the workbook.

FIGURE 12-21

	A	B	C	D	E
1	Scenario Summary for Equipment Repair				
2			Most Likely	Best Case	Worst Case
4	Changing Cells:				
5		Labor_cost_per_hour	$90.00	$85.00	$95.00
6		Parts_cost_per_job	$80.00	$75.00	$85.00
7		Hours_per_job	3.50	3.00	4.00
8	Result Cells:				
9		Cost_to_complete_job	$395.00	$330.00	$465.00
10					
11					
12					

Skills Review (continued)

4. Project figures using a data table.

   a. Activate the Equipment Repair sheet.

   b. Enter the label **Labor $** in cell D3.

   c. Format the label so that it is bold and right-aligned.

   d. In cell D4, enter **80**. Select the range D4:D8, then fill the range with values using a linear series in a column with a step value of 5.

   e. In cell E3, reference the job cost formula by entering **=B7**.

   f. Format the contents of cell E3 as hidden, entering the **;;;** Custom formatting type on the Number tab of the Format Cells dialog box.

   g. Generate the new job costs based on the varying labor costs. Select the range D3:E8 and create a data table. In the Data Table dialog box, make cell B3 (the labor cost) the column input cell.

   h. Format the range D4:E8 as currency with two decimal places.

   i. Enter your name in the center section of the worksheet footer, then save the workbook.

5. Use Goal Seek.

   a. Click cell B7, then open the Goal Seek dialog box.

   b. Assuming the labor rate and hours remain the same, determine what the parts cost per job would have to be so that the cost to complete the job is $350. (*Hint:* Enter a job cost of **350** as the To value, then enter **B4** as the By changing cell.) Write down the parts cost that Goal Seek finds.

   c. Click OK, then press CTRL+Z to reset the parts cost to its original value.

   d. Enter the parts cost that you found in Step 5b into cell A14, formatted as currency with no decimal places.

   e. Assuming the parts cost and hours remain the same, determine the labor cost per hour so that the cost to complete the job is $350. Press CTRL+Z to reset the labor cost to its original value. Enter the labor cost in cell A15.

   f. Save the workbook, then compare your worksheet to **FIGURE 12-22**.

FIGURE 12-22

	A	B	C	D	E	F	G	H	I	J	K	L	M
1	WTN Freight Transportation												
2													
3	Labor cost per hour	$90.00		Labor $									
4	Parts cost per job	$80.00		$80.00	$360.00								
5	Hours per job	3.50		$85.00	$377.50								
6				$90.00	$395.00								
7	Cost to complete job:	$395.00		$95.00	$412.50								
8				$100.00	$430.00								
9													
10													
11													
12													
13													
14	$35												
15	$77.14												
16													
17													
18													
19													
20													

Excel

Skills Review (continued)

6. **Find solutions using Solver.**

   a. Activate the Transportation Costs sheet, then open the Solver Parameters dialog box.

   b. Make B14 (the grand total cost) the objective cell, with a target value of 16,000.

   c. Use cells B6:D6 (the number of all scheduled trips) as the changing cells.

   d. Specify that cells B6:D6 must be integers. (*Hint:* Select int in the Add Constraint dialog box.)

   e. Specify that cells B6:D6 must be greater than or equal to 10.

   f. Use Solver to find a solution. Keep the Solver solution, then compare your worksheet to **FIGURE 12-23**.

FIGURE 12-23

	A	B	C	D	E	F	G	H	I	J	K	L	M
1	WTN Freight Transportation												
2													
3		Heavy	Standard	Small									
4	Labor Cost Per Trip	$110.00	$100.00	$95.00									
5	Parts Cost Per Trip	$150.00	$130.00	$100.00									
6	Trips Scheduled	23	33	13									
7													
8	Labor Cost Per Size	$2,483.89	$3,286.00	$1,252.63									
9	Parts Cost Per Size	$3,387.12	$4,271.79	$1,318.56									
10	Total Cost Per Size	$5,871.01	$7,557.79	$2,571.20									
11													
12	Total Labor Cost	$7,022.52											
13	Total Parts Cost	$8,977.48											
14	Grand Total Cost	$16,000.00											
15													
16													
17													
18													
19													
20													

   g. Enter your name in the center section of the worksheet footer, save the workbook, close the workbook, then submit the workbook to your instructor as directed.

7. **Manage data using a data model.**

   a. Open IL_EX_12-4.xlsx from the location where you store your Data Files, then save it as **IL_EX_12_Employee**.

   b. With the Employee sheet active, use Power Pivot to add the worksheet data to the data model.

   c. Switch to Worksheet view, activate the Routes sheet, then use Power Pivot to add the worksheet data to the data model.

   d. In Power Pivot, rename the Table1 sheet **Employee**, then name the Table2 sheet **Routes**.

   e. Create a relationship between the Employee # field in the Routes table and the Emp ID field in the Employee table.

   f. View the relationship between the tables in Diagram View and verify it is one to many.

g. Return to the workbook, activate the Employee sheet, then change the contents of cell B2 to **Concord** and cell D2 to **D. McKay**.

h. Return to the data model in Power Pivot, activate the Employee sheet, then refresh the worksheet data. (*Hint:* To return to the data model in Power Pivot, click the Manage button in the Data Model group.)

8. **Analyze data using Power Pivot.**

a. Activate the Routes sheet in the Power Pivot window, then add a measure in the calculation area to sum the Trip Cost data. (*Hint:* Click the first cell in the calculation area below the Trip Cost data, then use the AutoSum button in the Calculation group on the Home tab.)

b. Widen the Trip Cost column to fully display the Sum of Trip Cost, then format the value using the $ English (United States) Currency format and no decimal places.

c. Create a PivotTable on a new worksheet named **PivotTable** that adds the Location field from the Employee table to the Rows area, the Manager field from the Employee table to the Rows area, the Employee # field from the Routes table to the Rows area, the Trip Cost field from the Routes table to the Values area, and the Vehicle Size field from the Routes table to the Columns area.

d. Use a tool on the PivotTable Analyze tab to hide the Field Headers, then compare your PivotTable to **FIGURE 12-24**.

FIGURE 12-24

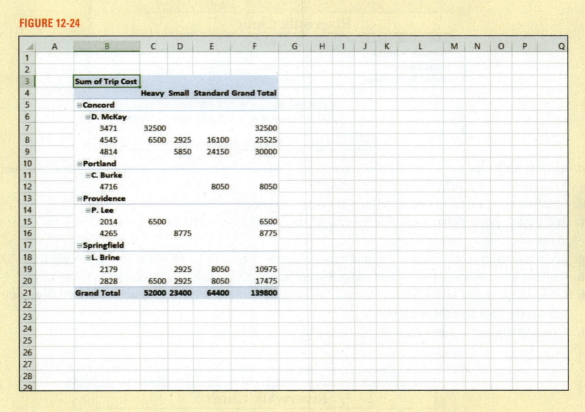

	Sum of Trip Cost	Heavy	Small	Standard	Grand Total
Concord					
D. McKay					
	3471	32500			32500
	4545	6500	2925	16100	25525
	4814		5850	24150	30000
Portland					
C. Burke					
	4716			8050	8050
Providence					
P. Lee					
	2014	6500			6500
	4265		8775		8775
Springfield					
L. Brine					
	2179		2925	8050	10975
	2828	6500	2925	8050	17475
Grand Total		52000	23400	64400	139800

e. Close Power Pivot, group the worksheets, add your name to the footer of the worksheets, ungroup the worksheets, save and close the workbook, submit the workbook to your instructor, then close Excel.

Excel

Independent Challenge 1

You are assisting Tony Sanchez, the office manager at Riverwalk Medical Clinic, with a disaster recovery plan for the medical records at the clinic. As part of that plan you are looking at two options for storing backup medical records. The first option is to purchase a storage facility, and the second is to use a third-party backup storage company that offers off-site small, medium, and large storage areas. In both cases, you want to keep your monthly payments below $1700. You decide to use Goal Seek to look at various interest rates for purchasing a storage facility and to use Solver to help find the best possible combination of third-party storage areas.

a. Start Excel, open IL_EX_12-5.xlsx from the location where you store your Data Files, then save it as **IL_EX_12_Records**.

b. With the Purchase sheet active, use Goal Seek to find the interest rate that produces a monthly payment of $16,500, and write down the interest rate that Goal Seek finds. Reset the interest rate to its original value, record the interest rate in cell A7, then enter **Interest rate for $16,500 monthly payment** in cell B7.

c. Use Goal Seek to find the interest rate that produces a monthly payment of $16,000. Reset the interest rate to its original value, record the interest rate in cell A8, then enter **Interest rate for $16,000 monthly payment** in cell B8. Compare your worksheet to FIGURE 12-25.

FIGURE 12-25

	A	B	C	D	E
1		Riverwalk Clinic			
2	Annual Interest Rate	5.75%			
3	Term in Months	48			
4	Loan Amount	$ 725,000			
5	Monthly Payment	$16,943.67			
6					
7		4.40% Interest rate for $16,500 monthly payment			
8		2.85% Interest rate for $16,000 monthly payment			
9					
10					

d. Activate the Rental sheet. Open Solver, then use the Set Objective To option to maximize the storage amount in cell B12. (*Hint:* Select Max in the Set the Objective To area.)

e. In Solver, use the quantity, cells B6:D6, as the changing cells.

f. Add a constraint to Solver specifying the quantity in cells B6:D6 must be integers. (*Hint:* Choose int as the operator in the Add Constraint dialog box.)

g. Add a constraint specifying that the total monthly payment amount in cell B11 is less than or equal to 17000.

h. Generate a solution using Solver and accept Solver's solution. Compare your worksheet to FIGURE 12-26.

i. Group the worksheets, then enter your name in the center footer section of both worksheets. Preview both worksheets, then save the workbook.

j. Close the workbook, then submit the workbook to your instructor.

FIGURE 12-26

	A	B	C	D	
1		Riverwalk Clinic			
2					
3		Large	Medium	Small	
4	Rental Fee	$ 4,200	$ 3,000	$ 2,400	
5	Capacity (cubic feet)	210	150	100	
6	Quantity	3	2	0	
7					
8	Monthly Payment	$ 11,604	$ 5,396	$ -	
9	Storage Capacity	580	270	0	
10					
11	Total Monthly Payment	$ 17,000			
12	Total Storage Capacity	850			
13					

Independent Challenge 2

As a senior financial analyst at North Shore CPA Services, you are researching various options for financing a $250,000 loan for the purchase of a new estate-planning facility. You haven't decided whether to finance the project for three, four, or five years. Each loan term carries a different interest rate. To help with the comparison, you summarize these options using a scenario summary. You will also create a two-input data table to analyze additional interest rates and terms.

a. Start Excel, open IL_EX_12-6.xlsx from the location where you store your Data Files, then save it as **IL_EX_12_Loan**.

b. Create cell names for cells B4:B11 based on the labels in cells A4:A11, using the Create Names from Selection dialog box.

c. Use Scenario Manager to create scenarios that calculate the monthly payment on a $250,000 loan under the three sets of loan possibilities listed below. (*Hint:* Create three scenarios, using cells B5:B6 as the changing cells.)

Scenario Name	Interest Rate	Term
5% 5 Year	.05	60
4.5% 4 Year	.045	48
4% 3 Year	.04	36

d. View each scenario and confirm that it performs as intended, then display the 5% 5 Year scenario.

e. Generate a scenario summary titled **Finance Options**. Use cells B9:B11 as the Result cells.

f. Delete the Current Values column in the report and the notes at the bottom of the report, row 1, and column A. Rename the sheet **Estate Planning Project**.

g. Activate the Loan sheet. Using **FIGURE 12-27** as a guide, enter the input values for a two-input data table with varying interest rates for 3-, 4-, and 5-year terms. Use a linear series to enter the interest rates.

h. Reference the monthly payment amount from cell B9 in cell A13, then format the contents of cell A13 so they are hidden.

i. Generate a data table, using cells A13:D22, that shows the effect of varying interest rates and loan terms on the monthly payments. (*Hint:* Use cell B6, Term in Months, as the Row input cell, and cell B5, the Annual Interest Rate, as the Column input cell.)

j. Format the range B14:D22 as currency with two decimal places.

k. Group the two worksheets, then enter your name in the center section of the grouped footer.

l. Save the workbook, close the workbook, submit the workbook to your instructor as directed, then close Excel.

FIGURE 12-27

	A	B	C	D	E
1	North Shore CPA Services				
2	Financing Options				
3					
4	Loan Amount	$250,000.00			
5	Annual Interest Rate	5.00%			
6	Term in Months	60			
7					
8					
9	Monthly Payment:	$4,717.81			
10	Total Payments:	$283,068.50			
11	Total Interest:	$33,068.50			
12					
13			36	48	60
14		3.00%			
15		3.25%			
16		3.50%			
17		3.75%			
18		4.00%			
19		4.25%			
20		4.50%			
21		4.75%			
22		5.00%			
23					

Excel

Visual Workshop

Open the file IL_EX_12-7.xlsx from the location where you store your Data Files, then save it as **IL_EX_12_Orders**. Using the two worksheets, create the data model shown in the Power Pivot window in **FIGURE 12-28**. (*Hint:* When entering the formula to calculate the balance, click each column header to enter the Total and Paid values.) Then, using the data model, create the PivotTable shown in **FIGURE 12-29**. (*Hint:* Create a one-to-many relationship between the ID field in the Customers table and the Cust_ID field in the Orders table, then create the PivotTable.) When you are finished, add your name to the center footer section of the PivotTable sheet, save the workbook, submit the workbook to your instructor as directed, then close Excel.

FIGURE 12-28

FIGURE 12-29

	A	B	C	D	E	F	G
3			Sum of Total	Sum of Balance			
4		⊟ Amy Folley					
5		⊟ 212-555-0100					
6		16398	$2,069	$0			
7		19377	$2,483	$283			
8		20937	$1,444	$44			
9		47805	$1,402	$0			
10		⊟ Corey Olsen					
11		⊟ 212-555-0115					
12		19921	$953	$53			
13		⊟ Gilbert Hahn					
14		⊟ 813-555-0195					
15		17344	$1,356	$0			
16		30934	$2,084	$84			
17		⊟ Jack Watson					
18		⊟ 305-555-0171					
19		20226	$2,500	$300			
20		40427	$845	$0			
21		43669	$2,120	$0			
22		⊟ Lisa Jones					
23		⊟ 239-555-0174					
24		17492	$1,306	$56			
25		19110	$1,509	$9			
26		31689	$1,101	$101			
27		41979	$2,021	$21			
28		⊟ Sally Wilkins					
29		⊟ 503-555-0134					
30		11972	$1,575	$75			
31		26667	$1,437	$87			
32		27552	$2,076	$76			
33		Grand Total	$28,281	$1,189			

Performing What-If Analysis

Index